Venice and the Veneto

(see maps on the inside covers, front and back)

THEGREENGUIDE
Venice
and the Veneto

Basilica di San Marco on Piazza San Marco / © M. Silvan / age fotostock

THE GREEN GUIDE **VENICE AND THE VENETO**

Editorial Director	Cynthia Ochterbeck
Updating and Layout	Buysschaert&Malerba, Milan
	Zino Malerba, Francesca Puglia
Contributing Writers	Judy Edelhoff, Jonathan P. Gilbert
Production Manager	Natasha George
Cartography	Michèle Cana
Interior Design	Chris Bell
Layout	Natasha George
Cover Design	Chris Bell, Christelle Le Déan
Contact Us	Michelin Travel and Lifestyle North America
	One Parkway South
	Greenville, SC 29615
	USA
	travel.lifestyle@us.michelin.com
	Michelin Travel Partner
	Hannay House
	39 Clarendon Road
	Watford, Herts WD17 1JA
	UK
	✆01923 205240
	travelpubsales@uk.michelin.com
	www.ViaMichelin.com
Special Sales	For information regarding bulk sales,
	customized editions and premium sales,
	please contact us at:
	travel.lifestyle@us.michelin.com

HOW TO USE THIS GUIDE

PLANNING YOUR TRIP

The blue-tabbed PLANNING YOUR TRIP section gives you **ideas for your trip** and **practical information** to help you organize it. You'll find tours, practical information, a host of outdoor activities, a calendar of events, information on shopping, sightseeing, kids' activities and more.

INTRODUCTION

The orange-tabbed INTRODUCTION section explores **Nature** from the lagoon to the impact of the built environment. The **History** section spans from the state's foundation to its ultimate decline. The **Art and Culture** section covers architecture, art, literature, traditions and folklore, while the **City Today** delves into modern Venice and the Veneto.

DISCOVERING

The green-tabbed DISCOVERING section features Venice and the Veneto's Principal Sights, arranged by region, featuring the most interesting local **Sights**, **Walking Tours**, nearby **Excursions**, and detailed **Driving Tours**.

ADDRESSES

We've selected the best hotels, restaurants, cafes, shops, nightlife and entertainment to fit all budgets. See the Legend on the cover flap for an explanation of the price categories. See the back of the guide for an index of locations for hotels and restaurants.

Sidebars

Throughout the guide you will find blue, orange and green-colored text boxes with lively anecdotes, detailed history and background information.

😊 A Bit of Advice 😊

Green advice boxes found in this guide contain practical tips and handy information relevant to your visit or to a sight in the Discovering section.

STAR RATINGS★★★

Michelin has given star ratings for more than 100 years. If you're pressed for time, we recommend you visit the ★★★ or ★★ sights first:

★★★ **Highly recommended**

★★ **Recommended**

★ **Interesting**

MAPS

- 😊 **Venice maps** with Principal Sights listed.
- 😊 **Veneto map**, **town plans** and **driving tours** in the Dolomites for trips out of La Serenissima.

All maps in this guide are oriented north, unless otherwise indicated by a directional arrow. The term "Local Map" refers to a map within the chapter or Tourism Region. A complete list of the maps found in the guide appears at the back of this book.

© Tibor Bognár / age fotostock

© A. Serrano / age fotostock

PLANNING YOUR TRIP

WELCOME TO THE CITY

CONTENTS

© Norbert Scanella / age fotostock

© Peter Barritt / age fotostock

EXPLORE VENICE

YOUR STAY IN THE CITY

Gardens in Prato della Valle, Padova
© Alberto Simonetti / istockphoto.com

Michelin Driving Tours

THE VENETO
ITALY ROUTE 4.

See the Michelin Guide Italy for even more driving tours in the surrounding regions of Lombardy and Romagna, and all the way south to Sicily.

FROM THE DOLOMITES TO VENICE AND TRIESTE

This spectacular route combines the natural majesty of the Dolomite mountains with the cultural and cul treasures of the Veneto and the Friuli-Venezia Giulia region – the latter occupying the north eastern corner of Italy with Trieste as its capital.

Local Veneto Trips

See the Veneto section of the guide for more routes and maps:

* VILLAS OF THE BRENTA
  * **Padua to Fusina, via Mirano**
* DOLOMITI
  * **Strada delle Dolomiti★★★**
  * **Val Pusteria area**

The route is approximately 500mi/ 800km long and requires at least 10 days, at least two of which should ideally be spent in Venice. From Venice head north to **Treviso**; the old centre, surrounded by waterways and what remains of the city walls, is a delight. From here **Portogruaro** has maintained the original layout of its old town and is justly famous for its Roman remains. In Friuli Venezia Giulia (*see ITALY Green Guide*) there are more fine Roman relics to enjoy at **Aquileia** before calling in at the seaside resort of **Grado**. Follow the coastline from here to **Trieste** with its blend of Italian and Central European culture. Be sure to savour the literary atmosphere in Caffè San Marco. Heading back north **Udine** boasts some excellent architecture. Back in the Veneto, pretty **Belluno**'s spectacular location is the gateway to the Dolomites. The route continues through the craggy and atmospheric **Dolomites** between its "capitals" of **Cortina d'Ampezzo** and **Bolzano**, ringing with the sounds of the German- or Latin-accented local dialect, before descending to **Trent**, dominated by the Buonconsiglio castle. The itinerary concludes in the beautiful Palladian town of **Vicenza**.

When and Where to Go

WHEN TO GO

Although Venice has its attractions all year round, **Spring** (mid-Apr–Jun) and **Autumn** (Sept–Oct) are the ideal times to visit. Mild temperatures (60°–70°F/15°–21°C) make sightseeing comfortable, although still crowded. The highlight of Winter is **Carnevale**, a moveable and highly colourful feast, leading up to Lent, but do note that hotels (and restaurants) are booked months in advance, and room prices reflect its popularity.

Summer brings hot, often humid, weather with intense sunlight, though at least the sea breezes mean it is not as scorching as on the mainland. Unless you are on the tightest budget, find a hotel with air-conditioned rooms and don't forget to bring along your anti-mosquito devices.

As well as insects, the city attracts the greater part of its 15 million visitors in summertime; the crowds threaten to overwhelm the city and make the main thoroughfares almost unbearable at peak periods. Make hotel reservations well in advance and expect very long lines at the main sights. Yet despite the crowds, the season's lengthy days and extended hours of operation are major draws.

Winter temperatures usually range from 30°F to 40°F and from just below freezing point to a few degrees above with overcast skies. Many connoisseurs of the city insist that this is the best time to see La Serenissima. The mists and fogs and even the floods (*see NATURE; and box opposite*) make the city particularly atmospheric, not to say downright melancholic, and of course the crowds have thinned out. On the other hand the cold and clinging damp can be uncomfortable and visitor opening hours may be reduced, with some establishments closing altogether for a week or two at a time. However, crisp clear winter days reward brave winter tourists.

Christmas in Venice is a magical time, with many churches festively decorated. Once again you will need to book well ahead and expect expensive room rates October through December generally are the wettest months, however it's unlikely that the *acqua alta* will be more than a mild nuisance during your stay. Having lived with the sea as their neighbour for all their lives, the Venetians are prepared.

WHERE TO GO
VENICE

It would be a shame to visit Venice and do nothing more than merely tick off an itinerary of great sights. As the French author, Jean-Louis Vaudoyer, once observed, "Nothing is simpler than to lose oneself in Venice and nothing is more fun than to be in this labyrinth." Yet, there are certain places and sights that demand a visit. If you only have a few days to spare here, we have made a few suggestions for making the most of *La Serenissima*. After ticking off the sights below we suggest simply wandering around the area you are in, exploring churches, bars and shops at will. You will almost certainly get lost in the narrow alleyways just as certainly as you will soon find your way back to a landmark.

Wellington boots

It is a curious and highly memorable sight to see the *Acqua Alta* (High Water) flooding the streets of Venice. The more flood-prone streets and squares are criss-crossed with wooden walkways and the city, which is usually so stylish, sees inhabitants and visitors alike wearing ungainly wellingtons, rubber boots, hip boots, and even plastic bags around their feet in an effort to keep dry.

Grand Canal

© Hiroshi Higuchi / GO Stock / GraphicObsession

Grand Canal★★★
and Piazza San Marco★★★

Go to the railway station and hop aboard Line 1 or the new (launched 2012) Art **Vaporetto**. If the weather is good, sit at the back in the open and watch the most glorious city High Street in the world go past. Get off at the Piazza San Marco. After marvelling at the architecture surrounding you from canal, then ground level, ascend the campanile to get a birds-eye view of the piazza. Take a tour of **St Mark's Basilica★★★** and/or the **Doges Palace★★★**, but only do both in one day if you have but a single day in Venice – otherwise it's a surfeit of riches in a few hours. Take a seat for a drink at one of the **grand cafes** in the piazza, but for value and the chance to mix with the locals, eat outside the square, snacking on *cichetti* in a *bacaro*.

Rialto★★

Go to the Rialto early in the morning, walk over the famous **Ponte di Rialto★★** and watch the markets in progress. Pop into one of the little bars around here and enjoy a coffee or a glass of wine at a ridiculously early hour, among the locals. From here it's just a five minute walk to the **Frari** church and almost opposite the **Scuola Grande di San Rocco**. Between them these two institutions are a pantheon of Venetian art.

Dorsoduro

The **Accademia★★★** is the city's main art gallery and houses a wonderful collection of Venetian paintings. If you don't know your Veronese from your Tiepolo, you can opt to watch seafaring vessels along the Zattere. Or wander over to the **Peggy Guggenheim Collection★★**, showing exclusively Modern and Contemporary Art, a two minute walk along the Grand Canal, and the second-most visited museum in the city, with not a Venetian Master in sight.

A five minute walk west brings you to the landmark church of **Santa Maria della Salute**, while a five minute walk south is the much-less visited **Squero di San Trovaso** where from across the canal you can glimpse gondolas being built and restored.

OUTLYING ISLANDS

Some tour representatives around the city will urge you to visit the island of **Murano**, world famous for its centuries-old glass blowing tradition. You definitely should go, though not with a glass company. Visit the excellent Glass Museum, a workshop, then the atmospheric Church of **Santi Maria e Donato**, perhaps the oldest in the lagoon.

You also have to make time for at least two more islands – a couple of hours on each will suffice. **Burano**, "the pearl of the lagoon" is like a tiny

Venice washed in a glorious rainbow of pastel shades with the occasional eye-popping colour scheme. **Torcello**, by contrast, is the island that time forgot, a dreamy overgrown, almost deserted place with a thousand-year old cathedral that is heart-achingly beautiful.

Finally, make the short journey across the lagoon to the church and monastery that you've seen countless times before in pictures of Venice, Palladio's splendid **San Giorgio Maggiore**. From the top of its campanile is the finest view in all Venice.

THE VENETO AND BEYOND

After a few days, particularly in crowds, Venice can start to feel claustrophobic. The hinterland is so full of cultural treasures and, if you have a little more time, natural scenery to explore, that it would be a shame not to venture out.

Day Trips

The richest city within easy distance of Venice is **Padova** *(Padua)*★★. Its historic centre is home to some of the most stunning historical and artistic sights in the Veneto, while its large student population gives it a lively buzz. You need two days to do it justice but an early start and late finish will cram in the highlights. Padua is linked to the city by the **Brenta Canal**, an attraction for its very popular day trip. Aboard a slow boat explore a selection of the great Italian **Villas of the Brenta**★★, which line this peaceful waterway (however, you cannot combine the Brenta and Padua in a single day).

If you are a fan of the Brenta Canal villas head for **Vicenza**★★, home of the great architect **Palladio**, where you can study more of his work. A small city, it can be seen easily in a day. **Verona**★★ is slightly further afield (75mi/120km) and like Padua requires two days to see it properly. It is the biggest city in the Veneto after Venice, and also the region's second richest

---

☺ Guided Tours ☺

There are any number of conventional guided tours of the city that are available to visitors, most of which include a guided walking tour and the option of a gondola ride. If you do hanker to ride in the city's most famous mode of transport then this is the cheapest way to do it, rather than negotiating for a private tour.

More unusual guided tours include: "Spicy Venice" – walking through the Rialto area, listening to the stories of Casanova and of libertine Venice in the 18C; and "Venetian Legends" – a walk through the districts of Castello and Cannaregio discovering the 'dark' side of the Venetian tradition.

🎫 Tickets can be bought at the tourist office – wear comfortable walking shoes!

---

artistic centre. A visit to the Roman Arena, Juliet's House and its scores of beautiful palazzi make the trip worthwhile.

Further afield

If you want to escape the dominance of Venice – which is prevalent in most of the Veneto – and swap narrow alleyways for mountains and meadows, then head north to the **Dolomiti**★★★.

Allow at least three nights of touring to see this majestic region. Call at the beautiful towns of **Bassano della Grappa**★★ and **Belluno**★ and the hilltop town of **Asolo**★. **Bolzano**★ is the principal city of the Dolomites and is well worth a visit. **Cortina d'Ampezzo**✳✳✳ is an excellent base for exploring the region, whether hillwalking in summer, or skiing in winter.

Know Before You Go

USEFUL WEBSITES

www.veneziaunica.it
This is the official website of Venice with useful links to the official websites of adjacent areas such as the Riviera del Brenta; a very good resource for events, attractions, etc. ℘ 041 2424.

www.comune.venezia.it
The official website of Venice town council is excellent for visitors as well as locals with interesting news items as well as its Tourism section.

www.gondolavenezia.it
Everything you ever wanted to know about this elegant mode of travel.

www.veniceworld.com
A hotel booking service that provides links to restaurants, transportation, events, entertainment.

www.visitmuve.it
This is the location for municipal museums (the museums of St. Mark's Square, Ca' Rezzonico, Palazzo Mocenigo, Casa Goldoni, Ca' Pesaro, Museo Fortuny, Museum of Natural History, the Clock Tower, museums of Burano Lace and Murano Glass). For all museums, tickets are available online or by phone at ℘892 234 *(call by vivatickets).*

www.chorusvenezia.org
Website for the 18 churches of the city connected with this group. (&see p28)

www.venetoinside.com
For information and reservations for visits in Veneto and Saint Mark's Basilica (April - November).

www.agendavenezia.org
Website offers a detailed daily overview of all exhibitions, events and other appointments of interest in Venice and the surrounding area.

ITALIAN TOURIST BOARD

The Italian Tourist Board is known as **Ente Nazionale Italiano per il Turismo** (ENIT). www.enit.it.

UK
1 Princes St., London W1B 2AY; ℘ 20 7408 1254. www.italiantouristboard.co.uk

USA
♦ 686 Park Avenue, New York, 3rd Floor, NY 10065; ℘(212) 245 5618.

Venissa wine estate in Mazzorbo, Burano

© M. Mionetto/MICHELIN

- 10850 Wilshire Blvd, Suite 575
  Los Angeles CA 90024;
  ℘(310) 820 1898.
- 3800 Division Street, Stone Park,
  Chicago IL 60165.
  ℘(312) 644 0996.

Canada
69 Yonge Street, Suite 1404.
Toronto Ontario M5E 1K3.
℘(416) 925 4882.

TOURIST OFFICES IN VENICE

The **Ufficio informazioni** and its branches provide brochures, maps and lists of hotels, youth hostels and campsites free of charge. The city centre tourist offices are located at the west end of the Procuratie Nuove, off Piazza San Marco; Airport Marco Polo, Piazzale Roma (Garage San Marco); and Santa Lucia Railway Station. All have the same telephone number as the main office. From the 1st February 2016 the Information Service for the City of Venice will be managed by the Company VELA S.P.A. For any information contact Hello Venezia. ℘041 2424. www.veneziaunica.it/en

INTERNATIONAL VISITORS
ITALIAN EMBASSIES ABROAD
- 14 Three Kings Yard,
  London W1Y 2EH, UK.
  ℘020 7312 2200.
  www.amblondra.esteri.it
- 3000 Whitehaven St, NW
  Washington, DC 20008, USA.
  ℘(202) 612 4400.
  www.ambwashingtondc.esteri.it
- 275 Slater Street, 21st floor,
  Ottawa, Ontario K1P 5H9, Canada;
  ℘(613) 232 2401/2/3.
  www.ambottawa.esteri.it

ITALIAN CONSULATES ABROAD
- Harp House 83-86, Farringdon
  Street, London EC4A 4BL.
  ℘020 7936 5900.
  www.conslondra.esteri.it
- 32 Melville Street, Edinburgh
  EH3 7HA, UK.
  ℘(0131) 226 3631.
  www.consedimburgo.esteri.it

Tourist Office
AZIENDA DI PROMOZIONE TURISTICA
© Gwen Cannon / MICHELIN

- 690 Park Avenue,
  New York, NY 10065, USA.
  ℘(212) 737 9100.
  www.consnewyork.esteri.it
- 3489 Drummond Street,
  Montreal, Quebec H3G 1X6
  Canada.
  ℘(514) 849 8351.
  www.consmontreal.esteri.it
- 136 Beverley Street, Toronto,
  Ontario, M5T 1Y5, Canada;
  ℘(416) 977 1566.
  www.constoronto.esteri.it

FOREIGN EMBASSIES AND CONSULATES IN ITALY
Australia
- **Consulate general**: 3rd Floor,
  Via Borgogna 2, Milan.
  ℘02 777 04 217.
- **Embassy**: Via Antonio Bosio 5,
  Rome. ℘06 85 27 21.
  www.italy.embassy.gov.au

Canada
- **Consulate**: Piazza Cavour 3,
  Milan. ℘02 626 94 238.
- **Embassy**: Via Zara 30, Rome.
  ℘06 85 44 42 911.
  www.canada.it

Ireland
- For **consulate** see UK below.
- **Embassy**: Villa Spada,
  Via Giacomo Medici 1, Rome.
  ℘06 58 52 381.
  www.dfa.ie/irish-embassy/italy

UK

- **Honorary consulate** in Venice: Piazzale Donatori di Sangue 2/5, Mestre.
  ☎041 5055 990.
- **British embassy**: Via XX Settembre 80a, Rome.
  ☎06 42 20 00 01.
  www.italiantouristboard.co.uk

USA

- **Consulate**: Via Principe Amedeo 2/10, Milan.
  ☎02 290 351.
  italian.milan.usconsulate.gov
- **Embassy**: Via Veneto 121, Rome.
  ☎06 46 741.
  italy.usembassy.gov

ENTRY REQUIREMENTS

British visitors travelling to Italy must be in possession of a valid national passport. Citizens of other European Union countries need only a national identity card. In case of loss or theft report to the embassy or consulate and the local police.

Entry visas are required for Australian, New Zealand, Canadian and US citizens (if the intended stay exceeds three months). Apply to the Italian Consulate (visa may be issued same day to personal callers; delay if submitted by mail).

US citizens may find the website www.travel.state.gov useful for information on visa requirements, customs regulations, medical care, etc.

CUSTOMS REGULATIONS

For the most up-to-date information on what you can and cannot import and export and duty-free allowances on alcohol, tobacco and other goods, visit www.hmce.gov.uk (and enter "Travel" in the Search option).
US citizens should visit www.cbp.gov for equivalent information.

HEALTH

As the UK is a member of the European Union, British subjects should obtain a **European Health Insurance Card (EHIC)** available from main post offices, before leaving home.

However the EHIC card only covers minimum medical expenses so separate travel and medical insurance is highly recommended.

ACCESSIBILITY

Sights in this guide marked with the ♿ symbol have full or near full access for wheelchairs. However, it is highly recommended that you call the sight in advance to determine the extent of their facilities. Quite understandably many Venetian historic monuments and attractions do not have lifts or wheelchair facilities, although some ramps were added in recent years. Wheelchairs may be loaded onto the vaporettos but not onto the gondolas. Information on accessibility for wheelchair visitors is available online at the Venice City Council website, www.comune.venezia. it or www.veneziacittapertutti.it.
☎ 041 27 48 144 or 96 55 440. This is an excellent resource (in English) listing suitable public transport, accommodation and attractions in some detail; for example ramps, accessible public toilets, and so on. It also says whether there are aids for blind or visually impaired visitors. There is more information on visitors with **impaired vision** on the City Council website at www. comune.venezia.it, although this is only in Italian.
UK travellers should contact:

- **Tourism for All UK** (formerly Holiday Care).
  ☎0845 124 9971.
  www.tourismforall.org.uk)
- **RADAR** (Royal Association for Disability and Rehabilitation), Ground Floor, CAN Mezzanine, 49-51 East Rd London N1 6AH.
  ☎020 7250 8181.
  www.radar.org.uk

Getting There and Getting Around

See p30 for details of accommodation taxes and Venice's unique definition of high and low season.

See p30 for details of accommodation taxes and Venice's unique definition of high and low season.

BY PLANE

Venice is served by dozens of international and domestic flights arriving at **Marco Polo Airport** (including budget Easyjet flights from the UK), about 10km/6mi (*20min*) from the city by vehicle. 041 26 06 111. www.veniceairport.it.
Six budget airlines, including Ryanair, use Treviso S Angelo airport (0422 315 111. www.trevisoairport.it) which is 30km/18mi north of Venice.

AIRPORT TRANSFERS

By Bus: Marco Polo airport is linked to Venice's Piazzale Roma by **ACTV bus** no 5 (€8, €15 AR, €14 for Airbus sea service, valid 90 minutes from the time of validation. www. veneziaunica.it. 041 24 24) and an **ATVO shuttle coach** (www.atvo.it). From Treviso airport ATVO buses run to Mestre Railway station and Venice (€12. Piazzale Roma) in time with departures and arrivals of Ryanair and

☺ Arriving in Venice ☺

The final stop in Venice for buses, taxis and cars is Piazzale Roma. From here you will have to walk with your luggage to the hotel. You can take the vaporetto service, but boats can be crowded and there's a fee for more than one bag.

Transavia flights. The journey takes around 1hr 10min.
By Taxi: Taxis are available from Marco Polo to Piazzale Roma (€40; 041 59 64. www.radiotaxivenezia.com).
By Water: Alilaguna boats cross the lagoon with a choice of two routes; the Red Line or the Blue Line, which between them serve all major parts of the city, including the Lido and Murano. The dock for Alilaguna (and private water taxis) is a 5 minute walk from the airport, or a 1 minute ride on the airport shuttle (€1).
As a rough guide as to the speed and cost of the service, it takes 70 minutes to reach Piazza San Marco and costs €15 (27 €round trip). For more detailed information on ticket prices and timetables, visit www. alilaguna.it. Private **water taxis** offer a much faster 35 minute door-to-door service, but are very expensive

Venice Simplon-Orient-Express

The Orient Express was the brainchild of the Belgian **Georges Nagelmackers**, who inaugurated the service in 1883. In 1906 the Simplon tunnel was excavated through the mountains between Switzerland and Italy (19.8km/12mi). The route could extend from Milan to Venice and on to Constantinople (56hr from Paris). After World War II, the legendary luxury train's financial problems eventually forced its closure in 1977. Revived in 1982, the trains have been restored to their former splendour, and include wood panelling, Lalique glass and Art Deco-style lamps. The Venice Simplon-Orient-Express leaves from London for Venice stopping in Paris. The full trip takes about 32hr, covering 1 715km/1 065mi. Other London routes go through Budapest, Prague or Vienna. Venice trains also depart for Istanbul; in 2013 a new Venice-Copenhagen-Stockholm route was launched.
For details, contact the office of **Venice Simplon-Orient-Express Ltd.** in the UK: 800 780 700, or www.belmond.com/venice-simplon-orient-express.

Highway Code

- In Italy vehicles drive on the **right-hand side** of the road.
- The **minimum driving age** is 18 years.
- **Seat belts** must be worn in the front and back of the vehicle. Drivers must wear **shoes**, carry **spare lights** and have a **red triangle** to be displayed in the event of a breakdown or accident.
- Emergency **road-rescue services** are offered by the **Automobile Club Italiano (ACI)**, ✆ 803 116.
- **Motorways** (*autostrade* – subject to tolls) and dual carriageways (*superstrade*) are indicated by green signs, ordinary roads by blue signs, and tourist sights by yellow or brown signs.
- Italian **motorway tolls** can be paid for with cash or with the **Viacard**, a magnetic card that is sold in Italy at the entrances and exits of motorways, in Autogrill restaurants and in the offices of the ACI (Automobile Club Italiano).
- The following **speed restrictions** are enforced:
  - 50kph/31mph in built-up areas.
  - 90–110kph/56–69mph on open country roads.
  - 90kph/56mph (600cc) to 130kph/81mph (excess of 1 000cc) on motorways, depending on engine capacity.
- **Fuel** is sold as *super* (4 star), *senza piombo* (unleaded 95 octane), *super plus* or *Euro plus* (unleaded 98 octane) and *gasolio* (diesel). Petrol (US: Gas) stations are usually open from 7am to 7pm. Many close at lunch time (12.30–3pm), as well as on Sundays and public holidays; many refuse payment by credit card.

(expect to pay at least €110). www.motoscafivenezia.it

BY SHIP

Venice Ferry Port is the busiest and most popular Southern European entrance to the Adriatic and Mediterranean Sea, handling around 500 major ship departures and 700 000 cruise passengers per year (most services run Apr–Oct only).

Venezia Lines (www.venezialines.com) operates from Venice to Slovenia (Piran, 2hr 30min) and several ports in Croatia: Mali Losinj 4hr 30min; Pula 3hr (then onto Lussino); Umago and Porec, 2hr 30mins; Rovinj, 2hr 45min; Rabac 4hr.

Viamare (www.viamare.com) also run ferries between Venice and Rabac. Both **Anek Lines** and **Minoan Lines** (www.minoan.gr) operate ferries from Venice to Patras and Igoumenitsa on the Greek mainland, and also to Corfu.

Book for all services with www.direct-ferries.co.uk, or www.aferry.co.uk. Many large **cruise operators** also call in at Venice. Some passenger cruise lines are Celebrity, MSC Italian Cruises, Princess, Carnival, Crystal, Cunard, Holland America, and Sea Cloud. Large ships generally use the main Marittima terminal, although this may change. It's about a 15min walk or a 5min taxi or shuttle-bus ride from the Piazzale Roma. Smaller ships also use this cruise terminal or they may use San Basilio terminal, on the Zattere promenade, fronting the Giudecca Canal, which is within easy walking distance or a short vaporetto ride from the Piazza.

BY TRAIN

Trenitalia, the Italian state railroad, runs its main line from Milan to Trieste via Brescia, Verona, Vicenza and Padova passes through Venice, www.trenitalia.com. Italo, a private company, launched high-speed trains, www.italotreno.it. A more luxurious alternative is the **Venice Simplon-Orient-Express Ltd**. Travelling at a leisurely pace in original 1920s and '30s carriages, the VSOE leaves from London and stops in Paris, Innsbruck, Verona and Venice (&see Box below).

BY COACH/BUS

Coach services from Victoria Coach Station, London, are organised by National Express/Eurolines, &44 (0) 371 818 181, www.eurolines.co.uk.
Alternatively visit your nearest National Express office or agent.

BY CAR
FORMALITIES

Nationals of the European Union require a valid **national driving licence**. Nationals of non-EU countries should get an **international driving licence**, obtainable in the US from the American Automobile Association (www.aaa.com). Other documents required include the vehicle's current **registration document** and a **green card** for insurance.

MAIN ROADS

Venice is situated off the A 4 Torino–Trieste road, reached from the south by the A 13 Bologna to Padua road. Exit at Mestre onto the SS 11, then cross the Ponte della Libertà to Piazzale Roma.

MAPS

Michelin Tourist and Motoring Atlas Italy and Michelin Maps *no. 705* Europe (1:3 000 000), *no. 735* Italy (1:1 000 000) and *no. 562* Northeast Italy (1:400 000) will make route planning easier.

PARKING
Mestre

Parking in San Giuliano starting from €12 per day. &041 53 22 632. www.avmspa.it.
Piazzale Roma

The municipal **ASM garage**, (&041 27 27 301. www.avmspa.it) at Piazzale

Roma costs €26 to €29 per day, depending on season and size of vehicle. Discounts available online (www.veneziaunica.it)
Another possibility at Piazzale Roma is the **Garage San Marco** (&041 52 32 213. mobile.garagesanmarco.it), which charges €30 (€28 online) for 24hr.

Tronchetto

To the west of Piazzale Roma, Interparking Italia (&041 52 07 555. www.veniceparking.it) on the island of **Tronchetto**—exit from the Liberty Bridge, serviced by vaporetto—charges cars, camper-vans and caravans around €21 for 24hr.

ON FOOT

The easiest way of getting around is on foot. Always carry a map but don't worry if you get lost—everyone does, and soon finds their way again. It is all part of the Venice experience.
Venice's system of house numbers can reach remarkable heights (up to almost 7 000), as these numbers refer to individually numbered addresses within the whole **sestière** rather than to a particular street or square. Even numbers are not always on one side of the street or odd ones on the other! Watch for the closest campo (square) and for yellow signs with directional arrows to major sights like the Rialto and Piazza San Marco.

ON WATER
VAPORETTO (WATERBUS)

&*See map of vaporetto routes on the inside back cover of the guide.*
As conventional cities use conventional buses, so Venice is served by **waterbuses**, run by **ACTV** (&041 27 22 111 or 041 24 24. www. actv.avmspa.it). These come in two kinds: the lumbering *vaporetto* (plural, *vaporetti)*, and, for longer distances, the faster *motoscafo* (motor boat, plural *motoscafi*).
Visitors should note that the name of a vaporetto stop does not necessarily mean that the waterbus will stop outside the monument after which it

is named – however it will always be in the close vicinity. Traffic on the Grand Canal is often congested and services may sometimes be erratic. A reduced service operates at night: it's best to check the timetables on display or visit www.actv.it for all timetable enquiries.

Single tickets may be purchased from kiosks or machines at each landing stage, from Hellovenezia ticket desks, and from shops displaying the ACTV sign. A single ticket costs €7,50 and allows 1hr of travel including a change in the same direction of travel, but *not* a return trip. Unless you are making a very fleeting visit it makes sense to buy a Tourist Travel Card (*biglietto turistico*), which allows unlimited travel for the following prices: 12hr €18; 24hr €20; 36hr €25; 48hr €30; 72hr €40; 7 days €60.

A three-day "youth card" is available to anyone aged between 15 and 29 in possession of a Rolling Venice Card (on sale at the www.veneziaunica. it ticket desks for €6) and allows 72 hours of travel for €20.

If you board without a ticket, you must request one immediately from the *marinaio* (sailor/attendant) in charge of the boarding gate. On-the-spot fines may be levied against passengers without a ticket.

Line 1 runs from Piazzale Roma and the railway station, the full length of the Grand Canal (14 stops) to Piazza San Marco and on to the Lido. It is known as the *accelerato*, although in some ways this is the slowest line.

Line 82 follows the same route as Line 1, but makes fewer stops and is therefore quicker. It runs from Tronchetto to Piazzale Roma, Giudecca, San Giorgio, San Marco and on to the Lido.

WATER TAXIS

Beware of touts out to overcharge the unsuspecting visitor! Use only authorised motor launches bearing a yellow registration number plate inscribed with the symbol of Venice on the boarding side. It is also worth ensuring that the meter is clearly visible and that charge rates are displayed.

There is a fixed starting price of €15 then a charge of €2 per minute. A ten minute ride across the city centre will cost approximately €70 (with small additional charges for night taxis, for carrying luggage and if you have more than four passengers in your group).

If you have any queries or wish to register a complaint contact the Azienda Trasporto Persone Venezia, S. Castello, 6385 ℘041 24 06 712 (Mon–Fri); 041 52 22 303 (Sat, Sun and public hols).

The following are authorised operators

♦ **Coop. Bucintoro, S. Croce, 328** ℘041 72 30 09

A typical waterbus

Actv 29

G. Rooney / age fotostock

- **Coop. Ducale, Isola Nova del Tronchetto, 14** ✆ 041 52 27 255
- **Coop. Motoscafi San Giorgio, S. Polo, 1151/a** ✆ 041 29 60 570
- **Coop. Motoscafi Taxi, Cannaregio, 85** ✆ 041 71 65 44
- **Coop. San Marco, S. Castello, 4512** ✆ 041 52 82 971
- **Coop. Trasbagagli, Santa Croce, 496c** ✆ 041 71 37 19

SELF DRIVE BOATS

A Venetian *topo* (open-topped motor boat), which can accommodate up to six people can be hired from two operators:

Brussa (*S. Cannaregio, 331* ✆ *041 71 57 87, brussaisboat.it*) by the Ponte delle Guglie, near the station. €20 per hour.

Cantiere Lizzio/Sport e Lavoro, (*Cannaregio, 2607A* ✆ *041 72 10 55*). €120 for the day.

Beware that although this is an unusual and exciting way to explore the city, Ventian lagoons and canals are busy waterways and you really should be an experienced boat driver.

GONDOLAS

For a relaxing trip on a gondola, be prepared to put your hand in your wallet: 30min along the canals during the daytime will cost you, and up to 6 other passengers, €80 (a musical serenade is extra).

Every additional 20min will be charged an extra €40.

A 35min trip by gondola at night (7pm–8am) costs €100, with an extra €50 for every further 20min.

Beware that although these are the official charges, they may also be subject to negotiation, depending on your own circumstances and where you want to go. You can decide how to reach your destination and ask the gondolier to follow the route you have chosen.

For contact details, contact the Istituzione per la Conservazione della Gondola e la Tutela del Gondoliere ✆ 041 52 85 075. For an official list of prices visit www.gondolavenezia.it/storia_tariffe.asp.

Gondolas and view of Isola di S. Giorgio Maggiore

© Gwen Cannon / MICHELIN

TRAGHETTI

You don't need to spend lots of money to ride in a gondola. Simply hop aboard a *traghetto* (gondola ferry). These operate at eight points along the Grand Canal (Ferrovia, San Marcuola, Santa Sofia, Riva del Carbon, San Tomà, San Samuele, Santa Maria del Giglio and Dogana). The relative absence of bridges across the Grand Canal (Calatrava, Scalzi, Rialto and Accademia), has given the traditional gondolier a continuing ferry role in Venice's day to day public transport system, a role that has been dramatically whittled down by the vaporettos.

The Venetian custom is to remain standing up. For less steady visitors however there is no compulsion to stand during the crossing; it is better to arrive seated than to be fished out of the Grand Canal!

A *traghetto* costs a mere €2 (slightly higher from San Samuele during exhibitions at Palazzo Grassi).

Times of operation are posted at the landing stages, though beware they finish quite early (before 8pm) and in winter services may be suspended completely.

Calendar of Events

Here is a selection of the most important and colourful annual events:

6 JANUARY
Regata della Befana – Epiphany boat race with contestants dressed as witches racing to a giant stocking at Rialto Bridge!

10 DAYS BEFORE LENT (FEB–MAR)
Carnevale – The year's most famous celebration featuring costumed revellers in masks throughout the city. www.carnevale.venezia.it. (👝see ART and CULTURE).

MARCH
Su e zo per i ponti – A non-competitive race through the streets of Venice. www.suezo.it/en/
Gusto in Scena – Food and wine tastings in Venice, usually in Scuola Grande San Giovanni Evangelista.

MAUNDY THURSDAY
Benediction – Candle-lighting procession outside Basilica di San Marco.

25 APRIL
Feast day of St Mark – Men give their sweethearts a *bòcolo* (a red rose).

MAY
Regata di Mestre and **Regata di Sant'Erasmo** – Regattas usually second and fourth Sundays at Mestre and the Island of Sant'Erasmo.
Vino in Villa – Conegliano hosts Prosecco Superiore DOCG winemakers with tastings in the San Salvatore Castle in Susegana. www.vinoinvilla.it. (👝see CONEGLIANO).
The **Vogalonga** – A non-competitive regatta open to foreign rowers around the islands. www.vogalonga.com.

ASCENSION DAY
The **Sensa** commemorates the Sposalizio del Mar. http://events.veneziaunica.it/it/content/festa-della-sensa (👝see Time Line 1177).

29 JUNE
Regata di Santi Giovanni e Paolo – Regatta on feast day of two saints.

JULY
Regata di Murano and **Regata di Malamocco** – Regattas in early/mid June on these islands.

THIRD SUNDAY IN JULY
Festa del Redentore. Feast of the Redeemer, commemorating the end of the plague in 1576, culminating in a huge fireworks display over the lagoon (👝see GIUDECCA).

AUGUST–EARLY SEPT
Regata di Pellestrina – Regatta early Aug. (👝see PELLESTRINA)
Venice Film Festival – glittering movie jamboree with top stars from all over the world jetting into the Lido (👝see IL LIDO).
Biennale – Odd numbered years for Art, even Numbered Years for Architecture, Dance and Theatre. International exhibitions of art and culture (👝see SANT'ELENA E SAN PITERO).

SEPTEMBER
Regata Storica – *First Sun in Sept.* Historic regatta re-enactment with a costumed pageant and races on the Grand Canal. www.regatastoricavenezia.it.
Regata di Burano and **Regata di San Michele**– Regattas usually third and fourth Sundays in Sept. (👝see BURANO and SAN MICHELE)

21 NOVEMBER
Feast of the Madonna della Salute - commemorating the end of the plague in 1576 with a bridge of boats across the Grand Canal to La Salute (👝see La SALUTE).

What to See and Do

OUTDOOR FUN

When you feel the need for a break from culture, you don't have far to go. Lido offers swimming, cycling and golf; Cavallino (6mi/10km east of Venice) boasts 9.5mi/15km of beaches and is said to be the largest open-air resort in Europe, while neighbouring Lido di Jesolo—not to be confused with Lido—is another huge beach strip with plenty of water sports on offer.

CYCLING

Cycling is not permitted in the historic centre but bikes are allowed on several of the lagoon islands (including Lido, Pellestrina, Sant'Erasmo), as well as mainland Venice (Mestre and Marghera) and Cavallino.

There are several places to hire bikes at the Lido and Cavallino. From the Lido, try www.venicebike rental.com and www.lidoonbike.it. Hire rates are around €9 per day.

GOLF

The nearest 18-hole golf course is Circolo Golf on The Lido (℘041 73 13 33. circologolfvenezia.it). Many big names have played here and Arnold Palmer holds the course record of 67.

FISHING

Ernest Hemingway once fished in the lagoon (even though he was more interested in duck shooting here!). For sport fishing call ℘041 98 48 71.

MOUNTAIN SPORTS

Cortina d'Ampezzo is the adventure capital of the Dolomites catering for just about every winter and summer mountain sport.

For one-stop adventure sports call at **The Cortina Adrenaline Center** (℘335 81 55 177. www. adrenalincenter.it) which offers canyoning, rafting, kayaking, bob sledding), mountain biking, snow rafting, trekking with snowshoes (and sled) and wilderness training.

Rock Climbing

For climbing and trekking contact the **Gruppo Guide Alpine Scuola di Alpinismo** in Cortina d'Ampezzo (℘0436 86 85 05 www.guidecortina.com).

Skiing and other winter sports

The Dolomites and the nearby Val pusteria (Pustertal) with its Kronplatz ski area, are blessed with many world-

---

Lord Byron In Venice

Lord Byron, the great poet, was famous for swimming in Venice as detailed in this letter he wrote in 1821: "*In 1818 the chevalier Mengaldo (a Gentleman of Bassano) a good swimmer, wished to swim with my friend Mr. Alexander Scott and myself. As he seemed particularly anxious on the subject, we indulged him. We all three started from the island of the Lido and swam to Venice. At the entrance of the Grand Canal, Scott and I were a good deal ahead, and we saw no more of our foreign friend, which however was of no consequence, as there was a gondola to hold his clothes and pick him up. Scott swam on past the Rialto, when he got out less from fatigue than from chill, having been for hours in the water without rest of stay except what is to be obtained by floating on one's back, this being the condition of our performance. I continued my course on to Santa Chiara, comprising the whole of the Grand Canal/beside the distance from the Lido, and got out where the laguna once more opened to Farina. I had been in the water by my watch without help or rest and never touching ground or boat for four hours and twenty minutes.*"

In fact Byron had covered a distance of around 4.5mi/7km!

class ski resorts with schools that cater for foreign visitors. Cortina d'Ampezzo is the most famous, most glamorous and has the widest range, but other top resorts include Vigo di Fassa, Canazei), St Ulrich/Ortisel, Selva Val Gardena, Bruneck (Dietenheim), Dobbiaco (Toblach) and San Martino di Castrozza (*see pages 240–246 for details*).

RIDING

The best place for horseriding is in the beautiful hills of the Colli Berici just south of Vicenza. Visit www.colliberici. com (then Sport/Equitazione) for details of various ranches and schools.

WATER SPORTS

Bathing

Go to the Lido, Cavallino or Lido di Jesolo for sea bathing. On Lido the best beaches have been annexed by the big hotels and if you want access to these you will have to pay. There are free public beaches at both the northern and southern extremities of the island. The water anywhere on the Lido is not particularly clean: the quality is better at Cavallino and Lido di Jesolo

Windsurfing

Windsurfs are for hire at Lido, Cavallino and Lido di Jesolo (www.unionlido.com).

ACTIVITIES FOR KIDS 🧑‍🧒

In this guide, sights of interest to children are indicated with a 🧑‍🧒 *symbol*. Venice isn't an obvious place to take children as there are no museums or attractions geared to them and there is little room to let off steam running around. Kicking or throwing a ball in the historic centre can have dire consequences with the city authorities, and feeding the pigeons was banned. However, for children of a certain age, a city with canals for main streets and boats instead of motor cars has a real fascination. Consider staying away from the centre, where younger ones will have running space. The glass blowers at **Murano★★** and

the **Natural History Museum** may captivate well-behaved youngsters, while a trip to the seaside is always a good idea. There is not so much space, and often a quieter atmosphere at Lido, but Cavallino and Lido di Jesolo are geared for families. The big attraction for kids at Jesolo is the Aqualandia **waterpark** (*Via Michelangelo Buonarroti ⏰Open Jun to mid-Sept daily 10am–6pm. €31, child 1m–1.4m €27. ☎0421 37 16 48. www.aqualandia.it*).

A little further east, at Caorle, there is another smaller water park, Parco Acquatico (*Viale Aldo Moro. ⏰Open late May to mid-Sept daily 10am–6pm. €20, child up to 1.4m €16. ☎042 181 423. www.aquafollie.it*). Caorle also has good beaches.

BOOKS
ART

Venetian Painting: a Concise History – John Steer (Thames and Hudson 1970)

The Stones of Venice – John Ruskin (Da Capo Press 1985)

Palladio and Palladianism – Robert Tavernor (Thames and Hudson 1991)

Palladio – JS Ackerman, P Dearborn Massar (Illustrator) (Penguin Books 1991)

Palladio's Villas – Paul Holberton (John Murray 1991)

Five Centuries of Music in Venice – HC Robbins Landon, John Julius Norwich (Thames and Hudson 1991)

Ruskin's Venice: The Stones Revisited – Sarah Quill, Alan Windsor (Introduction) (Ashgate Publ. 1999)

HISTORICAL REFERENCE

The Travels of Marco Polo – Marco Polo, R Latham (Trans) (Penguin Books 1965)

A History of Venice – John Julius Norwich (Penguin Books 1983)

The Venetian Empire – Jan Morris (Penguin Books 1990)

Venice Rediscovered – John Pemble (Oxford University Press 1996)

LITERATURE

Italian Journey – Goethe (Penguin Books 1970)

The Aspern Papers – Henry James, Anthony Curtis (Ed) (Penguin Books 1984)

The Wings of the Dove – Henry James, J Bayley (Ed), P Crick (Ed) (Penguin Books 1986)

The Desire and Pursuit of the Whole – Frederick Rolfe (Da Capo Press 1986)

Territorial Rights: Complete and Unabridged – Muriel Spark, Nigel Hawthorne (Narrator) (Chivers Audio Books 1990)

The Quest for Corvo – AJA Symons (Quartet Books 1993)

Across the River and into the Trees – Ernest Hemingway (Arrow 1994)

Thus was Adonis Murdered – Sarah Caudwell (Dell Publishing Company 1994)

A Literary Companion to Venice – Ian Littlewood (St Martin's Press 1995)

Dead Lagoon – Michael Dibdin (Faber and Faber 1995)

Death in Venice and Other Stories – Thomas Mann (Minerva 1996)

The Passion – Jeanette Winterson (Vintage 1996)

The Comfort of Strangers – Ian McEwan (Vintage 1997)

Volpone – Ben Jonson [can be found in *Volpone and Other Early Plays* – Ben Jonson, Lorna Hutson (Ed) (Penguin Books 1998)]

The Merchant of Venice – William Shakespeare, Jay L Halio (Ed) (Oxford Paperbacks 1998)

An Italian Journey – Jean Giono, J Cumming (Trans) (Northwestern University Press 1998)

Miss Garnet's Angel – Salley Vickers (HarperCollins 2001)

The City of Falling Angels – John Berendt (Companion Guides 1997)

OTHER GUIDES

Ghetto of Venice – Roberta Curiel, Bernard Dov Cooperman (Tauris Parke 1990)

Venice – Ian Littlewood (John Murray 1992)

Companion Guide to Venice – Hugh Honour (Companion Guides 1997)

Venice for Pleasure – JG Links (Pallas Athene 1999)

The Stones of Florence and Venice Observed – Mary McCarthy (Penguin Books 2000) Piazzale Roma.

FILMS

Il Ponte dei Sospiri (Bridge of Sighs) (1921) – A plot to assassinate the doge and romantic intrigues made this silent film a hit that even today delights.

Top Hat (1935) – Ginger Rogers and Fred Astaire dancing cheek to cheek and having a good time in La Serenissima.

Summertime (1955) – Romance sparks between Rossano Brazzi and Katharine Hepburn in *Summertime*. She falls in love and also into the canal (did her own stunt) at Campo San Barnaba!

From Russia with Love (1963) – Sean Connery as James Bond goes to Murano in search of a particular glassmaker. An amphibious gondola scatters pigeons in St Mark's Square!

Death in Venice (1971) – Based on the novella by Thomas Mann, Luchino Visconti directs Dirk Bogarde in the lead role; panoramic shots span the sultry lagoon and the Lido, particularly Hotel des Bains.

Don't Look Now (1973) – This psychic thriller is based on a story by Daphne du Maurier. Nicholas Roeg directs Donald Sutherland and Julie Christie.

Casanova (1976) – Fellini films the life and loves of the notorious Venetian rake.

Don Giovanni (1979) – A beautiful adaptation of Mozart's opera, populated by masked figures stepping out of swirling mists from boats in the Brenta Valley.

Indiana Jones and The Last Crusade (1989) – Indy jumps out of the library into Campo San Barnaba, in a cameo.

UNESCO

Cultural World Heritage Sites in Italy

18C Royal Palace at Caserta with the Park, the Aqueduct of Vanvitelli, and the San Leucio Complex (1997)

Arab-Norman Palermo and the Cathedral Churches of Cefalú and Monreale (2015)

Archaeological Area and the Patriarchal Basilica of Aquileia (1998)

Archaeological Area of Agrigento (1997)

Archaeological Areas of Pompei, Herculaneum and Torre Annunziata (1997)

Assisi, the Basilica of San Francesco and Other Franciscan Sites (2000)

Botanical Garden (Orto Botanico), Padua (1997)

Castel del Monte (1996)

Cathedral, Torre Civica and Piazza Grande, Modena (1997)

Church and Dominican Convent of Santa Maria delle Grazie (1980)

Cilento and Vallo di Diano National Park (1998)

City of Verona (2000)

City of Vicenza and the Palladian Villas of the Veneto (1994)

Costiera Amalfitana (1997)

Crespi d'Adda (1995)

Early Christian Monuments of Ravenna (1996)

Etruscan Necropolises of Cerveteri and Tarquinia (2004)

Ferrara, City of the Renaissance and its Po Delta (1995)

Genoa: Le Strade Nuove and the system of the Palazzi dei Rolli (2006)

Historic Centre of Florence (1982)

Historic Centre of Naples (1995)

Historic Centre of Rome, the Properties of the Holy See in that City Enjoying Extraterritorial Rights and San Paolo Fuori le Mura (1980)

Historic Centre of San Gimignano (1990)

Historic Centre of Siena (1995)

Historic Centre of the City of Pienza (1996)

Historic Centre of Urbino (1998)

Late-Baroque towns of the Val di Noto *(Southeastern Sicily)* (2002)

Longobards, Places of Power (2011)

Mantua and Sabbioneta (2008)

Medici Villas and Gardens in Tuscany (2013)

Piazza del Duomo, Pisa (1987)

Portovenere, Cinque Terre and the Islands *(Palmaria, Tino and Tinetto)* (1997)

Residences of the Royal House of Savoy (1997)

Rhaetian Railway in the Albula / Bernina Landscapes (2008)

Rock Drawings in Valcamonica (1979)

Sacri Monti of Piedmont and Lombardy (2003)

Su Nuraxi di Barumini (1997)

Syracuse and the Rocky Necropolis of Pantalica (2005)

The Trulli of Alberobello (1996)

The Sassi and the Park of the Rupestrian Churches of Matera (1993)

Val d'Orcia (2004)

Venice and its Lagoon (1987)

Villa Adriana (Tivoli) (1999)

Villa d'Este, Tivoli (2001)

Villa Romana del Casale (1997)

Vineyard Landscape of Piedmont: Langhe-Roero and Monferrato (2014)

Natural:

Isole Eolie *(Aeolian Islands)* (2000)

Monte San Giorgio (2003)

The Dolomites (2009)

Mount Etna (2013)

UNESCO

"Our cultural and natural heritage are both irreplaceable sources of life and inspiration", insists the United Nations Educational, Scientific and Cultural Organization (UNESCO). This non-profit group has helped preserve locations since 1972.

More than 180 State Parties have joined in protecting over 800 sites "of outstanding universal value" on the World Heritage List. Representatives from 21 countries, assisted by technical organisations, annually evaluate proposals. A site must be nominated by its home country. The protected cultural heritage may be monuments (buildings, sculptures, archaeological structures, etc.) with unique historic, artistic or scientific features; groups of buildings (such as religious communities and ancient cities); or sites (human settlements and exceptional landscapes), which are the combined works of man and the earth's beauty. Sites may celebrate the stages of geological history or the development of human cultures and creative genius. They may also honour significant ecological processes, superlative natural phenomena or provide a habitat for threatened species.

Well-known sites include: Australia's Great Barrier Reef (1981), India's Taj Mahal and Peru's Macchu Pichu (1983), the Vatican City and the United States' Statue of Liberty (1984), Canada's Rocky Mountain Parks (1984), Jordan's Petra (1985), The Great Wall of China and Greece's Acropolis (1987), Russia's Kremlin and Red Square (1990), England's Stonehenge (1986), Indonesia's Komodo National Park and France's Banks of the Seine (1991), Cambodia's Angor Wat (1992) and Japan's Hiroshima Peace Memorial (1996).

Italy's latest UNESCO sites are Tivoli's Villa Adriana (1999), Assisi's Basilica of San Francesco and Other Franciscan Sites (2000), the City of Verona (2000), the Aeolian Islands (2000), Tivoli's Villa d'Este (2001), Southeastern Sicily's late-Baroque towns of the Val di Noto (2002), the Sacri Monti of Piedmont and Lombardy (2003), Etruscan Necropolises of Cerveteri and Tarquinia (2004), Val d'Orcia (2004), and Syracuse and the Rocky Necropolis of Pantalica (2005), Genoa: Le Strade Nuove and the Palazzi dei Rolli (2006), the Rhaetian Railway in the Albula / Bernina Landscapes (2008), The Dolomites (2009), Mount Etna (2013), Zibibbo di Pantelleria (2014), Arab-Norman Palermo and the Cathedral Churches of Cefalú and Monreale (2015).

Blame it on the Bellboy (1992) – Mistaken identity in this comedy of hotel errors set in Venice.

Carrington (1995) – The painter, Dora Carrington (Emma Thompson) and the artist, Lytton Strachey (Jonathan Pryce) in WW1 England and on a visit to Venice.

Othello (1995) – Directed by Oliver Parker, Laurence Fishburne as Othello and Kenneth Branagh as Iago play out their tragic Shakespearian roles.

Everyone Says I Love You (1996) – Woody Allen directs and stars in the musical, set in New York, Venice (Scuola di San Rocco) and Paris.

Dangerous Beauty (1998) – Intellectual and courtesan Victoria Franco in 16C Venice.

The Talented Mr. Ripley (1999) – Anthony Minghella directs Matt Damon, Gwyneth Paltrow, Jude Law and Cate Blanchett, shot partly in Venice.

Pane e tulipani (Bread and Tulips) (2000) – A portrait of the real Venice, inhabited by mildly eccentric characters.

The Italian Job (2003) – This thriller begins with a bank heist in Venice, also is set in the Italian Alps.

Casino Royale (2006) – As James Bond, Daniel Craig finds the usual mayhem including an entire palazzo demolished into the Grand Canal!

Brideshead Revisited (2008) – Aristocratic memoirs, partly filmed in Venice, starring Emma Thompson, Michael Gambon and Greta Scacchi.

The Tourist (2010) – The canal chase scenes are more intriguing than the lack of chemistry between Angelina Jolie and Johnny Depp.

Shun Li and the Poet (Io Sono Li) (2011) – A delicate friendship between a Chinese immigrant and a poet fisherman, set in a bar and the silvery waters of Chioggia.

Merchant of Venice and *Othello* – Shakespeare's tragedy unfolds in various film versions from silent films to Al Pacino as Shylock (2004), while plays on film include a 1973 BBC videotaped production with Laurence Olivier in that role. National Theatre Live's production of *Othello* (2013) takes place in an outpost of Venice.

Otello – Opera on film includes Franco Zeffirelli's 1986 opera filmed on location, as well as the Metropolitan Opera (2012) and San Carlo (2014).

Basic Information

BUSINESS HOURS

SHOPS

Shops are generally open from 9am to 12.30/1pm and 1pm to 6pm, although many stay open during lunchtime. More shops are open in high season than in low season, and normally extend their business hours to accommodate the extra customers. Some businesses are closed on Mondays. *For bank opening times, see Money.*

MUSEUMS AND CHURCHES

The main churches in Venice are open 7am–noon and 4–6pm. Visitors should be dressed appropriately: long trousers for men; no bare shoulders or very short skirts for women. If you do not observe these conventions you may be refused entry. (Small change is useful for activating light time-switches). Museum times and days vary considerably; some also close on Mondays.

COMMUNICATIONS

The state telecommunication system is run by the **Compagnia Italiana Telecom (CIT)**. Telephone bureaux have banks of public telephones where customers pay for the line at the end of the trunk call (*Fondaco dei Tedeschi*). Reduced rates for national calls apply after 6.30pm and between 10pm and 8am for international calls.

PUBLIC PHONES

Public telephone boxes are to be found along streets and in some bars. They may be operated by phone cards (*see below*) and by telephone credit cards. To make a call, lift the receiver, insert payment, await a dial tone, punch in the required number and wait for a reply.

PHONE CARDS

These are sold in various denominations supplied by CIT offices and post offices as well as tobacconists (*tabaccaio* sign bearing a white T on a black background).

DIALLING CODES

For calls **within Venice**, dial the correspondent's number, including the 041 prefix code for Venice.
For calls to **other towns in Italy**, dial the code for the town or district beginning with an 0, followed by the correspondent's number.

For **international calls** dial 00 followed by the country code:

☏ +61 for Australia
☏ +1 for Canada
☏ +64 for New Zealand
☏ +44 for the UK
☏ +1 for the USA

The international code for Italy is +39, the code for Venice is 041 – note that you should no longer drop the first 0 of the area code.

INTERNET

Most good hotels (of 3-star status and above) will provide internet access to guests. There are relatively few other options, excluding occasional internet cafes around the city centre. The city has free wi-fi hot spots, which require registration (*www.cittadinanzadigitale.it*).

ELECTRICITY

The voltage is 220 ac, 50 cycles per second; the sockets are for two-pin plugs. It is advisable to take an adaptor for hair dryers, shavers, computers and other electrical equipment.

EMERGENCIES

EMERGENCY NUMBERS

General Emergency Services (equivalent of UK 999, US 911): **112**

MAIL

In Italy post offices are open 8.30am–2pm (noon Sat and last day of the month). The main post offices are at the Fondaco dei Tedeschi and just off Piazza San Marco, behind the Napoleon Wing by the Correr museum. Letters sent **poste restante** (*fermo posta*) can be collected from the main post office. Stamps are sold in post offices and tobacconists (*tabaccheria*).

MONEY

The unit of currency is the **euro** which is issued in notes (€5, €10, €20, €50, €100, €200 and €500) and in coins (1 cent, 2 cents, 5 cents, 10 cents, 20 cents, 50 cents, €1 and €2).

BANKS

ATMs (Bancomat) are plentiful in Venice. Banks are usually open Mon to Fri, 8.30am–1.30pm and 2.30pm–4pm. Some branches open in the city centre and shopping centres on Sat mornings, but most are closed on Sat, Sundays and public holidays. Some hotels will change travellers' cheques. Money can be changed in post offices, exchange bureaus and at railway stations and airports. Commission is always charged. Money withdrawn from Bancomat machines with a PIN incurs a lower commission charge than from a transaction in a bank.

CREDIT CARDS

Payment by credit card is widespread in shops, hotels and restaurants and at some petrol stations.

PHARMACIES

A pharmacy (*farmacia*) is identified by a red or green and white cross. When it is closed, it will advertise the names of the nearest on-duty chemist and a list of doctors on call.

PUBLIC HOLIDAYS

Public holidays (*giorni festivi*) include Saturdays and Sundays.

- ◆ January: 1 (New Year) and 6 (Epiphany)
- ◆ Easter: Sunday and Monday (*lunedì dell'Angelo*)
- ◆ April: 25 (St Mark's Day and liberation in 1945)
- ◆ May: 1
- ◆ 2 June – Republic of Italy holiday (*Festa della Repubblica Italiana*).
- ◆ August: 15 (Assumption – *Ferragosto*)
- ◆ November: 1
- ◆ December: 8 (Immaculate Conception), 25 and 26 (Christmas and St Stephen's day).

A working day is a *giorno feriale*.

REDUCED RATES

If you plan on visiting the interiors of Venice's more important churches, then it is sensible to obtain a **Chorus** pass in advance from the **Associazione**

Chiese di Venezia, San Polo, 2986, 30125 Venezia, Italy (☏041 27 50 462; www.chorusvenezia.org). This provides entry to 18 churches in Venice, is valid for one year, and costs €12. As admission to each individual church administered by Chorus costs €3, you will soon save money.

If you are a museum buff, consider buying a **MUVE Friend Card** (€45, valid 12 months) for entry to all Civic Museums. For details, ☏892 234. www.visitmuve.it.

Finally, if you wish to roll together churches, museums and *all* other sights, plus the option of transport, then consider purchasing the **Venezia Unica City Pass**, ☏041 24 24. This offers discounts on a number of tourist sights and facilities, such as transport, public toilets, car parks etc**.** The Venice Card offers unlimited use of public transport on land and water, free admission to 10 museums (including the Doges Palace, Museo Ebraico, la Fondazione Querini Stampalia), and the 16 Chorus-group churches, plus discounts on other admissions to exhibitions and events. The card is valid 7 days and costs €39.90. A Junior Venice card, for anyone aged six to 30 costs €29.90.

Another advantage of the Venice Card is that you can bypass queues. For further information on ticket offices and to purchase on-line visit www.veneziaunica.it..

The **Musei di Piazza San Marco** ticket provides access to the Palazzo Ducale, the Correr Museum, the Archeological Museum and the monumental halls of the Biblioteca Marciana: €19.

Museum Pass provides access to museums in Piazza San Marco, as well as to Ca' Rezzonico, Casa di Goldoni, Palazzo Mocenigo, Ca' Pesaro, the Natural History Museum, Museum of Glass (Murano) and Museum of Lace (Burano): €24. Valid for 6 months.

Youth Discounts
For €6, young people aged 6 to 29 can purchase a **Rolling Venice** card, which offers over 200 discounts at participating youth hostels, campsites, hotels, restaurants, university canteens, museums and shops, as well as reduced rates for public transport and the International Biennale of Art. The card is available from tourist offices and Venezia Unica Points outlets; visit www.veneziaunica.it for a list.

SMOKING
In line with the rest of Europe there is a ban on smoking in all public places, though some bars and cafes may have areas where it is possible to smoke.

TAXES
As of 2011, as was instituted also in Rome and Florence, even overnight guests are now taxed, per person, per night, which is applied for the first five nights. Likewise, high and low seasons have been completely redefined: in 2016, Venice classified February 1-November 30 as high season.

TIME
The time in Italy is the same as in the rest of mainland Europe (one hour ahead of the United Kingdom) and changes during the last weekend in March and October between summer time (*ora legale*) and winter time (*ora solare*).

TIPPING
With the exception of tourist honeypots, such as in and around the Piazza San Marco and around the Rialto, Venice is no more, nor any less tip-conscious than any other European tourist-oriented city. Restaurants often add a 12% service charge and *coperto* (cover charge for bread, pretzels etc) to the bill, in which case there is no need to tip further. Guides and taxi drivers will expect a tip of around 10 per cent (though this is by no means compulsory), porters, hotel maids and toilet attendants should be tipped a few coins.

Useful Words and Phrases

Basic

	Translation
si/no	yes/no
per favore	please
grazie	thank you
buongiorno	good morning
buona sera	good afternoon/evening
buona notte	goodnight
arrivederci	goodbye
scusi	excuse me
piccolo/un po'	small/a little
grande	large/big
meno	less
molto	much/very
più	more
basta!	enough!
quando?	when?
perché?	why?
perché	because
con/senza	with/without
l'aeroporto	the airport
la stazione	the station
un biglietto	a ticket
una scheda per il telefono	telephone card

Numbers

	Translation
1	uno
2	due
3	tre
4	quattro
5	cinque
6	sei
7	sette
8	otto
9	nove
10	dieci
11	undici
12	dodici
13	tredici
14	quattordici
15	quindici
16	sedici
17	diciassette
18	diciotto
19	diciannove
20	venti
30	trenta
40	quaranta
50	cinquanta
60	sessanta
70	settanta
80	ottanta
90	novanta
100	cento
1 000	mille
2 000	duemila

Time

	Translation
1.00 l'una	one
1.15 una e un quarto	one fifteen
1.30 un' ora e mezzo	one thirty
1.45 l'una e quaranta cinque	one forty-five
mattina	morning
pomeriggio	afternoon
sera	evening
ieri	yesterday
oggi	today
domani	tomorrow
una settimana	a week
lunedì	Monday
martedì	Tuesday
mercoledì	Wednesday
giovedì	Thursday
venerdì	Friday
sabato	Saturday
domenica	Sunday
inverno	winter
primavera	spring
estate	summer
autunno	autumn/fall

Food & Drink

	Translation
un piatto	a plate
un coltello	a knife
una forchetta	a fork
un cucchiaio	a spoon
il cibo	food

Gondoliers in traditional costume

© J. Frumm / hemis.fr

un piatto vegetariano	a vegetarian dish
un bicchiere	a glass
acqua	minerale
(gassata)	mineral water (fizzy)
vino rosso	red wine (bianco – white)
una birra (alla spina)	a beer (draught)
carne	meat
manzo/vitello	beef/veal
maiale	pork
agnello	lamb
prosciutto cotto (crudo)	cooked ham (cured)
pollo	chicken
pesce	fish (pesca – peach)
uova	eggs (uva – grapes)
verdura	green vegetables
burro	butter
formaggio	cheese
un dolce	a dessert
frutta	fruit
zucchero	sugar
sale/pepe	salt/pepper
senape	mustard
olio/aceto	oil/vinegar
si puo visitare?	can one visit?

On the Road

	Translation
il fiume	the river
un lago	a lake
un belvedere	a viewpoint
un bosco	a wood
l'autostrada	motorway
la patente	driving licence
un garage	repair garage
nel parcheggio	in the car park
benzina	petrol/gas
una gomma	a tyre
le luci	headlights
il parabrezza	the windscreen
il motore	the engine

Shopping

	Translation
un negozio	a shop
la posta	a post office
francobolli	stamps
macellaio	a butcher's
farmacia	a chemist's
sciroppo per la tosse	cough mixture
pastiglie per la gola	throat pastilles
cerotto	sticking plaster
scottato dal sole	sunburn
mal di pancia	stomach-ache
mal di testa	headache
punture di zanzara/ ape/vespa	mosquito bite/bee-/ wasp-sting
il panificio	a baker's
pane (integrale)	bread (wholemeal)
un supermercato	a supermarket
un giornale	a newspaper
pescivendolo	a fishmonger

Sightseeing

	Translation
si puo visitare?	can one visit?
chiuso/aperto	closed/open
destra/sinistra	right/left
nord/sud	north/south
est/ovest	east/west
la strada per ...?	the road for ...?
una vista	a view
al primo piano	on the first floor
tirare	pull
spingere	push
bussare	ring (the bell)
le luci	lights
le scale	stairs
l'ascensore	lift
i bagni per uomo/ per donna	WC facilities men's/ ladies'
una camera singola/ doppia/matrimoniale	a single room/with twin beds/double bed
con doccia/con bagno	with shower/bath
un giorno/una notte	one day/night

Urban Sites

	Translation
la città	the town
una chiesa	a church
il duomo	the cathedral
una cappella	a chapel
il chiostro	the cloisters
la navata	the nave
il coro	the choir or chancel
il transetto	the transept
la cripta	the crypt
un palazzo	a town house or mansion
una casa	a house
un castello	a castle
un monastero/ convento	an abbey/monastery
un cortile	a courtyard
un museo	a museum
una torre	a tower
un campanile	a belfry
una piazza	a square
un giardino	a garden
un parco	a park
una via/strada	a street/road
un ponte	a bridge

© R. Campillo / age fotostock

un molo	a pier or jetty
un cimitero	a cemetery
la barca	boat
il motoscafo	motor boat
il vaporetto	vaporetto
la spiaggia	the beach
il mare	the sea
pericolo	danger
vietato	prohibited or forbidden

USEFUL PHRASES

Parla inglese? – Do you speak English?
Entri! – Come in!
Non capisco – I do not understand
Dov'è...? – Where's…?
Parli piano per favore – Please speak slowly
Dove sono i bagni? – Where are the toilets?
A che ora parte il treno/l'autobus/ l'aereo...? – At what time does the train/bus/plane leave?
A che ora arriva il treno…? – At what time does the train… arrive?
Quanto costa? – How much does it cost?
Dove posso comprare un giornale inglese? – Where can I buy an English newspaper?
Dove posso cambiare i miei soldi? – Where can I change my money?
Posso pagare con una carta di credito? – May I pay with a credit card?

Rialto Bridge
© J. Arnold/age fotostock

The City Today

THE VENETIANS

To describe the countless faces of Venice and ignore the particular personality of the citizens who live here would present a misleading picture of the city: it would sustain the unfortunate, commonly held view of the place as a museum to which a cursory visit is made. To refute this, stroll down to Campo della Pescaria, linger in a bar in Campo San Luca over a glass of wine, or idle away on a bench in Campo San Giacomo dall'Orio to eavesdrop on a nearby conversation. Shopping around Sant'Elena will provide a glimpse of the living spirit of Venice. The best impressions of Venice are gleaned away from the obvious tourist areas.

Venetians can be unpredictable characters, both charming and astute (a quality sharpened by an age-old affinity for business), with a tendency to appear effusively genial in Italian and yet suspiciously distant in their native dialect.

THE CITY'S SPLIT PERSONALITY

Every visitor must formulate his or her own opinion of Venice: it may be a highly personal response to the unique atmosphere of this enchanting city; it may be one tainted by bad weather, high prices and at the height of summer a particular stretch of a canal can sometimes smell unpleasant – but it is not common and should not deter a single visitor. To stereotype the flavour of Venice would be detrimental to the magic of the place.

Just outside the tourist mainstream, a local resident is often ready to regale visitors with tales while the long-serving employee at a magnificent *palazzo* will enjoy sharing its enthralling history with whoever gives him the chance; the parish priest, in his sacristy, is happy to unlock secret doors to hidden treasures in his custody. Theirs is "the" Venetian personality too complex to be defined but too colourful to be ignored.

VENETIAN IDIOSYNCRASY

Historically, at least, the Venetian is born with a positive outlook on life that is maintained by an imperturbable nature in which emotional involvement is tempered by a certain indifference to anything that lies beyond the lagoon. This has led them to a noticeably predisposed state of tolerance, an innate quality acquired from a knowledge of different peoples distilled over the centuries. The blend of an almost Anglo-Saxon aplomb with boundless and all-embracing curiosity renders this personality even more fascinating.

Yet perhaps the attribute that most readily springs to mind is the pleasure the Venetian derives from gossiping, a pastime that delights all the more given the subtle sense of humour with which many Venetians are naturally and happily endowed, regardless of age, intellect or social class.

Jocular chatter is always conducted in dialect to allow quips and puns to sparkle and scintillate to full effect. It fills the bars and cafés, the shops and markets, but most of all the streets and squares, exchanged in passing or during a pause, which the Venetians take pleasure in granting themselves at every opportunity. Unlike citizens of other cities, Venetians are wholly sociable creatures, revelling in the advantages of sharing their environment with likeminded people who draw the calm and philosophical conclusion that only the truly essential priorities of life are worth worrying about, thus regarding the inconveniences of existence as relative. With a clear conscience and light heart, Venetians walk with a purposeful stride: it is clear when they are on their way somewhere, moving at a sustained speed, whether empty handed or earnestly pushing awkward carts up and over the bridges, heralded by a sprightly *"Atansion!"* from behind.

It is rare to meet an ill-intentioned Venetian, partly because the very structure of the city impedes criminal designs: where would you escape to?

Yet all is far from happy in this magnificent theme park of a city. The average age of Venetians is around 45, way older than most Italian cities, and over one third of the population is over 60. Unless they are employed directly in tourism there is little reason for youngsters to stay. Property is horribly expensive, damp and difficult to maintain and commuting against the tide of visitors coming the other way each day is a nightmare.

VENETIAN LEXICON

The living breath of Venice is its dialect. Accents have been used to facilitate pronunciation.

COLLOQUIAL TERMS

Baùta: a carnival mask comprising a black hood and a lace shawl
Brìcola: wooden pole used for mooring boats or, if roped to others, to delineate navigable channels
Carèga: chair
Ciàcola: gossip or chatter
Fèlze: the gondola awning set up in winter to protect the main seat
Ocio!: Look out!
Ostreghèta!: Good heavens!
Pantegàna: a large rat
Putèo: a child
Tòco/tochetìn: a piece/little piece

EATING AND DRINKING

Armelìn: apricot
Bacalà mantecà: boiled salt-cod, mixed with oil, garlic and parsley
Bàcaro: a Venetian bistro, usually crowded from early morning
Bagìgi: peanuts
Baìcoli: typical dry, flat, cutlet-shaped sweet biscuits
Bìgoi: wholemeal spaghetti, generally served in *salsa* with a lightly fried mixture of anchovies and onions
Bìsi: peas
Bussolài buranèi: an S- or ring-shaped biscuit from Burano
Càpe sànte: scallops
Cichèto: Venetian tidbit (salt-cod, marinated sardine or a meatball) that accompanies a glass of wine
Dìndio: turkey
Frìtole: carnival pancakes made with raisins and pine nuts
Lugànega: a long thin sausage
Narànsa: orange

Ombra, ombrèta: the traditional and much respected glass of wine taken standing at a bar
Parsùto: ham
Peòci: mussels
Pòmi: apple
Prosecco: dry sparkling wine
Rìsi e bìsi: rice and peas traditionally eaten during the Feast of St Mark
Sàrde in saòr: fried sardines, with a sweet-and-sour sauce of onions, vinegar, pine nuts and raisins
Sgropìn: lemon sorbet of vodka and *prosecco*, served usually after fish
Sprìz (Spritz): famous Venetian aperitif: white wine with a dash of bitters and soda water
Stracaganàse: dried chestnuts, literally translated as "jaw-acher"
Sopprèssa: fresh salami
Tiramisù: famous dessert made of biscuits soaked in coffee, layered with full-fat *mascarpone* cream cheese blended with egg and sugar, powdered with bitter cocoa.

PLACE NAMES

Altàna: a wooden roof-terrace or veranda
Assassini: a canal or street name alluding to where a murderer might have sought refuge
Beccarìe: butchers who have lent their name to streets, squares, bridges
Calle: plural calli, from the Latin *callis*, most streets in Venice bear this name (variations:*calli larghe*, *callette* and *calleselle*)
Campiello: a little *campo* or square
Campo: Venetian for a square; the only *piazza* in Venice is Piazza San Marco
Fiubèra: buckle sellers who have lent their name to streets or vaulted arcades where they once set up shop
Fondamenta: a road which runs parallel to a *rio* or canal
Fòntego: a warehouse where foreign merchants lodged
Fornèr: a common name identifying where the local bread ovens were

Italian coffee

Espresso – very short, dense, black and very strong
Caffè lungo/caffè americano – a short, strong espresso with added hot water
Caffè corretto – an espresso "corrected" with brandy or *grappa* (eau-de-vie)
Caffè macchiato – an espresso with a dash of milk, freddo (cold) or caldo (hot)
Cappuccino or **cappuccio** – an espresso topped with hot fluffy milk
Caffè latte – a glass of hot milk flavoured with an espresso coffee
Venice has some of its own coffee roasters (*torrefazioni*) that produce excellent coffee: Marchi; Girani; Doge; India; Venezia; and others.

Ice-cream flavours

Gelato is best at a specialist *gelateria* that is *artigianale* without additives.
Stracciatella – chocolate chip. **Gianduia** – dark or milk chocolate and hazelnut.
Fior di latte or **panna** – plain milk or cream. **Crema** – vanilla enriched with egg.
Cioccolato (fondente)– chocolate (bittersweet). **Nocciola** – hazelnut. **Frutta di bosco** – fruits of the forest (blueberries, blackberries etc). **Limone** – lemon sorbet. **Fragola** – strawberry. **Pistacchio** – made with bright green pistachio nuts. **Pesca** – peach. **Albicocca** – apricot. **Lampone** – raspberry.

Frezzerìa: commercial zone around St Mark's that was once the site of an arrow factory

Lista: the stretch of street in front of an ambassador's residence; diplomatic immunity is indicated by its white stone

Luganeghèr: grocery store

Megio: millet; alludes to grain (millet or wheat) warehouses storing supplies for times of hardship

Milìon: the nickname of Marco Polo's family, who lived over the Milion courtyard behind San Giovanni Grisostomo; also the title of the adventurer's travel experiences

Paradiso: this name given to a street or bridge refers to the lamps that were used on Good Friday to light the area of Santa Maria Formosa

Parrocchia: literally meaning "parish", this locality around a church serves as a subdivision of a *sestiere*

Pescarìa: a fish market

Piazzetta: little squares: the two in Venice are Piazzetta dei Leoncini and Piazzetta San Marco

Piovàn: common in Venetian topography; relating to a priest

Piscina: place where there used to be a pool or sheet of water

Pistòr: the baker who kneaded dough

Ponte: the 400 or so bridges in Venice are marked by this name

Ramo: a side street

Rialto: from the Latin *rivoaltus*, a word that indicates the islands from which the city originated

Rio terà: a street formed by a land-filled canal

Ruga: from the French *rue*, a synonym for street, usually one devoted to a commercial activity

Salizzarda: from the word *salizo* or paving stone; denotes a paved street

San Stae: the Venetian contraction of San Eustachio – St Eustace

San Stin: another Venetian contraction of San Stefanino

San Zan Degolà: refers to San Giovanni Decollato – the beheaded John the Baptist

Scaletèr: a doughnut seller, from the word *scaleta*, a doughnut with marks like a flight of steps

Sestieri: the six divisions of Venice: **Cannaregio:** from the Latin *cannarecium* or *canaleclum*, a marshy area where cane grows; **Castello:** alluding, perhaps, to the Roman fortification at Olivolo; **Dorsoduro:** includes the Giudecca and is named after the type of hill on which it developed;

San Marco, San Polo and
Santa Croce

Sottopòrtego: a vaulted passageway
running perpendicular to the
building's façade on the ground
floor; at one time lined with shops

Squèro: a boatyard where gondolas
are built and repaired

Tette: slang for breasts, applied to a
bridge or street where bare-
breasted women of easy virtue
used to lean out of windows

Zattere: the long *fondamenta* that
extends to the Giudecca Canal,
recalling the *zattere* or wood-
laden rafts which used to
stop there

VENETIAN WORDS IN THE ENGLISH LANGUAGE

Arsenal: a store for military equipment

Carpaccio: an appetizer of thinly
sliced raw beef

Ghetto: a socially restricted zone

Gondola: a type of boat or a cable car

Harlequin: a comic character/
buffoon/diamond pattern

Lagoon: an area of shallow water
divided from the sea by
sandy dunes

Lido: a fashionable beach resort/
public open-air swimming pool

Regatta: a boat race

FOOD AND WINE

Venice has traded with the world since
the dawn of time; throughout its history
the city has therefore been cosmopolitan
in every sense of the word. A thousand
different ethnic types have crowded the
streets and squares just as they have
populated the pictures of Titian and
Veronese. They have added colour to
the Venetian scene, idiom and dialect to
the vernacular language and, above all,
exotic spice to the indigenous cultural
and culinary traditions. The perfumes
and fragrances exchanged in Venice
have been blended and refined through
time, mixing exotic and local flavours.
Nothing has been lost. The multicol-
oured multitude of merchants has been
replaced with crowds of tourists, and so
the alchemy continues.

Social history has also played its part:
besides the gastronomic refinement
inherited from an aristocratic past, solid
peasant cooking still underpins many
local dishes, even if the poorest have
long since been enhanced or become
luxuries in modern times.

Tourism has nurtured a demand for restaurants that alternate between luxurious and anonymous "tourist" catering,
but the age-old rhythm of the city and
the convivial habits of its citizens still
survive and flourish: **un ombra di vin** (a
"shadow" or bit of wine) accompanied
by a **cichetto** (a tapas-like morsel) or
three, consumed in a **bacaro,** are life's
daily small luxuries for the locals.

Cichetti (the plural of cichetto) comprise all kinds of foods from sliced fried
vegetables to delicious garlic meatballs
(*polpette*), squid, salt-cod and prawns to
mini pizzas and bruschettas.

Fresh fish on sale in a market, Venice

© Yana Savostitskaya / Dreamstime.com

Pasta (and polenta)

Cannelloni – stuffed tubes, topped with tomato and bechamel sauce, baked in the oven

Farfalle – butterfly or bows

Fettuccine – thin tagliatelle served with various sauces

Fusilli – corkscrew pasta often served with heartier sauces

Gnocchi – dumplings made with potato and flour

Lasagne – sheets of pasta layered with meat, vegetables, or fish, with a tomato or bechamel sauce, and baked in the oven

Maccheroni – small tubes

Paglia e fieno – thin threads of egg and spinach pasta (literally meaning straw and hay)

Pappardelle – broad flat ribbons of freshly made pasta, very often served in a rich sauce (wild boar – *cinghiale*; hare – *lepre; porcini* mushrooms)

Pasta e fasòi – pasta served with Borlotti beans, typical family dish at home

Polenta – cornmeal porridge, also grilled or baked, accompanied by rich sauces.

Ravioli – cushions of freshly made egg pasta stuffed with meat, fish or spinach and cheese (*spinaci e ricotta); delicious with butter and sage (*burro e salvia*) or meat sauce (*al ragù*)

Spaghetti – long threads of pasta, often with shellfish (*frutta di mare*) or clams (*vongole*)

Tagliatelle – egg pasta in long ribbons

Tortellini – little pouches of egg pasta stuffed with meat, vegetables, or cheese, served with a sauce or in clear broth (*in brodo*)

When ordering a glass of wine "un ombra", specify "bianco" white, or for red, rosso.

SEAFOOD

Venetians are especially proud of their seafood. A traditional plate of *antipasto* offers a chance to relish a wonderful selection of local shellfish including **caparozzoli** (clams), **cozze** (mussels) **peòci** (mussels), **bòvoli** (sea snails) and **canòce** (shrimps), as well as **granseole** and **gransipori** (crab).

As a *primo* or starter, **bìgoi in salsa** (thick spaghetti cords served with lightly fried onions and anchovies) is one of the most popular first courses, (beware that after this you may be too full to eat any more!). In Northern Italy rice is more popular than pasta so look for many types of risotto. These are made with meat and/or fresh vegetables (**primavera**), grown locally in market gardens, or with fish, or **'in tecia'** – with cuttlefish.

Fish from the Adriatic is often served grilled, accompanied, in spring, by **castraùre** (young fried artichokes). Eels (**anguilla**, or **bisàto** in dialect), are not so common and are served either broiled or poached. Wild fowl and game are delicacies in winter months.

Vinegar is used in all kinds of ways, notably for pickling and for preparing **sarde in saòr**, a delicious sweet-and-sour sardine dish. Also popular is **seppie al nero**, cuttlefish in its own ink, a rich-tasting dish often served as risotto, the rice darkened from soaking up the ink! Another truly typical dish is **bacalà mantecato**, salt-cod beaten to a smooth cream with oil, garlic and parsley and served with polenta. It is often served as a cichetto, on bread or perhaps a cracker. Fried softshell lagoon crabs, **moeche**, are truly a delicacy.

MEAT DISHES

One of the most traditional *secondi* or main courses is **fegato alla veneziana**, (calf's liver and onions), a combination created in Venice but now popular everywhere. The defining factor for Venetians, however, is how thinly the meat is cut, and the long gentle cooking of the onions.

However no meat is as thinly cut as another Venetian invention, **carpaccio**, slices of raw beef served with olive oil and lemon. It was invented at Harry's Bar in Venice, where it was first served to the countess Amalia Nani Mocenigo in 1950 who, on doctor's orders, had requested raw meat. It was named carpaccio by Giuseppe Cipriani, the bar's owner, after the great Venetian painter because the colours reminded him of a favorite painting!

Another meat dish is **carne in tecia** – a braised beef stew, traditionally cooked in terracotta (tecia). Look also for duck and other waterfowl.

SOUPS AND VEGETABLES

For flavoursome country cooking, try **panàda veneziana**, a wholesome soup with bread, garlic, oil, bay leaf and Parmesan cheese, or **pastissàda**, of green vegetables, cheese, sausage, pasta or polenta bound together traditionally to use up leftovers. **Zuppa di Pesce** is a wholesome and hearty soup, of the market's mixed fish. Don't miss spring artichokes from the island of Sant'Erasmo, served raw and sliced very thinly, or the bottoms sauteed in olive oil with garlic. Also, pumpkin, beans, asparagus, chicory, and radicchio are great favourites among the locals.

DOLCI

For dessert, try the famous Veneto **tiramisu,** which combines biscuits, coffee, sweet marscapone cheese and eggs, dusted with cocoa. **St. Martin's Cake**, a sweet biscuit shaped like a man on horseback, appears in November.

Another very Venetian custom is to serve **baìcoli** biscuits, to dunk in hot chocolate or dessert wine; biscuits from Burano, **bussolài**, are moulded into ring or "S" shapes, called *essi buranèi*; or the **Veneziana**, a kind of brioche covered with chopped almonds and sugar. **Creme frite**, fried cream, has a pudding consistency. Carnival treats are often fried: **frìtole** are fritters flavoured with raisins and sometimes pine nuts. **Pìnsa**, a biscuit flavoured with fennel seeds, raisins, dried figs and candied peel, is a speciality baked at Epiphany.

SALUTI !

The most common drink in Venice (and the Veneto), after *un ombra* (*see page 113*), is a **spritz**, which is Prosecco with a dash of bitters and soda water; ask for *com Aperol* (an orange bitter made in Padova).

Venice's most famous cocktail is the **Bellini**, white peach juice and pulp with *Prosecco*; the **Tiziano**, substitutes strawberry grape juice; the **Mimosa**, orange juice; the **Rossini**, strawberry juice. Ernest Hemingway was a frequent visitor to **Harry's Bar**, where he would order his own special cocktail, the **Montgomery**, named after the famous general. It was made with one measure of vermouth to 15 measures of gin and is served only by that particular establishment. **Prosecco** wine from the Veneto's Conegliano Valdobbiadene is made primarily from the Giera grape, most popular in its sparking version, very light and very refreshing.

The king of the Veneto reds is **Amarone della Valpolicella** , from the province of Verona, a dense wine made from partially dried Corvina, Rondinella and Marinara grapes; also delicious and made from the same grapes is Recioto della Vapolicella and **Valpolicella**, slightly lower in alcohol content and more economical. Among other intriguing Veneto wines to try for red are **Bardolino** rand reds from the Colli Berici and other areas. For whites, try **Soave**, **Tai** and **Tocai**, although many are partial to whites from **Friuli** such as Schioppettino, Friulano, and Ribolla gialla.

Nature

The mainland of Italy reaches out a finger towards Venice, and the gap is spanned by the Ponte della Libertà (Freedom Bridge). Otherwise, the coast's profile cast in reflection across the Venetian lagoon looms with industrial developments at Mestre and Porto Marghera. These have grown around the timeless waters of the Brenta Naviglio, which flow peacefully into the lagoon at Malcontenta. The modern Tessera Airport and the prettified Jesolo beach huts betray the affluence of tourism.

THE VENETO

This area comprises mainly the vast alluvial Po Delta and its tributaries which are overlooked in the north by the Venetian Pre-Alps, and further north again in the **Cadore** district by the western massifs of the Dolomites. The highly-eroded limestone massif of the **Dolomites** extends across the Veneto and Trentino-Alto Adige. The Cadore is an agricultural region growing wheat, maize, mulberry bushes, olives, fruit trees and grapes. The industrial sector includes oil refineries, smelting works and chemical plants which are concentrated in the vicinity of Venice at Mestre-Marghera, as well as a large production of hydroelectric energy in the valleys of the Pre-Alps. The latter supplies the textile industry.

The landscape is punctuated by two small volcanic groups, the **Berici Mountains** south of Vicenza and the **Euganean Hills** thermal waters near Padua. The slopes of these blackish heights support vines and peach orchards, bordered by hot springs.

In the **Po Delta** and that of the Adige lie impoverished and desolate areas, subject to flooding. Following reclamation certain areas are farmed on an industrial scale for wheat and sugar beet. The coastline takes the form of lagoons (*lagune*) separated from the sea by spits of sand pierced by gaps (*porti*). It is one of these lagoons that both provides and threatens the survival of Venice.

THE VENETIAN LAGOON

The Venetian Lagoon extends over an area of 550sq km/213sq mi, making it the largest in Italy. It was formed at the end of the Ice Age by the convergence of flooded rivers, swollen by melted snow from the Alps and Apennines.

Today it provides a natural and complex habitat to wetland flora and fauna between the Cavallino coast to the northeast and the Lido and Chioggia to the southwest. Water levels are maintained by the sea: its tides constitute both an ever-present threat to the delicate make-up of the Venetian Lagoon while also providing its regular safeguard from stagnation. The sea merges with the canals' fresh water through three channels (**bocche di porto**) by the Lido, at Chioggia and Malamocco, where dikes were installed during the 19C and 20C.

A few lagoon terms

Bacino scolante: earth that carries rain and river water into the lagoon.

Barene: sandbanks protruding from the water and immersed at high tide.

Bricole: groups of colourful wooden masts roped together which mark out canals fit for navigation.

Ghebi: tiny canals that meander their way across the sandbanks.

Punto zero: standard reference for measuring the water level in the lagoon, established by the Punta della Salute tide gauge. The levels are usually 23cm/9.3in higher than the average sea level.

Valli da pesca: diked stretches of the lagoon set aside for fishing.

Velme: small strips of land which, unlike the *barene*, can be seen only at low tide, when they appear on the surface.

AN AGE-OLD PROBLEM

In the 12C, Europe enjoyed a long period of mild weather followed by a noticeable rise in temperature; then came torrential rains that caused high tides and flooding. The **River Brenta** broke its banks and water flooded a large part of the lagoon, depositing silt, mud and detritus. Malaria broke out. The Republic of Venice tried to defend itself by placing palisades along the coast, diverting the course of the rivers and building great dikes, but the lagoon continued to pose a threat. Over the ensuing centuries (15C–17C), major drainage programmes were implemented that affected the River Brenta, River Piave, River Livenza and River Sile. In 1896 the operation aimed at diverting the waters of the Brenta was finally completed, channelling them into the mouth of the Bacchiglione. Despite these measures, as water levels continue to rise and fall, the sand deposited in the lagoon by the rivers is buffeted back inland by the sea and the wind. Thus the sandbanks are formed and strengthened. All the while, caught between marine erosion and the rebuilding action of the rivers, the fate of Venice itself is at stake: after more than 1 000 years of existence, the city is slowly sinking.

The Venetian Lagoon can be likened to a sophisticated system that has achieved a subtle balance between excessive **sedimentation** (leading to the emergence of "new" land) and **erosion** (in which the deposits carried by the sea and rivers

are so scarce that a stretch of lagoon can turn into a stretch of sea). This is precisely the risk currently threatening the lagoon. About one quarter of the lagoon surface is rendered unnavigable by the existence of sandbanks or **barene**. Their importance is huge: they encourage the proliferation of a great many animal and vegetal species while attracting sediments that might otherwise be scattered in the water, contributing to reducing the swell.

About 4 000ha/15sq mi are taken up by the large inhabited islands and

Why do tides occur?

Gravitational forces caused by the earth's rotation around the sun and its relation to the moon are responsible for tides. Being nearer the earth, the moon exerts the greater force over changes in liquid levels and the movement of the oceans and seas. The strength of this force is affected by air pressure and winds. In the case of Venice, the greatest floods have always followed major sirocco storms. When the moon passes over the meridian of an area, it causes a high tide; when it is at 90° to that meridian, it produces a low tide. When the earth, moon and sun are aligned, the tide reaches its maximum levels.

Aerial view of the island of San Francesco del Deserto surrounded by the lagoon

© Guido Alberto Rossi / Tips Images

smaller, deserted ones, leaving another 40 000ha/155sq mi occupied by water. Anyone surprised at seeing how shallow a Venetian canal may be when drained of its water (from an average of 1–2m/3–7ft to a maximum depth of 8–10m/26–33ft) will understand why the seabed of the open lagoon is often exposed at low tide. Despite this lack of depth, which gives the lagoon its millpond appearance, a complex network of crisscrossed channels maintains currents and easy movement. Navigable areas are marked by lone wooden posts or groups of poles roped together, known as **bricole**. The deepest channels are those nearest the mouths of the ports, and as the distance from the sea increases, these rivulets become shallower and narrower (**ghebi**), dwindling across the sandbanks before disappearing into *chiari*, basins where salt water and rainwater mingle.

TIDES

Tidal changes occur every six hours, fluctuating between two high points per day. Low atmospheric pressure and the sirocco and bora winds are known to accentuate high tide, whereas high atmospheric pressure and northwesterly winds tend to bring on a low tide. In this case, some of the rivers may dry up. Sea water is thereby drawn into the lagoon through the three ports, flushing "new" water in and "old" water out, assisted by a current from the rivers on the opposite side. Parts affected by these tides are therefore known as the "living" lagoon, whereas sections little affected by this lifeline are referred to as the "dead" lagoon. These outlying parts tend towards marsh, channelled with canals, *ghebi* between fishing banks and diked lakes built by and for the fishing industry.

The health of the lagoon is totally dependent upon the influx of "new" water brought by the tides. However, the inflow of fresh water provided by the rivers that once maintained saline levels has been greatly reduced as the rivers have progressively been diverted. This diversion has also reduced the strength of current across the lagoon and allowed vast quantities of polluting material to be deposited.

In the 20C the problem was exacerbated by the growth of industrial sites around Mestre and Porto Marghera and the accommodation of petrol tankers and cruise ships, with obvious implications on the environment of the lagoon. The reduction in oxygenated water flowing through the canals of Venice is gradually eroding the ability of plant and marine life to survive. Only those organisms with short life cycles have had time to adapt, and so quantities of macroalgae (*ulva rigida*) and insects (mosquitoes and the like) have increased at a fantastic rate.

The tide along the coasts can fluctuate wildly; for it to be classified as tidal flooding, its level has to reach or exceed 1.10m/3ft 6in. The last such occurrence

High tides and flooding in Piazza San Marco

Manfred Bortoli/Sime/Photononstop

happened on 4 November 1966 when consequences were felt way beyond the shores of Venice: the Arno overflowed in Florence, with tragic results. That year an alarming prediction said that Venice might possibly disappear. Fortunately, radical action against further subsidence, including the closure of artesian wells on the mainland (1975), has proved the prophecy false.

Similar crises of this kind are documented as far back as 589. Contemporary personal accounts are terrifying. **Paolo Diacono** (c.720–799) wrote of the first flood tide: *"non in terra neque in aqua sumus viventes"* (neither on earth nor in water were we alive). Records from 1410 state that "almost one thousand people coming from the fair at Mestre and other places drowned".

Since the 17C the water level of the Venetian Lagoon has dropped by 60cm/24in. In past centuries, once every five years, the tide would rise above the damp-proof foundations made of Istrian stone that were built to protect the houses against salt deposits. Nowadays, in the lower areas, these foundations are immersed in water more than 40 times in a single year and the buildings can do very little to stall the degradation process.

VENICE, VICTIM OF THE TIDES

On 4 November 1966 the mareograph at Punta della Salute registered an exceptionally high tide of 1.94m/6ft. Medium to high tides usually reach a level of around 70cm/28in, flooding the Piazza San Marco and, with a further 30cm/12in, even narrow alley streets would be inundated. Between December and February the city can be the scene of very high tides indeed, estimated at around 90cm/36in. In 2012 acqua alta reached its fourth-highest level in recent history, 1.40 m.

At the end of the 18C, when the first part of the Riva degli Schiavoni promenade was completed, Venetian magistrates ordered that the letter "C" be engraved on the city houses and their foundations. The letter was to indicate the average level of the highest-known tides.

However, today it is difficult to spot these inscriptions since most of them are located under the level of the sea.

VENICE IN PERIL
FLOODING

The Centro Previsioni e Segnalazioni Maree provides warnings of impending danger and information on forecasts and tide tables. Tidal flooding tends to occur between April and December, and forecast warnings are issued about 48 hours in advance. Details are published in the *Gazzettino* and posted up on the landing stages of the vaporettos. Should the level threaten to exceed 1.10m/3ft 7in, 16 sirens sound five times for 10 seconds each time, three or four hours in advance of the high point.

Should high tide not exceed 1.20m/3ft 11in, the **AMAV** (Azienda Multiservizio Ambientale Venezia) sees to the laying of footbridges along prescribed routes. However, if the water level goes above this limit, then footbridges can become dangerous because they start to float. In the case of tidal flooding, the AMAV is unable to maintain its principal function (rubbish collection), because its boats are no longer able to pass under the bridges. Therefore it is responsible for laying down emergency footbridges. Meanwhile, the Venetian Municipality requests the population

What is an insula?

In the lagoon city, an *insula* is a tiny piece of territory which is circumscribed by a river or a canal. These *insule* are therefore linked to each other by a network of bridges. A small cluster of them is said to form a *sestiere*, one of Venice's six administrative divisions.

Marine Parade

The external surface of a **bricola** seems literally corroded by crustaceans, whereas within, bivalvular molluscs called *teredini* have taken up residence. Closest to the surface and buffeted by the tides are live crustaceans (*balani*) and green algae. Below, in calmer currents, live mussels (*mitili*). The submerged part is the kingdom of the sponges: the tube-shaped *ascidie* and the *hydrozoans*.

to just hang on to their household waste! In the UK, Venice in Peril (The British Committee for the Preservation of Venice) can help with forecasts and the latest news, ✆020 7736 6891, www.veniceinperil.org.

High tide, which is announced by the rather sinister sound of the sirens, floods the lowest-lying parts of the city not only by bursting the banks of St Mark's Basin and the canals and rivers of the city, but also by gushing out of the drains, cracks and manhole covers in Venice's streets and squares.

Today's concerns

In the past, land and water were clearly separated, with the lagoon acting as a link between the two, drawing on both to produce life and movement. However, the presence of factories, farms and areas inhabited by man have gradually changed the face of the *gronda*, the sloped land licking at the lagoon shores. Today, the lagoon has reached a sort of "standstill": it takes two weeks for waste material to leave the lagoon and end up in the open sea. Every year more than 1million m³/35.3million cu ft of solid matter is lost. Erosion, the sediments lost in the water, and the rising level of the sea all contribute to lowering the lagoon depths. This phenomenon is threatening the sandbanks known as **barene**, which are doomed to disappear by the year 2050 if drastic action is not taken to remedy the situation.

Water fluctuations and land subsidence

Variations in the level of the water are referred to as *eustatismo*. In the course of the last century, this phenomenon caused the waters of Venice to rise by 8cm/3.2in. This rise has led to dire consequences, aggravated by the effects of local subsidence, causing the land to drop, representing around 15cm/6.2in for the same period. Therefore, the city of Venice has "sunk" by around 23cm/9.2in since the end of the 19C.

Erosion

Erosion is the result of a number of factors: higher water levels, subsidence, digging for artificial canals, and the swell, which slowly increases while the seabed slumps and the sandbanks dwindle.

Pollution

Finally, to crown this somewhat pessimistic picture, pollution is responsible for the destruction of phanerogamic flora, invaluable sea-water plants whose roots serve to prevent erosion and stabilise the seabed. Water pollution has also killed the algae and other marine varieties which once thrived on sandbanks and mudflats and which are no longer able to attract sediments.

Tackling the problem

The risk of losing Venice through both tides and progressive de-population is so great that the Italian State has declared the salvation of the city to be a question of "pre-eminent national interest". The residents of Venice appear to be particularly concerned about high-to-medium tides, which cause flooding of the city. Consequently, a number of projects currently being examined or implemented are aimed at making these inhabited areas far safer. It is a highly delicate and complex situation: the city of Venice and the myriad islands are home to many buildings, monuments and works of art which cohabit in perfect harmony but, technically speaking, require different forms of intervention. On the San Marco and Tolentini islands, the stability of paved streets, bridges and houses was meticulously checked, as well as that of underground passages and sewage drains. In the lower sections, the paving has been raised (as is clearly visible on Campo San Zanipòlo) and the shores of the lagoon consolidated to cope more efficiently against tides below 100cm/40in (120cm/48in in Chioggia).

A project is under way to deal with exceptionally high tides by placing mobile barriers at the three entrances to the port. A prototype of this system, the MoSE (Experimental Electronic Module) comprises a huge mobile sluice-gate devised to regulate the movement of the tides. It was tested along the Canale di Treporti facing the Lido from 1988–1992. It is thought that the final project would need to provide 79 of these sluice-gates.

In the Experimental Centre for Hydraulic Models, at Voltabarozzo, near Padua, a simulated mock-up of the lagoon area allows studies to be carried out into projects for the harbour mouths, the safeguarding of the coastal region and of the jetties.

In the meantime, reconstruction of the coastal region of Cavallino and Pellestrina is being carried out. The coastal area has been consolidated with 2million m³/70.6 million cu ft of sand taken from the sea. These deposits were also used to reinforce sandbanks, which play a crucial role as they combat the swell and local winds while protecting the environment. In an attempt to increase their stability, these coastal dunes have been planted with *ammofila*, a variety of grass that thrives on sandy soil.

The north pier at Chioggia has been strengthened, 50km/31mi of canals have been dredged and the sediment obtained through this operation used to rebuild 300ha/740 acres of sandbanks. The restoration of sandbanks is achieved by fencing off a stretch of the lagoon with wooden masts. A large canvas sheet is then fixed to the poles and laid down over the sea depths. Sediments are poured into this artificial basin as well as water, which is then filtered by the canvas.

Further operations currently under way involve cleaning up the lagoon waters, gathering the macroalgae and salvaging the smaller islands such as Lazzaretto Vecchio.

The fight to save Venice

In 1966, the year in which record water levels were registered in Venice, UNESCO stressed the urgency of the fight to save this beautiful city and her lagoon.

A number of organisations and committees, both public and private, were set up to salvage and restore Venice's cultural heritage, namely the **Ufficio per la Salvaguardia di Venezia**.

The Head of the Monuments and Fine Arts Department is involved in the technical aspects of this undertaking and UNESCO oversees the allocation of funds raised by several private committees.

Fishing Areas

Known as **valli da pesca**, these stretches of the lagoon are used for fishing, taking into consideration the migratory movements of the fish. Because they have been diked, they are not exposed to the ebbing of the water. During the spring season, the fish (mainly eel, sea bass and gilt-head bream) congregate in the lagoon, attracted by the organic vegetation brought along by rivers and mountain waters after the thaw. In winter, when weather conditions are especially harsh, the fish try to swim back towards the sea, but on reaching the **chiaveghe** (structures with bulkheads built to regulate the flow of the sea water) they are caught and sorted by traditional methods. Among the various nets used for fishing, two in particular stand out: the *bilancione*, a huge trawl net suspended from four tall piers, and the *cogolo*, a cylindrical net consisting of several parts, ending in a cone.

Every year millions of euros are spent on rescue operations aimed at preserving the architectural, historical and artistic treasures of the city, as well as on scholarships for artisans and research. Each of these committees is directly concerned with a specific project on a regular basis. Among the many foreign organisations dedicated to saving Venice, the most important are **The Venice in Peril Fund** (Great Britain, www.veniceinperil.org/), **Save Venice** (United States, www.savevenice.org, **Comité Français pour la Sauvegarde de Venise** (France, www.cfsvenise.org).

LIFE FORMS

The lagoon comprises a vast and rich habitat for fauna and flora, part of which may even be glimpsed from the vaporetto between Venice and Burano or from a car driving through the section enclosed by the Cavallino coast. The best way, however, to appreciate the extent of vegetation and animal life thriving in this "watery plain" is to explore the sandbanks by boat.

The waters of the lagoon vary in salt concentration depending on their proximity to the river outlets, where the water is almost fresh. In the middle they tend to be brackish; near the ports, where the tides inject sea water, they are far saltier. At the same time, areas around the river deltas tend to be muddy, whereas by the port mouths the lagoon bed is sandy.

Fauna

At the lower end of the food chain, different types of **molluscs** breed successfully on the wooden piles or *bricole*.

Sluice-gates

These ambitious structures should be placed side by side to form a floating barrier linked to the seabed, rising and falling with the movement of the waves. Each gate, 20–30m/66–98ft long, 20m/66ft wide and 3–5m/10–16ft thick, contains compressed air controlled by valves, which enables the gate to be lowered.

The principal category is undoubtedly that of the **fish kingdom**, which has defined the very character of the lagoon, with its distinctive collection in shoals around sandbanks, and the interaction of human beings with this environment as they seek to exploit such rich resources. Crab and shrimp are central to the fishing industry and to Venetian cuisine. From a boat it soon becomes obvious where the fishing banks are situated as these attract various species of aquatic birds: wild duck (mallard and teal), tens of thousands of coots, herons and marsh harriers. Besides the common sparrows, swallows and blackbirds, the Venetian Lagoon is visited by special migratory birds, often with highly coloured plumage.

It is perhaps their beauty, strangeness and cleverness that is most fascinating: the black-whiskered bearded tit clings to the reeds; the reed warbler builds a floating nest between four reeds, which rises and falls with the tide; the kingfisher dives acrobatically and the moorhen nods her head in time to the rhythm of her strokes; little grebe pop out of the water only to dive quickly and silently below the surface again and emerge where least expected.

The very rich **bird life** of the lagoon also includes the cormorant, the inevitable sea-gull, the sea swallow, whose whirling wings and V-shaped tail allow it to swoop effortlessly time and again, and the little egret, recognisable by its elegant carriage and startlingly white feathers with which women adorned themselves at the beginning of the 20C. Even more beautiful is the black-winged stilt, whose sombre wings contrast with its white body and the red of its long legs; its thin, distinguished beak adds a touch of refinement.

Elegance seems to be a trait shared by all the birds of the lagoon, among which the mute swan must reign supreme.

There are numerous marsh harriers and hen harriers among the birds of prey.

Among the mammals, the rodent provides a somewhat harmful presence. The rat, the so-called *pantagena*, is at home anywhere, on the city squares as well as in rubbish dumps and attics.

Kingfisher

Cormorant

Coot

Black-winged stilt

Grey Heron

Little egret

Illustrations: M Dewynter (Kingfisher, Grey heron); R Corbel (Coot, Black-winged stilt, Little egret)

Flora

The **sandbanks** are abundantly cloaked in vegetation: glasswort, sea lavender and asters turn the mounds first green, then red, then blue, then grey. Rooted in the water are various reeds and rushes with long stalks and spiky flowers. On the beaches grow convolvulus with shiny dark-green leaves and pink flowers, and sea rocket with its violet blooms.

On the first dunes of shifting sands grows couch grass, a perennial member of the grass family. Farther back, tufts of coarse grass sprout among the spurges, with their long stalks of small lancet-like leaves and flowers with yellowish bracts. Tall bushy *gramineae* (*erianthus ravennae*) are also widely found.

Shrubs and trees grow beyond the dunes: along the Romea highway, south of Chioggia, between Santa Anna and Cavanella d'Adige, is the Bosco Nordio (Nordio Wood) of evergreen oaks. Even the market gardens form part of the vegetation of the lagoon, especially in the south at Chioggia, where red leaf chicory (*radicchio*) is grown, and north on Sant'Erasmo with its prized artichokes (*castraure*).

History

TIME LINE
LEGENDARY BEGINNINGS

It seems reasonable to turn to Homer when tracing the very ancient and uncertain origins of the Venetians. In the *Iliad* they arrived from Paflagonia to aid Priam. They were called the **Enetii**. Having abandoned their native land, these people arrived in the territory occupied by the Eugeneans, whom they put to flight. They founded the future Altino, from where they left for Torcello.

1000–700 BC	The Venetian civilisation known as *atestino* is founded around the city of Este.
530 BC	Etruscan colony of Spina established.
181 BC	Colony of Aquileia is founded.
42 AD	First dated documentation regarding the port of Altino.
400	From Padua, Altino, Concordia Sagittaria, Aquileia and Oderzo, the future inhabitants of Venice visit the lagoon solely for its provisions of salt and fish. In the 6C Cassiodoro (c.490–583) requests these watermen, fishermen and salt-workers to help supply Ravenna.
568	The Lombards descend into Italy. The Roman-Byzantine province of Venetia is gradually conquered.
639	Oderzo, the capital of Venetia, falls. The Byzantine governor moves to Cittanova, which takes the name **Heracleia**, from Emperor Heraclius. The Church of Santa Maria Assunta is built on the island of Torcello.
697	**Paoluccio Anafesto** is named the first doge.
742	Transfer of the ducal seat from Cittanova to Malamocco.
775	Olivolo, the present-day San Pietro di Castello, becomes a bishop's see. It is accountable to the patriarchate of Grado until 1451, when Lorenzo Giustinian is appointed First Patriarch of Venice.
810	Pepin, son of Charlemagne, is defeated after an attempted invasion of Dalmatia and the lagoon. Many inhabitants of the lagoon move to the Realtine Islands, where the dogate is established. In 811 **Agnello Partecipazio** or

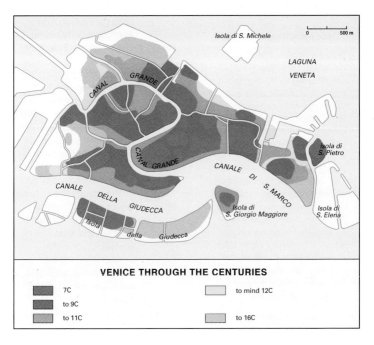

VENICE THROUGH THE CENTURIES

- 7C
- to 9C
- to 11C
- to mind 12C
- to 16C

"Particiaco" is elected doge. **Venice is born**.

During the 9C, when the dogeship was transferred, and for the three following centuries, Venice was made up of dozens of islands. The city was considerably smaller than it is today, however, because most of the land was below sea level.

THE INDEPENDENT CITY, RULER OF THE ADRIATIC

814 With the **Pax Nicephori (Treaty of Nicephorus)**, Charlemagne cedes his claims to the lagoon, and Venice guarantees her neutrality throughout the political struggles that were to rage in Italy during the eras of feudalism and the inter-city state rivalry.

828 The body of St Mark is stolen from Alexandria in Egypt and brought to Venice, where work begins on the construction of the first basilica the following year.

829 In his will Doge Giustiniano Particiaco calls for the construction of **San Marco**, which was to become the ducal chapel.

840 In the **Pactum Lotarii** (Peace of Lothar) the Byzantine ruler confirms the autonomy of Venice and assures her navy the control of the seas.

946 or 948 Narentine Slav pirates carry out the legendary abduction of the maidens (*see SAN ZACCARIA*).

976 The Venetians rebel against the repressive **Doge Pietro Candiano IV**, who chooses to ignore the maritime power base of Venice and instead engages foreign troops to conquer territories on the mainland, in order to enhance his own political standing and reputation. This provokes a fierce popular revolt culminating in the murder of the Doge (*see box, next page*). Fire

51

976: an witness account

Seized with panic, the doge, his wife and their young son sought safety by heading to the entrance of St Mark's. There they were stopped by noblemen. Pietro's promises to accept any compromise were of no avail. *"Affirming that he was... deserving of death, they shouted... that there could be no salvation for him. They immediately surrounded him and cruelly ran him through with the points of their swords so that his immortal spirit abandoned his bodily prison in search of the retreat of the blessed".* John Julius Norwich adds that, *"for what we know of Pietro Candiano IV, this happy final destination is somewhat improbable".*

damages St Mark's, the Doges' Palace and San Teodoro, destroying more than 300 houses, at the time built almost exclusively of wood.
Pietro Orseolo I is elected doge at **San Pietro di Castello**.

1000 After defeating the Croats and the Narentines, Venice assumes her role as ruler and protector of Dalmatia with the title *dux Dalmatinorum* (Duke of Dalmatia).

1032 The Venetians' strong spirit of independence precipitated a dislike for any government that resembled a monarchy and so, to avoid such a danger, the power of the doge is "split" between two ducal councillors, each one responsible for half of the city, with the Grand Canal as the dividing line.

11C In the second half of the century the new Basilica of St Mark is built, modelled upon the Basilica of the Apostles at Constantinople.

1081 Venice defends Byzantium from attack by the Norman Robert Guiscard.
The following year, the **Crisobollo** issued by the Byzantine Emperor, Alessio I Comneno, allows Venetians to trade freely throughout the empire and to open shops in Constantinople without having to pay duty on their goods.

1099 Venice defeats the Pisans near Rhodes, where the Venetian and Pisan fleets are taking part in the Crusades. The released Pisan prisoners undertake not to haunt the waters of Byzantium.

1104 The first nucleus of the Arsenal is created.
The following year the city is ravaged by fire.

1122–24 Under the dogeship of **Domenico Michiel**, Venice attacks and defeats the Egyptian fleet that was besieging Jaffa, taking possession of the merchant ships and their cargo of treasure trove and spices. She then goes on to participate in the victorious siege of Tyre, and the sacking of Byzantine ports in the Aegean and the Adriatic. These shows of force were crucial in restoring the reputation and political status enjoyed by the city before the King of Hungary had affirmed his power in Dalmatia, and in persuading the current Byzantine Emperor, **Giovanni Comneno**, to accept the fundamental independence of the city, recognised by his predecessors.

1143 The **Council of the Wise Men**, or *Consilium Sapientium*, is already in existence by this date. Thought to have consisted of 35 members presided over by the doge, this organisation was to evolve into the Great Council.

1145–53 Istria, already protected by Venice, now finds herself totally subjugated as the doge is proclaimed *totius Istriæ dominator*.

1171 Emergency measures are implemented by the Eastern Empire angered by the plundering of their trade ships by Venetian, Genoese and Pisan navies. The disastrous expedition of **Doge Vitale Michiel II**, whose crew was decimated by the plague, is judged very harshly by the Venetians, and leads to his murder. His successor, **Sebastiano Ziani** (1172), is elected under a system similar to that which later (1268) was sanctioned by law and lasted into the following centuries. During the dogeship of Vitale Michiel II, the six **sestieri** are created as subdivisions of the city, thereby facilitating the collection of taxes.

1175 Construction of a wooden Rialto Bridge.

Venetian Justice

Vitale Michiel II's assassin (1172) found refuge among the houses around San Zaccaria. The complicity of the Venetians in that area was severely punished: their houses were destroyed and the construction of any building in stone was prohibited. This law was eventually abolished in 1948.

1177 In Venice **Pope Alexander III** and **Frederick I (Barbarossa)** end the conflict between the city states and their antagonists, the Church and the Swabian Empire. According to legend, this is the occasion that saw Alexander III donate his ring in the Marriage of the Sea (*see box below*)

1178 Eleven men are nominated to elect the 40 electors of the doge, including six ducal councillors – one for each *sestiere*.

1201–04 **Fourth Crusade**. Doge **Enrico Dandolo**, a man of extraordinary energy despite being 90 and blind, attacks **Constantinople** (1203), which succumbs decisively to a second assault the following year. The Eastern Latin Empire is formed under an emperor nominated by six Venetians and six crusader barons.

Sensa, the Marriage to the Sea

According to one version of the legend, a fisherman obtained the "wedding ring" from St Mark on the night that Satan threatened to destroy Venice with a storm. Another legend relates that on Ascension Day, the doge solemnly proclaimed from the *Bucintoro* (state barge), in Latin *"We wed you, o sea, as a sign of true and perpetual dominion"*, casting a gold ring into the sea as he spoke. The ceremony began outside St Mark's, where the procession rallied before continuing on to the fort of San Andrea near the Lido. There the ring was cast into the sea. On his return, the doge stopped at San Nicolò on the Lido to attend Mass.

Piazza San Marco in 16C

©DEA/G. DAGLI ORTI/De Agostini Editore/ age fotostock

Spoils and lands are divided between the emperor, who took a quarter of the empire, the barons and the Venetians. Recognition is given to the doge's lordship over "a quarter and a half of the empire".

13C Around 1220 the **Quarantia**, a bench of 40 magistrates with judicial powers, is formed as part of the Great Council.

El Paron de la Repubblica

The **Great Council** held a quintessential position at the heart of the Venetian Republic, since it carried out all the duties of state. Not only did it pass laws, it also had the power to select the most important people in Venice. When it met in the chamber of the Doges' Palace, the doge would preside from the centre of the Tribunale or Bench of St Mark, while nobles seated upon armchairs would line the walls or fill rows of parallel benches down the length of the room.

1240 Venice besieges Ferrara, thus securing commercial control of the Po Valley.

1255 First dated documentation about the **Pregadi**, who are charged (*pregati*) with expressing opinions and fulfilling particular duties as members of the **Senate**. The Council of the Pregadi is appointed by the Great Council, to deal with questions of navigation and international politics, thus assuming both legislative and executive functions.

1257–70 Venice enters into conflict with Genoa. The Venetians defeat the Genoese at Acre, from where they brought the **Acrean pillars** now in front and to the right of the basilica.

The Eastern Latin Empire falls when the Byzantine Emperor, **Michele Paleologo III**, an ally of the Genoese, takes possession of Constantinople. The Genoese are subsequently bound by treaty (1270) to Louis IX of France, who

Lion's mouth, Palazzo Ducale

© E. Zane / MICHELIN

Bocca di Leone

The "lions' mouths" or "mouths of truth" (*see the example opposite*) were found along the streets or in the walls of public buildings. These lion-head masks were set with fierce expressions. The mouth was carved hollow to accommodate anonymous denunciations posted to the State. These denunciations were taken into account only if two witnesses were cited.

needs the Genoese fleet for the Crusades.

1268 New rules are drafted for the election of the doge. The Great Council has first to nominate the **Council of Forty**, charged with electing the next doge, by means of a 10-stage process of elections and drawing lots. The first doge appointed in this way is **Lorenzo Tiepolo**.

1284 The **gold ducat** is minted, equal in weight and gold content to the Florentine florin, which had been in circulation for 30 years (0.997g gold per 3.55g coin). The gold ducat was accepted currency until the fall of the Republic. When silver ducats were struck in 1561 the gold ducat became known as the *zecchino*.

1294–99 Venice is once more at war with Genoa. At the **Battle of Curzola** (1298) the victorious Genoese sustain grievous losses. The treaty signed in 1299 sanctions the Genoese dominance over the Riviera and that of the Venetians over the Adriatic.

1297 This is the year of the **Locking of the Great Council**, a reform that considerably increased the number of council members to more than 1 000, as well as tightening up the system for their selection. Current as well as former members have to conform to rigorous procedures. By 1323, nomination is standardised, membership is for life and passed down the generations. Later still, the Great Council degenerates into a corps for the Venetian nobility.

1308–13 Venice, dissatisfied with the duty levied on all the goods travelling through the Po Valley and wishing to consolidate its power over the area, attacks Ferrara. **Pope Clement V**, keen to defend his right of sovereignty over the city, issues from Avignon an **interdict** on Venice, which lasts until 1313.

1310 **Baiamonte Tiepolo**, a Venetian nobleman, tries to depose Doge Pietro Gradenigo. The revolt is suppressed with much bloodshed, and prompts the creation of a remarkable judicial body known as the **Council of Ten**, whose prime function is to protect constitutional institutions. Presided over by the doge, this body consisted of 10 members of the Senate and six wise men. It employed the service of secret police and informers to investigate suspicious citizens and deal with denunciations and charges of libel against the State posted in the **lions' mouths**.

1321 The poet **Dante Alighieri** stays in Venice in his capacity as ambassador to the Lords of Ravenna.

1347–48 A Venetian galley introduces the **plague** from Crimea, which was to decimate the densely populated city (over 100 000 inhabitants) by three-fifths.

1350–55 The conflict with Genoa continues.

In 1350, Venice is troubled by heavy traffic that often causes serious accidents; it is established that horses should be provided with "bell-collars to warn pedestrians of their passage".

DOGESHIP OF MARINO FALIER (1354–55)

Marino Falier was 80 when he was elected doge. Irascible and resentful, he began his dogeship under the worst of omens. The day he arrived in Venice, the **bucintoro**, the grandiose dogal barge, decorated with friezes and gold carvings, could not draw alongside its mooring because of fog; secondly, on arriving on the piazza, the doge entered the palace by passing between the two columns where outlaws were executed; lastly, he was offended by insults about

his wife scrawled on his chair by a young boy. Falier became even more viperish when he found out how lightly the culprit had been punished.

He decided to mete out punishment and exact his revenge by plotting murder on those members of the nobility whom he thought had betrayed him. The conspiracy was exposed in time. The doge was accused of treason and sentence passed for his execution. A black-draped portrait in the chamber of the Great Council, recording his unhappy rule, bears a defamatory but accurate inscription. (see PIAZZA SAN MARCO: Palazzo Ducale). The story of Marino Falier inspired both Byron and Swinburne (who both wrote works bearing the same title: Marino Falier), Donizetti (Marin Falier) and Delacroix.

1358 Dalmatia or "Schiavonia" is ceded to Hungary.

1378–81 A fourth offence is mounted by the Venetians against Genoa to liberate Chioggia from Genoese and then Paduan hands.

1386 Corfu comes under Venetian rule.

1389–1420 Venice gradually gains dominion over a vast territory corresponding, more or less, to the present areas of Veneto and Friuli.

1409 Venice regains possession of Dalmatia.

1410 Venice is badly hit by a high tide.

1424 Building begins on the Ca' d'Oro.

1425–54 During the dogeship of **Francesco Foscari**, by now head of an oligarchic system

Paradise Replaces the Coronation of the Virgin

In 1365 the Chamber of the Great Council was decorated with the fresco by Guariento (recorded 1338–70), representing The Coronation of the Virgin. After the fire, it was decided to "remake Paradise as it was before". After a first competition, won by Veronese and Bassano, the work was never executed. A second competition awarded the work to Tintoretto, who with his son Domenico in 1588–1592 painted the immense Paradise, reputed to be the largest canvas oil painting in the world.

De' Barbari map

© Museo Correr / Fondazione Musei Civici Venezia

(since 1423 the formula had been dropped which had once required the popular approval of the new doge; "If it is pleasing to you"), Venice is at war with the Lombards. **Carmagnola** takes part in the battles and, suspected of treason, is condemned by the Council of Ten to be beheaded between the columns of the Piazzetta. After three decades of battle, Venetian territory stretches as far as the River Adda.
In 1428 Venice is devastated by an exceptionally high tide.

1463–79 The capture of the Venetian Argosy by the Turks is one of several humiliations to which Venice has to succumb, including the loss of Cumae and Scutari in Albania that prompts an annual levy of 10 000 ducats. This tribute is finally abolished at the death of Mehmet II.

1472 **Caterina Cornaro** marries Giacomo Lusignano II, King of Cyprus, after whose death Queen Caterina is toppled by a coup d'état. (see *RIALTO*).

1490 The art of printing is introduced from Germany by **Aldo Manuzio**, who sets up his own printing press. It is famed for its refined

italic characters and for the intellectual nature of his books, stamped with a dolphin and an anchor.

1494 Charles VIII, King of France, arrives in Italy to conquer the Kingdom of Naples. The anti-French league, of which Venice was part, fails to defeat him in the **Battle of Fornovo** the following year.

1499 The Turks attack Lepanto. Antonio Grimani is defeated off the coast of Sapienza: in Venice he earns the epithet *"Antonio Grimani, ruin of the Christians"*. The Turks sack Friuli. The peace treaty of 1503 sanctions the loss of Lepanto, Modone and Corone.

1500 The **De' Barbari map** is published, providing a strangely evocative and realistic impression of the city.

1508 In order to split up Venetian territory, Julius II, Louis XII and Emperor Maximilian I form the **League of Cambrai**, in alliance with Spain, Hungary, the Duke of Savoy, the Duke of Ferrara and the Marquis of Mantua. After an initial defeat, Venice takes seven years to recover her possessions as far as the Adda.

1514	The Rialto market is destroyed by fire.
1516	The Jews are segregated in the Ghetto district.

DANGEROUS YEARS

1538	Andrea Doria, admiral under Emperor Charles V and a Venetian ally, is defeated at Prevesa. The Turks now control the seas.
1539	A secret service is set up by the **State Inquisitors**, the *Supreme Tribunale*, comprising three inquisitors: "the Red", a dogal councillor in a scarlet gown, and "the Blacks", two members of the Council of Ten. Working on information from informers, they take part in intrigue and counter-espionage.
1570	The Turks land in Cyprus and conquer Nicosia.
1571	After the siege and fall of Famagusta, **Marcantonio Bragadin**, the Venetian governor, is flayed alive by the Turks.

LEPANTO

Joined in the Holy League with the Pope and Spain, Venice confronted the Turks at Lepanto on 7 October 1571. The Christian fleet, commanded by **Sebastiano Venier**, comprised 202 galleys and six smaller ships, of which more than half were Venetian. The Turkish fleet comprised 208 galleys and a flotilla of 63 boats. The Turks were heavily defeated: 30 000 men were killed, 80 ships sunk and 140 captured. The League lost 7 600 men and 12 ships. Among the wounded Christians was **Miguel de Cervantes**, author of *Don Quixote*, who always considered the Battle of Lepanto the most important event not only of his life, but of all history. Cervantes believed that the injury to his left hand, which was permanently crippled, was "to the greater glory of his right one".

1573	Venice signs a treaty with the Turks that clinches control over Cyprus, which is abandoned and left to decline.
1577	Fire damages much of the Doges' Palace. Refurbishment is undertaken by Antonio da Ponte.

San Marco Basin *by Giovanni Antonio Canal, known as Canaletto*

©DEA/G. DAGLI ORTI/De Agostini Editore/ age fotostock

1587	The **Banco della Piazza**, the first public Venetian bank, is set up. The second, the **Banco Giro** (or Banco del Giro), is created in 1619 (⊙ see RIALTO).
1588	The Rialto Bridge is rebuilt in stone.
1593	The fortress of Palmanova is built, designed in the form of a nine-pointed star to defend the eastern borders against the Turks and Habsburgs. To commemorate the victory at the Battle of Lepanto, the foundation stone is laid down on 7 October.
1599–1604	The **River Po**, which deposits huge quantities of sediments around Chioggia, is diverted towards Goro.
1600	Once again, the city of Venice is flooded at high tide.

ANOTHER INTERDICT

In order to understand the relationship that existed between Venice and the Holy See, it is useful to note what the Venetians, who held themselves to be "first Venetian and then Christian", used to boldly claim: "We believe fully in St Mark, sufficiently in God and not at all in the Pope".

The Pope did not accept the right to religious freedom that Venice granted the Protestants. In 1605 the denunciation before the Council of Ten of two priests, accused of various crimes, proved to be the last straw. The Pope maintained that the two should have been handed over to the ecclesiastical authorities. On the Venetian side was a Servite priest, **Paolo Sarpi**, whose arguments seemed heretical to Rome. When the Pope threatened an interdict and excommunicated Venice, the city responded: "Your excommunication we regard as nothing and we care not a fig about it."

The interdict lasted for a year. Although the relationship between Venice and the Vatican normalised, Paolo Sarpi was the victim of an assassination attempt in 1607. Recovered from his wounds and

> ### The Libro d'Oro
>
> The Golden Book, first drawn up in the 16C, was the register of the civil status of Venetian nobility. Specific conditions for entry had to be fulfilled. Whoever was not high-born, and thus not inscribed, could not hold a government office.

surveying the dagger with which he had been stabbed, he is said to have declared: "I recognise the style of the Roman Church."

1609	**Galileo Galilei** presents the telescope to the doge.
1613–17	After raids by the **Uskoks**, pirates from Bosnia and Turkish Dalmatia protected by the Habsburgs, Venice goes to war over Istria and Friuli, which results in the Uskoks being deported to central Croatia.
1618	Spain instigates a complex conspiracy against Venice. The Council of Ten intervenes decisively as usual: one of the participants is sewn into a sack and thrown into the sea; another two are hung upside down on the gallows of the Piazzetta.
1622	**Antonio Foscarini**, the illustrious senator and ambassador to France and England, is found guilty of spying. He is condemned to death and succumbs to the usual treatment of being hung by one foot in the Piazzetta. Some time later, it is revealed that the accusations against Foscarini were false. The man who had spread these accusations is tried by the Three (⊙ see previous pages: 1539) and condemned to death. Venice makes public admission of her grave error. A state declaration

is sent to his family and to embassies, and copies are pasted around the city.

1628–30 Following the death of Ferdinand Gonzaga, Mantua is claimed both by the French, led by Charles of Gonzaga-Nevers, and the Habsburgs. It is under siege from German troops when Venice intervenes: the city is nevertheless lost to the French. Mantua is savagely ransacked as the **plague** ravages the region, decimating the local population and Germans, before spreading to Venice. In little more than a year, the Serenessima loses 50 000 inhabitants. When at last the contagion subsides, construction is begun on the Church of Santa Maria della Salute in fulfilment of a vow.

Draining the Rivers

Local authorities routinely undertake to dry out the city rivers to cleanse the water and restore bridges. It is only then that water depths and the hollowness of the river bed are apparent. Dark and malodorous, the waters tend to collect waste as well as objects that fall in by accident. Documents relating to this practice can be traced back to the late 13C and the early 14C. It has been established that these dredging operations have been carried out regularly since the 15C to renew the water and facilitate navigation. The main bodies in charge of implementing this work are the Magistratura del Piovego and the Savi alle Acque.

THE SULTAN'S HAREM AND THE WAR OF CANDIA (CRETE)

The Knights of Malta habitually committed acts of piracy of which Venice disapproved because they were detrimental to her relationship with the East. In 1644 the Knights attacked a Turkish galleon in the Aegean and captured part of the Sultan's harem. The Sultan avenged himself not by attacking Malta, but Candia – Crete was then known by the name of its capital – convinced that the Venetians were behind this act.

The war dragged on for over 20 years, despite the Turkish fleet having suffered a naval defeat, second only to Lepanto, in 1656. Finally, Captain **Francesco Morosini**, backed by 3 600 men, signed the surrender in 1699, with which Venice lost the island.

1684–99 Francesco Morosini, the ally of Austria and Russia, reconquers the Peloponnese peninsula, thereby acquiring the nickname "the Peloponnesian". Unfortunately, during this military operation, a Venetian mortar is fired at the Parthenon which, being used by the Turks to store their reserves of gunpowder, is severely damaged. He is elected doge in 1688. In 1699, although the former Venetian territories had not all been reclaimed, the Treaty of Carlowitz temporarily checks Turkish military campaigns.

18C AND DECLINE

Although in decline, when faced with a choice between alliance and independence, Venice once again opted for autonomy by refusing to side either with France or the Habsburgs in conflict for two centuries.

1714–18 Venice loses the Peloponnese forever in a final battle against the Turks, sealed by the **Treaty**

of Passarowitz, signed in 1718. She maintains possession of Istria, Dalmatia, the Ionian islands and a few territories in Albania.

1744–82 The *Murazzi* (protective wall around the lagoon) is built at Pellestrina and Sottomarina, 14m/46ft wide and 4.5m/14ft 8in higher than the average level of the tide. It is made with Istrian stone and pozzolana, a type of volcanic dust which has remarkable binding qualities when mixed with water, sand and lime.

1784 The Procurator **Andrea Tron**, nicknamed *el Paron* (the Leader) for his strong personality and political standing, which most citizens regarded as above the doge, laments that *"there are no shades of our old merchants among the citizens or subjects"* before the spread of *"weakness of character, overwhelming luxury, idle shows and presumptuous entertainment and vice"* in Venice.

1784–86 These are the years of the final naval incursions. Admiral **Angelo Emo** wages battles against pirates along the North African coast.

A BREAK WITH TRADITION AND THE DEMISE OF THE REPUBLIC

1789 The last doge to be elected, **Ludovico Manin**, ironically is the first not to be born of the old Venetian nobility, but of an émigré family from Friuli that had paid 100 000 ducats for inclusion in the **Golden Book** in 1651.

1792 The opera house reopens as **La Fenice**.
Before the decline of Venice, the city still shows consideration for its fragile lagoon. It defines a series of boundaries referred to as the "lagoon perimeter", inside which it was forbidden to carry out any activity that might endanger the natural habitat of the lake.

1797 **Napoleon** invades Venetian territory in 1796 while pursuing his Austrian enemy and successfully ejecting it from Italy – a possession he only maintains by posting troops in Verona and controlling access to the Brenner Pass. A temporary pact is made with the Austrians at Leoben (18 April 1797). This is ratified six months later on 18 October by the **Treaty of Campoformio** signed by Francis II, Emperor of Austria, and Napoleon Bonaparte. It confirms that Austria renounces her claim over Belgium and Lombardy to take possession of the Veneto as far as the Adige, Friuli, Istria, Dalmatia, the Po Valley and the islands in the Adriatic. France takes the Albanian coast and the Ionian islands. Venice is left with the former Papal States of Romagna, Ferrara and Bologna.
Venice's fate, in effect, is sealed by her resistance to ally herself to Napoleon. Not only does she show no remorse when anti-French feeling is stoked by the clergy during Easter week to the point of vicious rioting in Verona (a Venetian dominion), but she positively congratulates her officers for firing at a French patrol in the Adriatic and killing the French crew. Napoleon's exasperation is documented: *"I will have no*

Distinguishing Between Canals and Rivers

Although all Venetian waterways tend to be called canals, only three real canals exist in the city: Canal Grande, Canale della Giudecca and Canale di Cannaregio. Canals, which are wider, are tributaries of the lagoon, whereas the narrow rivers (*rii*) can be compared to streets: they are not linked to the sea and wend their way across the city along a sinuous, meandering course. The only exception is the Cannaregio *sestiere*, as any plan of Venice will show.

more Inquisition, no more Senate. I shall be an Attila to the State of Venice".

Without the reassurance of Venice's recapitulation, the government would have to be seized and war would be inevitable. The Senate meets for the last time on 29 April. By Friday 12 May, Napoleon's demands have to be conceded and the Great Council meets for a last, very tense sitting. A provisional government is approved by an "unconstitutional" Council falling short of its quorum of 600 by 63, many members having fled to their country estates on terra firma. Laying down the *cufieta*, the bonnet worn by the doge under his crown, Ludovico Manin turned with dignity to his servant: *"Take it away, I will have no further use for this"*.

AFTER THE FALL

1805 With the Treaty of Presburg, Napoleon formally reclaims Venice as part of the Kingdom of Italy.

1815 The Congress of Vienna establishes that Venice, the Veneto and Lombardy should belong to Austria.

1821 The Italians show unrest caused by the failed attempts to achieve unification. Anti-Austrian movements break out.

1839–53 Construction of the north and south dikes at Malamocco is completed.

1841 The railway bridge linking Venice to Mestre is built.

1844 The patriot founders of the secret organisation Esperia, Attilio and Emilio Bandiera, together with a sympathiser, Domenico Moro, are shot at Cosenza.

1847 The lawyer **Daniele Manin** and the writer **Niccolò Tommaseo** are awarded prizes by the 11th Congresso degli Scienziati.

1848 Daniele Manin is nominated President of the Republic of St Mark and begins reorganising a provisional government, before leading an insurrection against the Austrians supported by Niccolò Tommaseo. Both eminent men are subsequently exiled.

1854–58 Identical iron bridges are built near the Accademia and the station.

1866 After the Prussian defeat of the Austrians at Sadowa, Venice votes to be part of a unified Italy by a majority of 674 426 to 69.

1895 The **International Biennale of Art** is founded. Exhibition facilities are expanded through the 19C with the erection of various modern pavilions.

1902 The bell-tower of St Mark's collapses.

1915–18 Venice suffers several bomb attacks but her misfortunes are not caused only by the war: once again the city is flooded by the rising waters.

1932 First International Film Festival.

1933 Inauguration of the Ponte Littorio, now called the Ponte della Libertà.

1943–44 On July 25, 1943, the Italian Fascist government fell. German troops arrived in Italy on September 8, 1943. On September 16, Giuseppe Jona, president of the Jewish community of Venice, committed suicide rather than hand over the lists of the names of the Jewish community. 204 Jews were deported from Venice by the Nazis, only 8 returned from the death camps.

1953 Giuseppe Roncalli is appointed Patriarch of Venice before being elected **Pope John XXIII** and instigating the Second Vatican Council.

1953–69 Architect **Frank Lloyd Wright** (1869–1959) plans a student centre, the Masieri Memorial, to be built along the Grand Canal. In 1964 **Le Corbusier** (1887–1965) proposes designs for the Civil Hospital. **Louis Kahn** (1901–74) undertakes a project for a new Congress Hall. None of these undertakings sees the light of day.

1966 During November the high tide rises to an alarming level. The waters flood the *Murazzi* at Pellestrina and reach many of the city houses.

1969 Albino Luciani is appointed Patriarch of Venice and elected Pope in 1978, assuming the name **John Paul I**, which he bore until his death, a month later.

THE LAGOON LIVES ON

If the glory of Venice belongs to a bygone era, its lagoon provides a continuous link with the past, preserving a quality and style of life unique to its shores, regardless of the threat of subsidence or flooding. In 1925 alone, the Piazza San Marco, the "salon of Venice", was flooded eight times. Since then it has succumbed to inundation on more than 50 occasions.

Pollution, today's worst enemy

The 20C was the era of industrialisation. Marghera was created in the 1920s and, after the Second World War, the areas taken up by industrial activity expanded quite considerably. Oil was known to seep into the canal, threatening the ecological balance of the lagoon, whose precarious state was further endan-

Birdseed sellers out of work

Venetian officials first voted to outlaw pigeon feeding in 1997 but the Piazza San Marco was exempted because of the iconic status of the birds and their feeders. However by 2008 it had become clear that to make a significant reduction in the bird population, their most obvious food supply – St. Mark's official birdseed sellers – had to go.

Sergio Lafisca, the Venice health expert responsible for the Department of Prevention, estimates that there are about 130,000 pigeons living in Venice's historic centre. Aside from human health considerations (the birds are real and potential carriers of disease) the birds' droppings, claws and beaks cause significant damage to the monuments. In fact a recent report concluded that the pigeons costs each resident around €275 a year in terms of clean up and repairs.

gered by the draining of land to build industrial areas and Marco Polo Airport. Between 1950 and 1970, the waste turned out by refineries and by chemical and metallurgical factories at **Porto Marghera** would often end up in the lagoon. During the 1980s a number of purification plants were set up nearby and they now recycle an estimated 80% of the area's industrial refuse. Pollution, caused by excessive amounts of nitrogen and phosphates, chemical fertilisers and insecticides, and organic substances generated by industrial complexes and urban communities, destroys part of the lagoon flora and fauna, encourages the proliferation of algae and stunts that of the phanerogamic species, whose roots are extremely useful, since they prevent the onslaught of erosion.

1973	The Italian State declares that the preservation of Venice is of "pre-eminent national interest".
1988–92	The MoSE prototype, a huge mobile sluice-gate devised to regulate the movement of the tides, is installed in the lagoon waters on an experimental basis.
1989	The famous rock band **Pink Floyd** are invited to play in St Mark's Square. The council's gamble on bringing modern music to the heart of Venice backfires horribly as concert goers cause mayhem and thousands of pounds of damage. The city council resigns en bloc.
1996	The opera house **La Fenice** burns down on 29 January.
2001	Approval is given for the completion of the mobile tide barriers designed to protect the city.
2003	The reconstructed **La Fenice** opens to the public.
2004	The 650ft (200m) long cruise ship *Mona Lisa* runs aground in fog in St Mark's Basin, provoking fears of a major accident in the heart of Venice.
2008	Venice's fourth bridge across the Grand Canal, the **Ponte di Calatrava** is completed. **Pigeon feeding** in the Piazza is banned.
2010	In October a terrible storm strikes Vicenza. The areas that sustained the most damage were in the city and the surrounding environs, from Padua province to Verona province.
2011	Venice established a hotel tax for individuals.
2012	After ousting the previous director, Venice Film Festival announced a new director and streamlined its program.
2012	A cruise ship damages the port while docking, fueling the controversy over allowing large cruise ships into the lagoon.
2016	Work continues for the realization of MOSE (Modulo Sperimentale Elettromeccanico), a civil engineering, environmental and hydraulic project that aims to defend Venice and

> *"...a Venetian gondola? That singular conveyance, came down unchanged from ballad times, black as nothing else on earth except a coffin – what pictures it calls up of lawless, silent adventures in the slashing night; or even more, what visions of death itself, the bier and solemn rites and last soundless voyage! And has anyone remarked that the seat in such a bark, the arm-chair lacquered in coffin-black, and dully black-upholstered, is the softest, most luxurious, most relaxing seat in the world?"*
> Thomas Mann – *Death in Venice*

its waterways from flooding. The project calls for walls of mobile, submergible sluice gates to replace the harbour "mouths" (water passages that connect the lagoon with the open sea, and through which seawater flows in and out) at Lido, Malamocco and Chioggia, and can temporarily isolate the Venetian lagoon from the Adriatic sea during bad weather.

> "The bathing, on a calm day, must be the worst in Europe: water like hot saliva, cigar-ends floating into one's mouth, and shoals of jelly-fish."
>
> Robert Byron –
> The Road to Oxiana, 1937

THE TROUBLE WITH TOURISTS...

Henry James once remarked "There are some disagreeable things in Venice, but nothing so disagreeable as the visitors". It is a sentiment that many Venetians echo in private if not public.

In no other functioning major city on earth is the resident population so heavily outnumbered by visitors as it is in Venice. Some 62,000 live in the historic city (Centro storico), while another 31,000 live on other islands in the lagoon. Each year they are invaded by around 20 million visitors. No one knows the real total and this in itself is a problem for managing the infrastructure. According to the tourist board (in 2004), 6 million visitors spend one night or more in Venice every year. A further 15 million flood its streets and alleys only for the day, marching into the Piazza San Marco, perhaps paying a swift visit to the Basilica di San Marco, before heading out again. In fact It is said that around 80 percent of tourists don't even bother to visit a single monument while in Venice. Whatever the true figures, there is no doubt that day-trippers contribute little in economic terms and cause immense problems in terms of pollution and congestion. It helps to remember, like driving, stay to the right when walking. Venice of course is dependant on tourism, which accounts for 70 percent of its economy. However, on days when more than 60,000 visitors arrive, in a city where just 33,000 can be accommodated comfortably, entire systems are taxed from transport to pedestrian bridges and sidewalks. It is often said that the charm of Venice is more at risk from the tourist tidal wave than from sinking into the sea. The transport authority, ACTV, periodically experiments with new lines in response to citizens' complaints that (day-trip) tourists were cramming onto water buses, leaving residents stuck on dry land. People who live and work in Venice demand better transportation, paying a greatly reduced fare on (all) *vaporetti* than what tourists pay.

The city's approach has been to offer tourists a pass that offers significant savings when visiting over a number of days (plus it offers the privilege of jumping queues). Higher fees are paid for single trips or for a one-day pass. In June 2012 a new vaporetto line, Art Vaporetto, but was eliminated by 2014.

However, as of 2011, as was instituted also in Rome and Florence, even overnight guests are now taxed, per person, per night, which is applied for the first five nights. Likewise, high and low seasons have been completely redefined: in 2013, Venice classified February 1 -November 30 as high season.

Recent years have seen a tougher approach taken against misbehaving visitors. A previous mayor instituted regulations for decorum and fines for violations. Stewards patrol St Mark's Square and other historic sites and impose on-the-spot fines to tourists found picnicking, walking around bare-chested or barefooted and littering.

UNIQUE TO VENICE

The inhospitable nature of the lagoon, from which Venice sprung up as if by magic, has demanded of the Venetians an extraordinary ability to adjust

Gondola under repair

© khr128 / iStockphoto

to a particular lifestyle implemented through a rare spirit of initiative. To combat the waters, either too high or too low, and to make their way around the myriad islands, the Venetians built the gondola and hundreds of bridges; they also planted thousands of poles.

THE GONDOLA

No one knows exactly when the gondola was invented: the word *gundula* appears as early as 1094 in a decree of Doge Vitale Falier, although the reference relates to a massive boat equipped with a large crew of rowers – a far cry from the gondola we know today.

In the 14C, small boats covered with a central canopy bore metal decorations on the prow and stern. At the end of the century the vessel began to be made longer and lighter, the prow and stern were raised and the **felze** or cabin was added, affording shelter in bad weather. Some had decorated prows. Others were painted in bright colours and decked with satin, silk and gleaming brass. On the prow and stern stood painted cherubs bearing the coat of arms of the family to which the gondola belonged. From the 16C, boats were toned down by being painted black: a colour we might judge to be rather funereal, but in Venice red, not black, is the colour of mourning. Today the gondola is about 11m/36ft long, 1.42m/4ft wide and comprises 280 pieces of wood.

Building a gondola

The shipyards where gondolas are built and repaired are called **squeri**. At one time, each of these was allocated primarily to a family from Cadore in the Dolomites, hence the reason why their wooden galleried constructions resembled alpine houses (&see ACCADEMIA: Squero di San Trovaso).

The **ferro**, a sabre-toothed projection made of iron placed at the prow and stern, is without doubt the most crucial element of the gondola: implemented initially as a fender to safeguard against knocks, it serves as a counterweight to the gondoliere, and to align the boat around hazards in the narrowest passages. The curved fin is said to echo the dogal *corno* and to symbolise its power over the six **sestieri** represented by the six serrations. The tooth that "guards" the gondola itself is the Giudecca.

The **forcola** or rowlock, is an intricate piece of carving hewn from walnut, designed as a pivot that allows the oar maximum mobility. The oar is made of well-seasoned beech. Two bronze sea horses cleat the cords of the seats.

PALINE, DAME AND BRICOLE

Whether travelling by gondola, vaporetto or boat, there is always the risk of running aground. Navigable channels are identified by means of **bricole** – a series of large poles (*pali*) roped together – whereas the entrance to a canal or a junction is indicated by **dame**, which are smaller poles than the *bricole*. The **paline** are those thin individual poles that project from the water at odd intervals, to which private craft are tethered. They are particularly evocative if painted with coloured swirling stripes, outside some fine building to mark the landing stage of a patrician family in days gone by.

THE BRIDGES

The tussles of *su e zo per i ponti*, "up and down the bridges" (&see Calendar of Events, in Planning Your Trip), were once points of conflict among rival families.

Art and Culture

The history of architecture, art and culture in general in Venice cannot be divorced from the physical and geographical constraints that throughout the ages the Venetians have had to overcome with mastery and ingenuity. The city still bears the stamp of the former Byzantine Empire, but over the years the streets have also succumbed to the influence of Renaissance, Classical and Baroque architecture. Artists have played a role in forging the atmosphere of the city, while remaining faithful to the Venetian spirit.

ARCHITECTURE
BUILDING IN VENICE
Houses on piles

The city is not built on water, but in the water. It was built either on sandbanks above the water level, which gave rise to real islands, or on small sandy mounds which had remained at the water's surface.

In either case, great larch or oak **pali** are driven deep through the sand, mud or silt, forming an unstable lagoon floor, to the bedrock of hard clay. These 2–4m/6ft 6in–13ft piles are organised in concentric circles or spirals starting from the outer perimeter of the building to be constructed, at intervals of 60–80cm/24–32in. In this way the piles provide a base onto which a raft-like platform (*zattera*) of horizontal beams (*zatterone*) may be secured. To reinforce this wooden floor, it is lined with boulders of **Istrian stone** that provide a solid course for the brick and mortar on which it is possible to build.

The number of piles used can sometimes be considerable: 1 106 657 for the Church of Santa Maria della Salute, and 10 000 for the Rialto Bridge!

Building materials

Unfortunately, since the lagoon offers very little in terms of building materials, it is necessary to import these from other areas.

Most of the **timber** is brought from the Cadore forests and the Balkans. It is used not only for the foundation piles, but also for the frames and ceilings of the houses. Occasionally it is incorporated into masonry walls, not so much as reinforcement but rather as "shock absorbers": this procedure lends greater flexibility to the structure, which resolves some of the problems raised by the instability of the subsoil. **Marble**, used to front façades, is principally sourced from the Euganei Hills (*south of Padua*) or from Greece. **Istria limestone**, hard, white and marble-like, has the added advantage of being resistant to salt erosion; it is therefore frequently used in Venice for bridge copings and to face *palazzi*, churches, bell-towers etc. Only **brick**, which in Gothic times lent its charming pink hues to I Frari and many other quaint buildings in Venice, is made on-site from local clay.

Originality

All the houses, palaces and churches that have been erected in *La Serenissima* through the ages survive on these reinforced, drained, dried and consolidated areas reclaimed from the lagoon. It is almost as if the early Venetians made a pact with the lagoon that they would live with it rather than view it as a problem to be reckoned with. And so from the water rise mists and fogs that swirl and fade again to confer a thousand different moods on the urban landscape: one moment the millpond mirrors a perfect reflection and in another the choppy, churlish surface dissolves the shimmering profile according to whim. The lagoon intensifies the ethereal sunlight to sparkle and glitter and lend a festive air to the city, but it may also invade the landscape with a spirit of melancholy. Water consorts with the changing light and density of the air to exaggerate or deform the delicate stone lacework, the crenellated roof ornaments, the many recesses, loggias and arcades. However, poetic descriptions of atmosphere are

Campo

© Silvia Ganora / Dreamstime.com

an insubstantial preoccupation in comparison to the physical problems posed by the lagoon: it is rather the remoteness of mainland resources and the instability of the subsoil that preoccupy the Venetian authorities. Initially, it was the cost and transport of building materials that dictated a patron's choice and influenced an architect's design of a private palace or church. Up to the 16C, local brick had been the most obvious raw material available. However, when more sophisticated and reliable forms of transport were discovered, the economic factor became considerably less important. A second major element in the equation was the risk of subsidence. To reduce this threat, houses were erected no more than two or three storeys high, except in the Ghetto, where squat buildings had low ceilings so that the total weight was proportionally less. A constant reminder of instability was the angle at which certain palaces (Palazzo Dario) and bell-towers (Santo Stefano, San Barnaba) inclined, and the regularity with which the quays (Riva degli Schiavoni) and St Mark's Square flooded. Through determination, patience and perseverance in an unpredictable environment, strengthened by a spirit of enterprise and ambitious business acumen, the Venetians learned to construct and embellish their magnificent city. Yet despite everything

that has been accomplished and all the expertise acquired, the unpropitious site for this wonderful city means that it will forever be at the mercy of natural forces: the corrosive action of salt and water, and the instability of the lagoon floor.

The Campo

The *campi*, or squares, provide points at which all roads, streets, alleys and activity converge. It is at the very heart of community life, where housewives chat and hang out their washing and where children play in the open. It is not to be confused with the **corte**, a closed public courtyard with a single entrance, or with the **cortile**, a private courtyard hidden within a patrician town house.

The *campo*, sometimes dotted with a few trees, is encircled by fine patrician houses, Gothic or Renaissance in style, and blessed with its own church. At its centre, a well might occupy a choice spot. Given that the city was built on salty water and therefore had no natural drinking-water supply, rainwater had to be collected, purified and stored in cisterns that were excavated to a depth of 5–6m/16–20ft. The brick-lined tank collected water through several apertures in the *campo* floor, filtering it through fine river sand. Often the wellhead, the **vera da pozzo**, would have been paid for by a patron and would therefore have been sculpted as a work of art.

Domestic architecture

Throughout Venice, with the exception of the Grand Canal, palaces rub shoulders with modest houses. Simply built in pink brick or stone, most of these houses are low in height. A few retain their openwork external staircase, double façade and "double" front entrances: one on the street and one onto the canal with its "water porch". The inner courtyard is modelled on the Roman atrium: shaded in summer and protected from the wind in winter. On the first floor or **piano nobile**, a **portego** runs perpendicular to the main front, from the street, across the internal *cortile*, through the entire width of the house to open out onto a loggia on the canal side.

The **altana** is a veranda built on a tiled roof where typical Venetian high funnel-shaped chimneys, known as *fumaioli*, project; these distinctive features were immortalised by Carpaccio in his paintings. Forever short of space, the Venetians have made clever use of their rooftops by installing these charming terraces to increase their living area. The façades are enhanced with flower-decked balconies, small carved discs, ornamental reliefs and sculpted cornices. Down the side walls, houses with *barbacani* have corbelled projections to support the timber beams of upper floors (Calle del Paradiso).

The lack of space at ground level means that there are very few gardens in Venice, and those that do exist are small, sometimes consisting of a single tree or a few flower tubs, often jealously guarded from the public eye behind high walls.

CRAFTSMANSHIP VALUED
Veneto-Byzantine

The oldest monuments found in the Venetian Lagoon are on the island of Torcello: the **Cattedrale di Santa Maria Assunta** and the complex of **Santa Fosca** bear witness to the close ties that once allied Venice with Ravenna, the Western heir to a Byzantine legacy.

For several centuries Venice, through its conquests and trade links with the East, maintained a close relationship with Greece and Constantinople: the Basilica of St Mark, rebuilt in the 11C, was modelled on the 6C prototype of Byzantium churches, the Church of the Holy Apostles in Constantinople, destroyed in the 13C (the immense and sumptuous Hagia Sophia was built subsequently by the same architect along the same lines). St Mark's therefore directly transposes an expression of the Eastern Church, in terms of form, structure, volume and style, into the West.

This oriental Christianity was a major force in the fusion of an original "Veneto-Byzantine" style from the late Middle Ages onwards. The artistic iconography, strongly influenced by Byzantium, incorporates Islamic elements (decorative motifs, horseshoe arches), Palaeo-Christian features (*transennae*, capitals) and Roman details from sculpted fragments (marble blocks, column shafts, flat bricks) salvaged from villas along the Adriatic coast that had been destroyed during the barbarian invasions of the 5C and 6C.

Churches

The Byzantine-style churches like Santa Fosca, Torcello Cathedral, Santa Maria e Donato on Murano and St Mark's Basilica, best demonstrate the Eastern influence. This influence is clearly visible in the centrally planned Greek cross church or longitudinal hall church (nave

Altana

© T.Zane / MICHELIN

and two aisles) prefixed by a narthex (covered porch which evolved into an arched portico) but independent of a free-standing baptistry (like that at Torcello). Structurally, Byzantium provided the expertise to erect domes over open spaces unencumbered by piers; it inspired the use of precious marble column shafts crowned with variously shaped capitals (basket-shaped, inverted pyramid) and carved ornament (organic decoration such as foliage, symmetrically arranged animals). The practice in Ravenna (12C–13C) of applying decoration in the form of shallow relief, open fretwork, or *niello* (deeply cut engraving) and mosaic with flat gold backgrounds to both internal and external walls, was quick to be emulated by Venetian mosaicists, who copied subjects from the Old and New Testaments. Other features to be accommodated include Palaeo-Christian *transennae* (open-work window screens), *plutei* (marble tablets) and *paterae* (small carved discs) encircled within a twisted rope moulding, acanthus leaves and vine leaf tendrils, Palaeo-Christian figurative motifs (gryphons, eagles, peacocks and lions often quoted from embroideries or manuscript illuminations), marble ambos (pulpits before the chancel), and *iconostases* (screens in Greek churches separating the sanctuary from the nave).

The **Romanesque style**, which seems to appear in Venice during the 11C and 12C, is also in its own way modelled upon Byzantine art. The main forces at play were revived by the Lombard invasion from the northwest and from Ravenna in the south through which the Crusader armies would have passed.

Typical of the Venetian Romanesque style is the external appearance of high, solid, austere walls, pierced with tiny windows, relieved only by simple decoration afforded by blind arcading. The interior featured a raised nave, a vestige of Palaeo-Christian civilisation, and two aisles. Churches were planned as basilicas with a tall nave flanked by side aisles. In simple terms it is a compromise of "Western" Romanesque and "Eastern" Byzantine styles, and it is precisely from this period that Venice's oldest churches survive: San Giacomo (Rialto), San Nicolò dei Mendicoli, San Zan Degolà, San Giacomo dall'Orio and Sant'Eufemia (Giudecca). Although these churches were heavily rebuilt in the following centuries, many have retained their original massive, square, brick **campanile** or bell-tower, articulated with pilasters and blind arcading, capped with a loggia that screens the bells (San Barnaba). Only the roof, added later, differs from the original by being hexagonal, pyramidal or conical in shape. In some cases, the original church has long gone, but the Romanesque tower remains, as at San Zaccaria (⊙*illustration: see SAN ZACCARIA*) and San Samuele. All that survives of the famous 12C Sant'Apollonia monastery is its superb cloisters, a rare vestige of Romanesque architecture.

Domestic buildings

The **Veneto-Byzantine palazzo** is no doubt the most original product of 11C–13C Venetian architecture. Known as the *casa-fondaco* (from the Arabic

---

The Foreign Merchants of Venice

Venetian trade benefited from the different cultures brought over by foreign visitors to the city. In those days, a great many nationalities were living side by side, all engaged in commercial activities: Albanians, Armenians, Dalmatians, Jews, Greeks, Persians, Germans and Turks. In this context the storehouse (*fondaco*) played an essential role, as it was used for stocking goods and was seen as the heart of the business community. In Venice, the warehouses belonging to Persian, Turkish and German merchants were particularly active.

funduk, meaning depository or warehouse), this "storehouse" effectively combines the purpose of storage, commercial office and family home into one compact unit. The best preserved are the Fondaco dei Turchi, Ca' Farsetti, Palazzo Loredan and Ca' Da Mosto (*Ca'* being an abbreviation of *casa*, meaning house).

These houses further testify to the prodigiously rapid growth of the city's merchant aristocracy, empowered and enriched by maritime trade which, in turn, nurtured an interest and appreciation for Eastern Byzantine and Muslim craftsmanship.

As the need for defensive fortifications receded – on a scale seen at the first Doges' Palace – patrician town houses erected in the 11C began to conform to a set type that allowed for an easy and comfortable lifestyle. The structure would remain unchanged for several centuries to come, whereas its applied decoration would evolve according to contemporary taste. Split into three horizontal tiers, the main entrance into the storage or commercial area would have been on the canal side, through the *porta d'acqua*. On the first floor, the *piano nobile*, a continuous gallery or *loggia* would run the length of the façade between two solid walled towers, whereas at the top, a series of decorative crenellations would conceal the roofline. Only later would additional storeys sometimes be added.

Veneto-Byzantine arches have several forms: stilted round-headed arches (narrow arches with their springing line raised), horseshoe arches, Moorish ogee arches and high-pitched pointed "lancet" arches. These arches are often supported by highly prized marble shafts with decorated capitals, bearing Byzantine stylised and/or symmetrical foliage or animals. Further decoration might include Byzantine *paterae* illustrating real or mythical animals (peacocks, griffins etc) or medallions of different coloured marble, crosses or historical emblems.

Venetian Gothic

The term "Gothic", a label attributed in the 17C to the style developed by the barbarian Goths, assumes a distinctive meaning when applied to Venetian building design from the 1400s. For it is this delicate, ornamental, elegant style that has given the city its most distinctive characteristics and its architectural unity. It graces nearly all the *campi* and houses giving onto the banks of canals, styling a pointed arch or a loggia's filigree stonework. Unlike the structural changes that facilitated a new form of civil engineering in France, England and Germany, Venice merely used the Gothic style to ornament, flatter and decorate her buildings until the late 16C.

Churches

Politically, Venice was reinforcing her strength and autonomy. This prosperity allowed institutions to flourish both in the secular and religious domains, as demonstrated by the large-scale building projects undertaken by the principal monastic communities (I Frari, San Zanipòlo). With time, these were endowed by aristocratic patrons who wished to celebrate and publicise their wealth and standing (Madonna dell'Orto, Santo Stefano), entrusting to the churches their refined funerary monuments.

These were days in which the plague was rapidly spreading and they were characterised by a strong sense of urgency: poverty and charity were preached by the **Mendicant Orders**, and measures were taken to build monasteries and *scuole*, the characteristic Venetian institutions that sustained their confraternities in exchange for charity. Thus around 1245, with the benediction of **Doge Giacomo Tiepolo**, the Dominicans and Franciscans began erecting the city's most beautiful churches.

Exterior – From the 14C, designers of religious buildings began combining curved and rectilinear features in drafting their façades (San Giovanni in Bragora, I Frari, Scuola Vecchia della

Misericordia). Although the structures remained austerely simple, **porches** and **windows** suddenly became encrusted with Gothic features. The severe flat-brick west front was divided into three parts: the central, nave section soared high above the flanking aisles. Plain surfaces were relieved with decorative elements in white Istrian stone: portals were framed with engaged columns and pediments, hood mouldings articulated the gables, a cornice was supported by a frieze of niches that curved around the lateral walls. Only porches made in marble or white Istrian stone carry ornamentation: crowned by recessed arches with acanthus leaf motifs as well as elegant relief decoration such as cable fluting, knot-work and foliage, they are often flanked by statuettes or engaged columns. At the east end, apses proliferated and extruded to form chevets (I Frari, San Zanipòlo), whereas the tall square pink-brick *campanili* point skywards with a white marble open loggia (St Mark's, I Frari, Madonna dell'Orto).

Interior – The Gothic church, based on the T-shaped Latin cross to accommodate the long processions required by the liturgy down the nave, was abutted by aisles; at the east end, a wide transept could accommodate a chancel and numerous transept chapels endowed by private patrons (I Frari, San Zanipòlo). Sometimes the internal space was enclosed by a fine open timbered roof built by local shipwrights in the form of an inverted hull (Santo Stefano, San Giacomo dall'Orio) and articulated by arches painted with string-courses of acanthus leaves, or by carved wooden tie-beams.

Domestic buildings

Gothic-fronted *palazzi* enclose all the *campi* and line the secondary canals, but the most magnificent examples are to be found along the Grand Canal, which began to resemble a wonderful "triumphal waterway".

Fanciful creativity – The Venetian-Gothic **palazzo** was derived from the Byzantine model, retaining its three main characteristics: portico, loggia and decorative merlons. However, it now assumed a more noble, confident and sophisticated canon of ornamentation, which continued to be implemented until the fall of the Republic. As the patrician families stabilised their social status, they affected changes to their houses, most notably on the *piano nobile*. The simplicity of the earlier Veneto-Byzantine façades (portico and continuous loggia) was replaced by a centralised, more important arcaded loggia with cusped arches and quatrefoil motifs. In the corner section, single isolated windows interrupt the solid wall area now enhanced by the use of brick and stucco in two-tone colour combinations.

Interior layout – The *palazzo* is traditionally U-shaped in plan: a central block with perpendicular wings extended around a courtyard (*cortile*) with a well-head. Access to the *piano nobile* would have been via an open external stairway supported on Gothic arches up to a colonnaded portico with wooden architrave (Palazzo Centani). On the first floor, a broad passageway or, if enclosed, a reception hall (*portego*) ran the entire width of the house to open out onto the loggia on the canalside.

Extrovert beauty – Unlike the Florentine *palazzo*, austere, plain and impersonal, the Venetian façade may be seen as an extrovert, openly flaunting its charms to those who walk by. The windows, the eyes that open onto the outside world, are therefore natural vehicles for additional decoration.

Venice is still laden with oriental references both Christian and Muslim, and the characteristic loggias are strongly reminiscent of Palaeo-Christian stone fretwork; windows borrow from their Moorish counterparts a profile that echoes a cusped lancet and the temptation of inserting sculpted Byzantine *paterae* is still too great to resist.

By looking at the windows and their arched profiles, the various phases of Venetian Gothic may be discerned. Curvilinear arches of Moorish influ-

Cushion capital, Torcello
(9–10C)

Pluteus with peacocks
Torcello Cathedral (11C)

Composite capital, Torcello

Campanile di San Barnaba

Fretwork stone screen
San Alipio door, St Mark's

Patera with Pascal lamb

Drawings: © Rodolphe Corbel / MICHELIN

ence from the 14C sometimes rest on colonnettes (Corte del Million); early-15C three-cusped, four-light centred arches are often topped with a finial (Palazzo Duodo); late-15C Gothic or High Gothic arches, the most original and varied phase which might be compared with the French Flamboyant, grace the Doges' Palace. Here, one or more rows of quatrefoil oculi surmount the three-cusped arches of the loggias. The Ca' d'Oro, where **Marco d'Amadio**, a member of the **Bon** family, worked from 1421–61, is also expressive of this joyful, endearing exuberance.

Gothic sculpture

As with building, the first notable works of sculpture by known craftsmen date from this period. With **Pier Paolo** and **Jacobello dalle Masegne** (d.1403 and 1409 respectively) a style, explored by the School of Pisa, was evolved out of the static Byzantine tradition towards greater movement and expression, and mixed with a taste for Gothic ornament. Their work combines the use of delicate and complicated architectural elements with figurative statuary (iconostatis at St Mark's).

The Venetian School of Sculpture seemed unable truly to inspire the artistic community. *La Serenissima* was therefore forced to continue soliciting foreign artists or awarding commissions to craftsmen passing through the city.

Following in the footsteps of Pisa, Venice succumbed to the influence of Florentine art, to that of **Niccolò Lamberti** and to Sienese artists such as **Jacopo della Quercia**. **Marco Cozzi**, a remarkable woodcarver from Vicenza, created the splendid wooden chancel in the Church of the Frari, the only example of such work to survive in Venice.

Funerary monuments – The earliest 14C tombs consist of a simple sarcophagus with the recumbent figure of the deceased in front and the figures of the Madonna and Child and saints incorporated at the four corners; above, set into a recessed arch, is a lunette, painted or sometimes sculpted. Later a Gothic

baldaquin of stone drapery was added, seemingly suspended in the middle from the ceiling, its drapes drawn aside by figures (angels or warriors). It is in this vein that the Dalle Masegne brothers worked from the 14C to the 15C.

Portals – Almost all the 15C portals that adorn the Venetian churches are attributed to the architect **Bartolomeo Bon** (Santo Stefano, San Zanipòlo, Madonna dell'Orto, I Frari). Each is made of stone or marble to contrast dramatically with the main fabric of the brick building, and each is decorated with a series of hood mouldings and courses of twisted rope with cusps of foliage around the pointed ogee archway; elements are further embellished with acanthus leaves, the gable is surmounted with a free-standing statue, and inside the portal shelter small niches or aedicules. Bartolomeo Bon's unquestionable masterpiece is the elegant Porta della Carta, the main entrance to the Doges' Palace, executed in Flamboyant Gothic.

Venetian Renaissance

The success and popularity of the International Gothic canon was such that it delayed the adoption of Renaissance principles in Venice. However, once introduced, the style quickly took hold and soon graced the traditional structures with a new refined magnificence. During the 1400s, under the patronage of **Doge Francesco Foscari**, *La Serenissima's* civilisation changed direction: artistic links with Tuscany and Lombardy were strengthened and, after the fall of Constantinople in 1453, ties with the Eastern Empire were severed. Humanism flourished: it drew its inspiration from Hellenistic culture and was enriched by the sagacity of Greek scholars who had fled from Constantinople. In 1495 the printer **Aldo Manuzio** began publishing the Ancient Greek classics as the city witnessed the divide between **Scuole Grandi** and **Scuole Minori** (*see I CARMINI*). By the second half of the 15C, Florentine supremacy had dwindled. The new style, which originated from Tuscany,

San Giovanni in Brágora

Madonna dell'Orto

I Frari belltower

spread throughout Italy thanks to the wandering lifestyle of her artists, and gradually began to display regional characteristics – elements which Venice, in her inimitable fashion, absorbed and interpreted in her own way.

In the beginning

The earliest traces of the **Early Renaissance** are to be found in Venice's archways. The entrance to the Arsenale (1460) survives as the first full expression, complete with its Classical lions, mythological figures and Greek marble columns.

Three other examples showing the same characteristics include the portal of San Giobbe, one at the Gesuiti in the Zattere quarter, and the Foscari doorway at the Doges' Palace.

In terms of sculpture, the Florentine masters Donatello and Verrocchio endowed the Serenissima with only two works, both of major importance: an evocative wooden polychrome figure of John the Baptist (1438) at I Frari, and an impressive equestrian monument in bronze of the Condottiere Bartolomeo Colleoni from Bergamo (1458) that now stands in the *campo* in front of San Zanipòlo.

Lombardo dynasty – At the turn of the 15C, the spirit of innovation that was to animate contemporary sculpture and architecture was largely due to the genius and expertise of the **Lombardo family** – from Lombardy as their name clearly implies – and in particular to **Pietro** (1435–1515) and his two sons, **Antonio** and **Tullio**. Seeking to promote a complete re-evaluation of contemporary design and the widespread implementation of the new canon, the Lombardo family fashioned the highly public façade of the Scuola San Marco dominating its prime site, the Church of Santa Maria dei Miracoli and the unusual yet noble Ca' Dario giving onto the Grand Canal. In each case structural and decorative elements (porphyry medallions, marble rosettes) interact to form a perfectly balanced ensemble governed by a harmonious system of proportions.

Stone and marble replace the brick used earlier by Gothic builders. Façades may be asymmetrical, articulated with cornices, sculpted busts, figurative statues, pilasters – fluted or with cartouches of delicate graffiti (Classical reliefs featuring masks, the attributes of the Liberal Arts and the Gods of War) – friezes of vines or festoons of foliage, animals and *putti*.

In the field of sculpture, Pietro Lombardo undertook for San Zanipòlo a series of important and distinguished funerary monuments in Istrian stone to commemorate doges (those of Pietro Mocenigo, Pasquale Malipiero and Nicolò Marcello). Tullio, meanwhile, who worked extensively with his father, is responsible for the fine reliefs set into the front of the Scuola San Marco, and for the monuments to Giovanni Mocenigo and Andrea Vendramin in San Zanipòlo.

The Lombard tradition is reflected in the formal design of such memorials, as shown in the use of the triumphal arch on several levels with superimposed niches housing allegorical statues of the Virtues, acting as a cornice over the sarcophagus. On the other hand, the fine workmanship of the figurines, along with the poise and elegance of their stance, undeniably testify to Tuscan influence.

Mauro Codussi (1440–1504) – This architect from Bergamo, a contemporary of the Lombardo brothers, seemed happier to celebrate the decorative rather than the structural function of architecture and to this end returned to the Tuscan vernacular for inspiration. Despite adhering to the guidelines pronounced by the Humanist Alberti in his treatises on architecture for a Canon of Beauty formulated according to mathematical proportion and harmony of component parts (spatial organisation, symmetrical elevations, correct application of the Classical orders – Doric, Ionic and Corinthian – the use of rustication and niches), Codussi's designs appeared to lack homogeneity. Instead, he forged a personal style distinguished by semicircular pediments for the fronts of churches and the Scuola San Marco, which he completed, rustication on the ground floor of his *palazzi*, engaged columns and cornices to differentiate superior storeys, and circular oculi inserted between the coupled arches of an arcade supported on coupled columns.

His early projects, which included the Clocktower and the Church of San Giovanni Grisostomo, all showed trace elements of Byzantine styling (portico decoration, Greek cross floorplan), whereas his more mature works, the sumptuous *palazzi* Corner Spinelli and

Rialto Bridge over the Grand Canal *by Michele Marieschi*

©A. Dagli Orti/DEA/ age fotostock

Vendramin Calergi on the Grand Canal conformed to his distinctive style. This style developed into an even bolder statement at San Zaccaria and San Michele, his masterpiece, where marble or white Istrian stone were applied across all three carefully articulated sections of the elevation, both on the horizontal and vertical axes; the nave towers over the aisles linked with semicircular pediments, and friezes, shell niches and porphyry roundels provided ornamentation. Two additional designs by Codussi included Santa Maria Formosa and the beautiful Istrian stone campanile of San Pietro di Castello.

Antonio Rizzo – Antonio Rizzo (d.1499) was responsible for the internal (courtyard) façade of the Doges' Palace and the monumental Giant's Staircase faced in marble. Examples of his sculpture included the poised figures of Adam and Eve that once flanked the Foscari arch. He also varied the design of the archetypal funerary monument initiated at I Frari for Doge Nicolò Tron in 1473 by articulating it with five orders up to a semicircular pediment, and ornamenting it with several niches filled with free-standing figures.

Venetian High Renaissance

A heightened Classicism affirms itself only in the 16C, marking a distinctive, second phase of Renaissance design. Rome, which had displaced Florence, the capital of the arts at the beginning of the previous century, as the seedbed for new ideas, was badly damaged by Charles V's Imperial army, which sacked the Holy City in 1527. From 1530, Venice established herself as the model city of Italy. For a short period, she basked in the limelight, implementing a new Classicism that soon, alas, degenerated into Mannerism.

Arcaded porticoes proliferated at ground level with ever bigger openings, supporting ordered storeys above. Imposing *palazzi* with carefully articulated lines are rusticated the entire length of the ground floor, punctuated by large centrally planned openings and ornamented with masks. For the *piano nobile*, rectangular windows, framed with fluted or coupled columns, are pedimented with circular or triangular tympana in symmetrical formation; projecting balustraded balconies add to the sculptural effect. Below the

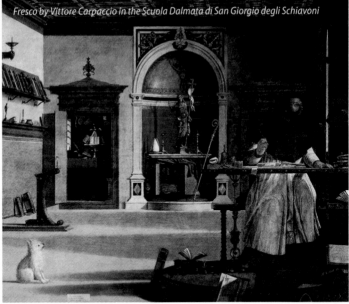

Fresco by Vittore Carpaccio in the Scuola Dalmata di San Giorgio degli Schiavoni

©De Agostini / Picture L/ age fotostock

entablature, the rhythm is maintained by a series of small oval apertures.

Sansovino, master of the Classical style – The Florentine-born Jacopo Tatti, known as Sansovino (1486–1570), an accomplished sculptor and architect, was responsible for introducing to Venice a Classical canon of design. Seeking refuge in Venice after the Sack of Rome (1527), where he had been apprenticed to Bramante and Raphael, Sansovino succeeded Bartolomeo Bon as *proto* or Chief Architect to St Mark's. He was thus entrusted with the Serenissima's ambitious plans for reconstruction and embellishment, beginning with the reorganisation of the Piazza San Marco. He drafted designs for the new Library, its portico based on an archaic model, the Fabbriche Nuove in the Rialto, Palazzo Corner della Ca' Granda on the Grand Canal, the elegant loggia at the foot of St Mark's campanile (for which he also produced the bronze statues and low-relief panels), the heavily rusticated, Tuscan- inspired Palazzo della Zecca, the imposing but incomplete Scuola Nuova della Misericordia and the Golden Staircase. Robust, but not overly austere, his initial projects (including Ca' Granda) show Sansovino completely at ease with the traditional Venetian vernacular style (buildings around the Piazza San Marco and the Piazzetta), enriching his Classical forms with original and majestic ornament; decorative detailing encrusts the portico arches and enhances the flat surfaces, whereas statuary, low-relief panels and festoons add a touch of fantasy and convey a vivid sense of movement.

To affirm Sansovino's brilliance as a sculptor, one need but cite the figures of Mars and Neptune that grace the Giant's Staircase and the highly expressive John the Baptist in I Frari – they speak for themselves.

Grandiose domestic buildings – At this time, the Grand Canal assumed its claim to be a true "triumphal way" fronted by ever more elegant and ennobled patrician houses.

Veronese Sanmicheli (1484–1559), having served his apprenticeship under Sansovino, earned recognition for his military projects (Fortress of Sant'Andrea on the Lido) and for his design of the Palazzo Corner Mocenigo in the San Polo *sestiere* and the Palazzo Grimani on the Grand Canal.

Andrea Palladio (1508–80) – Late in the 16C, the architect Andrea Palladio, a Paduan by birth, moved to Venice. He had established his reputation by designing villas in the Brenta Valley. His distinctive style, which is characterised by a balanced sense of proportion and formulated from a profound appreciation of Classical architecture, was applied to buildings that were designed to suit their purpose, their site and, most importantly, were practical to inhabit. Encouraged by the Humanist Trissino, Palladio visited Rome on several occasions to study Classical architecture in the context of theories outlined by Vitruvius (1C BC). In 1570, he published his theories based on observation in a treatise entitled *I Quattro Libri di Architettura* (*The Four Books on Architecture*). This grand opus was to have far-reaching consequences in the spreading of Classicism to the rest of Europe.

The essential principle of this "modern" Classicism is structural simplicity, achieved with the use of basic geometrical volumes of space (cube, sphere and pyramid) and symmetry. Designs for building elevations conform to the same rules, with a façade having a central portico (San Giorgio Maggiore). Palladio received commissions, in particular from the Serenissima's important and wealthy patrician families with estates in the hinterland (La Malcontenta on the Brenta). These variations on the villa design provide a new canon for informal domestic buildings that reflects both their function as country farm estates and their location: besides boasting pure Classical form and a sound knowledge of decoration as well as gardening, these houses blend in perfectly with the surrounding landscape. The scenery may therefore be enjoyed from the house and the house may be admired as a point of interest punctuating and enhancing the scenery. This consideration was later explored and developed in garden design by the 18C English exponents of Palladianism (Campbell, Burlington, Kent, Adam, Capability Brown and the like). Palladio based many of his villas on ancient pagan temples; only the domestic buildings have forsaken monumentality for utilitarian considerations.

In Venice itself, Palladio's sense of austerity and perfect harmony is reflected in his magnificent churches: San Giorgio Maggiore, Il Redentore, le Zitelle, San Francesco della Vigna. Recurring features in his architecture are long, slender engaged columns, Corinthian capitals, triangular pedimented porticoes borrowed from Roman temples, huge domes thrown into contrast by symmetrically arranged geometrical forms; whereas inside, the enclosed space is airy and light. After Palladio's death, Vincenzo Scamozzi saw a number of his master's projects to completion, ensuring the final effect was true to Palladio's vision, and thereby consolidating his reputation.

Vincenzo Scamozzi (1552–1616), born in Vicenza, also inherited Sansovino's projects for the redevelopment of the Piazza San Marco and erected the Procuratie Nuove (1586) modelled on the Classical example proffered by the former Library nearby. What is new however, is the interplay of decorative elements that pre-empt the advent of the Baroque. Also by Scamozzi is the Palazzo Contarini degli Scrigni on the Grand Canal.

Lo Scarpagnino completed the Fondacco dei Tedeschi and the Scuola di San Rocco initiated by Bartolomeo Bon. His style echoes that of Codussi (openings on the ground floor) although now there is a greater sense of movement and dramatic contrast, achieved in part by the use of free-standing columns that project from the façade. He was also involved in the rebuilding of the Palazzo dei Dieci Savi and the Fabbriche Vecchie in the Rialto district.

Spavento began the Classical façade onto the small Senators' courtyard of the Doges' Palace, while Guglielmo dei Grigi, better known by his epithet **il Bergamasco**, was working on the Palazzo Papadopoli and the Palazzo Camerlenghi on the Grand Canal.

High Renaissance Sculpture

Together with Palladio and Sansovino, the third important figure to import the artistic spirit of Michelangelo to Venice was **Alessandro Vittoria** (1525–1608). Famous for his austere and dignified portraits, Vittoria sculpted two lively representations of St Jerome, now at San Zanipòlo and I Frari. He demonstrated further skills in the art of applied decoration by executing the stucco ceiling of the Libreria Vecchia and the fine gilded coffered vault of the Golden Staircase in the Doges' Palace.

Other artists of note working during the 1500s include **Lorenzo Bregno**, to whom several funerary monuments are attributed (including that of Benedetto Pesaro) and the high altar at I Frari; **Girolamo Campagna** (bronze figures – I Frari and Correr Museum); **Tiziano Aspetti** (bronzes in Correr Museum, statues of Hercules and Atlantes flanking the Golden Staircase) and **Andrea Riccio** (bronzes in Correr Museum).

Venetian Baroque

Throughout the 17C the predilection for the Classical style was underpinned by the continued popularity of Palladian design. As a result, Venetian Baroque is more tempered than it ever was in Rome or elsewhere.

Baldassare Longhena (1598–1682) – This architect and sculptor is both the instigator and leading representative of Baroque art in the City of the Doges. His lasting legacy was to inspire a taste for stone and a solemn architectural language which, some say, verges on the whimsical. It is essentially Classical in inspiration but with charged ornamentation, frequently copied from examples in antiquity.

His undoubted masterpiece is the Church of the Salute. It is also the most eloquent embodiment of this peculiarly Venetian strain of Baroque: it exudes confidence and an air of triumph with its vast proportions, towering dome, sense of movement conveyed by modillions featuring curved scrolls, and crowds of angels and prophets.

Charged with designing the finest Baroque *palazzi* along the Grand Canal, Longhena turned to Sansovino for inspiration. He endowed both Ca' Rezzonico and Ca' Pesaro with grand

Palazzo Pisani Moretta along the Grand Canal

Chiesa dei Gesuati by Domenico Rossi

© Oleg Seleznev / Dreamstime.com

entrances, heavily rusticated ground floors, superimposed orders of tall windows deeply recessed into archways, separated by large columns and richly ornamented with masks. Particular emphasis is given to the *piano nobile*, with sharply defined architectural elements such as cornices, balustraded balconies, and dramatically sculpted *putti* or coats of arms. A similar boldness marks his high altars and commemorative monuments, of which perhaps the most exuberant is the sepulchre of Doge Giovanni Pesaro at I Frari.

After Longhena – Following the death of Longhena, the completion of his main projects was supervised by **Antonio Gaspari** (Ca' Pesaro) and **Giorgio Massari** (Ca' Rezzonico) (1687–1766), possibly Venice's greatest architect in the first half of the 18C. The remarkably exuberant ornamentation (deeply cut garlands of fruit, niches, entablatures, pediments, fluted columns, crowning statuary) is evidenced in the Church dell'Ospedaletto with its great and ponderous atlantes. The three churches designed by **Sardi**, a collaborator of Longhena, are Santa Maria del Giglio, which houses depictions of naval battles and is planned like a military fortress, Gli Scalzi and San Salvador. Two other Baroque churches are San Moisé by Tremignon (1668) and San Stae. Among the bell-towers are those of Santa Maria Formosa and All Saints.

The architect responsible for the great Church of the Gesuati (18C) is **Domenico Rossi**, who also designed its splendid white and green marble decoration imitating huge draperies falling into heavy folds. In contrast, the interior ceilings painted by **Giambattista Tiepolo** attain an unchallenged brilliance and lightness more often associated with Rococo. In sculpture, however, perhaps the main representative of the Venetian Baroque is the Flemish artist **Juste Le Court**, whose works include altar fronts, allegorical figures and panels of low relief (Santa Maria del Giglio).

Neo-Classicism

During the 18C, Venice improved her image by erecting new buildings and remodelling a number of existing ones. In counter-reaction to the Baroque, the city reverted to a pure form of Classicism that was to be labelled neo-Classicism – well before any revival had taken hold anywhere else in Europe. The emergence of rational thinking during the Age of Enlightenment had affected all disciplines, including architecture, and given birth to a novel trend dubbed neo-Classicism. One of the advocates of this new style was a Venetian Franciscan, **Carlo Lodoli**, who claimed *"only that which has a definite function or is born out of absolute necessity is worthy of existing in architecture"*; and so artists turned to Antiquity for inspiration.

Simple arcading, domes and pronaoi (projecting vestibules fronted with columns and pediments) grace monumental *palazzi* and churches. The linearity of each structural element is clearly defined and elaborate schemes for interior decoration are replaced by plain, simple arrangements based on the Palladian or the Baroque model. The buildings that best illustrate this trend are the Palazzo Grassi by Massari and the Napoleon Wing enclosing the Piazza San Marco.

The architects **Andrea Tirali** (1660–1737), **Scalfarotto**, **Visentini** and **Temanza** all implemented a neo-Classical style founded on simple form and basic geometry derived from Palladio (including the use of the pronaos); a sense of grandeur was imparted from **Giovanni Battista Piranese** (1720–78), the Venetian-born architect and engraver who studied Roman civilisation and published the famous *Carceri d'Invenzione* (c.1745).

Tirali employed neo-Classical principles in designing the façade of the Church of the Tolentini, endowing it with a large pronaos and Corinthian columns, a design that was to be inspirational later for other buildings. Other neo-Classical monuments of note include the Church of San Simeone Piccolo, erected in 1720 by Scalfarotto on a circular plan, with a gigantic porch copied from that of the Tolentini, and reached up a massive staircase. Unfortunately it is somewhat overwhelmed by the gigantic green dome and **Temanza**'s Church of the Maddalena, also built on a circular plan that is crowned by a great dome, but with a foreshortened pronaos.

Perhaps the figure who dominates the artistic output of the period, however, is **Giorgio Massari** (1686–1766), from whom we have inherited such grandiose statements as the Gesuati Church on the Zattere with its Palladian façade, the Church of the Pietà, and the main door of the Accademia (1760).

Antonio Canova (1757–1822) – The last great personality in the Serenissima's illustrious history of art is Canova who, in many ways, embodies the very essence of neo-Classicism in sculpture. Highly esteemed by his patrons at home and by Napoleon, Canova left the Republic to work in Rome and Paris, where the spirit of the style was distilled into painting by Jacques-Louis David, another imperial protégé.

His work exudes great purity and sensitivity. The velvety polish imparted to the white marble – his favourite material – together with the fluid compositions and elegant forms, in which line rather than texture is emphasised, combine to suggest fragile sensuality. Venice still retains a series of low reliefs in the style of the Antique and the famous group of *Daedalus and Icarus* (Correr Museum). His grandiose memorial can be visited in I Frari: it was executed by pupils and lies opposite the monument he designed for Titian.

From eclectic to modern times

The second half of the 19C was dominated by an eclectic assortment of revivalist styles in architecture: neo-Byzantine (Hotel Excelsior on the Lido, 1898–1908), neo-Romanesque, and

Orfeo *(1775 - 1776) by Antonio Canova in Museo Correr*

© Museo Correr / Fondazione Musei Civici Venezia

most especially neo-Gothic (Pescheria by Rupolo, 1907, Palazzo Cavalli-Franchetti by Camillo Boito, 1895); the curious Mulino Stucky on the Guidecca (1883), remodelled in the International Gothic canon, has high walls punctuated by a spired corner tower.

Since then, no particular trend has dominated Venice: only a few isolated personalities have had interesting projects built, now well integrated into the urban landscape. These include the residential districts around Sant' Elena from the 1920s, the railway station (1954) and the Savings Bank designed by Pier Luigi Nervi and Angelo Scattolin on Campo Manin (1968). Certain projects drafted by well-known personalities never got beyond the drawing board: a student hostel by the American Frank Lloyd Wright intended to stand on the Grand Canal (1953) and a public hospital by Le Corbusier (1964).

The area that accommodates the Biennale provides space for various contemporary experimental projects. Even if the gardens where the pavilions are built are dismissed as part of the urban environment, it is worth acknowledging the more original and obsolete: Hoffman's Austrian Pavilion (1933), the Venezuelan designed by Carlo Scarpa (1954) and the Finnish by Alvar Aalto (1956).

The most famous 20C Venetian sculptor is **Arturo Martini** (1889–1947).

ART
VENETIAN PAINTING

Venice's pictorial tradition has one constant: its profound sensuality achieved by a predilection for colour and for light, which lends a strong poetic touch to the landscape. It is an art that mirrors the personality of the lagoon city as a watery world where everything is suffused with light: the blur of the skyline, the shimmering volumes, the haze rising above the canals that adds a bluish tinge to the scene. It is this distinctive greyish light, opaque and iridescent at the same time, that inspired the artists of the 18C.

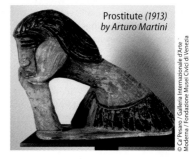

Prostitute *(1913)*
by Arturo Martini

© Ca' Pesaro / Galleria Internazionale d'Arte
Moderna / Fondazione Musei Civici di Venezia

Mosaics

The art of mosaic, inherited from the Romans, came to the lagoon long before the art of painting. In the 12C and 13C, Venice, inspired by the art of Ravenna, proceeded to arrange the mosaic murals from Torcello (*Last Judgement*), Murano and St Mark's Basilica. After the fall of Constantinople in 1204, Greek decorators and mosaic artists came to Venice to work on the great Golden Altarpiece and the mosaics in St Mark's. Consequently, the biblical iconography of the Eastern Church became markedly oriental, with Christ featuring as the central character (central apse), opening and closing a story which unfolded along walls, arches and cupolas, thus observing established biblical chronology (🕮 *see PIAZZA SAN MARCO*).

The use of mosaic continued throughout the city's history. The very last ones to grace San Marco were executed over a rather long period running from the 16C to the 19C. The assumption that early mosaics were more impressive can be explained by the simple fact that artisans were unable to arrange the small pieces of glass in a regular fashion: the myriad uneven surfaces lent "flexibility" to the mural. This effect was enhanced by the light, which caught irregularities, acting as a kaleidoscope of twirling colours and reflections. If all the pieces were aligned on a perfect flat plain, the effect would be dull and lifeless.

Quattrocento Primitives

A few artists began to paint in fresco in the 13C, a process that involves applying pigment to small sections of wet lime-plaster. Paintings from this period, however, if they have survived, are all badly damaged. As regards the style of these first Venetian frescoes, they soon conformed both in design and subject matter to Byzantine iconography, drawn for the most part from portable devotional icons typical of the Eastern Church, where the Madonna and Child usually occupy pride of place.

Paolo Veneziano

This artist, also known as Paolo da Venezia (active 1333–58), emerged as the first distinctive personality in Venetian painting, his name appearing with that of his son Giovanni on a *Coronation of the Virgin* (now in the Frick Collection in New York). Working in the Byzantine tradition, his painting showed him moving away from archaic stylisation (gold backgrounds, flat and confrontational compositions, hieratic attitudes) towards greater decorative refinement and distinctive use of line. This freedom of expression and sensitive treatment of Western subject matter forestalled the evolution of the International Gothic style characterised by graceful movement and elegant form. The work of **Lorenzo Veneziano**, traced to the years 1356–72, is characterised by expressive faces, vigorous bodies and a subtle use of strong, bold colours. (Note: he was not related to the two above; the epithet *Veneziano* simply means Venetian.)

Venetian International Gothic

At the beginning of the 15C, the work of **Gentile da Fabriano** and **Pisanello** and that of the Paduan **Guariento**, who were engaged in painting a cycle of frescoes in the Doges' Palace (destroyed by fire in the 16C), marks the city's endorsement of the "International Gothic". This was a refined, bejewelled style that combined Tuscan elements already assimilated in Padua (derived from sculpted Antique decoration on the one hand and by Giotto's cycle of frescoes in the Scrovegni Chapel on the other) with a more courtly style prac-

tised in Ferrara (notably portraiture). The stimulus provided by these two influences blended with the local, Venetian predilection for naturalism, elegant linearity, fluid movement and strong decorative appeal (even the gold-embroidered and brocade clothing is celebrated) led to a distinctive regional style akin to the International Gothic that flourished in Siena, Prague and Avignon.

Other painters worthy of note include **Nicolò di Pietro** (recorded 1394–1430), **Jacobello del Fiore** (recorded 1394–1439), a pupil of Gentile da Fabriano who practised a detailed and intricate style, and, most especially, **Michele Giambono** (recorded 1420–62) who produced highly refined works in which Eastern oriental influence can be felt (*St Crisogono* – San Trovaso, *St Michael* – Accademia).

A new pictorial tradition

By the mid-15C, attempts at perspective are reflected in the portrayal of floors and ceilings; depth of field is suggested in the background by landscape scenes or buildings.

The first hint of the Renaissance is to be found in the works of the **Vivarini** family from Murano. The shift in emphasis comes with the break of the generations: the earlier pictures have the same quality as Gothic goldsmithery and are markedly influenced by Byzantine iconography. These pictures are by the father, **Antonio** (active 1441–50), who worked with his brother-in-law, **Giovanni d'Alemagna** (*Triptych with Madonna and Child with Saints* – Accademia; polyptychs – San Zaccaria), and his brother **Bartolomeo** (*Triptych of St Mark* – I Frari). The son **Alvise**, however, shows an awareness of the Renaissance (*St Anthony of Padua* – Correr Museum; *Triumph of St Ambrose* – I Frari; *Christ Carrying the Cross* – San Zanipòlo) and his portraits show remarkable psychological depth. Strangely, in the following generation, **Marco Basaiti** (1470–1530), a pupil of Alvise Vivarini, is decidedly backward-looking in his delicate treatment of landscape and

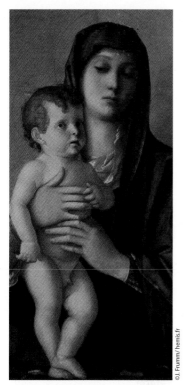

Madonna of the Small Trees *by Giovanni Bellini, Gallerie dell'Accademia*

©J. Frumm/hemis.fr

influences. The actual founder of the Venetian School is probably **Giovanni Bellini** (1430–1516), who admired Florentine painting for its pure, idealised forms, and Flemish painting for its clarity in terms of light and observed realism. He was markedly influenced by his master and brother-in-law, the Paduan-born **Andrea Mantegna** (1431–1506), who settled and worked in Venice. Mantegna was fascinated by Roman Antiquities which were commonly traded in Padua at the time, an interest acquired from his adoptive father, the painter-archaeologist Squarcione. From his study of relief carving, Mantegna forged a bold style that is completely uncompromising to the point of coldness, where perspective is almost obsessively defined, and details are drawn with scientific precision (*St Sebastian* – Accademia).

His style was, however, in some ways tempered by the example of **Antonello da Messina** who worked in Venice c.1475–76 (*Pietà* – Correr Museum) after learning to use oil paints from Flemish works. Giovanni adopted this medium and developed his own deeply sensitive style that is characterised by a playful suggestion of light, a delicate and harmonious use of colour, elegant rendering of form and a strong sense of realism derived from Mantegna. Landscape assumes a dominant role and is used to convey the atmosphere of the picture: it provides a context in which the figures appear as pawns, set below an expanse of sky relieved by drifting clouds. These expressions of mood are worked over and over again in countless Madonnas looking tenderly down at a sleeping cherub or a Christ Child in benediction (*Madonna degli Alberetti* – Accademia), in portrayals of the Dead Christ and many *Sacre Conversazioni* (*St Vincent Ferrer Polyptych* – San Zanipòlo).

Giovanni's brother **Gentile** (1429–1507) was the first artist to be nominated Venice's official painter, a position which underpinned a brilliant career. He emerged as a talented portrait painter (Doge Giovanni Mocenigo) and applied his observational skills to portraying

use of colour (*Vocation of the Sons of Zebedee* – Accademia).

Serenity in Early Renaissance Painting

Long after the flowering of the Renaissance in Florence in the early 1400s, during the latter half of the century, Venice's artists turned their attention to defining three-dimensional space and volume, and to an improved articulation of landscape and topographical views. They also gave up the abstract use of gold background and the Gothic taste for overly decorated and complicated pictures.

Bellini family

First Jacopo, the father (d.1470), followed by his two sons, Gentile and Giovanni, managed to emancipate Venetian painting from Byzantine and Gothic

views of Venice, known as **vedute**, which became an influential genre in itself in the 18C. The overall objective was for painting to be true to life: *The Procession of the Relics of the True Cross in Piazza San Marco* (Accademia), for example, is a factual or documentary representation of 15C Venice, even if the painter, conscientious in every detail, was careful to align the façades and order the attendant crowds.

The advent of High Renaissance

Vittore Carpaccio (1455–1526), following in the wake of Bellini and Antonello, suffuses a lesson learned from Flemish painting with his own personal creativity to execute the cycles of paintings commissioned by the "Scuole" (⦿*see I CARMINI: The Venetian Scuole*): *Miracle of the Relic of the True Cross at Rialto* for Scuola di San Giovanni Evangelista; *Legend of St Ursula* (Accademia) in which Brittany is represented as a Venetian Renaissance city; and *Legends of St George and St Jerome* for Scuola di San Giorgio degli Schiavoni, which depicts an exotic Orient. Carpaccio surpassed Bellini in sensitivity and in his inimitable talent for story-telling. His pictures are imaginatively populated with well-observed and delightful details: he even manages to reconcile his penchant for miniaturist precision with a love of broad views. In his landscapes, a key element in his paintings, are representations of a luxuriant, flowery vegetation, peopled with a host of animals (dogs, birds, rabbits, peacocks, parrots and deer). Renaissance buildings stand out, embellished with marble inlays that might have been designed by the Lombardo family, surrounded by numerous oriental motifs (palm trees, Moorish turbans). All of Carpaccio's works display the same distinctive features: boldness of line, luminosity, vivid colours, perfect sense of proportion, attention to detail and crowd scenes.

Giambattista Cima (1459–1518), known as Cima da Conegliano, drew on Giovanni Bellini for his strong, radiant light and on Carpaccio for his love of detail. His are the glorious portrayals of dignified figures, pictured in beautiful landscapes under broad open skies (*Madonna of the Orange Tree* – Accademia; *Adoration of the Shepherds* – I Carmini). By the close of the 15C, Venetian painting had reached the height of its artistic expression.

Reform

His name was Giorgio di Castelfranco but he went by the name of **Giorgione** (1475–1510). It was he who revolutionised the course of painting in the early 16C despite his short life. Giorgione is

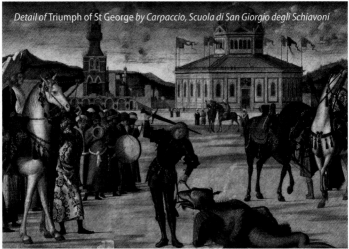

Detail of Triumph of St George by Carpaccio, Scuola di San Giorgio degli Schiavoni

©F. Ferruzzi / DEA/ age fotostock

considered the first "modern" artist in the history of painting.

A Renaissance man in every sense, he drew inspiration for his work from Humanist ideology, making it intellectual and sometimes shrouded in mystery, as well as open to controversial interpretation. Few works have been attributed to him with any certainty, and these are poetic in feel, almost dreamlike, but always charged with allusions to literature, music and philosophy: ephemerality and vulnerability are the subject of *The Tempest*; *La Vecchia* depicts the passage of time (both in the Accademia). His style appears more sensual than Classical. The landscape now plays an essential role in the painting; man is no longer the main subject, it is Nature itself that becomes the true protagonist – human drama is reduced to just one element in the force of Nature (such as in *The Tempest*).

Palma il Vecchio (1480–1528) followed in the same vein, although in later life he betrays the influence of Titian's handling of light, his juxtaposition of contrasting colour and the asymmetry of his altarpiece compositions. Palma il Vecchio specialised in *Sacre Conversazioni* (see SAN ZACCARIA) and painted the portrait of Paola Priuli (Querini-Stampaglia Collection). His art does not match that of the most talented masters but its appeal is one of spontaneity and exuberant colour.

The Venice-born **Lorenzo Lotto** (1480–1556) is another major early-16C painter with a distinctively personal style. Some pictures are disconcerting, while others show pyschological nuances or the influence of Dürer's scientific treatment of detail (Dürer visited Venice in c.1495) and the painter's liking for bold contrasts (*Portrait of a Young Gentleman in his Study* – Accademia). He avoided the sensual, colourful appeal of Giorgione and Titian, preferring to employ a rather frigid, angular style modelled on the precise, slightly archaic style of Alvise Vivarini.

16C masters and their pupils

In the 16C, Venetian painting affirmed its supremacy; this was the era of the great European masters and highly skilled painters who, thanks to their respective talents, succeeded in establishing a distinctive style that was to become the hallmark of Venice and which soon earned her European recognition.

Titian

Tiziano Vecellio, known as Titian (c.1485–1576), is unquestionably the most famous artist of his time. Born in

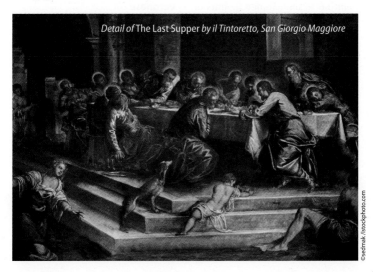

Detail of The Last Supper *by il Tintoretto, San Giorgio Maggiore*

©sedmak / istockphoto.com

Pieve di Cadore, he remained highly active until his death, aged 90. He served his apprenticeship under Giovanni Bellini and was subsequently influenced by Giorgione (some of whose works he completed) and then Raphael. The author of large altarpieces undertaken for churches (I Frari) and Scuole (La Carità) alike, he favoured colour over form and breathed life into his canvases with a dynamic handling of paint and bold composition (*The Assumption* – I Frari; *Martyrdom of St Lawrence* – Gesuiti). His reputation far outreached the realms of the lagoon city, and led to him being commissioned to paint portraits of all the leading lights of his time at the courts of Ferrara, Mantua, Florence and Urbino; he worked for the Pope, François I and Charles V, who knighted him in 1553. During the early part of his career, Titian's painting was fundamentally Classical in inspiration. However, between 1535 and 1545, he was seduced by Mannerism before reverting to a more dignified and serene style. At the end of his life, the melodramatic tension inherent in some compositions (*The Pietà* – Accademia) betrays the artist's mysticism at the imminence of death. In conclusion, Titian was largely responsible for reviving interest in the large altarpiece. He succeeded in taking painting to unimagined heights of monumentality by abandoning symmetry of composition (*Pesaro Altarpiece* – I Frari), opting for large contrasting blocks of colour, displaying a sure stroke and a perfect sense of harmony.

Il Tintoretto

Contemporary with Titian, Venice harboured the genius of Jacopo Comin, known as *il Tintoretto* (1518–94), the most original and most prolific of the Venetian masters. He was born the son of a dyer (hence his name) and never left Venice (save once, maybe, to visit Rome), but he never really enjoyed success in his lifetime. Tireless and passionate about his work, an ardent admirer of Michelangelo, he preferred biblical subjects to those of Classical Antiq-

uity (Scuola di San Rocco) and chose to portray common people instead of focusing on the excesses of the nobility. He developed a restless style: despite the interaction of rapid precise brush strokes and gentle soft touches, his work is always lyrical, a quality that is projected from his dynamic handling of paint and from the arrangement of figures in groups or alone, brought together by strong lines of composition (*Crucifixion* – Scuola di San Rocco). The use of chiaroscuro (strong contrasts of light and shade), juxtaposed complementary colours, elongated figures, daring foreshortening and a filtering light that blurs the contours of figures and architectural settings, all contribute to reinforcing the charged atmosphere of his Mannerist work.

His best pictures include the *Miracles of St Mark* painted for the Scuola di San Marco (Accademia), the *Marriage of Cana* (Santa Maria della Salute), *Paradise* (Doges' Palace, Grand Council Chamber), *The Triumph of Venice* (Doges' Palace), and *The Presentation of the Virgin in the Temple* (Madonna dell'Orto), not forgetting the 50 paintings, the largest cycle of its kind in Venice, executed for the Scuola di San Rocco, on which he worked for 23 years in collaboration with his son **Domenico Tintoretto**.

Veronese

In direct contrast with Tintoretto, **Paolo Caliari** (1528–88), born in Verona, hence his nickname *Veronese*, specialised in portraying the wealthy, opulent and carefree aristocracy of the Renaissance; in luminous colour (including the famous "Veronese green") that set off to theatrical effect the most sumptuous fabrics used for their clothing. His works in the main are endowed with optimism, fantasy and spontaneity, they seem permeated with spring light; towards the end of his life, however, Veronese's paintings change to more sombre and melancholic mood, muddied by the influence of Tintoretto's chiaroscuro and Bassano's style. Mythological scenes proliferate on the walls and ceilings of the Doges'

Palace (*Apotheosis of Venice*). The subject of *The Last Supper* was reworked by Veronese several times for the refectories of Venetian monasteries, including the famous, huge canvas *Christ in the House of Levi* (Accademia), commissioned for the Dominican monastery of San Zanipòlo. This was contrived as a depiction of an entirely profane meal, while providing an excellent pretext for a work of grandiose proportions. The magnificent decoration of San Sebastiano is another masterpiece, appropriate, perhaps, given that it was his chosen ultimate resting place.

Mannerism in Venice

Whereas Tintoretto forged his style from Titian and Michelangelo, and Veronese was heir to Bellini, Giorgione and Raphael, their legacy, like that of Titian, was both powerful and influential beyond the confines of Venice, for several generations. It also naturally led to Venetian Mannerism.

Titian had many followers: **Palma il Vecchio** (1480–1528); **Pordenone** (c.1483–1539), who worked successfully in Venice from 1535–38; **Paris Bordone** (1500–71), who delighted in Venetian Renaissance architecture (*Handing the Ring to the Doge* – Accademia; *Martyrdom of St Theodore* – San Salvador) and charged his canvases with vivid colours; the prolific **Palma il Giovane** (1544–1628), the grandson of Palma il Vecchio, with an eclectic style, who provided nearly all the city's churches with large-scale paintings.

An exponent of the sensuality and silky colours explored by Giorgione and Titian, **Andrea Schiavone** (c.1510–63) moved away from realism in favour of elongated form and restless movement typical of Mannerism, in the style of Parmigianino.

Impressed by Tintoretto's painting, **Jacopo Bassano** (Jacopo da Ponte, 1512–92) paints in a provincial style marked by an exaggerated preoccupation with naturalism (*St Jerome Meditating* – Accademia), while using light effects to suggest the intensity of the scene (*Nativity* – San Giorgio Maggiore).

His sons Leandro and Francesco shared this tradition of *maniera* painting, in which the pastoral and rustic element becomes the prime subject rather than the religious or profane content.

18C revival

Venetian painting, in decline during the 17C and overshadowed by the great personalities of the previous century and the Roman Baroque, enjoyed a new creative and glorious burst of energy during this period of lavish receptions in the Age of Enlightenment.

Decorative painting

Long after the taste for grandiose interior decoration had flourished in Rome and Florence during the 16C–17C, Venice revived her interest in the decorative art of Veronese found on the walls and ceilings of her churches and *palazzi* and in the Palladian villas along the Brenta. **Sebastiano Ricci** (1659–1734), the Baroque painter of rather sentimental religious pictures, reinforced his strong compositions with bright colour (*Madonna with Saints* – San Giorgio Maggiore). It was with **Giambattista Piazzetta** (1682–1754), who excelled in religious painting, that huge ceiling compositions became popular, and that figures began to be shown from below, aspiring to dizzy heights among the clouds, drawn awkwardly towards a mystical light (*Glorification of St Dominic* – San Zanipòlo). Influenced by Caravaggio, Piazzetta also painted genre pictures (featuring people from common, everyday life in mundane surroundings) with strong chiaroscuro (*The Fortune Teller* – Accademia).

Piazzetta influenced the greatest artist of the century: **Giambattista Tiepolo** (1696–1770), the pre-eminent genius of Venetian Baroque decoration and creator of huge compositions of great virtuosity full of delicate colour, golden light and infinite space. He painted vast altarpieces and covered entire ceilings with frescoes (Palazzo Labia, Scuola dei Carmini, Church of the Gesuiti, Ca' Rezzonico), turning his hand as easily to religious subjects (*Our Lady of Mount*

Carmel – I Carmini) as to mythological ones, including huge Virtues set before grandiose architectural backdrops.

Portraiture and Genre

Long-established patrician families and those of an aspiring bourgeoisie altered their household arrangements to reflect changes in lifestyle. In keeping with fashions elsewhere, it became acceptable to have informal, intimate and private rooms, separate from grandiose function or occasion rooms, in which to conduct everyday business, and this trend was reflected in contemporary art. Painters were asked to provide portraits that were both flattering and informal, a genre favoured by **Rosalba Carriera** (1675–1758), who produced delicate, vibrant pastels that earned her international fame (Ca' Rezzonico, Accademia), and **Alessandro Longhi**.

Around the same time, Venetians appeared to appreciate the small-scale interior scenes painted by **Pietro Longhi** (1702–85), such as masquerades, dances and duck hunting scenes (Hemingway's future pastime in Torcello), all revealing his acute powers of observation (Ca' Rezzonico, Querini-Stampalla Collection).

Topographical painters

Besides the *maniera* and genre scenes devoid of religious, allegorical or mythological meaning, landscape for its own sake began to provide artists with a worthy subject for easel pictures. In Venice, studies of the environment focused on the city herself, and it is for these views, *vedute* in Italian, that Antonio Canal (1697–1768), known as **Canaletto**, became so famous. In his pictures, he delineates in minute detail his on-the-spot observations of the city. Although his vision is almost photographic, he exaggerates perspective and paints huge, monumental buildings. He was also known to portray festivals and regattas. Unfortunately, most of his works are now exhibited in museums outside Italy and few can be admired in Venice itself. Canaletto

Portrait of the Artist's Sister Reading *(1909) by Umberto Boccioni*

inspired a great many artists, namely **Bernardo Bellotto** (1720–80), one of his pupils who was also a relative.

Quite distinct from Canaletto, **Francesco Guardi** (1712–93) was bewitched by the atmosphere of the lagoon city. His vision is not photographic; instead his bold use of paint succeeds in freezing the ripples of the water and the flickering light – a preoccupation that was to fascinate the English Romantic painter Turner and the French Impressionists a century later. Besides views of the lagoon, he also painted scenes of everyday life in the manner of Pietro Longhi: *Nuns' Parlour, Interval Time in the Foyer* (Ca' Rezzonico), as did his brother **Giovianni Antonio**.

Freed from the influence of his father, after painting the Stations of the Cross in San Polo, **Giovanni Domenico (Giandomenico) Tiepolo** (1727–1804) painted 18C Venetian society on the Brenta Riviera with humour and irony, depicting the holidaymakers as buffoons (Ca' Rezzonico: Villa Zianigo frescoes).

Modern and contemporary age

Between the 19C and the 20C Venetian painting continued on academic lines, ever faithful to the traditions set in the 18C with landscapes or urban scenes by Caffi and Ciardi, and fine portraits by Alessandro Milesi.

Motivated by mainstream developments in Europe during the early 20C, several painters produced interesting work (International Museum of Modern Art in Ca' Pesaro): **Federico Zandomeneghi** (1841–1917) who was born in Venice, worked with the Macchiaioli group before moving to Paris where he befriended Degas; **Umberto Boccioni** (1882–1916) was a founding member of the Futurist movement and painted in a style reminiscent of Signal (*The Grand Canal*); **Fragiacomo** was an Impressionist much inspired by Turner (*St Mark's Square*); **Casorati** was a Symbolist painter and portraitist.

Members of the **Burano School (Scuola di Burano)**, such as Moggioli, Gino Rossi, Sibellato and Semeghini, painted the islands of the lagoon, experimenting with techniques inspired by Van Gogh, Gauguin and Cézanne, and of the Post-Impressionists Bonnard and Vuillard.

LITERATURE
1200–1500

The history of Venetian literature begins in 1271 when "Master **Marco Polo**, a wise and noble citizen of Venice" embarked on a journey to the Orient. Despite his tender age, the 16 year-old decided to accompany his father Nic-

colò and uncle Matteo, both Levantine merchants, on a very long expedition to the court of "Kublai, the Great Khan of the Mongols". Never before had such an ambitious journey to those parts been undertaken by Westerners. Unfortunately the return journey was to prove Marco's undoing, for during one of the many naval battles between the Venetians and the Genoese, the explorer was taken prisoner by the enemy. As he languished in prison, he came to know a writer from Pisa, Rustichello, who undertook to set down on paper an account of the Venetian's experiences. So **The Book of the Wonders of the World** was born; it achieved success under the title *Il Milione*, an epithet given to Marco Polo when he described the quantities of gold he claimed to have seen. In the years that followed the death of the traveller, Venice appeared to dedicate itself less to literature than to commerce. Indeed, Venetian literary circles seem to have been affected by Humanism.

It was not until **Aldo Manuzio**, the *"ante litteram"* publisher, arrived in Venice that the situation changed. In 1499 he published the *Hypnerotomachia Poliphili*, an amusing, anonymous work written in an explosive style, using vernacular language bastardised from Venetian and Latin. Its success was modest but it seems to have heralded one of the most successful literary spells in Venice.

BEMBO TO GOLDONI: A PERIOD OF GREAT SPLENDOUR

A more conventional writer to be published by Aldo Manuzio was **Pietro Bembo**. Born into a very aristocratic family in Venice in 1470, Bembo remained the touchstone of literary developments for almost a century. His importance is largely due to *The Prose of Vulgar Language* which came out in 1528, and which contributed to the age-old debate over the use of vernacular language in literature. In it Bembo argued that he was violently opposed to the language adopted by Dante, and

Steven Wynn/istockphoto.com

Marco Polo

91

offered a convincing alternative that in part has influenced the evolution of Italian into the language of today.

The Paduan-born **Angelo Beolco** (1496), meanwhile, was moving in a different direction. His nickname, *il Ruzzante* (The Playful One), was derived from the peasant protagonist of his plays, whom the author often impersonated, and so the character and his creator became synonymous. The most famous play, *Il Parlamento del Ruzzante*, is a merciless portrait of peasant conditions at the time of a long and bloody war between the French and the Venetians.

Contemporary with Ruzzante was the unknown author of the **Veniexiana**, an entertaining comedy in dialect which depicted the vices and virtues (mainly the former) of the inhabitants of the lagoon city. Its significance, however, lies not so much in the amusing story it tells, full of melodramatic action, but in its marking a turning point in the cultural milieu of Venice. For between 1530 and 1540, the popular trend suddenly passed from foreign imported theatrical productions to the blossoming of "original" domestic plays.

This radical change was no doubt precipitated by the presence of **Pietro Aretino** who, as his surname suggests, was born in Arezzo. After a stay in Rome, Aretino reached Venice in 1527, just in time to publish *Il Marescalco* and *La Cortegiana*, two of the most popular and well-crafted comedies of the 16C. Their success was immediate and very well exploited by Aretino, who was astute enough to engage the new resources proffered by the printing press to increase his fame. This collaboration was, in fact, to make both the Tuscan and his publisher Marcotini a fortune. Aretino, furthermore, showed himself capable of using popular, vernacular language for literature to nothing short of tumultuous effect. His plays mocked and lampooned the authorities, attracting audiences from all walks of life, but most notably from among those in power who were anxious to know what was indeed being said. It was no surprise therefore, that he soon earned the epithet "the scourge of the princes". Thus during the 17C, the Republic's somewhat liberal attitude must have excused the considerable freedom of thought and action enjoyed in Venice: it is difficult otherwise to explain the success of Aretino and other such lax publications that would have been prohibited elsewhere. Venice became an important publishing centre, drawing all kinds of literary characters who wished to take particular care over typographical layouts and to oversee the output of their own book. Soon hundreds of printers mushroomed to service hundreds of authors, dependent one upon the other.

Comedy

The theatre became a passion for citizens of all social classes. Plays proliferated, almost all written and produced on the spot. Comedies enacted in dialect enjoyed the greatest popularity; these were often based around sets of particular carnival characters identified by their traditional mask and costume, such as **Harlequin**. The needs of a growing number of theatre devotees, coupled with those of an important and thriving port, founded the beginnings of a modern news-spreading media.

Journalism

The advent of journalism in Italy could only have been feasible in a milieu like Venice. In 1760 Gasparo Gozzi launched the magazine *La Gazzetta Veneta*, which appeared twice a week for about a year. Conceived along the lines of an English periodical, features included articles on orders of the day and useful practical information on life in the city (financial announcements, public notices, advertisement listings, stock exchange reports etc). It was in *La Gazzetta* that Goldoni published his first reviews on Rusteghi.

Carlo Goldoni (1707–93)

Goldoni's father was a doctor who wished his son to follow in his footsteps but when Carlo was aged 13, he ran away from school to join a ship in Rimini that was carrying a troupe of actors to Chioggia. From there he went on to join his mother in Venice. Goldoni resumed his studies and qualified as a lawyer. Lacking the will to succeed, however, he soon turned his hand at challenging the tradition of the Commedia dell'Arte to improvise dialogue along the lines of a given plot.

In 1743 Goldoni wrote the script for *La donna di Garbo*. In 1750 the provocative comedy playwright impudently waged a bet with his rival Pietro Chiari that in less than a year he could write 16 new comedies: in fact he wrote 17, including the splendid *La Bottega del Caffè* (*The Coffee Shop*), set in Venice and satirising the bourgeoisie. The ingredients were simple: he used colloquial language for immediacy and formulated rounded characters based on observation of real life. He avoided political incorrectness by importing his gentrified personalities from afar, able therefore to exaggerate their airs and graces. *Arlecchino, Servitore di due Padroni* (*Servant of Two Masters*), *La Locandiera* (*The Innkeeper*) are all constructed according to the same format. Goldoni died in France.

An account of Goldoni's stay in Venice can be found in the author's memoirs (*Memorie*).

HOW THE 18C AND 19C SAW VENICE

Venice as depicted by Goldoni, full of humour and moral integrity, was a vital place that attracted the talented, the eccentric and the curious. These included **Lorenzo da Ponte**, Mozart's celebrated librettist and author of the *Marriage of Figaro*, who lingered there for "a couple of years of adventurous libertinage", and that specialist master of licentiousness **Giacomo Casanova** (1725–98) who, between one amorous assignation and another, found time to write his interesting *Memoirs*.

Another reprobate of the same school, if the term is appropriate, the poet **Ugo Foscolo**, landed on the Riva degli Schiavoni in 1793. He stopped in the city for four years, during which he demon-

It would appear that the title of Marco Polo's book was in fact inspired by the word "Emilione", the nickname given to the family of the great navigator.

strated the true colour of his personality on numerous occasions. Abandoning his regular studies, he embarked on teaching himself the Greek and Latin classics to engineer his infiltration of the very refined salon of Isabella Teorochi Albrizzi, with whom he initiated a passionate affair, he aged 16 and she 34. In the meantime, he wrote the famous *Ode to the Liberator Bonaparte*; only the "liberator", in his political intrigue, paid no heed to the revolutionary ideals of the young Foscolo, but ceded Venice to Austria to further his own hegemonic aims. The repercussions on the writer were enormous, forcing him to seek refuge in Milan, where he devoted himself to drafting *The Last Letters of Jacopo Ortis*, a prose account of the delusion he had suffered. During his sojourn in Venice, however, Foscolo also became involved with **Melchiorre Cesarotti**, an important forerunner of the early Romantic movement.

Cesarotti was a tutor in an aristocratic household whose salon Foscolo frequently attended. In 1760 Cesarotti came across a collection of poems by Ossian, a legendary bard, published by a certain MacPherson: in six months, Cesarotti had translated them into Italian verse, which he published in 1763. *Le Poesie di Ossian,* as they appeared in Italian, shot Cesarotti to fame, oblivious of the fact that these "Ossianic poems" were to be one of those most famous cases of literary fraud to be uncovered over the last 200 years. **James MacPherson** (1736–96) claimed they were a translation of a series of surviving fragments of some ancient Gaelic mythical poetry when in fact they had been fabricated, for the most part, by the Scotsman himself. Poor Cesarotti was one of the many innocents to fall for the trick.

By the end of the century, the foundations of Italian Romanticism had been laid. The Piedmontese **Silvio Pellico**, the fervent patriot and anti-Austrian agitator, was soon to write his famous and doleful *Piombi*. In *Le mie Prigioni*, Pellico narrates his whole experience from the day of his arrest (13 October 1820) to that of his release (September 1830), thereby securing a place in the heart of the nation as a hero.

Throughout the Romantic period, Venice reigned supreme. This was not so much as a result of her literary output but rather because she continued to distract so many intellectuals, such as **Lord Byron**, on their travels through Italy, happy to meet up under the shaded porticoes of the Procuratie, a custom that was to extend well into the next century.

In 1886 the Russian author **Anton Chekhov** published a collection of short stories. *Story of a Stranger* recounts his overwhelming passion for Venice, to such an extent that he feels "intoxicated with life".

20TH CENTURY

The modern history of the lagoon city rests almost exclusively in the hands of foreigners, many of whom sought refuge there from persecution at home and soon enjoyed a protected social scene. Not only were there no Venetian-born writers of note to emerge,

few Italians were attracted to the decadent beauty of *La Serenissima*. **Gabriele d'Annunzio** was a notable exception. **Marcel Proust** arrived in 1900, inevitably accompanied by his mother, with whom he began translating the English writer **John Ruskin**, author of the famous *Stones of Venice*, while refining his own literary style. Proust's sojourn was a particularly happy one: reflecting in *A la recherche du temps perdu*, he writes *"However did the images of Venice give me such joy and confidence as to render me indifferent to death"*.

The reflections of **Thomas Mann** are of a very different order: in *Death in Venice*, the city is portrayed as being in a state of decay. The protagonist of the novel is Gustav von Aschenbach, a German writer who, after a lifetime of rigorous discipline, feels attracted by a city described as crumbling and overrun with cholera.

In 1918 the Viennese author **Arthur Schnitzler** wrote *Casanova in Spa*, a book set in Venice and loosely based on his amorous adventures.

Among the most recent illustrious visitors to the city was **Ernest Hemingway** who set down his suitcases in the Hotel Gritti in 1948. He loved to be called "Papa" and while away the time with glasses of Montgomery, a strong Martini, at Harry's Bar. Far removed from the more rugged places associated with the writer, Hemingway once confessed to his translator Ferdinanda Pivano: *"Sitting by the Grand Canal and writing near where Mr Byron, Mr Browning and Mr D'Annunzio wrote makes Mr Papa feel he has arrived at where he is meant to be"*.

The same year saw the publication of *Cantos* by the American poet **Ezra Pound**, who died in Venice (⊙ *see SAN ZANIPÒLO: Cemetery*) and who wrote about the city in Canto LXXVI.

In the early sixties, the Italian author **Giorgio Bassani** used the Ghetto district as a backdrop to his novel *Il Giardino dei Finzi Contini*, which was made into a famous film by **Vittorio de Sica**. The Russian writer **Josif Brodskij**, who received the Nobel Prize for Lit-

Ernest Hemingway in Piazza San Marco

E. Hemingway Photograph Collection, John Fitzgerald Kennedy Library, Boston

---

Literary Venice

Travellers with a keen eye and a writer's pen have provided many accounts of life in the lagoon city. In his notes about Italy (1729), **Charles Louis de Montesquieu** offers a sketchy description of Venice that nonetheless lists a great many figures (six *sestieri*, seven parishes, 25 houses for monks and 36 for nuns, 500 bridges, 20 000 residents etc). **Goethe's portrayal** is infused with sentiment: *"I suddenly felt that I too reigned supreme over the Adriatic, as do all Venetians as soon as they set foot on their gondola...".* (*Italian Journey*, 1829). In his diary about Italy (1857), **Herman Melville** presents the reader with an interesting medley of thoughts, impressions and fleeting images: *"Shimmering silver thuribles swaying softly, scattering incense over the heads of the faithful ... The rich, deep complexion of the women painted by Titian is indeed close to nature ...".*

---

erature in 1987, was fascinated by Venetian water and canals, a passion he recounted in *Watermark*.

Another Slav author who evokes the lagoon city was Polish-born **Gustaw Herling** who, in *Portrait of Venice* (1994), evokes his "sentimental involvement with Venice".

MUSIC
PRELUDE TO VIVALDI
Renaissance

Whereas in Rome a brilliant revival in music flourished under the auspices of **Giovanni Pierluigi da Palestrina** (1525–94), who headed a polyphonic school dedicated to sacred music, patronage in Venice was limited to more secular applications. Perhaps the turning point is marked by the Flemish **Willaert** (c.1490–1562), the choirmaster at St Mark's, who set a trend that was to be continued by his pupil Andrea Gabrieli.

Andrea Gabrieli (c.1510–86) – Organist at St Mark's, Gabrieli emerged as an important composer and influential teacher of organ and choral music in the Venetian tradition. His innovative use of the *concertato* (a small group of instruments or voices), contrasted with the *ripieno* (a larger body of musicians), forestalled the implementation of the *concerto* form developed and exploited later by Corelli. This allowed Gabrieli to experiment with harmony and dissonance by combining various "parts" for choir, or the human voice with instruments. His most lasting contribution is

a large body of choral works for both sacred (motets for four to 12 voices, masses for six voices, the *Psalms of David* for six voices) and secular texts (madrigals for three to 12 voices).

Giovanni Gabrieli (c.1557–1612) – Andrea's nephew Giovanni inherited the position of organist at St Mark's and further propagated the fame of the Venetian School abroad (the Dutch master Sweelinck, Hans Leo Hassler, Heinrich Schutz, Bach's precursor and founder of German church music, were already pupils). Among his compositions, which comprised sacred, secular and instrumental pieces, the most notable are his motets, the **Sacred Symphonies**. His more avant-garde works include **sonatas** for violin, which he used to explore antiphonal effects: at the time the violin was the instrument that best sustained the popular taste for monophonic music (following a single line of notes). By adding a **basso continuo** or figured bass line, with long drawn notes, he was able to develop harmonies with the accompaniment, thereby providing sustained and textured melody. This Gabrieli applied not only to choral arrangements but to instrumental pieces for two violins and clavichord or cello.

The Baroque Period

With the 17C began another rich and fruitful period for Venetian music. Melodrama became a formal genre; formulated from accounts of contemporary historical events or legends, exaggerated stories were re-enacted to audiences in elaborately contrived stage settings. Francesco Cavalli (1602–76), a chorister at St Mark's, Marc'Antonio Cesti (1623–69) and Giovanni Legrenzi (1626–90), choirmaster at St Mark's, all collaborated at an operatic school in Venice which, in 1637, opened the first commercial opera house, San Cassiano. Here Monteverdi's operas were later performed.

The 18th Century

By the mid-1700s, Venice was renowned for the more typically Neapolitan kind of comic operas by **Baldassarre Galuppi** (💿see BURANO), who, together with Giovanni Platti (1700–63), contributed to the development of the sonata (literally meaning "sounded", implying music that is instrumental rather than sung) for strings and keyboard. In response to works by the Bach dynasty in Germany, they composed pieces for one (harpsichord) or two instruments (harpsichord and violin) in homophonic (several lines of notes moving in chords) and polyphonic (several lines of notes each with its own distinctive pattern) arrangements in several movements (usually three).

The harpsichord enjoyed particular favour, despite the advent of the piano, developed by Bartolomeo Cristofori (1655–1732) by substituting hammers for quills. Among the most famous players of the harpsichord, besides Galuppi and Platti, were the two **Marcello** brothers, **Benedetto** (1686–1739), who also composed sacred music and concertos for five instruments, and **Alessandro** (1684–1750), who wrote sonatas for violin and basso continuo and concertos for oboe and strings that hitherto have been attributed to Benedetto. Also active in Venice in this period was **Tomaso Albinoni** (1671–1750), who more closely followed in the German Baroque tradition and foreshadows Vivaldi in his instrumental compositions.

ANTONIO VIVALDI (1678–1741)

It is undoubtedly Vivaldi who best epitomises Venetian music: even JS Bach (1685–1750) drew openly on the compositions of the *"Prete Rosso"* (💿see SAN GIORGIO degli SCHIAVONI), who was literally rediscovered in the mid-20C, after years of oblivion.

Vivaldi was a prolific composer, using a three-movement form of the concerto, *allegro-adagio-allegro*, and freeing up the *Sonata da Camera* as a series of contrasting descriptive passages as in the *Four Seasons*, the *Goldfinch* and *Night concerti*. Altogether, Vivaldi composed over 500 concertos for violin, viola d'amore, cello, mandolin, flute, oboe, bassoon, trumpet, cornet and string orchestra.

His parents

Giovanni Battista Vivaldi, father of Antonio, was a professional barber and musician: this would be surprising today, but many Venetians of the time combined both professions. Giovanni Battista, nicknamed *il Rosso* after the colour of his auburn hair, obviously a family trait, was a violin virtuoso in 17C Venice, more specifically in the area around **San Martino** where most of the city's musicians congregated at the Scuola, the *Sovvegno di Santa Cecilia*, whose patron naturally was St Cecilia.

Camilla Calicchio, the mother of Antonio, was born in the area around **San Giovanni in Bràgora** (💿see ARSENALE), where Antonio was baptised a second time, having been subjected to the formalities of a blessing at home on 4 March 1678, shortly after his birth, when it appeared that he might not survive.

Il Prete Rosso

Antonio was ordained at **San Giovanni Novo**, even though he dedicated himself to the cause of music rather than to the priesthood, content to remain a secular priest or abbot. He took up residence in Fondamenta del Dose, near the Ponte del Paradiso, before abandoning the Castello *sestiere* in favour of

St Mark's, where he lived on the Riva del Carbon. When he left these lodgings in 1740 it was to leave Venice completely, dying in poverty in Vienna the following year.

The Musician

Vivaldi's main musical activity is associated first and foremost with the Pietà and the Theatre of San Angelo.

The Pietà was one of the great **foundling hospitals** which, between the 17C and 18C, doubled as one of the musical conservatories of Venice, each having its own church where concerts were held. These "hospitals" functioned as charitable institutions and orphanages for girls (*ospitaliere*), who received an education and, if gifted, musical instruction to enable them to take part in the choirs and orchestras of which the establishments were so proud.

Associated as it is with the fame of Vivaldi, the Pietà became the best known of the hospital-churches. Standing on the Riva degli Schiavoni it cannot be mistaken or missed, although the present church is not the original one where Vivaldi had been music teacher and composer. The former church stood where the Metropole Hotel now stands, slightly to the right of the present church.

The San Angelo Theatre no longer exists. It was there that the violin virtuoso acted as musical director, impresario, composer and performed more secular works.

AFTER VIVALDI

The musical splendour of Venice, which regaled contemporary ears for three centuries and continues to survive today in churches and concert halls, faded with the passing of its most illustrious representative. In more recent times, one interesting composer emerges from the Venetian and German traditions and that is **Ermanno Wolf-Ferrari** (1876–1948), who was particularly impressed by Mozart's operatic works and inspired by the theatre of Goldoni: both influences are evident

> ### Famous organ-builders
>
> **Gaetano Callido** (1727–1813) built about 400 organs throughout the Veneto, Dalmatia and even the Holy Land: all three organs at St Mark's were restored by him in 1766. Four years later, he was appointed the official, permanent organ-maker to the city. His sons Agostino and Antonio continued to practise their father's craft until 1821.

in his own life's opus *Gioielli della Madonna, Le Donne Curiose, I Quattro rusteghi, Il Campiello,* etc.

Yet more recently still, the city has resumed its role as a lively and innovative artistic centre by playing host to such experimental musicians as **Bruno Maderna** (1920–73) and **Luigi Nono** (1924–90).

Venice was also the birthplace of the conductor Giuseppe Sinopoli (1946–2001), who was to become an authority on Mahler's work.

> ### 17C Opera
>
> During the 17C, thanks to Claudio Monteverdi, who conducted the choir at San Marco, Venice became known as the world's leading centre for operatic art, placing herself ahead of Florence and Mantua. In those days, the lagoon city boasted a total of 17 theatres.

VENETIAN BY ADOPTION

Tribute should also be paid to visiting composers who died in Venice.

Claudio Monteverdi (1567–1643) was one genius who breathed personality and characterisation into opera: he lies buried at I Frari (◐*see I FRARI*). **Domenico Cimarosa** (1749–1801), often regarded as the Italian Mozart, died in Campo Sant' Angelo (◐*see La FENICE*). The apparently aloof and detached **Igor**

Venice in Music

From *The Four Seasons* by Vivaldi to traditional Venetian songs, music heard for the first time in Venice will evoke memories of its canals and piazzas. The works of classical and traditional music below embody a particularly Venetian flavour.

- Various artists, *Musiche veneziane per voce e strumenti,* Claves
- Various artists, *Music of the Tintoretto Age,* Edelweiss
- Various artists, *A Piano Recital for Venice,* Edelweiss
- Various artists, *Voice and Lute in Venice in the 16th Century,* Edelweiss
- Various artists, *Musiche veneziane per voce e strumenti (Teresa Berganza),* Claves
- Various artists, *Musiche veneziane per trombe e tromboni,* Claves
- Various artists, *Souvenirs de Venise: The Songmakers' Almanac,* Hyperion
- Tomaso Albinoni, *Musiche veneziane,* Claves
- Andrea and Giovanni Gabrieli, *Musica organistica,* Tactus
- Giovanni Gabrieli, *Sinfonie sacre,* Oiseau-lyre
- Baldassarre Galuppi, *Musiche veneziane: concerti e sinfonie,* Claves
- Baldassarre Galuppi, *Musiche veneziane: passatempo al cembalo,* Claves
- Baldassarre Galuppi; Antonio Vivaldi, *Musiche veneziane: Magnificat; Gloria,* Claves
- Alessandro Marcello, *Concerto in re minore per oboe, archi e organo,* Philips
- Monteverdi, Rigatti, Grandi, Cavalli, *Venetian Vespers,* Archiv
- Antonio Vivaldi, *The Four Seasons*
- Antonio Vivaldi, *Musiche veneziane: Six Concertos for Flute,* Claves
- Antonio Vivaldi, *Musiche veneziane: concerti,* Claves

Venetian music – The *Concerto in D minor for oboe, strings and organ* by Alessandro Marcello was long attributed to his brother Benedetto. This well-known piece of music accompanied the Italian film *The Anonymous Venetian*, which starred Tony Musante and Florinda Bolkan.

Stravinsky (1882–1971) is buried in the cemetery of San Michele.

However, it was **Richard Wagner** (1813–83), possibly the most controversial composer in musical history, who most desired to be adopted by his beloved Venice. The maestro died on 13 February in the Palazzo Vendramin Calergi (&see *Il CANAL GRANDE*) in the company of his wife, Cosima, and the gondolier Gigio Trevisan, nicknamed Ganassete.

During Wagner's peaceful stay in Venice, he would go to St Mark's Square daily where, seated at Quadri's or Florian's, he was sometimes recognised by the leader of the municipal band who would ask him to conduct: Wagner would agree, happy to direct his own compositions for the Venetians. It was here that Wagner composed the second act of *Tristan* (the English horn part having been inspired by the evening song of the gondoliers), wrote part of *Parsifal* and initiated work on the *Maestri cantori* inspired by Titian's *Assumption* that he so admired at I Frari.

CARNEVALE (CARNIVAL)

During the 18C, the Venice Carnival opened at the beginning of October and ended on the Tuesday preceding Lent, with only one short interruption for Christmas festivities. In those days, masks were worn throughout the carnival but they were also used in other circumstances: during the Fiera della Sensa lasting for two weeks, on the occasion of doges' elections and their sons' weddings, and when famous personalities arrived in town.

The culmination of Carnival is 10 days before Lent (Feb–Mar) with the "volo dell'angelo" or "flight of the angel". In this ceremony, an acrobat descends the bell-tower of St Mark's and glides over the piazza to the Doges' Palace by means of two ropes. In the past, the acrobat was dressed as a Turk rather than an angel. The trend now is to begin Carnival festivities earlier, in hopes of relieving the crush of the crowds in the final week. The city has even consulted with Rome and Viareggio, in particular, to upgrade their celebrations to take some of the pressure off Venice.

"BUONGIORNO, SIORA MASCARA"

A key feature of Carnival is the mask. It is said that masks were first introduced to Venice in 1204 when Doge Enrico Dandolo brought veiled Muslim women back to Venice after his conquest of Constantinople. As in Mozart's opera *Don Giovanni* (Act 2), masked people greeted each other routinely with the saying "Buongiorno Siora Mascara" during the 17C. To go about one's business dressed in the *baùta* – a mask complete with its hooded black shawl – was so normal that a formal request was lodged by the clergy for Venetians to remove their disguise at least in church.

RETURN OF THE CARNIVAL

The greater the decline of Venice, the sharper her sense of fun. Come 1797 when the French assumed power, thus ending the glory of the Venetian Republic for all time, the city continued her revelries, thriving on her taste for jokes and riddles, laughter and carnival, which was eventually revived late in the 19C.

Even when this modern carnival was reinstated, with an open invitation to all to congregate in Piazza San Marco – the only time the space is truly filled by the crowds – it was a masked attendance. Whether it be with the *baùta*, the full-length cloak (*tabarro*), the three-horned hat (*tricorno*) or the long-nosed mask (*maschera a becco*) that doctors used to wear during the plague epidemics, the rule of the game is always the same: never investigate the identity of the person wearing the mask.

The need to don a mask seems to come as second nature to a Venetian. Maybe because, in the words of Silvio Ceccat: *"The streets are narrow, the population is small. You meet someone at every corner. Everyone knows everyone else's business. Today there are no cars to protect anonymity as yesterday there were no coaches in which to hide … People used to and still do feel naked in Venice. So naked, indeed, that clothes are not enough and hence the need for the mask …".*

Today's festivities are organised by the city and include various colourful historic pageants and performances, with grand balls by invitation.

Carnival participants

© Olivier Harand / Fotolia.com

Colourful houses along the canal, Burano
© Norbert Scanella / age fotostock

The Districts of Venice

&*Map on inside covers, front and back.*

Il Canal Grande★★★

Arguably the most famous, the most beautiful, and certainly the most unusual High Street in the world, the Grand Canal bisects the island of Venice in the form of an inverted S. It is only 3km/2mi long though packs so much in that it feels much bigger. Other vital statistics are that it is between 30m/98ft and 70m/229ft wide and on average it is 5.5m/18ft deep). When he was living in Palazzo Mocenigo, Lord Byron was in the habit of swimming across the Grand Canal. Mark Twain described the appearance of the canal in moonlight as magical; Goethe felt himself to be "Lord of the Adriatic" here; and Dickens, convinced the ghost of Shylock roamed the bridges of the city, felt the spirit of Shakespeare strongly in Venice. A short journey along the canal will undoubtedly leave as magical an impression on modern-day travellers as it did on its illustrious visitors of the past.

A BIT OF HISTORY

The origins of the Grand Canal, which may once have been a branch of the River Medoacus (⊙ *see VILLAS OF THE BRENTA*), are lost in time. The *traghetti*

▷ **Location:** Two vaporetti lines travel up and down the Grand Canal from one end to the other: line **1** serves nearly all the stations; line **2**, which is faster, makes only a few stops. From midnight until around 5am, the night vaporetto, **N**, takes over the service (*see p19*).
Sit at the back in the open air for the best views. If you can't get a seat at the back, wait for the next boat – it won't be long.

▷ **Don't Miss:** There are so many great landmarks to pick out, but the Rialto Bridge is the most famous.

▷ **Timing:** It takes around 35–40min non-stop by vaporetto from Santa Lucia (Ferrovia Scalzi) to Piazza San Marco, but you could easily spend a full day (and longer) hopping on or off at places of interest.

(gondolas which cross the river) have provided a ferry service between the banks of the canal since the year 1000: some of the existing landing stages have been in place since the 13C, many either serving mills that were operated by the

Aerial view of the Grand Canal

© Guido Alberto Rossi / Tips Images

The Fourth Bridge

Venice acquired a new bridge in 2008 to much fanfare – its fourth across the Grand Canal was the first in more than 70 years. It was designed by Santiago Calatrava, the Spanish engineer and designer famous for his grandiose modernist works in Valencia. The exquisitely modern arched truss bridge, a single sleek span between the Santa Lucia railway station and Piazzale Roma, shows no visible means of support. To integrate it somewhat with the vernacular architecture it is partly built of local Istrian marble, Venice's most important raw material.

Controversy dogged the project. Many questioned whether this was the best location to build a new bridge, the contrast of its bold modern design, it was way over the original budget, there were safety issues, it was behind schedule, and, incomprehensibly it was not accessible to wheelchairs. The span is approached by illuminated glass steps and, belatedly, provision was made for disabled users.

The **Ponte della Costituzione (Constitution Bridge)**, informally called **Ponte di Calatrava**, was named for its opening date, which was the 60th anniversary of the Italian constitution.

tides or *squeri* where the gondolas were built; then there were the workshops for the Guild of Wool Weavers and Cloth-makers, which employed the poor to card, finish, dye and press the textiles. It is along the canal especially that the beauty of the city unfolds: façades of vibrant colours, resplendent with gilding, exude the festive spirit and optimism of the Venetians, who have never known the threat of oppression, not even in the Middle Ages, when the rest of the world had to build fortresses to defend themselves. The *palazzi* that flank the Grand Canal are the Venetian nobility's expression of pride and self-satisfaction: they were the only people who could vouchsafe a piece of this water garden (&see Il GHETTO: Palazzo Labia). Commercial, banking and state enterprises have been in operation along the canal since the Renaissance; churches and *palazzi* were being built right up until the Republic breathed its last breath.

LEFT BANK - FROM SAN MARCO TO PIAZZALE ROMA

 🕲 **Good to know** – The vaporetto stops mentioned are those used by line 1, which we recommend you take for this tour.

Palazzo Corner della Ca' Granda

Nowadays this Renaissance palace is used as the police headquarters (*Prefettura*). It was built for the nephew of Caterina Cornaro by Sansovino (1486–1570). The rusticated ground floor has a three-arch portico; elegantly aligned arched windows on the upper floors alternate with paired columns.

Next door, the little red house was used by **Canova** as his studio (1770s) and during the First World War by the controversial, poet, novelist and Fascist politician, **Gabriele d'Annunzio**.

Palazzo Cavalli Franchetti

Between the Giglio and Accademia stops. The splendid façade of this late-15C *palazzo*, complete with delicate tracery work, five-arched windows with intersecting tracery and quatrefoil motifs, casts its intricate reflection across the Grand Canal. It was rebuilt towards the end of the 19C.

Ponte dell'Accademia

Venice had to wait until 1854 for its second crossing of the Grand Canal after the Rialto Bridge. The original iron construction, restricted in height, hindered the passage of the vaporettos; the bridge was therefore replaced

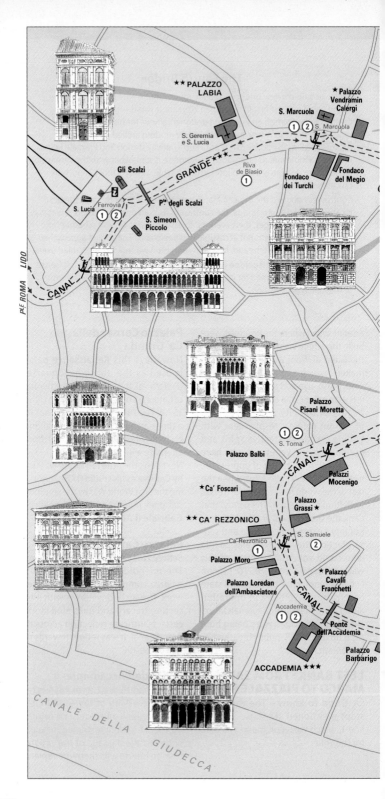

★★ PALAZZO LABIA

★ Palazzo Vendramin Calergi

S. Marcuola

① ② S. Marcuola

S. Geremia e S. Lucia

GRANDE ★★★

Gli Scalzi

Riva de Biasio

①

Fondaco del Megio

Fondaco dei Turchi

S. Lucia

Ferrovia

① ②

P.te degli Scalzi

PLE ROMA LIDO

CANAL

S. Simeon Piccolo

Palazzo Pisani Moretta

① ②

S. Toma'

Palazzo Balbi

CANAL

Palazzi Mocenigo

★ Ca' Foscari

Palazzo Grassi ★

★★ CA' REZZONICO

Ca'Rezzonico

①

S. Samuele

②

Palazzo Moro

★ Palazzo Cavalli Franchetti

Palazzo Loredan dell'Ambasciatore

CANAL

Accademia

① ②

Ponte dell'Accademia

Palazzo Barbarigo

ACCADEMIA ★★★

CANALE DELLA GIUDECCA

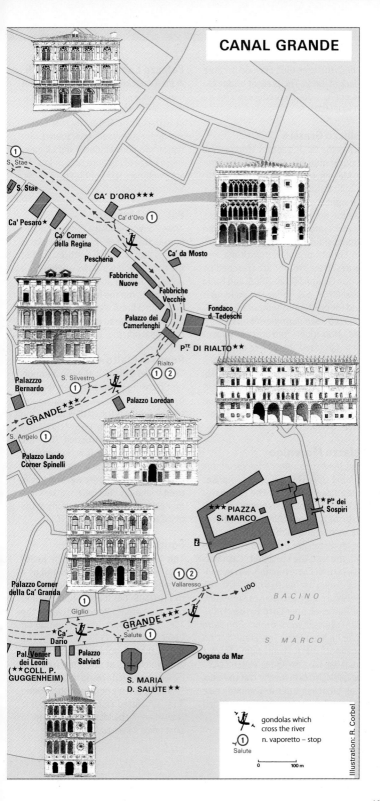

CANAL GRANDE

S. Stae

S. Stae

Ca' Pesaro ★

Ca' Corner
della Regina

CA' D'ORO ★★★

Ca'd'Oro ①

Pescheria

Ca' da Mosto

Fabbriche
Nuove

Fabbriche
Vecchie

Palazzo dei
Camerlenghi

Fondaco
d. Tedeschi

P^TE DI RIALTO ★★

Palazzzo
Bernardo

S. Silvestro

Rialto
① ②

GRANDE ★★★

Palazzo Loredan

S. Angelo ①

Palazzo Lando
Corner Spinelli

★★★ PIAZZA
S. MARCO

★★ P^ta dei
Sospiri

① ②
Vallaresso

→ LIDO

B A C I N O

Palazzo Corner
della Ca' Granda

①
Giglio

GRANDE ★★★

D I

★ Ca'
Dario

Salute ①

S. M A R C O

Pal. Venier
dei Leoni
(★★ COLL. P.
GUGGENHEIM)

Palazzo
Salviati

Dogana da Mar

S. MARIA
D. SALUTE ★★

gondolas which
cross the river

① n. vaporetto – stop
Salute

0   100 m

Illustration: R. Corbel

in 1932, this time built of wood because of lack of funds. The present bridge is a copy of its wooden predecessor (&see ACCADEMIA).

Palazzo Grassi★

Facing the Ca' Rezzonico stop (or San Samuele stop). Erected in 1749 by Giorgio Massari, this last Venetian palace to be built before the fall of the Republic is designed with all the majesty of neo-Classical domestic architecture. Inside, the courtyard has a fine colonnade and a grand staircase frescoed by Alessandro Longhi populated with masked figures. Other rooms are frescoed by Jacopo Guarana (1720–1808) and Fabio Canal (1703–67). Today the building is used for prestigious temporary exhibitions (©*Open during exhibitions only; Wed–Mon 10am–7pm (last entrance at 6pm).* ©*Closed, 24–25 Dec and 1 Jan.* ☞€15 (€20 inc Punta della Dogana). ☞*Guided tours available in english.* ℘041 20 01 057. www.palazzograssi.it) and is also home to a very good cafe run by Rosa Salva pasticceria and bookshop. &*See La Fenice.*

Palazzo Mocenigo

After the bend in the canal, facing the S. Tomà stop. This building comprises four adjacent *palazzi*. The first dates back to 1579, when it was rebuilt according to the designs of Alessandro Vittoria. The second and third buildings, which are identical, are from the end of the 16C; the last, the so-called "Casa Vecchia," a Gothic construction, was remodelled during the first half of the 17C. The furnished palace also houses a museum. The Romantic poet **Lord Byron** (1788–1824) started work on his *Don Juan* while he lived here. This English "Don Giovanni" often swam home from a day at San Lazzaro (&*see SAN LAZZARO degli ARMENI*) or an evening at the Lido, a habit that instituted a swimming race that was held until 1949 and rewarded by the Byron Cup.

Palazzo Lando Corner Spinelli

At the S. Angelo stop. Erected in 1490, this Renaissance *palazzo* was most probably designed by Mauro Codussi. The façade in Istrian stone is heavily rusticated. The upper storeys are punctuated with typical two-light windows, and a Renaissance frieze of festoons runs below the attic windows. It resembles the Palazzo Vendramin Calergi.

Palazzo Loredan

After S. Silvestro. Also a *fondaco* (warehouse), this Veneto-Byzantine *palazzo* retains some original features: part of the portico and windows opening out onto the loggia, interlaced with *pateras* (discs), run the length of the *piano nobile* (first floor). Palazzo Loredan and the nearby Palazzo Farsetti now house municipal offices.

Ponte di Rialto★★

The **Rialto Bridge** is the most important crossing point between the two banks of the Grand Canal. Although today's bridge is the sixth version – the original was built in 1175 – this is the first stone-built construction. The work of Antonio da Ponte, it was opened in 1591. The shops which are housed in the symmetrical arcades were originally used by money changers, bankers and moneylenders, in close proximity to the first Zecca (Mint – &*see RIALTO*).

Fondaco dei Tedeschi

This 13C *palazzo* served as the headquarters of German traders and as a warehouse for their goods. Devastated by fire (1505–08), it was rebuilt by Giorgio Spavento (in Venice between the 15C and 16C) and by Scarpagnino (in Venice between 1505 and 1549). The façade that overlooks the Grand Canal, and which was at one time frescoed by Giorgione (c.1476–1510) and Titian (1490–1576), has a portico on the ground floor, as befitted a *fondaco* (warehouse). Nowadays the building houses the main post office (&*see La FENICE*).

Ca' da Mosto

After the second bend in the canal. Erected in the 13C, this Veneto-Byzantine *palazzo* was the birthplace of Alvise da Mosto (1432–88), the great navigator who explored the western coast of Africa. The portico betrays the building's dual function as house and warehouse. Note the first-floor ceiling decorated with circular coffering or patera. Between the 16C and 18C, the *palazzo* served as the city's finest hotel, the **Leon Bianco**.

Ca' d'Oro★★★

Just after the stop of the same name. The *palazzo*'s façade, in the ornate Gothic style, presents a colonnade lapped by the water's edge and, on the upper floors, two enclosed loggias with arched windows, interlaced with intersecting tracery and quatrefoils. Oddly, this decorative feature is not centred in the façade. The right section consists of a blank wall between single-arched windows. Cordons of marble accentuate the corners (*see CA' D'ORO*).

Palazzo Vendramin Calergi★

After the S. Stae stop. This Renaissance palace, commissioned by the noble family of Loredan al Codussi, who worked in the city between 1502 and 1504, is a magnificent synthesis of Byzantine and Gothic architectural features. From 1844 it was home to the Duchesse de Berry, the daughter-in-law of Charles X of France. **Richard Wagner** lived here, composing the second act of *Tristan and Isolde* between 1858 and 1859. Although the composer died in the Palazzo Vendramin, where he had also worked on *Parsifal*, his memory is enshrined in the **Museo Richard Wagner** (*Open by appointment only. 041 27 60 407. www.casinovenezia.it*). The *palazzo* currently serves as the more formal of two municipal casinos.

San Marcuola

After the stop of the same name. This church is quite distinctive from others overlooking the Grand Canal: the roughly-bricked façade remains incomplete. Interestingly, this façade is actually the side of the church. Although its present appearance is Baroque in style, the church is altogether much older (*see IL GHETTO*).

The wide Cannaregio canal then flows into the Grand Canal.

Palazzo Labia★

Just after the confluence near the Riva di Biasio stop. This elegant 18C residence on the corner of the Cannaregio Canal is slightly set back from the Grand Canal. The ground floor is rusticated, with Ionic and Corinthian pilasters on the two floors above: the large windows open out onto balconies. The eagles which protrude from under the roof refer to the heraldry of the Labia family (*see Il GHETTO*).

San Geremia e Santa Lucia

From the water, all that can be seen of this church is the Chapel of Santa Lucia, which houses the remains of the Sicilian martyr (*see Il GHETTO*).

Ponte degli Scalzi

Originally built in 1858, the bridge, named after the "discalced" (meaning unshod and pertaining to religious orders, such as the Carmelites and Franciscans), was designed by the same civil engineer, Neville, as the first Accademia Bridge. It was rebuilt in 1934.

Gli Scalzi

Juste after le pont. This Baroque church was designed by Longhena (1598–1682). Its most distinctive features are the niches in the façade (1672–78), which are adorned with statues and framed with paired columns (*see Il GHETTO*).

Stazione di Santa Lucia

Described by Gustav von Aschenbach, the main character in *Death in Venice*, as the "tradesmen's entrance" to the city, the station has served as the gateway to the city since 1860 when the first station was built. The present building was erected in 1954.

Piazzale Roma

The main link to *terra firma* (mainlaind), the bus terminal and a car park are located here; the tram T1 to Mestre opened in 2014. The vaporetto heads back towards San Marco/Lido.

In 2008, a fourth bridge – for pedestrians – crossed the Grand Canal. Designed by Spanish architect **Santiago Calatrava**, this glass-and-steel structure links the station directly with the piazzale.

RIGHT BANK – FROM PIAZZALE ROMA TO LA DOGANA DA MAR

🕙 **Good to know**– The vaporetto stops mentioned are those used by line 1, which we recommend for this tour.

San Simeone Piccolo

Before the Ferrovia stop. This is the first eye-catching landmark after the station. Distinctive features include a Corinthian *pronaos* (front portico) up a flight of steps and a green dome. The church was designed by Scalfarotto (c.1700–64) in the tradition set by Palladio and Longhena.

Fondaco dei Turchi

Facing the S. Marcuola stop. Dating to the 13C, this Veneto-Byzantine *fondaco* was built as a private house and turned into commercial premises in 1621. Its current appearance is largely due to its restoration in the late-19C. With the side towers framing the façade, the portico and the floor above are laced with arches. Between 1621 and 1838 the warehouse was used by Turks, hence its name. The building houses the Natural History Museum (🕙*see I FRARI*).

Fondaco del Megio

Separated from the Fondaco dei Turchi by the Rio dei Turchi. This distinctive building, with walls of roughly hewn brick and tiny windows, dates to the 15C. Note the lion below the ornate crenellation. The structure was used as a grain store, notably for millet (*miglio = megio* – hence the name).

San Stae

At the stop of the same name. Dedicated to St Eustace, this church was completely renovated during the 17C. The elaborate Baroque façade (1709), dominated by a pedimented bay set between two roughcast wings, is attributed to Domenico Rossi (1678–1742). Its broken tympanum, crowned with statues over the entrance, is original. Inside a single nave are works by Piazzetta (1683–1754), Ricci (1659–1734) and Tiepolo (1696–1770) that forestall a shift in style towards the Rococo. Doge Alvise Mocenigo is buried here.

Ca' Pesaro★

At the death of Baldassare Longhena (1682), completion of the building was assigned to Antonio Gaspari (c.1670–c.1730). Unusual is its diamond-pointed rustication of the ground floor and row of lions' heads. On the second and third floors, great arched windows with single columns grace an open loggia.

Today, the building is home to the Museum of Oriental Art and the International Gallery of Modern Art (🕙*see RIALTO*).

Ca' Corner della Regina

San Stae and Rialto Mercato stops Designed by Domenico Rossi (1678–1742), the heavily rusticated ground floor gives way to plainer upper storeys punctuated by balconies and windows framed with columns. The home of Monte di Pietà bank until 1969, this building then hosted the ASAC (the Venice Biennale's historical contemporary art archives) from 1975 to 2010, and in 2011 became the Venetian headquarters for Fondazione Prada, hosting various cultural activities focused mainly on contemporary art and cinema (🕙*Open during exhibitions or free by reservation at least 7 days in advance for groups of at least 6 people.* 📞*02 56 66 2611. www.fondazioneprada.org/visit/visit-venezia/*). (🕙*see RIALTO*).

Pescheria

After the Ca' d'Oro stop. The portico of this neo-Gothic building, which dates back to the beginning of the 20C, now holds the famous fish market, hence the name (*see RIALTO*).

Fabbriche Nuove

This rather plain building on the bend of the Grand Canal was designed by **Sansovino**. Its rusticated ground floor at one time would have consisted of *magazzini* (small shops) and warehousing. The first floor was occupied by magistrates' courts (*see RIALTO*).

Fabbriche Vecchie

Destroyed by fire, the warehouses were rebuilt by Scarpagnino (active in Venice between 1505 and 1549). Even the "old workshops" boast their own columned portico (*see RIALTO*).

Palazzo dei Camerlenghi

Just before the Rialto. Situated in the lee of the bridge, this Renaissance palace was designed by Guglielmo dei Grigi, known as Bergamasco (active in Venice between c.1515–30), for the Camerlenghi, who were government officials responsible for the State's financial affairs. The pentagonal building has large windows aligned below a frieze of festoons.

Palazzo Bernardo

After the S. Silvestro stop. Gothic in style (1442), the building boasts splendid five-arched windows, pointed on the first floor, and quatrefoils on the second floor.

Palazzo Pisani Moretta

Between the S. Angelo and S. Tomà stops. Also late Gothic, the Palazzo Pisani Moretta dates from the second half of the 15C. Like Palazzo Bernardo, the windows have five lights and intersecting tracery that enclose quatrefoils on the upper floors.

Palazzo Balbi

After S. Tomà, on the corner of Rio Foscari. The façade of this *palazzo*, which is attributed to Alessandro Vittoria (1525–c.1600), is divided into three sections. Above a rusticated ground floor, the central bay is pierced by an arrangement of three arched windows.

Ca' Foscari★

The glorious façade of this *palazzo* rises above the Grand Canal at the junction with the Rio Foscari. Perfect symmetry aligns the three orders of arched windows that alternate with single light openings and stonework. The original 14C building was rebuilt closer to the water's edge after 1550. Nowadays it is part of the university (*see I CARMINI*).

Ca' Rezzonico★★

At the stop of the same name. This house was the last palace designed by Longhena, who lived to see only the completion of the first floor, before Massari took over. Note the extensive embellishment of the *piano nobile* and the fine configuration of balconies. It presently contains the Museum of 18C Venice (*see I CARMINI*) and collections of Venetian finery related to the Carnival.

Palazzo Moro

After the Ca' Rezzonico stop. This 16C *palazzo* is austere in its simplicity. Here the Moro family resided, one of whom suffered the tragic marriage that was to inspire **Shakespeare** (1564–1616) to write *Othello*, and portray the famous "Moor of Venice".

Palazzo Loredan dell'Ambasciatore

Next to the Palazzo Moro. Otherwise known as "The Ambassador's House," the late-Gothic Palazzo Loredan has splendid arched windows.

Accademia★★★

At the Accademia stop. The Academy of Fine Arts has been housed here since the beginning of the 19C. The adjoining church, rebuilt between 1441 and

Santa Maria della Salute

© B. Gardel/hemis.fr

1452, has been subject to considerable restoration, most famously by Palladio (1508–80) (☝ *see ACCADEMIA*).

Palazzo Barbarigo

The mosaics that decorate the façade depict Charles V in Titian's studio and Henry III of France on Murano. These were installed by the glass-blowers and mosaic-makers responsible for the reconstruction of the 16C palace in the late-19C. This building provided **Henry James** with inspiration for his novel *The Wings of the Dove*. In 2007 it opened its doors as a splendid art-deco-inspired luxury hotel.

Palazzo Venier dei Leoni

A a scale model in the Correr Museum shows how this palace was intended to look by its designer Lorenzo Boschetti in 1749. Financial problems forced the Venier family to stop work and all that survives of the original is its rusticated ground floor. Its large stone lion, is a link to a story that the Venier family once kept a pet lion in the garden!

The building currently houses the world-famous **Peggy Guggenheim Collection** of modern art (☝ *see La SALUTE, Collezione Peggy Guggenheim*).

Ca' Dario★

This small, late-15C *palazzo* is most distinctively embellished with polychrome marble decoration. It was built by the Lombardo family for Giovanni Dario, the secretary to the Senate of the Republic at the Sultan's court.

Palazzo Salviati

Facing the Giglio stop. Like Palazzo Barbarigo, the 19C Palazzo Salviati was owned by glass-makers who provided its fine mosaics.

Santa Maria della Salute★★

The massive white structure with its distinctive spiral volutes (the so-called *orecchioni*, or big ears) is visible from afar. Designed by Longhena, it was erected upon the wishes of the doge as a gesture of supplication to end the plague of 1630, a story recounted in the Italian novel by Alessandro Manzoni, *I Promessi Sposi* (☝ *see La SALUTE*).

Dogana da Mar

This extension of the Dorsoduro district served to unload goods and duty was levied here. On its tower two Atlantes support the weight of the World and the figure of Fortune, dates to the second half of the 17C (☝ *see La SALUTE*).

Piazza San Marco★★★

"The finest drawing room in Europe" according to Napoleon, **St Mark's Square** is the daily destination for tens of thousands of visitors. Beyond the columns of St Mark and St Theodore, the gondolas and vaporettos come and go, noisy crowds gather around the souvenir stalls and musicians play to the habitués of the legendary cafes. Tourists follow their tour guide's raised umbrella into the basilica or loiter under the porticoes, bewitched by windows of sparkling jewellery and glass. For centuries the passing of the hours has been ceremoniously sounded by the Moors on the clock tower and the mighty bells of the campanile.

A BIT OF HISTORY

A canal once ran in front of the basilica but by covering it over in 1160, the length of the piazza was tripled. The columns of St Mark and St Theodore (*see below*) were erected in the piazzetta, and the entire architectural complex, as adapted, became the setting before which Pope Alexander III met with the

- **Michelin Map:** (◨, FGX) Vaporetto: S. Marco
- **Location:** The square is the heart of the city. All central streets lead to here and it houses the two must-visit sights of the Basilica di San Marco, with its landmark Campanile, and the Palazzo Ducale (Doges' Palace).
- **Don't Miss:** The piazza when an orchestra is playing outdoors near Caffè Florian: a thoroughly romantic, magical experience.
- **Timing:** For the basilica, the Doges' Palace and the museums allow at least a half day. The early hours of the morning and evening in spring and autumn, are preferable to peak Carnevale and midday summer crowds.
- **Kids:** The view from the campanile across the rooftops and the lagoon, or boarding a gondola from in front of the Doges Palace, or a vaporetto ride.
- **Also See:** *La FENICE, RIALTO, SAN ZACCARIA.*

Basilica di San Marco on Piazza San Marco

B. Gardel/ hemis.fr

113

The Moors of Venice

Although the two bronze moors have been striking the clock tower bell for half a millennium they have still only put a slight dent in it. An ancient superstition has it that stroking their exposed nether regions confers sexual potency. It is said that in the 19C a workman was knocked clean off the tower by one of the Moors hammers – whether he had "provoked" the Moors by touching them is not recorded!

German king Frederick Barbarossa (1177).

The great Florentine sculptor and architect Jacopo Sansovino (1486–1570) redesigned the piazza, linking it to the piazzetta. He is also responsible for the **Library**. Towards the close of the 16C, attention was turned to the redevelopment of the south side of the piazza and old buildings were removed to make way for the **Procuratie Nuove**.

The present trachyte paving was designed by Andrea Tirali (c.1657–1737), who also resurfaced the area known as the **Piazzetta dei Leoncini**, named after the two lions by Giovanni Bonazza (1654–1736). Tirali then conceived the idea of accenting lines of perspective in the piazza by inlaying four "fasciae" in Carrara marble in concentric geometrical formation. Two such bands converge on the Basilica; the other two running oblique to the first pair are aligned with the columns of St Mark and St Theodore. At their speculative point of intersection stands the square base of the campanile (this is best appreciated from above). It remained little changed until the spectacular collapse of the campanile

The only *piazza* in Venice

St Mark's Square is the only square in all Venice to bear the more distinguished title of *piazza*. Every other Venetian square is a mere *campo* or a smaller *campiello*!

on 14 July 1902. Miraculously, the only damage incurred was to Sansovino's Loggetta and to a small part of the Biblioteca Marciana. By 1911, the new campanile, which is an exact reproduction of the old one had restored the square's traditional appearance.

SAINT MARK'S SQUARE★★★

La Serenissima's iconic square is most dramatic when approached from the lagoon. Disembark from the vaporetto on the riva at San Zaccaria or San Marco Vallaresso, so that you can gradually discover this miracle of architecture, colours and light. Two columns mark the entrance to the square, the stone lace of the Doge's Palace, the tall majestic bell tower and, of course, the fabulous St Mark's Basilica.

Piazzetta San Marco

This extension of St Mark's Square, between the Doges' Palace and the Biblioteca Nazionale Marciana, overlooks the sea through a magnificent portal framed by the two **Colonne di Marco e Todaro**. These two column shafts used as pedestals for St Mark and St Theodore were brought back from the East in 1172, although their specific provenance remains uncertain. The second is a copy, the original being in the courtyard in the Doges' Palace. The lion, which the Venetians identify with their Evangelist-Saint, could be a chimera.

Biblioteca – *see p131.

Piazza San Marco

The vast trapezoidal space (176m/577ft in length, 82m/269ft maximum width) is harmoniously framed by the porticos of the Procuratie, originally intended to house the procurators of San Marco: to the north, the Procuratie Vecchie faces the Procuratie Nuove. On the west side, the **Napoleonic Wing** (Ala Napoleonica, or Nuovissima), which links them, was built in a neoclassical style in the early 19C by order of Napoleon on the site of the San Geminiano church, which had been rebuilt by Sansovino in the 16C. The only traces that remain of this building's past existence are the famous plan

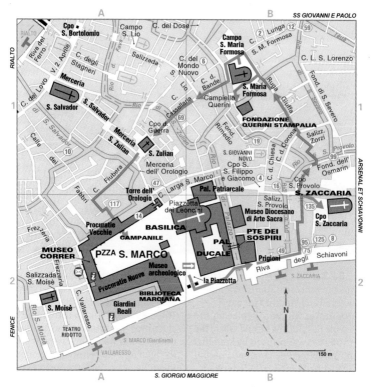

SAN MARCO

Famous Bars

In the arcaded portico of the Procuratie Vecchie is the **Caffè Quadri** (**8**, **FX** Y), which was founded by Giorgio Quadri in 1775 to serve Turkish coffee.

Opposite, on the other side of the piazza, is the older **Caffè Florian** (**8** **FX** Z), also named after its first proprietor, Floriano Francesconi, which was opened in 1720. Its most renowned previous habitués have included the playwright **Carlo Goldoni** (1707–93) and the neo-Classical sculptor **Antonio Canova** (1757–1822).

West of the Procuratie Nuove, on Calle Vallaresso, sits famed **Harry's Bar**, haunt of the glitterati and most famously patronised by Ernest Hemingway.

Beware that the price of a drink in all of these places is extremely high. However think of it more as an entrance ticket to a theatrical entertainment rather than the price of a mere refreshment!

Piazza San Marco

© Alija/istockphoto.com

by **De' Barbari** *(see Museo Correr p129)* and the representations by Antonio Visentini and Vincenzo Coronelli.

Procuratie Nuove – Replacing the Orseolo hospice, the second seat of the Procurators was planned by Scamozzi and completed by Longhena during the first half of the 17C. Under Napoleon, the Procuratie Nuove became the **Palazzo Reale**. *Under the arches of the Napoleonic Wing* is the entrance to the **Museo Correr** (♿*see p129*).

Procuratie Vecchie – The original residence of the Procurators in the 12C, these ancient loggias were initially Veneto-Byzantine in style before being rebuilt up to the first floor probably by Scarpagnino or possibly by **Mauro Codussi**. Still incomplete, they were damaged by fire in 1512, after which first Bartolomeo Bon (active c.1463–1529) then Guglielmo Grigi (active c.1515–30) added their mark, before Sansovino (1486–1570) completed work in 1532.

Torre dell'Orologio – ⏱*Visit by guided tours only ages 6 and older (book in advance);in English, Mon–Wed 10, 11am and Thu–Sun 2, 3pm. ⊶€12 Museums of St Mark's Square ticket. (♿Correr Museum). ✆848 082 000 or (+39) 041 427 30 892 (from abroad), or book online at torreorologio.visitmuve. it.* Designed by Codussi, the clock tower was erected between 1496 and 1499,

and constitutes the main entrance to the **Mercerie**, Venice's principal shopping street (♿*see RIALTO*).

The building's striking astronomical clock probably attracts less attention than the two Moors (1497) who sound the hour on a big bell at the top of the tower. Below it stands the lion passant of St Mark, set against a starry background. Below this tier comes a Virgin and Child before whom, on Ascension Day, appear mechanical figurines of the Three Wise Men and an angel. To the left, the Roman numerals tell the hour while the minutes are marked out at intervals of five to the right.

A tour of the Renaissance Tower enables visitors to get a close view of the clock mechanism, restored 2012–2014 with the assistance of Piaget (♿cover your ears if you are there on the hour!); it ends on terraces which afford a magnificent view of St. Mark's Square and the lagoon.

Piazzetta dei Leoncini

On the left of the basilica's facade.
This small area tucked between the Basilica, the Palazzo Patriarcale and the side of the former Church of San Basso was designed by Longhena. Its name is derived from the red marble lions from Verona, sculpted by Giovanni Bonazza (1722).

BASILICA DI SAN MARCO★★★ (SAINT MARK'S BASILICA)

"Peace unto you, Mark, my Evangelist. Here rests your body," the angel said to St Mark near the Rialto, as the Evangelist was journeying from Aquileia to Rome. Almost another 800 years were to elapse before the legendary prophecy was fulfilled: the symbol of St Mark has been synonymous with the Venetian flag ever since.

According to legend – In Egypt, around the year 800, two merchants set out for Alexandria with the intention of stealing the saint's body as it was felt that the relics would bestow upon Venice the prestige needed to "compete" with Rome or, at least, would affirm its politico-religious independence from the capital. The body was taken in a chest aboard a Venetian vessel. On arrival in Venice, the precious relic was placed in the chapel of a castle belonging to Doge Giustiniano Partecipazio, and subsequently consecrated in 832 as the first church dedicated to St Mark.

History of the church – As a result of the arrival of the relics of San Marco, the first patron saint of Venice, San Teodoro (*Todaro* in dialect), was demoted, if not forgotten.

After the fire of 976, which seriously damaged the church, St. Mark's body was lost. But, on the occasion of the consecration of the third church to be erected on this site (25 June 1094), a part of a pilaster in the right transept crumbled to reveal a human arm.

The sacred relic was removed to the crypt and later buried below the high altar.

The 11C basilica is modelled upon the Church of the Holy Apostles in Constantinople. It came to be the pride of the Venetians: **Doge Domenico Selvo** (1071–84) would ask merchants travelling to the East to bring back marble and other stone pieces (alabaster, jasper, porphyry, serpentine) for its embellishment. Indeed this was how the mosaics in the domes and the vaults came about.

Exterior

Silhouetted against the sky are the Basilica's five 13C Byzantine domes which culminate in a cross over the lantern. The lateral façades face onto Piazzetta dei Leoncini and Piazzetta San Marco.

West front – It is divided by a terrace with a balustrade that continues around the sides. The two parts display the same structure of five arches, which open in portals on the lower register. Note, in particular, the mosaics of the first arch (from the left), the only original ones remaining (1260–70): it depicts the deposition of the relics of St Mark in the church. You will also notice the third arch, where the Months, the signs of the Zodiac, the Virtues and the Beatitudes are represented, but also, more surprisingly, traditional Venetian trades: the man with crutches on the left shows the basilica's architect ruing the imperfection of its realization. ☺ **Good to know** – The best time to closely examine the mosaics of the lower exterior is when the basilica is closed to the public.

North facade – Walk down the left flank, overlooking Piazzetta dei Leoncini, to admire the Porta dei Fiori (4th arch, on the corner) with its Romanesque relief of *The Nativity*.

South facade – The south side abuts the Doges' Palace on the piazzetta. The first arch is framed by two columns surmounted with Romanesque griffins; the second arch contains the door to the Baptistry, framed with the **Acrean pillars** (1). Syrian in origin, two of the 6C columns have white marble shafts; the one nearest the piazzetta is of porphyry. This porphyry column is also known as the **pietra del bando**, the proclamation stone from where laws would be announced. In 1902, when the campanile collapsed, this pedestal was damaged while protecting the corner of the Basilica. On the corner nearest the Palace stand the famous 4C **Tetrarchs★** (2) or Moors sometimes upheld to allude to the Emperors Diocletian, Maximilian, Valerian and Constantine. They are otherwise said to be Saracens who, according to legend, were turned to stone when trying to steal the treasure of St Mark.

Atrium

🕐 Open Mon–Sat 9.30am–5pm (Oct–Easter Pala d'Oro and Treasury 9.45am–4pm); Sun and hols 2–5pm (Easter–Nov 5pm). 🕐 No tours hols. 👓 Basilica free. Pala d'Oro €2,50. Treasury €3. ✎ Guided tours (1.30hr) of the mosaics, Apr–Oct everyday 11.30am (ww.venetoinside.com). 👥 Clothes must be appropriate for a place of worship; no large bags (leave these in the Ateneo San Basso (Piazzetta dei Leoncini); no photography or video cameras. ✆ 041 27 08 311. www.basilicasanmarco.it.

Enter the basilica through the large atrium that would have been reserved for the unbaptised and new converts. Decked with mosaics that relate stories from the Old Testament, these herald others inside the church that illustrate incidents from the New Testament.

At the end of the Fourth Crusade (1201–04), Venice entered a phase of self-esteem on the wave of victory after the conquest of Constantinople. Romanesque and early Christian iconography in these early mosaics are borrowed from 5C–6C illuminated manuscripts that appear to have reached Venice with the Fourth Crusade.

▶ Start with the right dome, and follow towards the left:

The Creation according to Genesis (3)

These are the oldest mosaics in the atrium: in three concentric circles, in an anticlockwise direction, they tell the story of Genesis, beginning with the dove, the smallest mosaic, to the east. In synthesis with the tradition of the Eastern Church, based upon the Gospel of St John (The word was God…), the figure of the Creator is that of Christ, beardless, to signify the period before the Incarnation. Each stage of the Creation is attended by the angels which gradually increase in numbers as the days go by.

Note, on the day of the creation of the animals, the lions before God that symbolise Venice's atmosphere of pride and self-congratulation; on the day on which the Creator blesses the seventh angel – the day of rest and the day that Adam and Eve were chased from the Garden of Paradise – how they are depicted dressed in clothes. On the eighth day, Christ is born, heralding the beginning of a new Creation.

The Arch of Noah (4) depicts the story of Noah and the Flood: notice the ark's little window during the deluge. Continuing with the iconographic theme initiated in the entrance, the mosaics of the Arch of Paradise (5), designed in part by Tintoretto (1518–94) and Aliense (1556–1629), exalt the mission of the Church as the Salvation of Man by means of the Cross, Paradise and Hell; represented as symbols that break with the narrative of the Old Testament stories illustrated previously. Before passing through the doorway, it is worth looking up at the vault, where St Mark in Ecstasy is based on a cartoon by **Titian** (1490–1576).

In the niches on either side of the doorway stand the Madonna, Apostles and Evangelists; the ornamentation is Byzantine.

The story of Noah continues in the next arch with a particularly beautiful depiction of the Tower of Babel (6), marking a prelude to the division of the human race.

Story of Abraham (7)

The mosaics in the second dome comprise one cycle, dedicated to the life of Abraham. Between the various scenes are lunettes which illustrate God's promises to Abraham. In the next arch, Abraham is depicted with the confirmation in writing, as the prefiguration of Christ.

Story of Joseph (8)

The last dome on the left and the next two in the left arm illustrate the story of Joseph. In order to portray a person who is dreaming – in this case the Pharaoh – the mosaic artists resorted to a sort of bubble that unfurls. The second and third dome of this series postdate the first by about 20 years, which explains why the images and landscapes appear richer and more vibrant.

Story of Moses (9)

In the last dome of the atrium, this part of the biblical cycle concludes with the life of Moses.

Above the door, the Madonna presents her Son, flanked by St John and St Mark. This concludes the Old Testament cycle and serves as a link to the New Testament by encouraging the visitor to carry on "reading" inside the Basilica.

Basilica

The tour proceeds in a single direction, entrance to the treasury and the Pala d'Oro (fee) being optional.
We recommend that you first visit the building. After you return to the atrium, turn left (before you exit onto the square!) to reach the gallery and the Museo di San Marco.

It is difficult to say what is most striking about St Mark's: is it the brightness of this unique mosaic "tapestry", on which Byzantine tile setters began working in 1071? Is it the oriental atmosphere? Or even the floor (12C), with its depictions of animals and geometric pat-

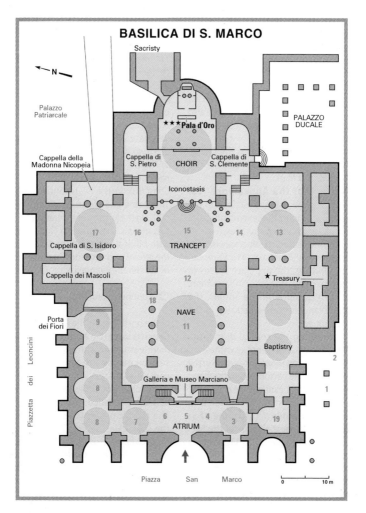

BASILICA DI S. MARCO

Sacristy

← N

Palazzo Patriarcale

★★★ **Pala d'Oro**

PALAZZO DUCALE

Cappella della Madonna Nicopeia

Cappella di S. Pietro — **CHOIR** — Cappella di S. Clemente

Iconostasis

17 16 **15** 14 13

Cappella di S. Isidoro

TRANCEPT

Cappella dei Mascoli

12

★ Treasury

18

Porta dei Fiori

9

NAVE

11

Baptistry

8

8

10

Galleria e Museo Marciano

8 7 6 **5** 4 3 19 2

ATRIUM

1

Piazzetta   dei   Leoncini

Piazza   San   Marco

0   10 m

terns, whose undulations, caused by the marble character of the site, add to the feeling that you are at the heart of a mysterious and sacred past? Built on a Greek cross plan, the basilica has a raised chancel that is separated from the central nave by an iconostasis.

Mosaics★★★

Visitors are advised to view the mosaics inside St Mark's when the basilica is illuminated; no visits during Mass.

As a general orientation, the lower part of the walls depict the saints, the middle section is reserved for the Apostles and the domes are dedicated to the Creator. The key to each story is held in the dome of the apse from where the story unfolds chronologically. Christ as Pantocrator towers over the four patrons of Venice: St Nicholas, St Peter, St Mark and St Ermagora, with the area above the atrium given over to the Last Judgement. These last mosaics are also the most recent, dating as they do from the 16C.

The entrance door depicts the *Deesis*, the Saviour in benediction between the Virgin and St Mark.

The **Arch of the Apocalypse** (10) illustrates the visions described in the Gospel of St John; the seven candelabra symbolise the seven churches.

The dome nearest the doorway is dedicated to the *Pentecost* (11). Between the windows, the populace listens to the preaching of St Peter in Jerusalem; to correspond with the angels, the Four Evangelists are illustrated in the pendentives.

Approaching the central dome, the **West Arch** (12) presents a synthesis of the *Passion* and *Death of Christ*. Worthy of note are the cartouches in the hand of the Judeans, bearing Pilate and Christ. In the right transept, illuminated by a Gothic rose window, the **Dome of St Leonard** (13) or the Saints of the Sacrament, is decorated with 13C mosaics representing St Nicholas, St Clement, St Blaise and St Leonard. The **South Arch** (14) has Byzantine mosaics which depict the *Temptations of Christ* and *His Entry*

into Jerusalem, the *Last Supper* and the *Washing of the Feet.*

In the centre is the **Dome of the Ascension** (15). This encapsulates the most important moments in the story of the Salvation. Witnesses to the *Ascension* include the Apostles, the Madonna and, between the windows, the Virtues and some of the Beatitudes. Christ in benediction dominates the scene. Beneath the pendentives which depict the Four Evangelists are the Four Rivers of the Earth.

The **Presbytery Dome** is dedicated to the Season of Advent, dominated by Emmanuel in the company of Prophets, with the Virgin in the middle. The decoration of this dome dates back to the beginning of 1100. Symbols of the Evangelists adorn the pendentives.

The mosaics on the **North Arch** (16) designed by Tintoretto show *St Michael with Sword Drawn* with the *Last Supper* on the left and the *Marriage at Cana* on the right. In the centre, the *Healing of the Leper* is taken from a cartoon by Veronese (1528–88), the *Healing of the Bleeding Woman* and the *Resurrection of Naim's Widow's Son* are based on cartoons by Salviati (1520/25–75). The *Christ in Glory* is a 19C reconstruction.

The **Dome of St John the Evangelist** (17) is in the left arm of the transept. The 13C mosaics reproduce a Greek cross with biblical verses on the *Sermon on the Mount* and episodes from the Life of St John the Evangelist.

Continue along the left aisle.

In the north aisle is the **Capital of the Crucifixion** (18), a white and black marble structure with a pyramidal roof surmounted by an agate. The crucifix contained therein, coming from Constantinople, would have been the cause of much bloodshed.

The mosaic panels (c.1230) opposite the side aisles depict *Christ Blessing the Prophets* – Hosea, Joel, Micah and Jeremiah (*in the left aisle*) and Ezekiel, Solomon, the Madonna in prayer, David and Isaiah (*in the right aisle*).

Pala d'Oro★★★

The **Golden Altarpiece** is preceded by a ciborium on **columns of alabaster★★** inscribed with reliefs inspired by the Gospels and the Apocrypha. The exact date and provenance of these reliefs remain uncertain, but are usually classified as 5C–6C Greek (from Ravenna), Syrian, Egyptian or Coptic. Contained within the high altar rest the remains of St Mark and, beyond, towers the great altarpiece.

Commissioned and made in Constantinople in the 10C, the Golden Altarpiece is a masterpiece of the goldsmith's craft. Gleaming with precious stones set among enamelled panels, it continued to be embellished with new and valuable sections until the 14C.

The top section is dominated by the figure of the Archangel Michael in the centre, framed between scenes (starting from the left) of the *Entry into Jerusalem*, the *Resurrection*, the *Crucifixion*, the *Ascension*, the *Pentecost* and the *Death of the Virgin*. The focal point of the lower section is Christ Pantocrator (the Ruler of the Universe) flanked by the figures of the Evangelists. Below, the Virgin appears between the Empress Irene and the Emperor Giovanni Commeno, Prophets, Apostles and Angels. On either side, the iconographic cycle continues with episodes from the lives of Christ and St Mark.

In the apse, the doors to the tabernacle and to the sacristy are by Sansovino.

Chapels

Grouped around the presbytery it is worth stopping to look at the **iconostasis** (openwork screen) in polychrome marble. Eight columns support an architrave bearing figures of the **Apostles**, the **Madonna** and **John the Baptist** by Dalle Masegne (14C–15C). This great line is broken in the middle by a bronze and silver **Crucifix**. At either end, the iconostasis terminates with a pulpit, each reconstructed in the 14C. The **Double Pulpit** on the left comprises two sections from which lessons are read from the Gospels (*upper tier*) and the Epistles (*lower tier*). To honour

the Word of God, it is crowned with a fine golden cupola which is decidedly oriental in style. The pulpit on the right, the **Pulpit of the Reliquary**, was where the relics would be displayed and where the newly elected doge would make his first appearance.

Both chapels dedicated to **St Clement** (*right apse*) and **St Peter** (*left apse*) are screened off by their own iconostasis; the one for St Clement, complete with statues, is by Dalle Masegne. Outside each chapel, the wall is covered with mosaics (12C) illustrating episodes from the lives of St Mark and St Peter respectively; inside the domed vault of each are representations of the saints to whom each chapel is dedicated (St Peter is 13C).

The window on the right wall of the Chapel of St Clement enabled the doge to follow functions and services being held in church without leaving the comfortable confines of his palace apartments.

In the **Chapel of the Madonna Nicopeia** is a particularly venerated image of the Madonna and Child, called *Nicopeia* (meaning the Bringer of Victory or Leader), because she served as the standard of the Byzantine army. Coming from Constantinople, the figure may have been brought to Venice as booty from the Fourth Crusade.

The **Chapel of St Isidore** is off the transept, whose end wall bears *Mary's Genealogical Tree*, which dates back to the end of the 12C.

The next chapel, the **Mascoli Chapel**, is dedicated to the members of the confraternity of male worshippers. The mosaics are the work of Giambono (active 1420–62), Andrea del Castagno (c.1421–57), Jacopo Bellini (c.1396–c.1470) and **Andrea Mantegna** (1431–1506).

Treasury★

This priceless collection of religious objects, reliquaries and ornaments, which came into Venice's possession after the conquest of Constantinople in 1204, includes one particularly notable exhibit, the *Artophoron*, an 11C container for the Bread of the Eucharist, in the shape of a church, crowned with oriental-style domes.

Baptistery

⏱ *Open for prayer only.*
The baptistery is divided into three interconnecting areas; 14C mosaics recount the life of John the Baptist and the Infant Jesus. The most famous panel shows *Salome Dancing before Herod*. The baptismal font is by Sansovino (1486–1570), who is buried here, before the altar. The mosaics in the **Cappella Zen** (19), the funeral chapel of Cardinal Zen who died in 1501, date from the 13C.

Museo di San Marco

Access to the atrium (on the right) is via a steep staircase. ⏱ *Open year-round daily 9.45am–4.45pm.* €5. ℘041 27 08 311. www.museosanmarco.it.
Access to the Marciano Museum is via the Gallery, from where there is a marvellous view of the mosaics and an opportunity to look out over the piazza from the balcony. The museum houses tapestries, mosaics and some interesting documents relating to the history of the Basilica. The greatest draw for visitors must be the **gilded bronze horses★★**. They arrived in Venice as part of the booty from the Fourth Crusade but undoubtedly date back to a much earlier period, although opinion on their origin is divided as to whether they are 4C–3C BC Greek or 4C Roman works.
Given pride of place on the balcony, these wonderful equestrian statues were taken to Paris by Napoleon after his crushing Italian campaign, but returned in 1815. In 1974 they were removed from their original position for restoration and replaced with copies.

IL CAMPANILE★★

♿⏱*Open mid-Jul–mid-Sept, 8.30am–9.30pm; April/Easter–Jun and mid-Sept–Oct, 9am–7pm; rest of the year 9.30am–3.45pm.* €8. ℘041 27 08 311. www.basilicasanmarco.it.
Although the present bell-tower was erected at the beginning of the 20C (🕮 *see A Bit of History*), it was rebuilt according to its predecessor's early-16C

designs by Bartolomeo Bon in brick. The tower stands 96m/315ft high, culminating in a golden angel weather-vane that turns in the wind.
The campanile is articulated as if by a gigantic order of pilasters, up to an arched white marble section, pierced by a four-light loggia where the bells hang. Above a balustraded section, the four sides rise cleanly to a pyramid.
At the top, from where **Galileo Galilei** once extended his telescope (1609), a magnificent **view★★** stretches from the Giudecca Canal to the Grand Canal across roofs and chimneytops to the islands in the lagoon.

Loggetta Sansoviniana

At the base of the tower, and facing St Mark's, the richly decorated Sansovino Loggetta comprises three arches supported on columns reminiscent of a triumphal arch; columns also frame the niches that accommodate the figures of Minerva, Apollo, Mercury and Peace. The reliefs above depict (*from left to right*), the Island of Candia, Venice as an allegory of Justice, and the island of Cyprus. The terrace at the front is enclosed by a balustrade, broken in the middle by a bronze gate designed by Antonio Gai (1686–1769).
The present *loggetta* was first built during the early part of the 16C by **Jacopo Tatti Sansovino** and rebuilt after the collapse of the campanile.
😊 On the right side of the basilica, near the Porta della Carta, stand the remains of a tower decorated with low-relief sculptures; as they are not directly at eye level, they tend to elude the attention of visitors. However, if you bend down a little, you will notice one in particular that is located under the Tetrarchs, just on the right. It represents two putti escaping from the jaws of two dragons. They are pictured framing a 13C inscription, believed to be one of the very first texts written in Venetian dialect.

Piazzetta San Marco and Palazzo Ducale from the lagoon

© Silvio Verrecchia / iStockphoto

PALAZZO DUCALE★★★ (Doges' Palace)

&. ⊙ *Open daily 8.30am–7pm (5.30pm Nov–Easter); last admission 1hr before closing.* ⊙ *Closed 1 Jan and 25 Dec.* ⊛€19. *Museo Correr, Museo Archeologico Nazionale, Monumental Rooms of Biblioteca Marciana or Museum Pass (& see p30).*

⌁ *Itinerari Segreti (Secret itinerary) tickets book online (€20). For Musei al Chiaro di Luna see www.visitmuve.it/moonlight.* ☏ *041 27 15 911. palazzoducale.visitmuve.it.*

The size, wealth of decoration and extreme attention to detail of every nook and cranny and every decorative element of this building express the soul and history of the city. The origins of this Byzantine, Gothic and Renaissance palace go back almost as far as those of Venice itself. In 810 **Doge Agnello Partecipazio** decided that the seat of his public offices should be located on the site of the present Doges' Palace. At the time, the buildings, which included the Church of St Mark, were more of a citadel than a government office. The need for a fortified residence gradually gave way towards one with an institutional role, with loggias and porticoes on the outside, and a host of offices inside where various affairs of State could be conducted by the doge's staff.

Exterior

The harmony of the structural whole is striking: the "hollow" spaces of the portico and the loggia contrast with blocks of "solid" masonry in the upper section of the building. The effect is mitigated, however, by the rose-coloured tint of the upper floor and the darkness of the multi-arched lower floors.

The narrative function of the mosaics inside the basilica is transposed here onto the sculptural iconography that adorns the capitals, the corners of the *palazzo* and its pillars. Decorating the palace are allegorical figures representing the Vices and Virtues, the Ages of Man and Signs of the Zodiac, all charged with moral example.

Façade on the Piazzetta

The façade onto the piazzetta rises from an arcade of 18 pointed arches along the ground floor, supported on baseless columns. The first-floor loggia also runs continuously along the façade, the horizontal emphasis accentuated by the balustrade and sequence of 34 roundels between the ogive, cusped arches, punctured with quatrefoil cutouts. From between the two red marble columns, public announcements of capital sentences were made, later to be carried out between the columns of St Mark and St Theodore in the square below.

The two upper storeys, which together are as tall as the two lower floors, seem lost in solid wall. From a distance, the building appears a distinctively soft shade of pinky-rose, with surface relief at closer proximity, provided by the interplay of terra-cotta and white bricks disposed in diamond patterns. Its massiveness is further offset by the delicate line of gables along the top.

On the first floor, the central balcony overlooking the piazzetta is 16C (artists unknown). The portrait above it is of **Doge Andrea Gritti** (1523–38) and at each corner is a sculptural group: that projecting into the square shows the *Judgement of Solomon,* an allegory of Wisdom, thought to be by Bartolomeo Bon (active 1441–64), beyond which stands the Porta della Carta.

Porta della Carta★★ – The **"Paper Doorway"** is the entrance to the palace per se. Flamboyant Gothic in style, it was constructed by Giovanni and Bartolomeo Bon between 1438 and 1442. Explanations for the name have been attributed to the many scribes who used the entrance, which also served the archives (*cartarum*). The superimposed niches are occupied by the four Cardinal Virtues sculpted by Antonio Bregno (c.1418–c.1503). Above the doorway, kneeling before the winged lion, is the Doge Francesco Foscari, who was in power when the portal was constructed. Above the window, in the roundel, is St Mark, overlooked by Justice on the pinnacle.

Facade overlooking Il Molo

To reach the canal quayside from the Piazzetta San Marco, walk round the full length of both sides of the palace.

The façade overlooking the Basin stretches between the corner sculpture groups of (*left*) *Adam, Eve and the Serpent* (late 14C) – an allegory of Sin – surmounted by the figures of Tobias and the Angel Raphael (late 14C) and *The Drunkenness of Noah* (14C–15C), a symbol of the virtue of compassion (*near the Paglia Bridge*).

The second capital from the left, known as the Capital of the Sages (*dei Sapienti*), is inscribed with the date 1344, the year in which this wing was constructed. The central balcony on the second floor was inserted in the early 15C, designed by Dalle Masegne.

The last two, more decorative, windows appear out of alignment with the others because of the internal room arrangement.

To the right, the **Ponte della Paglia** (literally translated as the Bridge of Straw) precedes that second and much more famous bridge across the canal.

Ponte dei Sospiri★★

Universally known, the Bridge of Sighs owes its name to Romantic literary notions: overwhelmed by the enchanting view from the windows of this bridge, it was across here that prisoners would be led to the courtroom to learn of their fate.

The bridge, constructed in Istrian stone, links the palace with the Prigioni Nuove (New Prisons). It was built during the dogeship of **Marino Grimani** (1595–1605) and bears his coat of arms. Inside, the bridge is divided into two passages through which visitors pass on their tour of the Doges' Palace. Given the number of rooms and the length of the tour, it is easy to lose one's bearings and to cross the bridge without realising it, so beware!

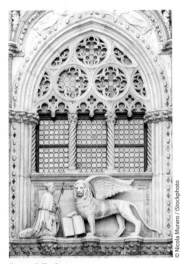

Porta della Carta

© Nicola Muraro / iStockphoto

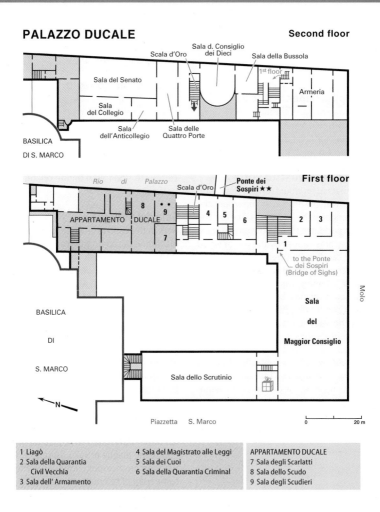

PALAZZO DUCALE — Second floor

- Sala d. Consiglio dei Dieci
- Scala d'Oro
- Sala della Bussola
- 1st floor
- Armeria
- Sala del Senato
- Sala del Collegio
- Sala dell'Anticollegio
- Sala delle Quattro Porte

BASILICA DI S. MARCO

First floor

- Rio di Palazzo
- Scala d'Oro
- **Ponte dei Sospiri ★★**
- APPARTAMENTO DUCALE
- 8
- 9
- 4
- 5
- 6
- 2
- 3
- 7
- 1
- to the Ponte dei Sospiri (Bridge of Sighs)
- BASILICA DI S. MARCO
- Molo
- **Sala del Maggior Consiglio**
- **N**
- Sala dello Scrutinio
- Piazzetta S. Marco
- 0   20 m

1 Liagò	4 Sala del Magistrato alle Leggi	APPARTAMENTO DUCALE
2 Sala della Quarantia Civil Vecchia	5 Sala dei Cuoi	7 Sala degli Scarlatti
3 Sala dell' Armamento	6 Sala della Quarantia Criminal	8 Sala dello Scudo
		9 Sala degli Scudieri

DOGE'S PALACE INTERIOR

The entrance to the Palazzo is to the right of the Porta della Carta (through which visitors pass on their way out). The courtyard is graced with a fine mid-16C well-head, the mid-15C **Porticato Foscari** leading through to the **Foscari Arch**, and the **Scala dei Giganti** directly opposite. The Giants' Staircase, constructed at the end of the 15C, was designed by Antonio Rizzo (c.1440–99) and is dominated by two magnificent statues of Mars and Neptune (the gods of War and Sea) by Sansovino (1486–1570). It was at the top of these stairs that the doges used to be crowned. The well-heads in the courtyard date to the mid-16C; the east end façade, designed by Rizzo, is early Renaissance in style.

From the portico, take the **Scala d'Oro** or Golden Staircase up to the second floor. Sansovino initiated work on the staircase during the reign of **Doge Andrea Gritti** (1523–38), although work was not to be completed by Scarpagnino (recorded in Venice 1505–49) until after the appointment of Lorenzo Priuli (1556–59): note the coats of arms of the two doges on the large arch. Its Baroque-sounding name comes from reference to the rich stucco decoration in white and gold around Giovan Battista Franco's (1498–1561) frescoes depicting *The Glorification of the Defence of Cyprus and*

125

Crete and *The Virtues Necessary for Good Government*. The portrait in the atrium of Doge Gerolamo Priuli was painted by Tintoretto.

L'Appartamento Ducale

Follow the signs through to the Ducal Appartment, where a *Pietà* by Giovanni Bellini and the famous *Lion* by Vittore Carpaccio are displayed.

Sala delle Quattro Porte

Ambassadors would wait for their audience with the doge in this first room, the Chamber of the Four Doors. The decoration postdates 1574, following one of the many fires caused by the use of wood and candles. Propped up on the easel is *Venice Receiving the Homage of Neptune*, a famous canvas by Tiepolo. The frescoed ceiling is by Tintoretto and the four doorways by Palladio. The paintings on the walls depict allegorical scenes or historical subjects.

Among these, *Doge Antonio Grimani in Adoration before the Faith and St Mark in Glory* was started by Titian and finished by his nephew. The painting, commemorating a visit made by Henry III, King of France, in 1574, depicts the Triumphal Arch designed by Palladio that would

---

Law and Order Venetian Style

After Florence, Venice was the second state in the world to abolish torture and the first to abolish slavery. However, treatment of prisoners was guided more by diplomatic and political acumen than piety. The "law of the repentent" *ante litteram* applied to informers, whereby anyone with a relation accused of a minor crime could ensure their release from prison if they revealed valuable information that led to the capture and conviction of an assassin. Murder, religious theft, crimes against children, criminal offences against the State, return from exile or causing pollution, however, resulted in capital punishment.

---

have been made of papier mâché, a material commonly used to create temporary stage sets for special occasions.

Sala dell'Anticollegio

An antechamber for diplomatic delegations, the room houses the *Return of Jacob with Family* by Jacopo Bassano (c.1517–92) and the *Rape of Europa* by Veronese (*facing the windows*). The paintings on either side of the doors are by Tintoretto. The fresco on the ceiling is by Veronese.

Sala del Collegio

Here in the College Chamber the doge, his throne raised on the wooden platform, presided over meetings. The "Full College" dealt with legal matters that were subsequently presented to the Senate, and political relationships between Venice and foreign courts on diplomatic missions. The stalls date to 1575. The paintings decorating the gilded wooden ceiling exalt the city; above the throne, the great panel depicting Doge Sebastiano Venier is also by Veronese. The paintings on the wall with the clock set in black Belgian marble are by Tintoretto: left of the clock, *Alvise Mocenigo Thanking the Redeemer* commemorates the votive plea for an end to the plague of 1576. Tintoretto's painting on the door continues in the same spirit of celebration.

Sala del Senato

Here in the Senate Chamber, or "Pregadi Chamber," members of the Senate were asked (*pregati*) to submit written request to participate in the meetings. The assembly presided here over all matters of State. The decor, refurbished after the fire of 1574, is peopled with doges and patron saints, in audience before the Redeemer or the Virgin. In the central panel of the ceiling Tintoretto depicted *The Triumph of Venice*. Behind the throne hangs a work of Palma il Giovane. In the painter's *Allegory of Victory over the League of Cambrai*, Venice appears as a young warrior on the attack, preceded by the lion. The pulpit was used by those taking part in the debates.

Sala del Maggior Consiglio

© Palazzo Ducale / Fondazione Musei Civici di Venezia

Sala del Consiglio dei Dieci

The powerful and notorious council, whose origins go back as far as 1310, used to meet in this Chamber of the Council of Ten. On the ceiling preside allegories of good government and the power of the Republic: most notable is Veronese's *Juno Offering the Doge's Corno*; the central painting of Jove is a copy after Veronese: the original, "stolen" by Napoleon, is now in the Louvre in Paris.

On the walls two important historical events are depicted: *The Peace of Bologna between Pope Clement VII and Emperor Charles V* by Marco Vecellio (1545–1611), a cousin of Titian (*left*), and *Pope Alexander III Blesses Doge Sebastiano Ziani after the Battle of Salvore* by Francesco da Ponte, also known as Bassano (1549–92), and his brother Leandro (1557–1622) (*right*).

Sala della Bussola

The Ballot Chamber was also the waiting room for those who were to be interrogated by the heads (*capi*) of the Council of Ten. To the left of the ballot box is a painting by Marco Vecellio. Beside the exit door is the wooden hatch that allowed the secret denunciations to be removed from the **bocca di leone** or lion's mouth outside. Ceiling paintings are largely by followers of Veronese, although the central painting of St Mark is a copy; the original is in the Louvre.

Armeria

The various rooms making up the Armoury house objects such as trophies, relics of war, and the suit of armour of the infamous *condottiere* Gattamelata identified by the badge with a cat on the knee, and instruments of torture. The room dedicated to Francesco Morosini is marked with the sign CX, the Council of Ten's monogram.

Sala del Maggior Consiglio

The enormous Grand Council Chamber is perhaps the highlight of the tour. Here and in the nearby Sala dello Scrutinio, the new doge was elected. Except for the undamaged 14C Guariente fresco the *Coronation of the Virgin*, now in the Sala del Armamento, the paintings destroyed by the fire of 1577 were swiftly replaced with more magnificent decoration. The subject of the long wall overlooking the Basin is the Fourth Crusade. Other notable paintings are those by Carlo Saraceni and Jean Le Clerc, Palma il Giovane, Domenico Tintoretto, Andrea Micheli (also known as Vicentino) and Federico Zuccari. The vast painting behind the throne was executed by Tintoretto, his son and followers.

Below the ceiling are portraits of the 76 doges who governed Venice between 804 and 1554, almost all by Domenico Tintoretto. **Marino Falier** who, in the 14C, conspired against the State and was beheaded, is remembered rather unfa-

127

vourably. Portraits of the last 39 doges, spanning the years 1556–1797, are in the Scrutinio.

The trussed wooden ceiling is dominated by Veronese's *Apotheosis of Venice* (1582). Other paintings on the ceiling celebrate Venice's victory in battle.

Sala dello Scrutinio

Here the *scrutinio* (counting) of the votes took place. The series of portraits of the governors of Venice concludes with the last doge, **Ludovico Manin** (1789–97), who ceded to Napoleon, which marked the subjugation of the Serenissima.The decoration of this room celebrates grandiose events in Venice's history.

The ceiling comprises five large paintings, the most noteworthy being *The Naval Victory of the Venetians over the Pisans at Rodi* by Vicentino and *The Venetian Victory over the Genoese at Trapani* by Giovanni Bellini. The partition wall dividing this room from the **Sala della Quarantia Civil Nuova** bears Palma il Giovane's *Last Judgement*, which replaced Tintoretto's painting destroyed during the fire. Just before the prisons, the **Sala del Magistrato alle Leggi** preserves *The Mocking of Christ* by the Flemish master Quentin Metsys (1466–1530) and the only works by Hieronymus Bosch (c.1450–1516) in Italy.

Prigioni Nuove – Steps lead up to the Bridge of Sighs and beyond to the New Prisons on the other side of the canal. These prisons also served as the seat of the magistrature of the **Signori di Notte al Criminal**, a sort of vice squad. Note the graffiti inscribed on the stone walls.

Sala dei Censori

Lined with wooden seats, this chamber, known as the Censors' Chamber, accommodated a judiciary body. The paintings, mostly by Domenico Tintoretto, consist of formal portraits of magistrating censors.

Sala dell'Avogaria

The last room of the tour, the Avogaria Chamber, was the seat of another part of the former magistrature, whose members, the *avogadori*, consisted of lawyers appointed by the State. Their duty was to ensure that the law was obeyed. It is unusual for such portraits to have been presented in this way, a practice that hitherto was reserved for religious subjects. The tour concludes with the **Sala dello Scrigno** and the **Sala della Milizia da Mar**.

PALACE CORRIDORS (ITINERARI SEGRETI/ SECRET ITINERARY)

€20. 848 082 000 or palazzoducale.visitmuve.it. Guided morning tours (1.15hr) en anglais (9.55, 10.45 and 11.35am); following visits you can continue along the standard route for Palazzo Ducale.

The various magistrates that had seats in the palace operated in an environment that was anything but ostentatious. Many of the activities, most of which were secret, took place in very restricted surroundings just off the grand chambers. Linked by a maze of hidden stairs and passageways, these still exude an air of mystery.

The **Cancelleria segreta** (Secret Chancellery), which resembles a ship's deck, is ornamented with the chancellor's coats of arms. The impressive **Sala delle Torture** (Torture Room) betrays the more intolerant, if not more characteristic face of the Republic (*see p26*). The prison cells located in the Palace were referred to as the **Pozzi e Piombi** (Wells and Leads): the *pozzi* were the deep, damp dungeons for hardened criminals; the *piombi*, so-called because they were roofed in lead, were for those imprisoned for a couple of months. Life in the cells was not necessarily that severe: prisoners were allowed to bring some furniture and a little money with them. Punishment was intended to induce remorse by exerted psychological pressure rather than by inflicting physical suffering.

It was from the *piombi* that **Giacomo Casanova** (1725–98) made his daring escape, emerging onto the roof above the Grand Council Chamber. From here one can picture the view over Venice in former times when it was almost entirely built of wood.

After the fire of 1577, Antonio da Ponte was given only 16 months to complete the Palace's reconstruction. He drew upon the skills of the *arsenalotti* who were capable of assembling a ship in one day.

In the **Sala dei Tre Capi del Consiglio dei Dieci**, the magistrates (*capi*) who had been elected from the Council of Ten to preside over court cases would meet. Of particular interest on the ceiling are *Virtue Driving Away Vice* (*centre*) by Zelotti, and two paintings in the corner panels by Veronese.

In the **Sala dei Tre Inquisatori** (Inquisitors' Chamber) officials would pass judgement on crimes against the State. The ceiling features paintings by Tintoretto.

MUSEUMS

Museo Correr★★, Museo Archeologico and Biblioteca Marciana

Entry to the public Piazza San Marco, Ala Napoleonica, Scalone monumentale. ⊙*Open Mar–Oct 10am–7pm (ticket office closes at 6pm); Nov–Mar 10am–5pm (ticket office closes at 4pm).* ⊙*Closed 1 Jan and 25 Dec.* ⊚€19 (ticket valid for all the musems of the Piazza San Marco: Museo Correr★★, Museo Archeologico and Biblioteca Marciana)(◔ see p29). ☏848 082 000 or (+39) 041 427 30 892 (from abroad). www.museiciviciveneziani.it.

Museo Correr★★

This museum takes its name from **Teodoro Correr** (1750–1830), a Venetian gentleman who bequeathed his rich collection of artifacts relating to the history and art of the Serenissima to the city. The tour proceeds up the magnificent 19C staircase, through the neo-Classical **Sale Canoviane** (Canova Rooms) and on to the **History, Arts, Crafts** and **Games** Departments (*first floor*). Among its historical maps, the Museo Correr boasts one of the famous **De' Barbari** maps (c.1445–1515). Important paintings include the vivid,

Salone da Ballo, Museo Correr

typically Venetian works of the German artist, Joseph Heintz the Younger (c.1600–78), most notably *Bull Baiting in Campo San Polo*. Among the sculptures by **Antonio Canova** (1757–1822) are his *Orpheus and Eurydice* and the celebrated *Daedalus and Icarus*. Other works, by Francesco Hayez (1791–1882) betray Canova's influence.

Beyond the dining room, with its particularly neo-Classical decoration, objects testify to the nobility and rich symbolism of the city's history: exhibits include doges' *corni* (caps), staffs of command, and *manine* (modelled hands used, along with the ballot urn, for counting votes in the lengthy procedure in electing a doge).

More paintings include works by Vicentino, Vassillachi, and Longhi. The *Lion of St Mark's* attributed to Michele Giambono represents Venice in one of its most typical allegories.

The **Libreria dei Teatini**, complete with 17C furnishings, accommodates books from the Teatini Convent. The **Sale dei Costumi** (Costume Rooms) contain official 17C and 18C garments worn by senators and procurators.

The **Collezione Numismatica** (Numismatic Collection) comprises coinage minted by the Republic, including the famous *zecchino* and a painting by Tintoretto.

A whole room is dedicated to the **Bucintoro**, the doge's ship aboard which the ceremony of **The Marriage with the Sea** took place. Measuring 35m/115ft long and 7m/23ft wide and propelled by 168 rowers, the ship was so tall and threfore so unstable that it could sail safely only in the calmest conditions.

Exhibits relevant to the Arsenale include a map, engravings and banners.

The section "Venice and the Sea" is followed by one dedicated to war, which includes the weaponry and armour from the Corer and Morosini Armouries.

From here, ascend to the second floor, and on to the **Quadreria** (Paintings Section), which presents a synthesis of the Venetian School of painting up to the early 16C.

Among Veneto-Byzantine examples is perhaps the earliest Venetian painting on wood, the lid of a wooden chest.

The following rooms are dedicated to **Paolo Veneziano** (c.1290–1362) and **Lorenzo Veneziano** (1356–72) and **Jacobello dalle Masegne**. Among the other Gothic artists represented here is **Stefano Veneziano**. In Venice **International Gothic** arrived at the beginning of the 15C. Examples include the paintings of Michele Giambono (active 1420–62) and Jacobello del Fiore (c.1370–1439).

The suggestive *Pietàa*, marked by brittle form and metallic colour, is the work of **Cosmè Tura** (c.1430–1495), who came from Ferrara. *Portrait of a Young Man*, characterised by strong contrasting colours, is attributed to another 15C artist from Ferrara, Antonio da Crevalcore.

The next room is dedicated to **Bartolomeo Vivarini** from Murano. His works betray the strong influence of Mantegna. His use of gold-leaf background, however, is more archaic and Byzantine in style.

Particularly worthy of note from the 15C Flemish School is an *Adoration of the Magi* by **Brueghel the Younger** (1564–1638), a Holy scene set in a Northern landscape blanketed with snow. The

Two Venetian Ladies *(c.1495) by Vittore Carpaccio*

influence of Northern oil paintings on Italian art is suggested in a *Pietà*★★, the only work here by **Antonello da Messina** (c.1430–79), who visited Venice in 1475/6. The two other Flemish works in the room are by Hugo van der Goes and Dieric Bouts. One painting from the later 15C and 16C **Flemish School** is the *Temptations of St Anthony* by a follower of Hieronymus Bosch; its complex symbolism adds a disquieting, nightmarish dimension to the subject.

The **Bellinis** are gathered together in one room: they include the *Crucifixion* by **Jacopo** (1400–c.70), the *Portrait of Doge Giovanni Mocenigo* by Gentile (1429–1507) and four works by **Giovanni** (1430–1516).

Alvise Vivarini and Venetian painters from the late 15C forestall the works of **Vittore Carpaccio**, one of Venice's most acclaimed artists. His enigmatic *Two Venetian Ladies* are apparently animated by a private joke, their slightly dismissive expressions giving rise to various explanations. The *Gentleman in the Red Cap*★★ is presently attributed to a painter from Ferrara/Bologna, although in the past it was thought to have been executed by Lotto (c.1480–1556), Giovanni Bellini or Carpaccio.

The evolution of art through the **High Renaissance** continues with **Lorenzo**

Lotto (*Madonna with the Christ Child at her Breast*), before being interrupted by displays of works by 16C and 17C Greek *Madonneri* (painters depicting the Madonna in the traditional manner) and 15C and 16C majolica extending to the room beyond the Manin Library.

Museo Archeologico

The Archaeological Museum is housed in the **Procuratie Nuove**, two doors away from the Biblioteca Marciana. It holds Greek sculpture, Egyptian and Roman fragments and a collection of coins and medals.

Start in the loggia containing the Greek inscriptions and pass through the coins and medals section before reaching the most ancient Archaic pieces, such as the famous **Grimani** Greek statues (5C–4C BC); sculpture from the 5C–4C BC including the Classical and Hellenistic phases; small sculptures from the times of Alexander the Great to the 1C BC; Assyrian-Babylonian and Egyptian antiquities; Cypriot and Mycenaen vases; early Venetian ceramics and Etruscan *buccheri* (clay drinking vessels).

Biblioteca Nazionale Marciana★

As the first example of Classical architecture in Venice, this prestigious seat of Venetian culture is almost as glorious as its neighbour, the Doges' Palace. Over the Doric portico runs the loggia, its windows framed by Ionic columns, true to the Classical architectural canon of orders. **Sansovino** worked on the library from 1537. On his death, the project was completed by Scamozzi.

The Biblioteca's sculptural decoration draws on Classical mythology: the keystones of the arches are marked by leonine and mythological heads, and statues in various expressive poses overlook the piazzetta from the balustrade.

Inside, the Reading Room is located off the **Zecca** (Mint) courtyard.

With its two flights, the **staircase** is reminiscent of the Scala d'Oro (◔ *see Palazzo Ducale*). The vaulted ceiling and cupola stucco decoration are by **Alessandro Vittoria**, the frescoes are by **Battista Franco** (*first flight*) and Battista del Moro

(*second flight*). The thematic iconography is defined by a neo-Platonic concept of Man, who, influenced by cosmic forces (*first flight*) and fashioned by the Virtues (*second flight*) finally arrives at Universal Knowledge, symbolised by the book and the circle.

First floor – An important exhibit is the famous map of Venice by **Jacopo De' Barbari**, executed in 1500, the other version being in the Museo Correr. Nearby is the *Mappamondo* (1457–59) by Fra Mauro, the Camaldolite monk from San Michele in Isola. His planisphere is painted in colour and gold on parchment stuck down on wood.

Vestibule – Sansovino intended the Vestibule as a salon for Humanist lectures. Instead, it was turned into the Republic's Sculpture Museum when the Patriarch of Aquileia, Giovanni Grimani, donated his collection of sculpture and statuary to Venice; some pieces have overflowed into the Archaeological Museum (◔ *see below*).

On the ceiling, *Wisdom*, painted by Titian, has been inserted into a *trompe l'oeil* perspective by Cristoforo and Stefano Rosa, executed around 1559.

Salone Sansoviniano – At the heart of the original Library, the Sansovino Room houses the codices and manuscripts bequeathed to the Republic by **Cardinale Bessarione** (1403–72), the famous Greek Humanist. The grotesque ceiling decoration, the work of Battista Franco, is completed with 21 tondos illustrating mythological subjects, virtues and disciplines against a gold background. The artists responsible for this ultimate "manifestation of Mannerism in Venice" are Giovanni De Mio, author of the first trio (◔ *best viewed walking backwards away from the entrance);* Giuseppe Porta, known as Salviati (second trio); Battista Franco, (third trio); Giulio Licinio, whose third tondo, in poor condition, was replaced with one by Bernardo Strozzi depicting Sculpture; Giambattista Zelotti, whose third painting was also replaced, this time by a panel representing the *Nile, Atlas, Geometry* and *Astrology* by Padovanino, Veronese and Andrea Schiavone. Portraits of philosophers line the walls, including two by Veronese (*door side*); four by Tintoretto (*left*), then two by Schiavone, and another two by Tintoretto, although the attribution of the one on the right is uncertain (*end wall*). One by Salviati, one by Franco and one by Lambert Sustris adorn the right wall.

Museo Diocesano di Arte Sacra

At the end of Piazzetta dei Leoncini, take Calle Canonica, then just after the bridge, turn right onto Fondamenta S. Apollonia. ◷*Open year-round Tue–Sun 10am–6pm.* ﹩€5. ℘041 24 13 817. *www.veneziaupt.org.*

Romanesque in style, the building was once part of the Benedictine Convent of Sant'Apollonia (12C–13C); its cloisters so inspired D'Annunzio that he described it in his work *Il Fuoco* (The Fire). Its arches have double-arched lintels supported along the longer sides by paired columns. The well-head in the centre is 13C. Fragments of Roman, Byzantine and Veneto-Byzantine (9C–11C) stonework line the walls.

Originally conceived by the Patriarch of Venice, **Albino Luciani** (1912–78), and Pope Giovanni Paolo, whose reign lasted just one month, the museum of religious art houses paintings and sculptures, sacred objects and congregational banners from deconsecrated churches. Its collection boasts works by artists such as Antonio Zanchi, Palma il Giovane and Jacopo Guarana.

◣◥WALKING TOUR

⚲Circuit starting from St Mark's Square, shown in green on the map on p115.

Leave St Mark's Square via the Piazzetta and turn left onto the Riva alongside the Doge's Palace: beyond the **Paglia Bridge**, (Ponte della Paglia) always crowded with photographers immortalizing the **Bridge of Sighs (Ponte dei Sospiri)**, you will arrive at the **Riva degli Schiavoni** that you will follow until **Calle del Vin**. At **Campo San Provolo**, turn right to join Campo San Zaccaria, passing

beneath a Venetian Gothic marble portal. Note the bas-relief of the Virgin and Child Enthroned with Saints.

Campo San Zaccaria★★

San Zaccaria is a stone's throw from St Mark's and as a result there are numerous restaurants, pizzerias, souvenir and *passemenerie* (trimming) shops in the area. As the distance from the church increases, so the numbers of tourists thin out and the district becomes quieter and more frequented by locals. At its heart lies the attractive and atmospheric Campo Santa Maria Formosa and its busy market. Dotted with shops specialising in typical Venetian goods, this area is perfect for a leisurely stroll.

San Zaccaria★★

◷*Open year-round Mon–Sat 10am–noon and 4pm–6pm. Sun 4pm–6pm.* ℘041 52 21 257.

The original church, founded in the 9C, has been partly incorporated into the new church: the right aisle was created from the left aisle of the old church. The present church, dating from the 15C, was built by Gambello and completed, on his death, by Codussi.

The splendid white façade incorporates three tiers of round-headed windows, niches and semicircular pediment. Contrived from a variety of architectural styles, its tall Gothic proportions are cloaked in Renaissance detail. At ground level the lower section is set with square polychrome panels that run horizontally. Above this, a continuous frieze of shell-headed flat niches introduce a vertical element that is then carried through the upper sections, accented first with three windows, then two and finally by a single central oculus. The Gothic configuration of tall nave and side aisles cede to Codussi's more Classical idiom: projecting piers give way to free-standing paired columns that extend up to a cornice, crowned with free-standing figures – far removed from the statue of *St Zaccarias* by Alessandro Vittorio above the main door.

The stunning interior is covered in paintings, the most important of which is Giovanni Bellini's *Sacra Conversazione* (1505) over the second altar on the left. On the lower left wall are two panels (1500) by Palma il Giovane.

The church is dedicated to Zacharias, the father of St John the Baptist and legend has it that his body lies beneath the right aisle.

The **Cappella del Coro** is hung with works by Tintoretto, Tiepolo and Palma il Vecchio; a pair of organ panels painted by Palma il Giovane; a *Crucifixion* attributed to Van Dyck and a *Resurrection* by Domenico Tintoretto.

In the **Cappella d'Oro**, also known as the Chapel of St Tarasius, the vault is frescoed by Andrea del Castagno and Francesco da Faenza, and the three Gothic polyptychs are by Antonio Vivarini and his collaborator. At the foot of the altar are the remains of the mosaic from the apse of the 12C Romanesque-Byzantine chapel. A little farther back (*protected by glass*) are mosaics from the 9C church. Stairs descend into the very atmospheric crypt, which is between 1 000 and 1 200 years old. It is almost permanently submerged in water and holds the watery graves of several early doges.

▶ Follow Salizzada San Provolo and proceed straight to the canal; turn left for the Diocesan Museum of Religious Art. Alternatively, return to Campo Santi Filippo e Giacomo and take Calle della Chiesa, turn left before the canal and follow the water's edge through Campiello Querini and onto Campo Santa Maria Formosa.

Campo Santa Maria Formosa

This busy square is a main thoroughfare situated between the tourist honeypots of St Mark's Square and the Church of Santi Giovanni e Paolo.

Fondazione Querini Stampalia Onlus★

🕐Open year-round Tue–Sun 10am–6pm. ⊜€10. ℘041 27 11 411. www.querinistampalia.it.

Housed in a modern building, this museum, which contains a library and occasionally hosts temporary exhibitions, is of interest to visitors seeking to imbibe the atmosphere of a Venice long disappeared, when life in the city was synonymous with art.

Works of art on display here include paintings by Palma il Giovane, Luca Giordano, Tiepolo, plus a clay model for a sculpture of *Letizia Ramolino Bonaparte* by Antonio Canova.

Particularly noteworthy are the **series of panels★★** by Pietro Longhi, predominantly devoted to the sacraments and hunting; the *Scenes of Public Life in Venice★★* by Gabriele Bella and the evocative *Presentation of Jesus in the Temple* by Giovanni Bellini.

Everyday Venetian life of the period is well depicted in the paintings *The Boxing Match* after Antonio Stom and *The Frozen Lagoon by the Fondamenta Nuove* by an anonymous 18C Venetian painter.

Santa Maria Formosa

🕐Open year-round Tue–Sat 10.30am–4.30pm (4pm Mon). 🕐Closed 1 Jan, Easter, 15 Aug and 25 Dec. ⊜€3 or Chorus Pass. ℘041 27 50 462. www.chorusvenezia.org.

The original 7C church built here was dedicated, according to legend, to St Magnus, to whom the Madonna appeared in the form of a shapely buxom (*formosa*) woman. It was rebuilt by Codussi between 1492 and 1504 and embellished with a new façade in 1604 and a new canal frontage in 1542, financed by a noble Venetian family, the Cappellos. The 17C campanile retains, above the entrance, a grimacing mask and its original pinnacle.

On passing through the main entrance, note on the left the *Madonna di Lepanto* (1571), which once graced the naval ship commanded by Sebastiano Venier.

The interior, in the form of a Latin cross, includes two chapels: the Chapel of the Scuola dei Bombardieri (mortar foundries), which contains a *San Barnaba and Saints* by Palma il Vecchio (c.1480–1528), and a *Madonna of the Misericordia* by Bartolomeo Vivarini; and the Chapel of the Scuola dei Casselleri (trunks and chest makers).

Rialto★★

Situated in the heart of the commercial area, the Rialto Bridge crosses the Grand Canal and continues the long line of shops that snakes its way from St Mark's Square, along the Mercerie, as far as the side stalls and market in the **San Polo** district. Given the overwhelming hustle and bustle of the small workshops and local bars, it is easy to forget the long history of the Rialto, and the fact that it was once the seat of government in Venice.

PONTE DI RIALTO★★

Built c.1175, the first bridge over the Grand Canal was a significant factor in the commercial development of the area. The wooden bridge had to be replaced several times following its deliberate destruction during the uprisings led by Baiamonte Tiepolo, and twice more when it collapsed. Its design was ever more complicated by the requirements of the boatmen and the shopkeepers already established here.

Palladio proposed a cumbersome Roman-style design with three arches, but this was dismissed on the grounds that it might hinder canal traffic. Some 80 years later, this consideration became less of an issue as restrictions were imposed upon larger ships using the Grand Canal.

The new construction, designed by **Antonio da Ponte** (1512–97), was sim-

- **Michelin Map:** (4, FU) Vaporetto: Rialto, San Marco
- **Location:** Signposts all over the city centre point visitors towards the Rialto and in summer, at least, there is a near continual procession of tourists making their way between the Rialto and St Mark's Square. The districts described in these four walks are both the heart and stomach of Venice. The Rialto Bridge can be reached easily on foot from any district due to the abundant signs. If you are travelling by vaporetto, lines **1** and **2** will drop you just downstream of the bridge. In addition to Rialto, line 1 also stops at Stae and San Silvestro on the right bank of the Grand Canal.
- **Don't Miss:** On the left bank the Mercerie; on the right, the market around the Campi San Giacomo and the Pescheria, and the Ca' Pesaro modern art gallery.
- **Timing:** Enjoy the animation of the right bank in the morning when the markets are in full swing.
- **Also See:** *La FENICE, PIAZZA SAN MARCO, SAN ZACCARIA, SAN ZANIPÒLO.*

Rialto Bridge over the Grand Canal at dusk

© Cosmo Condina / Tips Images

plified to a single span, thereby ensuring ease of use by boats and barges as well as safeguarding a flow of water that prevented stagnation and maintained the delicate equilibrium of the lagoon.

The present bridge consists of a single stone archway, 28m/92ft long and 7.5m/25ft high, which supports a central graduated alley lined with commercial units, flanked on either side by a narrower parallel passageway. Access from one aisle of shops to another is from either end of the bridge or via transverse arches in the middle. The whole complex is sheltered by a sloping roof. The Rialto was to remain the only means of crossing from one bank of the Grand Canal to the other until the mid-19C, when the Accademia Bridge and the Scalzi Bridge were built, and in 2008 the fourth bridge 'Calatrava' was erected.

🐾 WALKING TOURS

1 RIALTO TO PIAZZA SAN MARCO VIA THE MERCERIE★

♿Tour marked in green on map p136.

The large number of shops selling a variety of goods gives rise to the name of this historic commercial street. The *mercerie* (traditionally these were haberdashers selling cloth, ribbons and other merchandise, but the name is now a catch-all term) provide access between St Mark's and the Rialto. In the past, this was the route chosen by nobles intending to make a triumphal entry into the Piazza San Marco. The Mercerie are as busy today as they were in the Middle Ages, and fall into three main sections, starting from the clock tower: Merceria dell'Orologio, Merceria di San Zulian and Merceria di San Salvador.

Note at Merceria dell'Orologio 149, a relief recording the event that spread panic among the rebels led by Baiamonte Tiepolo, who disbanded when a stone mortar was dropped on a standard-bearer.

▶ Take the Salizada Pio X, which continues on from the bridge.

Campo San Bartolomeo

This *campo* is a busy crossroads between St Mark's, the Rialto, the Accademia and the Strada Nuova. Bars and tourist shops surround the square, which is dominated by a spirited late-19C **statue of Goldoni** (♿*see p86*).

From the *campo*, on your right, the Merceria Due Aprile leads to the **Campo San Salvador**. Then turn left before the church onto Merceria San Salvador, which follows Merceria San Zulian (to the campo of the same name) and finally becomes Merceria dell'Orologio which opens onto St Mark's Square under the clock tower. Just before the square, on the left *(at No. 149)*, a bas-relief depicts an event that caused panic in the column of rebels led by **Baiamonte Tiepolo**, when a housekeeper dropped a stone mortar on the standard-bearer.

2 TOWARDS STRADA NUOVA

♿*Tour in green on map p136.*

This busy but attractive urban route between the Accademia and the Mercerie makes its way past all kinds of shops.

▶ Starting from the bridge, join the Campo San Bortolomio as in the previous tour, but this time turn left.

Fondaco dei Tedeschi

What once served an association of German traders – the most powerful trading group in the city from the 13C onwards – now houses the main post office headquarters. Destroyed in a fire in 1505, the Fondaco (warehouse) was rebuilt by Giorgio Spavento and Scarpagnino, who conceived the idea of a square courtyard. The frescoes that adorn the façade facing the Grand Canal are the work of **Giorgione** and the earliest-known works by Titian. One of the reasons why the two artists received the frescos commission was because they had helped the firefighters to put out the flames. More of the frescoes, subsequently removed from the Fondaco, can be seen in the Ca' d'Oro (♿*see p172*).

Not Just Pedestrian Traffic

In the Middle Ages, the main means of transport in Venice was on horseback; movement through the streets became impossible given the number of horses. In 1291, it was decreed that horsemen should dismount their charges in Campo San Salvador before continuing on foot and that, in any event, horses should not be allowed into the Piazza. Instead, they had to be left by the clock tower, where (as hard as it might be to imagine) stood a copse of elder.

▷ Continue straight ahead on Salizada San Giovanni Grisostomo.

San Giovanni Grisostomo

Shoehorned between the houses into a narrow passageway is the simple yet remarkable reddish façade of the **Church of St John Chrysostom**. Founded in 1080, the church was given its current appearance by **Mauro Codussi** and his son Domenico, who completed the project after his father's death. The compact and well-proportioned interior, dominated by a dome resting on four piers,

is in the form of a Greek cross. In the first chapel on the right is a painting by **Giovanni Bellini**; the second chapel is dedicated to St Joseph, with an altarpiece by Johann Karl Loth. The presbytery is literally plastered with 17C scenes from the life of the church's patron saint, coupled with episodes from the life of Christ. The central section, by Sebastiano del Piombo, depicts the saints John Chrysostom, Paul, John the Baptist, Liberale, Mary Magdelene, Cecilia and Catherine. In the left transept, the marble *Coronation of the Virgin* is by Tullio Lombardo.

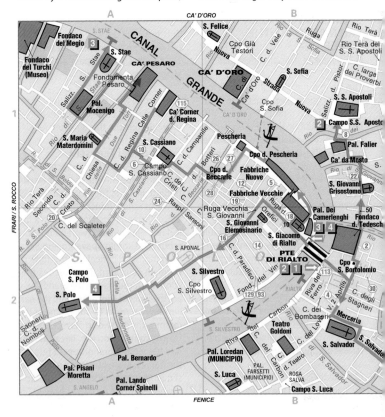

Continue, veering left, until you reach Rio dei Santissimi Apostoli, alongside which runs a pleasant sottoportego that passes under the Palazzo Falier. The campo of the same name opens out on the other side of the bridge. Continue straight ahead to Campo dei Santissimi Apostoli.

Campo dei Santissimi Apostoli

This square is the start of the Strada Nuova, and as such it serves as a busy thoroughfare, with shops and bars in almost all the nearby *calli*. Only one side of the rectangular **Church of All Saints** (*dei Santi Apostoli*), rebuilt in the 16C and restored in the 18C, opens onto the square. Its tall campanile is detached from the church. Inside, the 15C **Corner Chapel**, attributed to Codussi, contains the *Communion of St Lucy* by Tiepolo. On the left wall of the presbytery is a depiction drafted by Veronese (1528–88)

and executed by Heredes Pauli; in the chapel on the right are a series of early-14C Byzantine-style frescoes. On the far side of the canal stands the 13C **Palazzo Falier** (**4**, **FTU**; *map p136*, **B1**), named after its most eminent resident, **Doge Marino Falier**. At ground level, the portico shelters shops and restaurants; the two superior levels are decorated with pateras and arcaded windows.

③ FROM THE RIALTO TO SAN STAE VIA THE MARKETS
Tour in green on map p136.

Continuing along **Ruga degli Orefic** – flanked by arcades lined with stalls selling souvenirs, gadgetry, vests printed with the names of famous footballers, and postcards – you will approach a very busy district, particularly in the mornings when tourists and locals alike come here to shop in the market and neighbouring shops. Venetians like to intersperse this

activity with a few breaks at the bar of one of the area's many *bàcari* to enjoy an *òmbra* of white wine or *prosecco* accompanied by tasty *crostini*.

Campo San Giacomo di Rialto

This fruit and vegetable market hotspot, which is bordered on one side by the eponymous church and on the other by the Fabbriche Vecchie, opens out on the right of the Ruga degli Orefici.

San Giacomo di Rialto

Partially hidden by the stalls and the market in Campo San Giacomo di Rialto, this church is best viewed when approaching the Rialto from the San Polo *sestiere*.

San Giacomo di Rialto is considered to be the oldest church in Venice: according to one document (albeit of dubious authenticity) the city was born on 25 March 421 when three consuls arrived from Padua to establish a commercial seat at the Rialto. This church was built to celebrate the event. Its present appearance dates from the 11C, when it was rebuilt to accommodate local residents drawn to the market in the square. The façade boasts some striking features, namely the clock (despite being a 1938 reproduction), the campanile, which houses the clock and the bells, and the 14C portico.

The interior is planned as a Greek cross. Its original Greek marble columns survive, complete with 11C Veneto-Byzantine capitals carved with organic decoration. On the left is an altar by Scamozzi and bronzes by Gerolamo Campagna, who was responsible for the altar in the famous lagoon Church of San Giorgio Maggiore. On the right is an *Annunciation* by Marco Vecellio (a cousin of Titian). The main altar is by Alessandro Vittoria.

The **Banco Giro**, Venice's first public bank, was founded in 1619, just off the square. The building is now occupied by the Bancogiro restaurant.

In addition to being home to banks and the magistrature, the Rialto has always been a commercial area, as the names of the *fondamenta*, *campi* and *calli*, such as

olio (oil), *pesce* (fish), *vino* (wine), *spezie* (spices), *polli* (chicken), *beccarie* (meat) and *luganegheri* (sausage), testify to this day.

Fabbriche Vecchie

This building, set back from the Fabbriche Nuove, was designed by Scarpagnino, as was much of the surrounding area, which was destroyed by fire in 1514. The ground floor is rusticated, broken by an open colonnade; the upper floors, punctuated by simple windows, seem lightweight and less imposing.

Fabbriche Nuove

These premises, directly overlooking the bend of the Grand Canal, were designed by Sansovino. As the rusticated ground floor is interrupted by its portico, so the upper storeys are articulated by windows framed with pilasters and surmounted with pediments.

Campo della Pescaria

Under the porticoes of an impressive building (in fact it is of modern construction, dating from 1907) the Rialto's famous fish market takes place daily (7am–2pm except Sundays and holidays). A vivacious atmosphere generally pervades the **Campo delle Beccarie** (**A**, **EU;** *map p136*, **B1**) which, at one time, housed the public slaughterhouse, and now shelters a traditional Venetian *bacaro* (wine bar) and various market stalls.

▶ To reach the Campo San Cassiano, follow signs for the "Ferrovia" crossing the bridge over the Rio delle Beccarie, turning left onto Calle dei Boteri then right onto Calle dei Cristi.

San Cassiano

Although the origins of this church are rooted in the 9C, it has been subjected to restoration and its present appearance largely reflects a 17C remodelling. The interior has three aisles separated by columns hung with red and grey damask drapes. The right chapel off the apse houses three works by Leandro Bassano and one by Palma il Giovane. In the presbytery are three works by Tintoretto.

▶ Once you have crossed the Rio di San Cassiano, turn right, beyond the Sottoportego de la Siora Bettina, onto Calle della Regina, which becomes Calle Cornèr reaching the Grand Canal.

Ca' Corner della Regina

It was here, in the house of her brother, that **Caterina Cornaro**, Queen of Cyprus, resided after her fall from grace. The *palazzo* was then fashioned in the Gothic style. The present building, dating from the 18C, is decorated with frescoes, in the style of Tiepolo, that recount the unhappy events of her life.

▶ Retrace your steps towards Calle della Regina, then turn right into the ramo of the same name.

Santa Maria Materdomini

With its distinctive five-arched window, the church is set slightly back from the square and the 14C–15C Palazzo Zane. Influenced by the Tuscan style, it is an expression of Renaissance design: the simple Istrian stone façade, hemmed in between the houses, has been attributed to Sansovino, although the overall project may owe more to **Pietro Lombardo** and **Codussi**.

The ordered, simple marble-faced interior comprises three aisles and a domed apse. The most striking paintings are the large-scale dramatic renderings by **Tintoretto** in the left transept and a *Last Supper* (*opposite*) attributed to Bonifacio de' Pitati.

The exquisite altarpiece in the second bay on the right is also worthy of note. Painted by **Vincenzo Catena,** a close associate of Giorgione and Bellini, the scene shows *St Christina of Bolsena* emerging from Lake Bolsena on the millstone that was meant to have drowned her. The fine terracotta *Madonna* by the main altar is 15C by Nicolò di Pietro Paradisi. The more subtle early-16C marble altarpieces (*right of the entrance and left of the main altar*) are carved by Lorenzo Bregna. In the presbytery is a delicate relief by the Lombardo brothers.

▶ On the right of the campo, turn right into the calle that passes under two sottoporteghi to reach Calle del Ravanoo. Turn left, then right onto Fondamenta Pesaro.

Ca' Pesaro★

🕐*Open Apr–Oct Tue–Sun 10am–6pm; rest of the year 10am–5pm.* 🕐*Closed 1 Jan, 1 May and 25 Dec.* ✆€10 (inc ticket with the Museo di Arte Orientale) or Museum Pass (👣*see p30*). ✆*848 082 000 or 041 427 30 892 (from abroad). www.capesaro.visitmuve.it.*

This *palazzo* was commissioned by the Pesaro family. Initiated by Longhena, it was completed by Francesco Antonio Gaspari and now houses an important collection of oriental art and a museum of modern art (👣*see II CANAL GRANDE*).

Museo d'Arte Orientale – The Museum of Oriental Art is housed on the upper floor of the *palazzo* and contains Japanese armour from the Edo Period (1615–1868), swords, lacquer-work, puppets, musical instruments and Chinese porcelain.

Galleria Internazionale di Arte Moderna – This gallery hosts important modern art from the end of the 19C onwards, notably from the Futurist movement. On display are works by Klinger (1857–1920), Chagall (1877–1985), Klimt (1862–1918), Bonnard (1867–1947), Matisse (1869–1954), Kandinsky (1866–1944), Klee (1879–1940), Tanguy (1900–55), Henry Moore (1898–1986), Mirò (1893–1983), Ernst (1891–1976), Boccioni (1882–1916), Rosso (1858–1928), De Pisis (1896–1956), Morandi (1890–1964), De Chirico (1888–1978), Casorati (1883–1963), Carrà (1881–1966), Sironi (1885–1961) and Pizzinato (1910–). There is also a permanent exhibition featuring works by Guglielmo Ciardi (1842–1917), who perpetuated the Venetian landscape tradition. Works from the latter half of the 19C include Venetian pieces by Luigi Nono (1850–1918), Alessandro Milesi (1856–1945) and Giacomo Favretto (1849–87).

Palazzo Mocenigo

🕐 Open Tue–Sun 10am–5pm (Nov–Mar 4pm). 🕐 Closed 1 Jan, 1 May, 25 Dec. €8 or Museum Pass (♿ see p30). ☎041 72 17 98. mocenigo.visitmuve.it.
The Palazzo Mocenigo was the residence from the 17C onwards of the San Stae branch of the Mocenigo family, one of the most important families of the Venetian patriciate, seven members of which became doges between 1414 and 1778. Their portraits hang in the entrance. It is a large building of gothic origin extensively rebuilt at the beginning of the 17C, when it attained its present appearance.

This museum provides an idea of Venetian life among the noble classes in the 17C and 18C. Today the interiors are used to display fabrics and costumes belonging to the **Centro Studi di Storia del Tessuto e del Costume**, a foundation dedicated to the study and conservation of fabrics and costumes. On show are a range of woven materials and textiles dating back as far as the early days of the Republic. The section dedicated to perfume extends out along a route through eight rooms: the museum exhibits original tools, texts and a collection of perfume bottles.

Chiesa San Stae

🕐 Open Tue–Sat 1.45–4.30pm (4pm Mon) . 🕐 Closed 1 Jan, Easter, 15 Aug and 25 Dec. €3 or Chorus Pass. ☎041 27 50 462. www.chorusvenezia.org.
This single-nave church dedicated to St Eustace houses, among others, works by Piazzetta, Ricci and Tiepolo, as well as the tomb of doge **Alvise I Mocenigo.** The church regularly hosts temporary exhibitions, as does the little Scuola dell'Arte de Tiraono et Battioro (1711).

▷ The campo opens onto the Grand Canal and the jetty for vaporetti 1 and 82. There is the option, if you take the Salizada then turn left onto Calle del Tentor, to join the promenade des Frari next to the Campo San Giacomo dell'Orio..

④ FROM THE RIALTO TO CAMPO SAN POLO

As on the previous tour, leave the bridge via Ruga degli Orefici, then turn left onto Ruga Vecchia San Giovanni.

San Giovanni Elemosinario

🕐 Open Mon–Sat 10.30am–1.15pm. 🕐 Closed 1 Jan, Easter, 15 Aug and 25 Dec. €3 or Chorus Pass. ☎041 27 50 462. www.chorusvenezia.org.
The origins of this ancient church, built in the shape of a Greek cross, date back to 1071, although the original building was destroyed by fire in 1514. The church was rebuilt, possibly by Lo Scarpagnino, and completed in 1531. It now houses works by Jacopo Palma il Giovane and Il Pordenone (c.1484–1539) – also responsible for the frescoes in the dome, – as well as an altarpiece by Titian on the high altar.

▷ From the Campo Sant'Aponal, take Calle del Perdon, which runs into Calle della Madonetta, which opens onto the vast Campo San Polo.

Campo San Polo

This huge amphitheatre-plan *campo* hosts lots of public events, including an outdoor summer cinema, thus continuing a very old tradition; bulls were run in the past, depicted in a painting at the Museo Correr. The square is surrounded by some fine buildings, including the two Venetian Gothic-style **palazzi Soranzo** (Nos. 2169 and 2170), and the nearby Baroque-style **palazzo Tiepolo Maffetti**, with a Herculean head decorating its portal. On the oppostie corner, the **palazzo Corner Mocenigo**, built by Sanmicheli in the 16C, today houses the Customs officials (Guardia di Finanza). The church of **San Polo** (🕐 Open Tue–Sat 10.30am–4.30 pm; 4pm Mon). 🕐 Closed 1 Jan, Easter, 15 Aug and 25 Dec. €3 or Chorus Pass. ☎041 27 50 462; www.chorusvenezia.org) dates to at least the 9C. Inside, major works of art include the Assumption of the Virgin, and a Last Supper by Tintoretto, as well as works by Tiepolo, Giandomenico and Veronese.

La Fenice★

Occupying the loop of the Grand Canal this is a very lively part of Venice. As well as the city's famous opera house, the area has plenty of good shops; for books try the Campo San Luca and for masks, look between Campo Manin and Campo Sant'Angelo. The route between St Mark's and Campo Santo Stefano boasts many elegant shops and hotels, and around the Church of San Moisé are art, glass and bookbinding workshops.

WALKING TOUR

Tour starting from St Mark's Square marked in green on map p142.

▷ Leave the square by passing under the Ala Napoleonica, continue ahead and take, slightly to the left, Calle Seconda, a street lined with designer boutiques that soon becomes Salizada San Moisè.

San Moisè

Undoubtedly, the most striking feature of this church is its façade: built by Longhena's pupil **Alessandro Tremignon** in the 17C with the help of the Flemish artist Meyring, a disciple of Bernini, it is the epitome of excess. Divided into three sections both horizontally and vertically, the edifice features every sort of adornment on the front. The lower tier is designed as a triumphal arch, dominated by memorials to members of the Fini family.

The interior is also Baroque. Its sense of dramatic gesture is conveyed in Tintoretto's *Christ Washing his Disciples' Feet* (in the chapel). ○Open year-round Mon–Sat 9.30am–12.30pm.

▷ In front of the square take the campo la Calle Larga 22 Marzo, lined with shops, restaurants and hotels, then turn right onto Calle delle Veste until you reach Campo San Fantin, which is located beyond the rio.

◔ **Michelin Map:**
(8, EX) Vaporetto: S. Marco, S. Maria del Giglio, S. Samuele, S. Angelo or Rialto

▷ **Location** The area in the immediate vicinity of the theatre is known as the "seven campi between the bridges," a reference to the Campi di San Bartolomeo, San Salvador, San Luca, Manin, Sant'Angelo, Santo Stefano and San Vidal, situated between the Rialto Bridge and Accademia Bridge. Although the theatre occupies a fairly quiet setting, it is edged by a bustling commercial hub of restaurants and shops.

◈ **Don't Miss:** The designer boutiques and street entertainers along the Calle Larga 22 Marzo.

○ **Timing:** Allow 2hrs for the itinerary and another 1hr for a guided tour of the theatre.

◔ **Also See:** *PIAZZA SAN MARCO, RIALTO.*

Campo San Fantin

The Renaissance church **Chiesa San Fantin** was begun by Scarpagnino (active in Venice between 1505 and 1549) and completed by Sansovino. Inside are two works by Palma il Giovane (1544–1628).

Gran Teatro La Fenice★ – ⅍○*Open year-round daily 9.30am–6pm unless the theatre is being used for other purposes.* ○ *Closed 1 Jan, 1 May and 25 Dec.* ◉€10. *Guided tours on reservation (€13).* ☎041 78 66 75. *www.teatrolafenice.it* . Situated in a secluded and picturesque little square of Campo San Fantin, the opera house and music-theatre was inaugurated in 1792 after its predecessor (1673) burned down in 1774. Construction was initiated by Giannantonio Selva (1751–1819), a friend of Canova, who won the commission in a competition. Almost completely destroyed by fire in 1836, it was rebuilt and renamed La Fenice (The Phoenix) in honour of its emergence from the ashes. Neo-Classical in style, La Fenice had two façades and two entrances, including one overlooking the canal. It is not difficult to imagine the difficulties posed by the spatial requirements of the auditorium, which was much bigger than the apparently narrow façade, a problem overcome by means of an ingenious series of stairways.

This "jewel box of a theatre" (Isaac Sterne) burned down again on 29 January 1996 when it was closed for restoration. Damage was exacerbated by the fact that fire services were unable to reach the scene along normal routes as neighbouring canals had been drained for cleaning. John Berendt gives a fascinating account of the event in his book *The City of Falling Angels* (*see Further Reading in Planning Your Trip*). Special funds were set up by the Italian government, the Venice in Peril Fund and the American Save Venice Com-mittee. Reconstructed to architect Aldo Rossi's plan, the theatre reopened on 14 December 2003.

Good to know – The Calle dei Bar-caroli (between the Ateneo and the church) leads from the Campo San Fan-tin to the **Rio dei Barcaroli**. A plaque on the side of the palace commemorates the young **Mozart**'s stay here in 1771 during the Carnevale.

Chiesa San Fantin – This Renaissance building, begun by **Scarpagnino** and completed by Sansovino, houses two paintings by **Palma Giovani**.

Scuola di San Fantin – This building, now the Ateneo Veneto, was formerly the site of the College of St Jerome, also known as the college "of the hang men", as its members had the thankless task of accompanying those sentenced to death to their place of execution. The facade is by **Alessandro Vittoria** (c.1580).

Return to the Calle Larga 22 Marzo and turn right. It is followed by the twisting Calle delle Ostreghe.

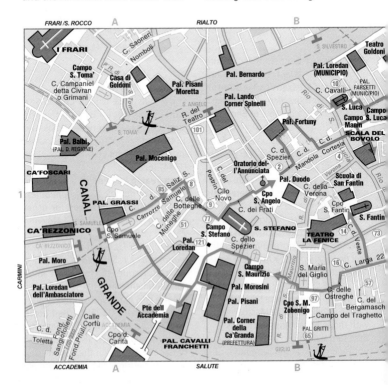

Chiesa Santa Maria del Giglio (or Zobenigo)

🕐*Open year-round Tue–Sat 10.30am–4.30pm (4pm Mon).* 🕐*Closed 1 Jan, Easter, 15 Aug and 25 Dec.* 🎫€3 *or Chorus Pass. www.chorusvenezia.org*

The church of St. Mary of the Lily stands on a pleasant campo that opens onto the Grand Canal near the traghetto that carries its name. Its majestic facade, the work of Giuseppe Sardi, is reminiscent of that of San Moisè in its style and exuberant decoration. This one is a tribute to the glory of the 'Sea Captain' Antonio Barbaro and his family, statues of whose most illustrious members stand on either side of the door. Construction of the bell tower (18C) stopped quickly in a sort of pavilion, which today houses a souvenir shop.

The church houses a painting by Rubens, Madonna and Child with St. John, and *The Four Evangelists (behind the altar, under the organ)* are by Tintoretto. The two Annunciation sculptures flanking the altar are by Meyring.

Famous Premieres

Celebrated works that have been performed for the first time in the Fenice include *Tancredi* (1813), *Sigismondo* (1814) and *Semiramide* (1823) by **Gioachino Rossini**, and *Ernani* (1844), *Attila* (1846), *Rigoletto* (1851), *La Traviata* (1853) and *Simon Boccanegra* (1857) by **Giuseppe Verdi**.

▶ Walk alongside the church and cross the Rio San Maurizio on the righthand side of the Ponte Duodo and take Calle Zaguri, at the end of Campiello della Feltrina.

Campo San Maurizio

The peace of this square is usually only broken by the busy 3-day antiques market which descends here four times a year (consult the official tourist board website, under "events" for dates). To the right of the church is a view of the

The Renaissance Palazzo

Based on Roman originals, the Italian *palazzo* was designed to fulfil commercial and residential demands. Arranged around a central courtyard, it most often comprises three storeys. The ground floor was used for storage or shops (*magazzini*) that opened out onto the street; this level tends to be heavily rusticated. The first floor, or *piano nobile*, was used by the occupying family as living quarters: externally lighter in texture, the interior had high ceilings and large windows providing ample light and ventilation. The top storey, below the roof and much lower in proportion, served as quarters for servants and children.

campanile of Santo Stefano. The former **Scuola degli Albanesi**, with its Renaissance reliefs, sits on the left. Previous residents of the *palazzo* opposite include the novelist Alessandro Manzoni (1785–1873) and Giorgio Baffo (1694–1768), who wrote salacious poetry in Venetian dialect.

▶ Take Calle del Piovan, then Calle del Spezier to lead you to Campo Santo Stefano.

Campo Santo Stefano

This *campo* is one of the most elegant squares in the city. Dominated by a church in which concerts are regularly given, this lively meeting place is animated by busy outdoor cafes and people making their way to and from the Accademia Bridge. It's a perfect venue for an early evening stroll or *passeggiata*. Towering over the square is a monument (1882) to **Niccolò Tommaseo** (1802–74, journalist and essayist).

Overlooking the square is the **Palazzo Loredan**, now home to the Venetian Institute of Science, Arts and Letters and its prestigious library (⊙*guided tours by request at.* ☎*041 24 07 711. www.istitutoveneto.it*). In 1536 the Loredan family commissioned Scarpagnino (active in Venice between 1505 and 1549) to rebuild the palace recently acquired from the Mocenigo family. Note its Palladian northern façade.

Straight ahead is the **Palazzo Pisani**, one of the largest private palaces in the city, on the square of the same name. Having been acquired by a noble family between the 17C and 18C, Girolamo Frigimelica (1653–1732) was commis-

sioned to remodel the building. The *palazzo* is now the home of the **Benedetto Marcello Music Conservatory**. **Palazzo Morosini**, which dates to the 14C and was restored at the end of the 17C by Antonio Gaspari.

Former residents include Francesco Morosini, Doge between 1688 and 1694. The *palazzo* is now the home of the New Consortium of Venice, a group of 40 companies set up in 2005 with a remit to save the city from the encroaching sea.

Palazzo Grassi★
⌂*See p108.*

▶ Turn right onto Calle Crosera, which follows Calle delle Botteghe, which leads to Campo Santo Stefano, facing the church.

Santo Stefano★
⊙*Open year-round Tue–Sat 10.30am–4.30pm (4pm Mon).*
⊙*Closed 1 Jan, Easter, 15 Aug, 25 Dec.*
∞€*3 or Chorus Pass.* ☎*041 27 50 462. www.chorusvenezia.org.*

Gothic in style, the church comprises a central vaulted nave flanked by lower side bays. Construction of St Stephen's and the adjacent convent was begun in the latter half of the 13C; the church, however, was modified in the 15C. The campanile (60m/196ft 10in high) is one of the most famous in Venice. Building on the lower section was resumed in 1544; when it collapsed in 1585, it was the new masonry that crumbled, hit by lightning so violent that the bells melted. Further damage incurred by subsidence between the 17C and 18C has left the tower leaning at an angle, as do all the other bell-towers in Venice. Like other churches in Venice, St Stephen's is a pantheon to the glory of the city: it contains the tombs of **Giovanni Gabrieli** (composer and organist) and of **Francesco Morosini** (doge 1688–94), as well as Baldassare Longhena's monument to Capt. Bartolomeo d'Alviano. In the sacristy hang works by Tintoretto: in the *Last Supper*, the dog and cat allude to the dispute raging between the Catholic and Protestant Churches over belief in the mystery of the Eucharist.

▷ Take Calle Santo Stefano which becomes Calle le Frati.

Campo Sant'Angelo

This rather austere square en route between St Mark's and the Accademia, is bordered by some handsome *palazzi* overlooking the canal.

The **Oratorio dell'Annunciata** (Oratory of the Annunziata) has replaced the church that gave the square its name, formerly associated with the Scuola dei Zoti, the guild for disabled sailors.

The plaque on the wall of **Palazzo Duodo** commemorates the composer, Domenico Cimarosa (1749–1801), who died here.

The Gothic portal on the bridge leads into the cloisters of St Stephen (now the headquarters of the Regional Accountancy Board).

▷ Rio Terrà della Mandola branches left off Calle dello Spezièr and leads to the Palazzo Fortuny.

Palazzo Fortuny

Dating to the 15C, the building boasts two mullioned windows with five arches. The Palazzo Pesaro degli Orfei was acquired by the painter, photographer, stage designer and textile designer, **Mariano Fortuny y Madrazo** (1871–1949), in 1899. Formerly a music school, it is now the **Museo Fortuny** (&✆ *Open during exhibitions only; Wed–Mon 10am–6pm.* ✆*Closed Tue, 1 Jan, 25 Dec.* ☞€*10.* ✆*848 082 000 or (+39) 041*

427 30 892 from abroad. www.fortuny. visitmuve.it) devoted to the artist's work. The *calle* that leads from Campo Sant'Angelo to Campo Manin is always busy with people coming and going, usually distracted by the many shops along the way.

▷ The bridge over the Rio di San Luca leads into the modern Campo Manin.

Campo Manin

Few features distinguish this square other than the monument to **Daniele Manin** (1875), the shops down along one side and the **Cassa di Risparmio di Venezia**, designed by **Pierluigi Nervi** (1891–1979) and Angelo Scattolin, which provides an idea of modern Venetian architecture.

Scala del Bovolo★

✆*Open year-round daily 10am-1.30pm and 2–6pm.* ✆*Closed 1 Jan, 1 Nov, 15 Aug and 25 and 26 Dec.* ☞€*7 (visit the Tintoretto room in the Oratorio dei Crociferi, roughly 20 mins on foot from the Scala del Bovolo,* &*see p170.* ✆*041 30 39 211. ww.scalacontarinidelbovolo.com).*

The delicate spiral **Bovolo Staircase** is all the more impressive, situated as it is off a tiny, peaceful courtyard overlooked by private houses. The staircase (*bovolo* in Venetian dialect), which seems to har-

A. Copson/ age fotostock

Scala del Bovolo

monise with a composite style drawn from both Gothic and Renaissance styles, is attributed to Giovanni Candi, who died in 1506. Encased in a tower, it provides access to the *palazzo*'s loggias. From the top extends a lovely, if somewhat disorientating **view★★** over the Venetian rooftops.

▶ Return to the Campo Manin and walk along the lefthand side of the Caisse d'Épargne down the Ramo di Salizada then the Campiello della Chiesa on your left.

San Luca

The **Church of St Luke** (San Luca) contains the *Virgin in Glory Appearing to St Luke While Writing the Gospel* by Veronese (1528–88). When the floor was repaved at the beginning of the 20C, the gravestones of those buried there, including the writer Aretino, were not relaid.

▶ Retrace your steps then turn left onto the Salizada San Luca.

Campo San Luca

This lively *campo* is one of the most popular meeting places in Venice. It is lined with cafés, well-known stores, bookshops, travel agencies, fast-food outlets and a host of shops in the immediate vicinity.
Calle Goldoni leads from the Campo San Luca to Piazza San Marco via the **Bacino Orseolo**, where several of the city's gleaming black gondolas dock.

▶ Leave the campo on the left via Calle del Forno, then turn right onto the Calle del Teatro de la Commedia.

Also off the Campo, on the opposite side, is Calle del Teatro is the **Teatro Goldoni**, the theatre named for Italy's famed playwright, Carlo Goldoni. Once a city of many theatres, today, La Fenice, the Goldoni and the Teatro Màlibran are among the few active theatres.

Campo San Salvador

Ce petit *campo* ne manque pas d'animation du fait de sa proximité avec les **Mercerie** reliant la place Saint-Marc au pont du Rialto.

San Salvador – The 7C Church of San Salvador was consecrated by Pope Alexander III during his visit to Venice to meet Barbarossa in 1177. Despite having been subjected to various phases of rebuilding, the 17C façade survives with a cannon ball embedded in the masonry since 1849. The main layout was designed by Spavento, who combines an assured use of Classical structural elements with refined sculptural ornament, a style that foreshadows Mannerism and the bold Classicism of Palladio. Inside, three square bays are aligned to form a nave, each cubic space rising to a semicircular dome. A number of significant paintings include the main altarpiece, *The Transfiguration* by Titian (c.1490–1576) and, in the last bay on the right before the transept, his *Annunciation*. To the right of the main chapel hangs *The Martyrdom of St Theodoric* by Paris Bordone (1500–71). In the Santissimo Chapel on the left of the main altar is *The Disciples at Emmaus* by Giovanni Bellini (c.1432–1516); the organ doors (*by the side door*) are painted by Titian's brother, Francesco Vecellio (1475–1560).
Telecom Italia Future Centre – ⊙*Open year-round Tue-Sun 10am–6pm.* ⊙*Closed 1 Jan, 25 Dec.* ✆*041 94 77 70. www.telecomfuturecentre.it.* Housed in the beautifully restored cloister of the San Salvador convent adjacent to the San Salvador church, is a showcase of Telecom Italia, Italy's leading telephone company.
Scuola Grande San Todaro – *On the square on the corner of Calle del Lovo – no charge.* This former adult college dedicated to St Theodore hosts a permanent exhibition 'Vivaldi and his times'. Venetian musicians perform several times a week (*see "On the Town" in "Addresses"*).

▶ Continuing straight ahead on the Merceria Due Aprile, you will arrive at the Campo San Bortolomio (Bartolomeo) which leads to the Rialto Bridge, while if you turn right after the church, you will rejoin St Mark's Square via the Mercerie (𝕝*see RIALTO*).

Accademia★★★

This area, named after its famous Academy of Fine Art, is permanently thronged by people on the move: locals going about their everyday business; visitors arriving on the vaporetti, drawn to the art treasures; students milling outside the nearby university, lending a bohemian atmosphere to the area. Whatever your business here it is always worth stopping for a short break at one of the bars or trattorias.

GALLERIE DELL'ACCADEMIA★★★

Open year-round 8.15am–7.15pm (2pm Mon), last admission 45min before closing. The gallery limits the number of people allowed in at any one time, so if you are visiting at a busy time of year, book ahead either online or by telephone. Closed 1 Jan, 1 May and 25 Dec. €12, more during temp exhibits. 041 52 00 345. www.gallerieaccademia.org.

The **Academy of Fine Art** exhibits what is arguably the city's most important collection of artworks. A €26 million restoration to the museum and adjacent Academy of Fine Arts more than doubled the museum's exhibition area adding 30 rooms in December 2013. Visitor services were improved, including a cafeteria. Visitors now have access to a court designed by Andrea Palladio (1561-63). The collection encapsulates the development of Venetian painting from the 14C to the 18C, in a complex of buildings converted in the 19C. These structures include the Monastery of Lateran Canons, designed by Andrea Palladio (1508–80), the Church of La Carità, an atmospheric building that was redesigned by Bartolomeo Bon (recorded 1441–64), and the Scuola Santa Maria della Carità, the first Scuola Grande, which was erected in 1260 (see *I CARMINI: The Venetian Scuole*). The tour starts in the large Sala Capitolare at the top of the 18C staircase.

Michelin Map: (**7**, DX) Vaporetto: Accademia or Zattere

Location: The Accademia area is served on the Grand Canal by a stop of the same name located just in front of the Gallerie (vaporetti **1, 2** and **N**). The Gallerie dell'Accademia is situated just at the end of the Ponte dell'Accademia, which can be reached via the Campo Santo Stefano. The surrounding area stretches between the Grand Canal and the Zattere. The north side of the area is dominated by the Gallerie dell'Accademia, the south side boasts the Zattere, the long promenade that overlooks the Giudecca canal and Giudecca island. Boats depart frequently from the Zattere for the airport.

Don't Miss: The Accademia Gallery, of course, and the picturesque gondola dockyard, Squero di San Trovaso.

Timing: Allow 2hrs for the Academy Gallery and 1hr for the area.

Also See: Neighbouring sights: *I CARMINI, La SALUTE.*

Room I

The Sala Capitolare (chapter house) is the place where, from the 15C, the Scuola Grande of the Santa Maria della Carità used to meet. This large room has a gilded panelled ceiling by Marco Cozzi (1484), divided into sections with a cherub in each. The figure of God in the central tondo, attributed to Alvise **Vivarini** (1445–1505), replaces that of the Madonna della Misericordia, the patron who would have occupied the section originally. The room is devoted to Venetian Gothic masters from the 14C and the first half of the 15C, including Paolo Veneziano (*Coronation of the*

GALLERIE DELL'ACCADEMIA

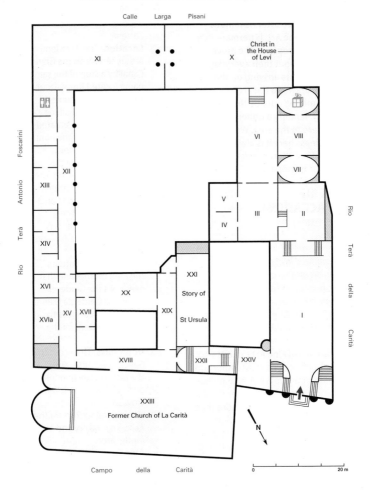

Calle   Larga   Pisani

Christ in
the House
of Levi

XI   X

Foscarini   Antonio   Terà   Rio

XII

XIII

XIV

XVI

XVIa   XV   XVII

XX

XIX

XVIII

XXI

Story of

St Ursula

VI   VIII

VII

V

III   II

IV

XXII   XXIV

I

XXIII

Former Church of La Carità

Rio   Terà   della   Carità

N

Campo   della   Carità

0   20 m

Virgin at the top of the stairs straight ahead) and Lorenzo Veneziano. The huge painting, *Coronation of the Virgin in Paradise*, at the end of the room, is by Jacobello del Fiore (*right*). Note Michele Giambino's works also on display here; Giambino, who worked between 1420 and 1462, is the most important artist to work in the International Gothic style in Venice.

Room II

This room displays eight important 15C altarpieces. On the entrance wall: the *Crucifixion and Apotheosis of the Ten Thousand Martyrs of Mount Ararat*

by **Vittore Carpaccio** (c.1465–c.1526) depicts the legendary massacre of the Roman soldiers betrayed by their own captains after beating the Armenian rebels (*right*). On the wall to the right hang the famous *Virgin and Child with Saints*, also known as the *Pala di San Giobbe*, by **Giovanni Bellini** (c.1470–1516) taken from the Church of San Giobbe; the *Agony in the Garden* by Marco Basaiti (c.1470–c.1530) (*right*) and the *Presentation of Christ in the Temple* by Vittorio Carpaccio (*left*).

On the end wall: the *Madonna of the Orange Tree* by Cima da Conegliano (1459–1517) (*right*) hangs alongside his

Incredulity of St Thomas and the Great Bishop in which the three figures are silhouetted against the sky with a village in the distance (*left*).

The *Calling of the Sons of Zebedee*, by Marco Basaiti, is a particularly beautiful and engaging treatment of the subject of Christ recruiting his Apostles, the variety of scenery with the focus on the water and the magical quality of the colour (*centre*).

On the wall to the left: the *Mourning of the Dead Christ* by Giovanni Bellini and assistants (*right*) and the *Madonna with Child Enthroned* by Cima da Conegliano (*left*).

Room III

This room contains works by Sebastiano del Piombo, Cima da Conegliano and Giovanni Bellini.

▷ Cross to the far end for access to the small adjoining Rooms IV and V, among the most important rooms in the gallery.

Room IV

One of his most important works, Giovanni Bellini's *Madonna with Child between St Catherine and Mary Magdalene* depicts four figures thrown into relief by a strong transverse light that lifts them out of the darkness; note, however, the suggestion of serene beauty and tender spirituality so typical of Bellini. Also by Bellini are his the *Madonna and the Seraphim*, and *Pietà*, which was painted when the artist was considerably older. In contrast, is the *Portrait of a Young Man* by the Dutch artist Hans Memling (c.1435-94) with its sharp delineation of features and characterisation; lost in tranquil meditation, the young man's face is embued with inner calm. A famous work by Giorgione, *the Old Woman* is a compelling portrait, appealing yet uncompromising. Self-explanatory, it has been described as a "hymn to fleeing youth," touched with the inevitable sadness of realised awareness, highlighted by the inscription in the cartouche *col tempo* ("with time"). The picture is especially charged with

meaning if one considers how Giorgione's untimely death in 1510 from the plague cut short a life full of promise.

Room V

This room is dedicated primarily to rotating exhibits of 17–19C art.

Room VI

This long room houses works by Tintoretto (1518–94) and Veronese (1528–88). A Virgin and Child (c1560) by Titian shows a burning bush in the dsiance.

Room VII

This little room is home to the famous 1524 *Portait of a Young Gentleman in his Study* by **Lorenzo Lotto** (c.1480–1577), in which the sitter's concentration seems to have been interrupted by a thought or a memory; distracted from his reading, his long delicate fingers idly flick through the pages as he muses perhaps upon the passing of time, staring into the distance, his pale, chiselled face contrasting with his black coat.

Admire works by Vasari, Palma il Vecchio and Titian in **Room VIII**; then proceed to Room IX, which shows works of the Lombard school.

Room X

The *Madonna with Child Enthroned* by Veronese (*left of the entrance*) recalls the Pesaro altarpiece in the Frari (◑*see I FRARI*). The *Pietà* by Titian (1490–1576) was intended by the artist for his own tomb; unfinished on his death, it was complete by Palma the younger, who indicated this on the note.

Nearby hangs one of Veronese's most important works in the museum, *Betrothal of St Catherine*.

Opposite the entrance hang Tintoretto's canvases depicting the life of St Mark. From left to right: *St Mark's Dream* (in fact the dream of St Mark's son, Dominic), *St Mark Saves a Saracen, St Mark Liberates a Slave* – the oblique lighting effects heighten the drama of the scene with St Mark falling head first; the *Theft of the Body of St Mark* (the final panel in the series, the *Finding of the Body of St Mark* is now in the Brera Collection in Milan). Note how the figures in the foreground appear thrown into relief by the use of chiaroscuro, where forms, picked out by strong light, are contrasted against another recessed into shadow; here phantom-like figures fade into the darkness, sloping off in search of safety in the palace.

The whole of the right wall is taken by Veronese's controversial *Christ in the House of Levi*, conceived as a *Last Supper* (1573) for the refectory of Santi Giovanni e Paolo (&see SAN ZANIPÒLO). Shortly after the painting was unveiled, Veronese was summoned before a tribunal of the Inquisition on a charge of heresy for not adhering to the description of the event as related in the Gospels. Veronese defended himself on the grounds of artistic licence. He promptly changed the painting's title to suit a more secular subject that might also justify the painter's predilection for such opulent textures as brocade, glass and gold.

Rooms XI to XIX

Rooms XI-XVI host temporary exhibitions, which may result in some works being unavailable for viewing. This room accommodates works by **Giambattista Tiepolo** (1696–1770) including the frieze that depicts the *Castigation of the Serpents* and the fresco pendentives from the Scalzi Church (destroyed in 1915). *Dinner in the House of Simon* by **Bernardo Strozzi** (1581–1644) is particularly vibrant, notably animated by the expressive face of the figure filling the chalice. The *Crucifixion of St Peter* composed around its strong diagonal axes by Luca Giordano (1643–1705) is also here.

On the left wall hangs the masterpiece by Bonifacio de' Pitati (c.1487–1553). The *Rich Man Epulone* projects domestic life of the wealthy; rich with incidental detail and contrasting personality, populated with musicians, a beggar bitten by a dog, huntsmen and lovers converging in a wood, as a fire rages on the right. **Room XII** is dedicated to landscape painting from the late 17C and early 18C, including works by Marco Ricci,

Giuseppe Zais and Francesco Zuccarelli. Access to the two side rooms, **Rooms XIII** features several works by Tintoretto, including his portrait of the Procurator Jacopo Soranzo, all showing how his style varied as influenced by other artists. Through Room XII, **XIV** shows works from the 16C and 17C. The corridor then becomes **Room XV**, which leads to side rooms on the left **(Room XVII)**, full of the most typical Venetian paintings: a single **Canaletto** (1697–1768) – although a prolific Venetian painter, all save a handful of his works hang in collections abroad, having been sold to foreign gentlemen on the Grand Tour or requisitioned by Napoleon; Bernardo Bellotto (1721–80); Francesco **Guardi** (1712–93); Giambattista Piazzetta (1683–1754); Rosalba Carriera (1675–1758), whose series of informal pastel portraits are provocative studies of personality; Pietro Longhi (1702–85) (the famous *Dancing Lesson*). **Room XVIa** accommodates works from the 18C, including the *Fortune Teller* by Giambattista Piazzetta.

Room XVIII serves as a passageway into **Room XXIII**, the old Church of La Carità, which now contains works from the 15C/16C Venetian School.

The *Annunciation* by Antonello de Saliba (active 1497–1535), displayed in **Room XIX**, is, in fact, a copy of a work bearing the same title in the Galleria Nazionale di Palermo in Sicily, executed by Antonello da Messina, Da Saliba's uncle.

▶ Access to Room XX is through Room XIX. Near here will be future access to the Palladian courtyard.

Room XX

This room contains the famous collection of paintings illustrating the story of the *Miracles of the Relic of the True Cross*, executed by various artists between the 15C and 16C, for the Scuola di San Giovanni Evangelista.

The *Procession in St Mark's Square* by Gentile Bellini (1429–1507) covers the wall facing the entrance. The work is an important representation of the square in the mid-15C (&see *PIAZZA SAN MARCO*). Other paintings by Gentile Bellini on the right wall include (*from left to right*) the *Healing of Pietro de' Ludovici* and the *Miracle of the Cross on the Ponte di San Lorenzo* in which Andrea Vendramin is shown retrieving the Reliquary of the True Cross from the canal. Note that Caterina Cornaro (&see *RIALTO: Ca' Corer della Regina*) is just visible on the left-hand side of the latter work. On the same wall hangs a work by Giovanni Mansueti (active in Venice from 1485 to c.1526): the *Healing of Benvegnudo's Daughter of San Polo* sets the scene in a beautiful Renaissance interior (*right*). Carpaccio's *Miracle of the Relic of the True Cross at Rialto* can be seen on the entrance wall. Interestingly, the subject of the painting – the miraculous healing of a madman taking place on the first-floor loggia on the left – seems secondary to the profusion of topographical detail showing Venice at the end of the 15C: the wooden Rialto Bridge, the Fondaco dei Tedeschi on the right as it was before the events of 1505 (&see *La FENICE*), the Ca' da Mosto (&see *Il CANAL GRANDE*) and the bell-towers of San Giovanni Grisostomo and the Church of All Saints (&see *RIALTO*).

Room XXI

This room contains the colourful and magical series of canvases by **Carpaccio** that retell the *Story of St Ursula* (1491–98).

▶ Start with the wall facing the entrance (left) and proceed clockwise.

The first panel, *Arrival of the English Ambassadors,* shows the ambassadors arriving at the (Catholic) court in Brittany bearing a proposal of marriage from their English (pagan) prince, Hereus. Ursula (*to the right*) is shown dictating her conditions of marriage (including his baptism and promise to undertake a pilgrimage accompanied by Ursula and a large number of virgins), in the presence of her wet nurse seated on the steps. The next scene shows *The English Ambassadors Taking their Leave*, in which the king

hands over the reply: it may well be that it is being written up by the scribe who is concentrating on his task.

In the *Return of the Ambassadors* the cortège bringing the reply to the king is followed by a crowd to the edge of the lagoon, the towers suggestive of the Arsenale. Among noteworthy details: the central scene is almost theatrical, the eye caught by the handsome youth turning away as if affronted; the figure sitting on the bank is the "Steward," whose duty it is to herald the arrival of the ambassadors, invited by the doge, with music, while a monkey on the right watches a guinea fowl.

The *Meeting of Ursula and Hereus and the Departure of the Pilgrims* is a composite scene, divided by the pennant, showing the prince taking his leave; Hereus and Ursula bid farewell to the rulers of Brittany before departing for Rome. Note the sharp contrast between the harsh, darkened representation of the English capital on the left and the colourful Breton town on the right, represented according to Humanist ideals.

In *Ursula's Dream* the scene is more compact, set in Ursula's room where the light reveals more domestic details: reminiscent of *St Augustine in his Studio* (&see *SAN GIORGIO degli SCHIAVONI*), the angel reaches out for the palm of martyrdom. The *Meeting of the Pilgrims with Pope Cyriac under the Walls of Rome* takes place against the background of the Castel Sant'Angelo, between two groups of virgin pilgrims (Ursula's companions) to the left and the prelates to the right. In the centre, the betrothed are waiting to be crowned. Note Carpaccio's delight in using strong and contrasting colours, notably red and white.

The *Arrival in Cologne* depicts how, on their arrival in the city, Ursula and her father, who has joined the pilgrims, learn that the city is in the hands of the Huns.

Ursula's eventful life on earth concludes with the *Martyrdom of the Pilgrims and Ursula's Funeral,* in which the two scenes are separated by the column. In the centre the warrior is removing blood from his sword. The final panel in the cycle, however, showing the *Apotheosis of St Ursula and her Companions*, is perhaps the saddest. **Room XXII**, a small circular room, displays bas reliefs and sculptures. In **Room XXIII**, the *St George* by **Andrea Mantegna** (1431–1506) is one of only two paintings by the master who so influenced Bellini and consequently the evolution of Venetian painting. The knight is a synthesis of Humanism. *Madonna under the Trees* by Giovanni Bellini refers to the trees that serve as foreground to the landscape, channelling perspective across the countryside to distant snow-capped peaks. The *Allegories*, by Giovanni Bellin, is a particularly exquisite small painting intended as a decorative panel to set into a piece of furniture or mirror. *The Tempest* by **Giorgione** (c.1467–1510) is the crystallisation of a state of mind in a poetic narrative "fantasy picture" with the three figures, the ruins, the water and the village dramatically caught in an iridescent green flash of lightning.

Room XXIV, on the way out, is the former Sala dell'Albergo. Restored in 2013 with funds from Save Venice, it has the only intact 15C ceiling in Venice and houses works commissioned specifically for this room, including one of the collection's highlights: Titian's *Presentation of the Virgin to the Temple* (1530s).

👣 WALKING TOUR

🕐 *Tour leaving from the Accademia marked in green on the map opposite.*

On exiting the Accademia, leave the Campo della Carità on your left via the Calle Contarini Corfù. This leads to Fondamenta Priuli bordering the Rio di San Trovàso that crosses the Ponte delle Maravegie straight to Calle della Toletta, named for the plank bridges (tola) that were used in the past by Venetians to cross the canals.

This busy and peaceful area has small streets linked together by narrow passageways, many of which have a sottoportego. Little bars provide pleasant places to take a break. This is everyday Venice, frequented by a bustling crowd of employees and students on their way from the Ponte dell'Accademia to nearby Campo San Barnaba (🕐 *see I CARMINI*).

▶ The Calle delle Eremite on your left leads to the rio of the same name. Turn left alongside the latter on the Fondamenta delle Eremite or the Fondamenta di Borgo until you reach the Rio Ognissanti. Turn left onto the Fondamenta Bontini.

Rio Ognissanti

This canal is lined on either bank with gardens, visible through the railings and the openings in the walls, situated at the rear of the palace whose facade looks over the Zattere, towards the island of Giudecca (it is one of these palaces that P.-M. Pasinetti locates the action of one his novels. At the end of the quay, the Campo San Trovàso, like (almost) all the campo in Venice, is graced with a well with a finely crafted edge.

Chiesa San Trovaso

Entrance on the canal side. The church is dedicated to two saints (Gervasius and Protasius, the protomartyrs of Milan) whose names have been contracted to "Trovaso." Built in the 9C, the original church was totally remodelled by architects of the Palladian School between the 16C and 17C. Built in the plan of a Latin cross, it has a single nave with side chapels. In the presbytery, a chapel off to the right, hangs *Christ Crucified between the Two Marys,* by Jacopo Tintoretto's son Domenico (c.1560–1635) and *St Chrysogonus on Horseback* by Michele Giambono (active 1420–62). Other paintings by the Tintorettos as well as works by Palma il Giovane (1548–1628) and Andrea Vicentino (end 15C–early 16C) grace the church.

▶ After you have crossed the bridge, turn right onto the Fondamenta Nani. You will see, on the opposite bank, at the confluence of the Rio Ognissanti, a very strange building.

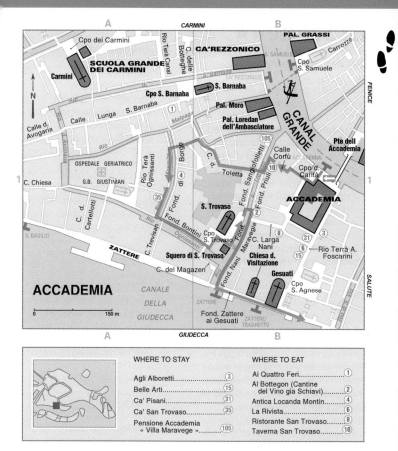

Squero di San Trovaso

This is one of the few *squeri* still in operation in Venice and is certainly the most famous, not least because of its unusual building. In a city of elegantly refined Byzantine *palazzi*, this seems idiosyncratic. Built of wood, with its geraniums tumbling from the balcony in summertime, it looks more like an alpine chalet. This picturesque little boatyard continues to function as a dockyard where gondolas are built and repaired, often in the open air, visible from the opposite side of the canal. (*www.squerosantrovaso.com*)

▶ Turn left onto Fondamenta Zattere ai Gesuati.

Chiesa della Visitazione

Near the Gesuati, the Church of the Visitation was built in its present form between the 15C and the beginning of the 16C. It boast two fine ceiling paintings by **Giambattista Tiepolo**.

Gesuati

🕐*Open year-round Mon–Sat 10.30am–4.30pm.* 🕐*Closed 1 Jan, Easter, 15 Aug and 25 Dec.* ✆€3 or Chorus Pass. 📞*041 27 50 462. www.chorusvenezia.org.*

The Church of Santa Maria del Rosario ai Gesuati is a famous landmark on the Zattere from the water. The Madonna of the Rosary was honoured by a 14C order of laymen, the Clerici apostolici S Hieronymi, distinct from the Jesuit brotherhood. Architect Giorgio Massari (c.1686–1766) created the new façade borrowing elements from the Church of San Giorgio Maggiore. Highlights of the luminous interior include the *Crucifixion* by Tintoretto, *Three Saints* by Piazzetta (1683–1754) and a *Madonna* by **Giambattista Tiepolo**.

La Salute★★

Despite the hordes of tourists visiting the landmark church of Santa Maria della Salute and the famous Guggenheim Collection of modern art, this corner of the **Dorsoduro** district is otherwise very peaceful. It is mostly residential, with not many shops, cafes and wine bars (to be found in the adjacent San Trovaso and San Barnaba districts). Foreign artists' workshops and the nearby Anglican Church, along with the numerous American and British tourists, give these streets an Anglo-American flavour; some of the street directions are even given in English.

●●WALKING TOUR

Le Zattere★

A walk along these *fondamente* provides exactly the kind of thrilling view that might be expected from a long balcony with a perfect prospect over the Giudecca Canal to the island of Giudecca itself on the other side.

The name Zattere was coined from the transportation of wood on rafts or *zattere* along here in the 17C.

The buildings evoke a past that involved both hard physical work and profound religious faith: the former **Magazzini del Sale**, a 14C warehouse used to store salt (*sale*) produced in Venice; the former Convent and **Church of the Spirito Santo**, from where the bridge of boats stretched across the water for the Feast of the Redentore; the **Ospedale degli Incurabili** (Hospital for Incurables), which later served as a home for abandoned children and as a musical conservatory.

The route is dotted with cafes which, in spring and summer, set tables outside on wooden platforms over the water.

Dogana da Mar

Dating to the 15C, the Dogana da Mar originally served as the customs point for goods arriving by sea. Fashioned to resemble a ship's hull, the building's

- **Michelin Map:** Vaporettto: Salute, Accademia
- **Location:** The tip of Dorsoduro, the "bow" of the city at the confluence of the Grand Canal and the Giudecca Canal has both quiet streets and the airy Zattere promenade. The walk can be combined easily with that around the Accademia area (see p147), which is why it begins from the Zattere. Vaporetti stops on the Grand Canal: Accademia (lines 1 and 2) and Salute (line 1). The night vaporetto does not stop at Salute. On Zattere: vaporetti **5.1, 5.2, 10, 6, 8** and **2** and, from midnight, the night vaporetto all stop at Zattere.
- **Don't Miss:** Sitting on the broad steps of La Salute to take in the sights and sounds of the Grand Canal. Stroll and watch ships passing along the Zattere.
- **Timing:** Allow about 3hrs for the walking tour, plus another hour for the Guggenheim Collection.
- **Also See:** *ACCADEMIA*.

present appearance dates from the 17C. A statue of *Fortune* towers over a golden globe, representing the world, supported by two Atlantes.

Punta della Dogana – ⊙*Open year-round Wed–Mon 10am–7pm (last entrance at 6pm).* ⊙*Closed, 24, 25 Dec and 1 Jan.* ⊛€15 (€ 20 with Palazzo Grassi). ●●*Guided tours available in english.* ℘*041 20 01 057. www.palazzograssi.it.* Opened in 2009, this museum houses contemporary art from the François Pinault Collection. Dogana Café serves breakfast, snacks, and drinks.

A must-see, located near the Punta della Dogana, Fondazione Vedova (Fondazione Vedova. ⊙*Open May 29–Nov 1; 10.30am*

–6pm. *Closed Tue.* *041 241 0833.* *€8. www.fondazionevedova.org.*

Santa Maria della Salute★★

Open year-round daily 9am–noon and 3–5.30pm. €4 (Sacrestia). basilicasalutevenezia.it.

The Basilica of Santa Maria della Salute is one of the most important and obvious points of reference on the skyline of Venice. It is also very dear to the Venetians: in 1630, when their city was racked by plague, they pledged a solemn vow to erect a church should the epidemic subside. Their prayers were answered and, in 1631, **Baldassare Longhena**, the pre-eminent Venetian Baroque architect of the day, was commissioned to develop the project.

This impressive basilica is rendered all the more majestic by its magnificent flight of steps up to the entrance. Dominated by the towering central dome, the great round volume emerges from an octagonal base: a geometric shape that radiates to eight façades presided over by a figure flanked by two angels over each pediment. Like Palladio before him, Longhena uses Classical architectural forms to build bold outlines and articulate every subsidiary part of his design: he employs figurative sculpture to punctuate profiles, to relieve flat planes and to reiterate the human dimension. The proliferation of statues at every level is a reminder that Longhena was born into a family of stonecarvers. Akin to a free-standing sculpture, the church occupies a prominent position from every viewing angle.

At the apex is a figure of the Madonna clutching the baton of the *Capitano da*

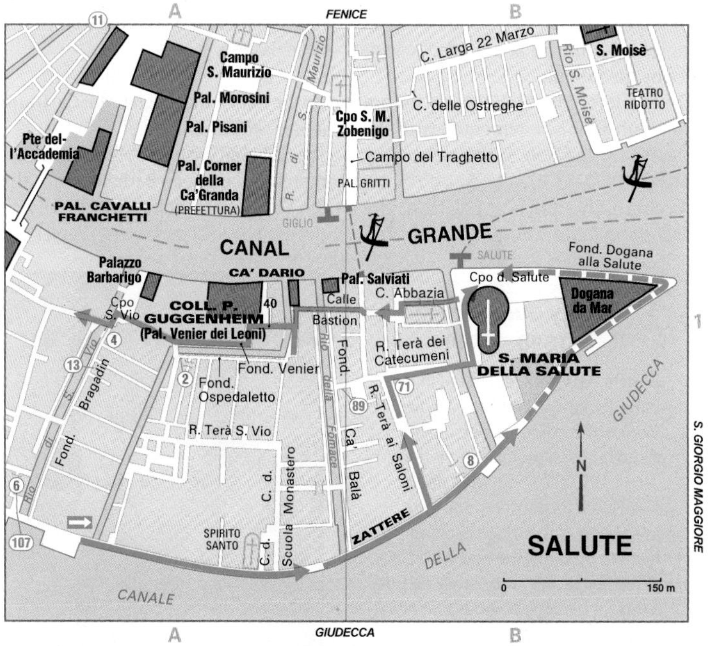

WHERE TO STAY

American Dinesen.............. 13
B&B Cà Fujiyama 11
Istituto Suore Salesie.......... 71
Messner.............................. 89
Pensione La Calcina.......... 107

WHERE TO EAT

Ai Gondolieri....................... 2
Cantinone Storico................ 4
La Piscina........................... 6
Lineadombra........................ 8

STREET INDEX

San Cristoforo (Calle)...........40

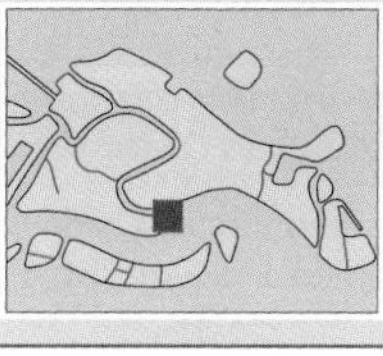

Mar (Captain-General of the Sea), poised above the balustraded lantern. Note also the figure of the patron presiding over the main pediment of the façade.

On the smaller dome stands St Mark, flanked by the weathervanes of the two *campanili* beyond, marking the far end of the church. At the drum level, great concentric volutes, also known as *orecchioni* (big ears), link the lower level of the outer section with the dome.

The interior is dictated by the main cupola, with the central area opening out into six chapels. The polychrome marble floor converges on a central circle of five roses which, together with the other roses of the wider circle, suggest the idea of a rosary. The central inscription in Latin states that it is from here that the health (*salute*) and salvation accorded to Venice emanates: tradition has it that the city was born on the Feast of the Annunciation (25 March 421) to signify the protection accorded to Venice by the Virgin.

On the left side, the last bay before the high altar is ornamented with the *Descent of the Holy Spirit,* painted by **Titian** (1490–1576) in 1555.

At the high altar is a 12C icon, the *Madonna della Salute,* also referred to as *Mesopanditissa* because it came from a place of the same name in Candia (Crete). The sculptural group above (1670–74) represents Venice, liberated from the plague, at the Virgin's feet: it is the work of the Flemish artist Juste Le Court (1627–79). The Plague is depicted, being chased away by the angel.

The sacristy boasts a wealth of treasures, the most eye-catching being the *Wedding at Cana* by **Tintoretto** (1518–94), in which the artist has included himself (as the first Apostle on the left), his friends and their wives.

The various depictions of the *Madonna in Prayer* are by **Sassoferrato**.

On leaving the sacristy, in the corridor before the chapels (*right*), are three notable altarpieces by **Luca Giordano**.

▷ Leave the Campo della Salute by crossing the rio of the same name and take Calle Abbazia, which becomes Calle Bastion.

On the right is the magnificent **Ca' Dario** (⌒see GRAND CANAL).

The Calle San Cristoforo leads to the harmonious Campiello Barbaro which the Rio Ospedaletto follows, bordered on the right by the Fondamenta Venièr and

Peggy Guggenheim (1898–1979)

Born in New York, educated in Paris, worked in London and died in Venice: this colourful personality has done much to popularise modern art. In 1939 she decided to open a museum for contemporary art in London, but during the period leading up to the Second World War, when she resolved to "buy a picture a day," it became obvious that it was safer to return home. In October 1942, when she opened her gallery "Art of This Century" in New York with a collection of Cubist, Abstract and Surrealist art, she wrote "I wore one of my Tanguy earrings and one made by Calder, in order to show my impartiality between Surrealist and Abstract art." She was briefly married to Max Ernst, the Dadaist and Surrealist.

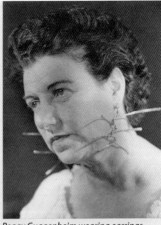

Peggy Guggenheim wearing earrings made for her by Alexander Calder

Collezione Peggy Guggenheim

© Peggy Guggenheim Collection, Venice. Ph. David Heald

on the other side by the Fondamenta Ospedaletto. Take the latter to admire, through the railings, one of these surprising gardens that Venice conceals. But the Peggy Guggenheim collection is situated on the other bank.

Collezione Peggy Guggenheim★★

♿🕐Open year-round Wed–Mon 10am–6pm. 🕐Closed 25 Dec. ◉€15. ✆041 24 05 411.
www.guggenheim-venice.it.

The Peggy Guggenheim Collection is housed in the incomplete **Palazzo Venier dei Leoni** (1749), which was designed by Lorenzo Boschetti, the architect of the Church of St Barnabas (👁see Il CANAL GRANDE). The entrance is through a peaceful garden, in whose surrounding wall are two stones that mark the final resting places of the owner and her beloved dogs. Peggy was the niece of American industrialist, Solomon R Guggenheim, who instigated the museum of the same name in the famous spiral building by Frank Lloyd Wright in New York. She began assembling her Venice collection in 1938, acquired the *palazzo* after the Second World War and lived there adding to it until her death in 1979, when, according to her express wishes, both the *palazzo* and the collection it housed were handed over to the Solomon Guggenheim Foundation.

The museum is arranged thematically, displaying parallel collections of Abstract and Surrealist works by the same artists. Particularly strong in Surrealist art , the gallery contains works by **Braque** (1882–1963); **Picasso** (1881–1973); Mondrian (1872–1944); Boccioni (1882–1916); **Brancusi** (1876–1957); **Kandinsky** (1866–1944); **Chagall** (1887–1985) – including *The Rain*; Balla (1871–1958) – including *Abstract Speed+Noise*; Severini (1883–1966) – including *Sea = Ballerina*; **Mirò** (1893–1983); De Chirico (1888–1978) – including *The Red Tower*; **Max Ernst** (1891–1976); Klee (1879–1940); Magritte (1898–1967) – including *Empire of Light*; Dali (1904–89); **Pollock** (1912–56); **Calder** (1898–1976) – including *Mobile*; Vasarely (1908–90) and **Moore** (1898–1986). Look out for the 23 sculptures designed by Picasso and executed by Egidio Costantini (1964), positioned in the window to maximize their transparency against the dark water of the Grand Canal beyond.

The Guggenheim also holds the **Mattioli Collection**, which includes 26 masterpieces by the Futurist painters Carrà (1881–1966) – including *La Galleria di Milano*; Severini – including *Ballerina in Blu*; Boccioni; and other important masters such as Morandi (1890–1964); Sironi (1885–1961); and Modigliani (1884–1920).

Outside, *The Angel of the City,* a sculpture by Marino Marini (1901–80), stands guard over the Grand Canal.

Schiavoni and Arsenale★★

Beyond St Mark's Square, the formidable Arsenal symbolizes the naval power of la Serenissima. A walk along the little streets that slumber under the high walls will allow you to discover a different Venice, in an area that was long inhabited by the Dalmatians, who built their "Scuola", decorated with an amazing cycle of paintings by Vittore Carpaccio, here.

◗◖WALKING TOUR

⚘Tour leaving from Riva degli Schiavoni marked in green on the map on p161. Access on foot from St Mark's Square or via vaporetto (San Zaccaria stop).

Riva degli Schiavoni

The name of "Slavonians' quay " is a reminder that it was here, on the edge of the St Mark's Basin (canale San Marco), that ships from Dalmatia (Schiavona or Slavonia), which was for a long time partly Venetian, used to moor. It doubtless also evokes the fact that it was the district chosen by the Dalmatians, who formed a very important community here after the region's annexation by the Republic of Venice. Lined with hotels and restaurants, the riva is largely open onto the lagoon and affords some beautiful views. The narrow strip of land of the Lido, facing the island of San Giorgio Maggiore, partially conceals the island of Giudecca, which seems to close the lagoon; on the right, the dome of the Salute marks the entrance to the Grand Canal, while on the way back, your eye is drawn to the bell tower that seems to emerge from the Doge's Palace. You will also enjoy watching the comings and goings of the many different kinds of boats, particularly their manoeuvrings as they approach the jetties, between which glide little skiffs. A few majestic cruise liners advance silently on the water, guided by their tugs, to get to their mooring points on the Giudecca

- 🚶 **Michelin Map:** (⑨, HV) Vaporetto: S. Zaccaria, Riva degli Schiavoni
- ▷ **Location:** Venice's Arsenal is situated on the east of St Mark's Square; the area described here is demarcated by the Arsenal walls and the rii dei Greci, di San Lorenzo e di Santa Giustina, which separate it from the heart of the sestiere de Castello. Vaporetto stops on the St Mark's Basin: San Zaccaria (lines **1** and **2**) and Arsenale (line **1**).
- ◉ **Don't Miss:** Carpaccio's series of *St. George* paintings in the Scuola.
- ◷ **Timing:** Allow 3hrs.
- 🚶 **Also See:** *SAN ZACCARIA.*

canal, or, on the contrary, to reach the open sea beyond the Lido.

La Pietà

On the Riva, between the Rio dei Greci and the Rio della Pietà. ◷*Open year-round Thu 10.15am–1pm and 2–5pm.* ✆€3. www.pietavenezia.org or www.chiesavaldi.it.

Edging Riva degli Schiavoi, Santa Maria della Visitazione is better known as "La Pietà" (the merciful one) after its hospice for abandoned children, dedicated in the 14C. From afar, the church's white façade with its broad pediment supported on columns, finally added in 1906, is its distinguishing feature. Initially the church would have been integrated within the institutional complex, but in the 18C, when it was all to be remodelled by Giorgio Massari, it was decided that the church should be designed as a concert hall, given that the orphans' education was oriented towards music, at one time under the leadership of **Antonio Vivaldi**.

The internal structure is vaulted to optimise the acoustics. The orchestra and the choir are positioned along the side walls. Music is the theme of the superb frescoes on the ceiling and concerts are often staged here.

▷ After the second rio, la Riva becomes Ca' di Dio, then crosses the Rio dell'Arsenale to arrive at the Campo San Biagio, on which stands the Museo Storico Navale (museum of naval history).

🕴🕴 Museo Storico Navale★

The Museum is currently closed for renovation, but we visited the pavilion ships at rio della Tana Castello 2162 (near the marine museum) ⏱*Open year-round Mon.–Thu. 8.45am–1.30pm, Fri 8.45am–5pm; Sat.– Sun. and public hols 10am–5pm.* ⊚*€5.* ☎*041 24 41 399. www.marina.difesa.it/storiacultura/ ufficiostorico/musei/museostoricove.*

ight any boat enthusiast and prove a veritable treasure trove to anyone intrigued by Venice's shipbuilding industry. The museum comprises five floors and houses a large collection of artifacts: a torpedo, taffrail lights, mortars, cannons, firearms and sabres and scale models of the city and her fortresses.

As you enter, the **ground floor** holds cannons, various weaponry and a room with models. Note the large lanterns from Venetian flagships.

On the **first floor** are displays of wooden sculptures that decorated the galleys, coats of arms, naval weaponry, nautical instruments (including compasses and octants), parchment *portolani* (pilots' charts and navigation material specifying details of coastal areas, harbours, anchorages and dangerous waters), engravings, models of ships, fine examples of galleys' broadsides, the supposed remains of Lazzaro Mocenigo's flagship which disappeared in the Dardanelles in 1657 and a model of the state barge, the *Bucintoro* (♿*see PIAZZA SAN MARCO: Museo Correr*). The **second floor** is dedicated to naval history during the 19C and 20C and includes scale models and naval uniforms.

The **third floor** displays an extensive collection of ex-votos (offerings given by mariners to a church in thanks or commemoration of an event), a luxury vessel

from the 18C, gondolas (including Peggy Guggenheim's) and a model of a working boatyard, the Squero di San Trovaso (♿*see ACCADEMIA*). One room is devoted to models of Asian giunca and sampans. On the **fourth floor** there is a shell collection, plus sections on Vikings and the Swedish navy and its relationship with Venice. The rescue expedition of the airship *Italia* is also remembered here.

Arsenale★

Some parts of the Arsenal are open to the public for events, exhibitions and concerts, especially during the Biennale. arsenale.comune.venezia.it.

A naval base, depository for arms, and maintenance shop, the Arsenal served as the main shipyard, the heart of the Venetian State. Enclosed within medieval walls, it has two main entrances along the Rio dell'Arsenale: the **land entrance**, a grand Renaissance triumphal arch, constitutes the most important gateway, dating to c.1460, and presided over by the lions from Ancient Greece (Athens and Piraeus) brought over by Francesco Morosini after his victory over Morea in 1687. The **water entrance**, through which the vaporetto passes, is marked by two towers rebuilt in 1686.

The first recorded dockyard in Venice, the **Arsenale Vecchio**, dates to about 1104 when the demands of the Crusades stimulated shipbuilding. At one time, there were 24 active boatyards. In the 14C, the Arsenal was extended towards the southeast (**Arsenale Nuovo**). Altogether

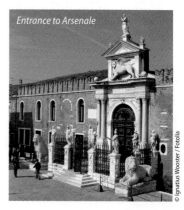
Entrance to Arsenale
© Ignatius Wooster / Fotolia

16 000 *marangoni*, men apprenticed as joiners and trained as shipwrights, were employed. The boat-building techniques were highly advanced, and the Venetians were already implementing production lines. During the second half of the 15C, the **Arsenale Nuovissimo** was extended to the north of the area – on the Galeazzi Canal (1564). Destroyed during the French occupation of 1797, the Arsenal was rebuilt by the Austrians between 1814 and 1830. After the Venetians attacked it in 1848, the area was abandoned during the third Austrian occupation (1849–66). Restructuring work began in the late 19C, and continued to 1914.

The street names serve as a reminder of the various trades and activities: Calle della Pegola (fish), Calle dei Bombardieri (cannon-ball foundries), Calle del Piombo (lead), and Calle delle Ancore (anchors). Mills churned out hemp rope; other structures included sail lofts, artillery warehouses and slipways.

Along the canal lies the **Scalo del Bucintoro** (*second on the right after the towers*), designed by **Sanmicheli** (1484–1559). This dock was home to **Bucintoro**, a magnificent state barge built for the Doge (*see PIAZZA SAN MARCO: Museo Correr*) by the **arsenalotti**, special artisans who worked in teams.

On entering the **Galeazzi Canal** the first building on the right is the **Complesso degli Squadratori**. Skeletons of the ships were squared here.

▷ After the bend, turn left onto Calle del Bastion and Calle delle Muneghette until you reach the peaceful Campiello Due Pozzi. Then turn left onto Calle del Mandolin, then right onto Calle dei Scudi, which leads to the Campo delle Gatte. Continuing on, Salizada de le Gatte and Salizada San Francesco, lined with small shops, lead to the church of San Francesco della Vign.

Coming from the south is particularly interesting as the route passes between the columns of an unusual 19C portico, of a delicate pinkish-brown colour, which links the naval headquarters with the Renaissance Palazzo Gritti, otherwise known as *La Nunziatura* (the Nunciature). Originally owned by **Doge Andrea Gritti** (1523–38), it was ceded by the Republic to Pope Pius IV (1559–65), who allowed it to be used by Apostolic delegates.

San Francesco della Vigna★

🕐*Open 8am–noon and 3–6pm.*

The name comes from the fact that there were vineyards here when the Franciscans first erected the church, begun in 1534. The main façade features a crowning pediment by **Palladio**. The *campanile* is one of the highest in Venice. Works of note include the *Four Evangelists* by **Giovanni Battista Tiepolo**, a *Virgin with Child* by **Veronese** and a *Madonna with Child and Saints* by **Giovanni Bellini**.

The church also accommodates the tomb of **Doge Marc'Antonio Trevisan** (1553–54). Its masterpiece is **Madonna and Child Enthroned★** painted in 1450 by the monk **Antonio da Negroponte**.

▷ Leave the Campo via Calle San Francesco, which leads on from the front of the church.

🕙 Good to know – If you turn around, you will get a fine view of the facade designed by Palladio, harmoniously framed by the houses lining the street. Keep going straight ahead until you get to the Rio di Santa Giustina to see the island of San Michele and its black cypress trees emerging above the brick walls of the cemetery. Turn left alongside the rio and you will arrive at the **Campo Santa Giustina**.

▷ Follow Calle del Fontego, then, bearing slightly to the left, Calle Zorzi va in Corte Nuova, after a sottoportego, which leads to the tranquil Corte Nuova and the Rio Sant'Agostino. Cross the bridge and turn left onto Fondamenta San Giorgio degli Schiavoni.

Popular and authentic, this part of the Castello district behind the Riva degli Schiavoni, mostly frequented by locals, has a unique Venetian charm: here elderly people sit on chairs outside their front doors and enjoy the cool of the

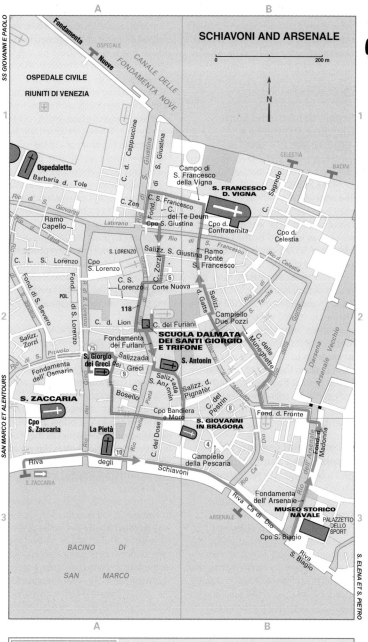

SCHIAVONI AND ARSENALE

0 —————— 200 m

N

WHERE TO STAY

Liassidi Palace..................75

STREET INDEX

S. Giorgio degli Schiavoni
(Fondamenta)..............118

WHERE TO EAT

Al Covo......................4
Alle Alpi da Dante..............6
Corte Sconta....................8
Da Remigio....................9
MET..........................10

evening while commenting on the news, cats bask on a campiello, while children chase a ball while dreaming of a future in the *Squadra Azzurra*.

▶ Cross the first bridge.

Scuola dalmata dei Santi Giorgio e Trifone★★★

♿🕐*Open Mon 2.45–6pm, Tue – Sun 9.15am–1pm and 2.45–6pm; Sun and hols 9.15am–1pm .* 👓€5. 📞*041 52 28 828.*

The original 15C buildings were remodelled by Giovanni de Zan in 1551, but the layout of the interior was retained. The *scuola* was founded by the Confraternity of the Schiavoni who, for the most part, traded with the Levant from here. Their patron saints were the three protectors of their homeland, St George, St Tryphon and St Jerome. In 1502 **Vittore Carpaccio** started working on his cycle of paintings, intended for the upper hall. The *Cycle of St George*★★★ took the artist five years to complete. It was moved downstairs in the 16C, to the intimate well-lit ground-floor gallery, which with its fine wooden ceiling, provided an ideal location to best show off the paintings' warm colours.

Cycle of Saint George, Saint Tryphon and Saint Jerome

😊 *It is best to read the panels from the left wall even if this does not follow the chronological order of execution.* (*In fact Carpaccio started painting episodes from the Life of St Jerome*).

St George and the Dragon catches the very moment when the knight attacks the dragon: the event is narrated pictorially with all the romance of heroic chivalry. The noble bearing of the saint and his steed, the dignified composure of the emotional princess and the architectural precision of the composition are true to the idealised legend, but contrast sharply with the macabre portrayal of skulls and hideously mutilated bodies.

The Triumph of St George dramatically depicts the saint on the point of killing the wounded dragon: the exotic figures are set against a background of Renais-

sance architecture, although the centrally planned temple is not positioned in the actual centre as this would have disturbed the harmony of the composition. In the next scene, *St George Baptising the Heathen King and Queen*, the group of musicians previously seen are present again as witnesses to the solemnity of the occasion; the picture is tempered only by the timorous hesitant pose of the saint. The pre-eminent significance given to the chivalry of St George may be due to the financial support given to the Scuola by the Knights of Rhodes, who considered the saint to embody all the ideals of the perfect knight.

St Tryphon Exorcising the Daughter of the Emperor Gordianus is a rare representation of the saint. Painted by Carpaccio and his assistants, the master's touch is recognisable in the architectural details and the distinctive personalities of the figures.

The two small paintings, the *Agony in the Garden* and the *Vocation of St Matthew*, are exceptions to the cycles dedicated to the lives of the Scuola's three patron saints, and serve as a prelude to episodes in the life of St Jerome.

The first canvas, *St Jerome leading his Lion into a Monastery*, offers a humorous depiction of the monks as they flee from the beast, which is more concerned with obediently following St Jerome. The building in the background is the Scuola di San Rocco.

By contrast there is no such animation or humour in the *Funeral of St Jerome*, only solemn tragedy. Set in the peaceful, ordered precinct of a monastery, the composition centres on the saint laid out on the floor, attended by monks. A basic, yet serene, sense of inevitability pervades the scene, suggested by the animals in the courtyard that represent the continuous natural rhythm of life and death.

St Augustine in his Study also alludes to the legend of St Jerome: the Venetian version of the story tells of St Augustine wishing to address a letter on a matter of theology to St Jerome, who had already died. His divine presence appeared in St Augustine's study admonishing him for his presumption (a Venetian edition of the letter was published in 1485). The study is flooded with natural light that highlights every detail including the dog's bemusement. The quality of rendering and exquisite attention to the furnishings, especially the open door into a second room, are reminiscent of Flemish domestic interior painting. The facial traits of St Augustine are, in fact, those of Cardinal Bessarione (1402–72), a scholar of Greek Humanism.

A variety of works in silver are displayed in the sacristy and in the upper hall.

Chiesa Sant'Antonin

Founded in the 7C, this church was built by Longhena. The bell tower, which dates from the mid-18C, is surmounted by an oriental-style dome.

▷ Follow Salizada Sant'Antonin, then turn left onto Salizada dei Pignatèr.

Campo Bandiera e Moro

℘ 041 52 05 906.
www.sgbattistainbragora.it.

Although it practically backs onto the Riva degli Schiavoni, this campo surrounded by beautiful palaces has a tranquil atmosphere. It was here that Attilio and Emilio Bandiera, heroes of the Risorgimento were born, and the campo is named in tribute to them and to Domenico Moro, another patriot.

San Giovanni in Bràgora★ – The interior of this late 15C church comprises a nave with a trussed ceiling and two aisles. In the left aisle, near the font, a copy of deed confirming the baptism of Antonio Vivaldi is displayed. The highlight is the **Baptism of Christ★★** by Cima da Conegliano (c.1459–c.1517). Also on view are works by **Alvise Vivarini**, Palma il Giovane (1544–1628) and Paris Bordone (1500–71). A stylised, truly Gothic *Madonna and Child with St John and St Andrew★* (1478) by Alvise's uncle, Bartolomeo Vivarini (1432–c.1491) and *St Andrew with St Martin and St Jerome*, the work of Francesco Bissolo (c.1470–1554), are also featured.

▷ Leave the Campo via Calle della Pietà, which beyond the rio becomes Calle dietro la Pietà. Calle Bosello on the right leads to Calle de la Madonna. Follow this on the left until you reach Rio dei Greci. Turn left before the rio onto the Fondamenta.

San Giorgio dei Greci

🕓 Open Mon and Wed–Sat 9am–12.30pm and 2.30–4.30pm, Sun 9am–1pm. 🕓 Closed Tue and during Mass. ℘ 041 52 39 569.

A closed complex designed by Longhena and a gently leaning tower comprise a 16C church and college buildings reserved for its Greek Orthodox community, and an icon museum. Founded originally by a colony of Greeks, a confraternity evolved to form the **Scuola di San Niccolò**. After the fall of Constantinople in 1453, its numbers increased greatly. The long narrow façade with its prominent pediment owes much to the influence of Sansovino. The cupola was added in 1571.

Inside, the great rectangular space is sealed by a magnificent **iconostasis★** embellished with holy figures against a gold background that screens off the apsed area. Beyond here is reserved for the clergy. The walls are lined with wooden stalls for use by the congregation during the long Orthodox rituals.

Museo di Icone Bizantine-postbizantine – ♿ 🕓 Open year-round daily 9am–5pm. 🕓 Closed 1 Jan and 25 Dec. ⚲ €4. ℘ 041 52 26 581. www.istitutoellenico.org.

The museum houses a rich collection of Byzantine and post-Byzantine icons and paintings portraying various religious subjects, exquisite illuminated manuscripts and religious artifacts.

Return along Salizzada dei Greci past **San Antonin** (**9**, **HV**), a church which dates back to the 7C but which was rebuilt by Longhena. The mid-17C campanile rises to an Eastern-style cupola. Continue onto Campo Bandiera e Moro with its church, **San Giovanni in Bràgora★** (♿ see ARSENALE), where Vivaldi was baptised, before turning back towards Riva degli Schiavoni.

▷ To get back to St Mark's Squre, cross the bridge and continue straight ahead.

Santi Giovanni e Paolo★★

This area is striking not only for its majestic architecture but also for the broad range of activity in the district, from the busy commerce of the *calli* between Campo di Santi Giovanni e Paolo (Zanipolo) and Campo Santi Apostoli to the tranquillity of Campo dei Gesuiti and the Fondamenta Nuove. From here, the view extends over the choppy waters of the lagoon to the cemetery of San Michele, disturbed only by the passing of the water-buses.

﹉﹎WALKING TOUR

Tour marked in green on map p168.

Continuing on from the previous walk, starting from San Giorgio dei Greci, follow the Rio di San Lorenzo on the right until you reach the Campo di San Lorenzo. Follow the Calle Larga San Lorenzo, then turn right onto the Calle Cappello until you reach the point where Calle del Caffetièr becomes Barbaria delle Tole. Turn left onto the latter.

Church of the Ospedaletto (Santa Maria dei Derelitti – *Guided tour by advance reservation and for groups only . 041 30 39 211. www.scalacontarinidelbovolo.com.* Along **Barbaria delle Tole** (the street owes its name to the timber or "tole" yard that was here and that exported to "Barbary"), this church, also called **Santa Maria dei Derelitti**, has a particularly extravagant Baroque facade designed by Longhena. Built from 1575 with an altar by **Andrea Palladio**, it has a colourful painted interior. Long renowned for its choirs made up of young orphans, led by prestigious musicians (such as **Domenico Cimarosa**), it has retained a music room, which is a real rococo gem.

Location: Part of the sestieri of Castello and Cannaregio, San Zanipolo (Giovanni e Paolo) is bounded on the north by the Fondamenta Nuove, on the east by the Rio di Santa Giustina, separating it from the Church of San Francesco della Vigna (*SCHIAVONI AND ARSENALE*), on the west by the canal de la Misericordia and on the south by the rii di Santa Marina and di San Giovanni Laterano. To get there, follow signs for "Ospedale" from anywhere on the left bank of the Grand Canal. The only area in the centre of Venice to back on to neither the Grand Canal nor St Mark's Basin, it is served by stops on the north lagoon: Celestia, Ospedale and Fondamenta Nuove (lines **4.1/4.2, 5.1, 5.2, 9, 12, 14 and N**, serving the islands of Murano, Burano and Torcello).

Don't Miss: The churches of Santi Giovanni e Paolo and Santa Maria dei Miracoli and the cemetery.

Timing: Allow half a day to enjoy this area.

Also See: Neighbouring sights: *CA' D'ORO; RIALTO*.

The road becomes Salizada Santi Giovanni e Paolo, which continues alongside the church to the Campo di Santi Giovanni e Paolo.

Campo di Santi Giovanni e Paolo

The name *Zaniplo* is a contraction of the names John and Paul in dialect, the two saints to whom the square is dedicated. **Equestrian monument to Bartolomeo Colleoni★★** – The proud gait of Colleoni – a mercenary soldier – his face set with a wilful expression, contrasts powerfully with the restless disposition of the horse. The commission for such a major monument was awarded to **Verrocchio** by competition. As the master died before it had been cast, Alessandro Leopardi oversaw the project and added the base. Inspiration came from the *Gattamelata* by Donatello in Padua, which, is ranked among the highest of its genre. The decorative **well-head** is attributed to Sansovino, who was also responsible for the side of the Scuola di San Marco that faces onto the canal.

Basilica dei Santi Giovanni e Paolo★★

Open year-round daily 9am–6pm.
No visits during Mass. and hols
€2,50. 041 52 35 913.
www.basilicasantigiovanniepaolo.it
One of the largest churches in Venice, San Zanipolo was founded by Dominican friars late in the 13C, but not consecrated until 1430.

The incomplete façade comprises at ground level a central pointed arch flanked by three blind arches; above, the width is divided vertically by plain piers rising up to niches on the roof line with statues of the Dominican Saints. On either side of the main portal, designed by Bartolomeo Bon, are the two sarcophagi of the Doges Jacopo and Lorenzo Tiepolo.

Interior

The well-lit lofty nave leads to an apse pierced by slender double lancet Gothic windows. In the form of a Latin cross, the church has three aisles and five apses. Huge columns carry great beams that support arches and the cross vaults.
The internal façade commemorates the **Mocenigo Doges**: (*centre*) Alvise I (**1**); (*left*) Pietro – (**2**) monument by Pietro Lombardo; (*right*) Giovanni – (**3**) monument by Tullio Lombardo.
Along the left aisle is the altar to St Jerome (**4**), its statue a work by Alessandro Vittoria; the pyramid nearby is in memory of the Bandiera brothers (**5**), supporters of Mazzini's *Young Italy*, who were gunned down in 1844.

At the altar to St Peter Martyr (altarpiece after Titian) is the monument to **Doge Niccolò Marcello** (**6**) by Pietro Lombardo; that to **Doge Tommaso Mocenigo** (**7**) with its great baldaquin, is the work (1423) of Niccolò Lamberti and Giovanni di Martino.
Flanking the double arch are two statues by Antonio Lombardo. Before the sacristy is the Renaissance monument to **Doge Pasquale Malipiero** (**8**) by Pietro Lombardo.
The **sacristy** is full of ornate decoration. Before turning into the transept are three panels of a *Polyptych* (**9**) by Bartolomeo Vivarini.
In the left transept, above the entrance to the Chapel of the Rosary but below the great clock, is a monument to **Doge Antonio Venier**.
The **Cappella del Rosario** (Chapel of the Rosary or Lepanto Chapel) was built as a mark of gratitude for the great victory over the Turks.
On the walls are depictions by Padovanino and Benedetto Caliari. Opposite the altar, Veronese has painted himself in the guise of the man standing beyond the column. Beyond the apsed chapels on the left, the central apse is replete with other **funerary monuments**.
Immediately on the left is that of **Doge Marco Corner** (**10**) by Nino Pisano, followed by the sepulchre of **Doge Andrea Vendramin** (**11**), a majestic work by Tullio Lombardo.

The Condottiere

Bartolomeo Colleoni (1400–76) was one of many mercenary soldiers (*condottieri*) engaged by the Venetian Republic to defend and acquire her territories. A native of Bergamo, Colleoni served Venice for a long time, with considerable success. He also served Francesco Sforza. Returning to the Republic of Venice, he was relegated to Malpaga Castle, where he died. His tomb is housed in the Colleoni Chapel in Bergamo.

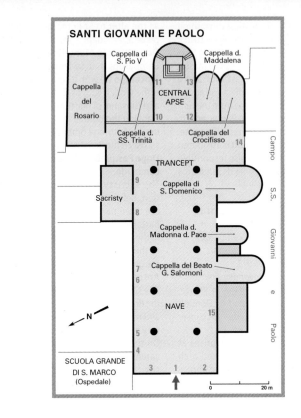

SANTI GIOVANNI E PAOLO

Cappella di S. Pio V

Cappella d. Maddalena

Cappella del Rosario

11 **13** CENTRAL APSE

10 **12**

Cappella d. SS. Trinità

Cappella del Crocifisso **14**

Campo

TRANCEPT

9

Cappella di S. Domenico

Sacristy

8

S.S.

Cappella d. Madonna d. Pace

Giovanni

7
6

Cappella del Beato G. Salomoni

e

NAVE

15

Paolo

N

5

4

SCUOLA GRANDE DI S. MARCO (Ospedale)

3 **1** **2**

0 20 m

On the right is the funerary monument to **Doge Michele Morosini** (1382) (**12**) from the workshops of Dalle Masegne. Here also is that of **Doge Leonardo Loredan**.

The first apsidal chapel on the right is dedicated to **Mary Magdalene**. The *Four Evangelists* are frescoed by Palma il Giovane; on the right wall is the monument to the **Sea-Captain Vittor Pisani** (1324–80); on the left is a particularly haunting piece known as *Vanity* or *The Conceited Woman* (17C), depicting a young girl looking at her reflection in a mirror and seeing Death.

In the adjacent **Cappella del Crocifisso** (Chapel of the Crucifix), the *Grieving Virgin* and *John the Baptist* are by Alessandro Vittoria.

In the right arm of the transept, the **stained glass** (**14**) evidences intense colour.

The **Cappella di San Domenico** (Chapel of St Dominic), in the right aisle, houses the *Glory of St Dominic* by Piazzetta (1683–1754). Before the **Cappella della Madonna della Pace** (Chapel of the Madonna of Peace) stands the **Valier monument** (1705–08), the largest of the Doge monuments. The chapel houses a Byzantine icon and works by Leandro Bassano (*left wall*), Aliense (*right wall*) and Palma il Giovane (*vault*).

In front of the Baroque **Cappella del Beato Giacomo Salomoni** is the tombstone of Ludovico Diedo who died in 1466, a fine example of *niello* engraving. Over the next altar sits an early *Polyptych* (**15**) by Giovanni Bellini.

The final monument comprises an urn said to contain the skin of Captain Marcantonio Bragadin, who was flayed alive by the Turks in 1571 after the surrender of Famagusta.

Scuola Grande di San Marco

© Anna Kurzaeva/istockphoto.com

Scuola Grande di San Marco★

🕐*Open year-round Tue–Sat
9.30am–1pm and 2–5pm.* 📞*041 52 94
323. www.scuolagrandesanmarco.it.*

This ancient **Scuola**, founded in 1260,
was transferred here from its original
seat in Santa Croce in 1438. Destroyed
in the fire of 1485, it was reconstructed
by Lombardo, and his sons Antonio
and Tullio, before being completed by
Lombardo's arch rival, Mauro Codussi.
It has reverted to the purpose for which
it was founded; at the beginning of the
19C, the building was transformed into
a hospital, first for military and now general civic use.

At ground level, the **façade** boasts an
effective series of *trompe l'oeil* panels;
two bold lions guard the left entrance
and, to their right, two groups of
figures crowd around St Mark healing and baptising Anianus, a cobbler
from Alexandria.

The **Sala dell'Albergo** now accommodates the medical library and several
large pictures, one by Palma il Vecchio
and one by Jacopo and Domenico Tintoretto. Before leaving the room, note
the lion with the closed Gospel, a conceit
alluding to whether Venice, at the time,
was at war or at peace.

The **Sala Capitolare**, also known as the
Sala San Marco, has a blue and gold ceiling bearing the symbols of the Scuole.
The lion in the centre holds an open Gospel. The large panel behind the altar is
the work of Palma il Giovane. Those to

each side are by Jacopo and Domenico
Tintoretto, as is the painting on the
opposite wall.

In addition to the antique medical
instruments, there are also some valuable 16C texts on display in the Sala
Capitolare, some of which were illustrated by Titian.

🔹 Leave the square via Fondamenta
dei Mendicanti that skirts the rio of the
same name. When you arrive at the
lagoon, turn left onto the quay.

Fondamenta Nuove

The Fondamenta Nuove, which runs
alongside the lagoon, was constructed
at the end of the 16C. Today water-buses
(vaporettos) depart from here for the
islands of San Michele, Murano, Burano
and Torcello. Venice's main theatre, the
Teatro Fondamenta Nuove, is to be
found near the Sacca della Misericordia.

🔹 After crossing the Rio dei Gesuiti,
turn left onto Salizada dei Specchieri,
which heads into the urban fabric.

Gesuiti★

The Jesuit church stands in a peaceful
square. It is all the more striking for its
white marble Baroque façade, decorated
with numerous statues, which include
one of the *Virgin*, to which it is dedicated, over the pediment. The present
building was erected between 1715 and
1729 on the site of the ancient Church

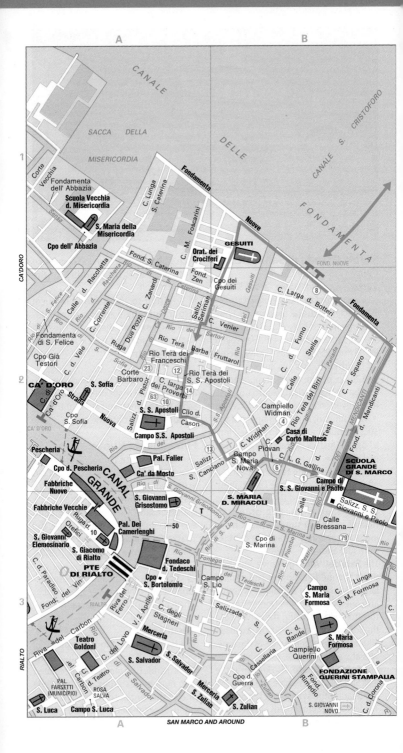

SAN MARCO AND AROUND

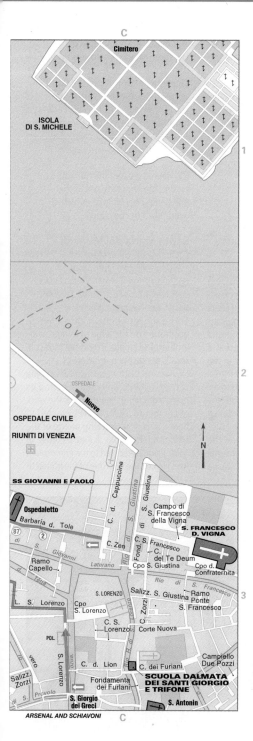

of Santa Maria dei Crociferi (1150). The sumptuous interior is enhanced by the white and gold stucco ceiling, the two central sections of which are by Francesco Fontebasso. Over the first altar on the left sits *The Martyrdom of St Lawrence* by Titian; in the left transept is the *Assumption of the Virgin* by Tintoretto. In the sacristy is a cycle of paintings by Palma il Giovane which, among other things, narrates stories from the Bible and of the True Cross.

Oratorio dei Crociferi★

⏱*Open only by reservation Fri–Sat 10am–1pm and 2–5pm.* ✒*€7 (inc. Scala Contarini del Bovolo) (*⃝ *see p145).* ☎*041 30 39 211. www.scalacontarinidelbovolo.com.*
Adjoining the Church of the Jesuits, the Oratory of the Crossbearers dates from the 13C. It was run by the Crutched Friars (*Fratres Cruciferi*), an Order of mendicant friars that was eventually suppressed in 1656. The hospital also served as a refuge for those who had fought in the Crusades. In 1414, it was transformed into a hospice for 12 destitute old ladies. Much of its decoration, on the history of the Crutched Friars, was undertaken between 1583 and 1592 by Palma il Giovane. Included in the painting on the end wall is **Doge Renier Zen**, a principal benefactor of the hospital of Santa Maria dei Crociferi.

On either side of the altar, two paintings depict the foundation of the Order. The three canvases on the left wall illustrate scenes from the life of **Pasquale Cicogna**, Procurator of St Mark's and Doge. Above the doors are represented *The Flagellation* and *The Dead Christ*. In homage to the Virgin, to whom the chapel is dedicated, the ceiling has been decorated with the *Assumption*.

▷ Having crossed the rio, walk around the church to get to the tiny Campo dei Miracoli, which is overlooked by the church.

Santa Maria dei Miracoli★

⏱*Open year-round Mon–Sat 10.30am–4.30pm (4pm Mon).*
⏱*Closed 1 Jan, Easter, 15 Aug, 25 Dec.* ✒*€3 or Chorus Pass.* ☎*041 27 50 462. www.chorusvenezia.org.*
This exquisite Renaissance church, positioned on the edge of a canal overlooking the small Campo dei Miracoli, recalls the distinctive nature of 14C Tuscan design both in terms of its crisply carved architectural ornament and its marble detailing. The church is the work of Lombardo (⃝ *see above*), erected to house a miracle-working image of the Madonna by Nicolò di Pietro (1409). In 1489, it was dedicated to the *Immacolata* (the Virgin), the doctrine of the Immacu-

Santa Maria dei Miracoli

San Michele in Isola

© Banet12/istockphoto.com

late Conception having been proclaimed 12 years before this.

The **interior**, especially the barrel vault, resembles a casket. Prophets and patriarchs are depicted in the 50 compartments of the coffered ceiling (*best appreciated with the mirror provided for this purpose*).

Casa di Corto Maltese

Rio Terà dei Biri, Cannaregio 5394/B.
⚬━ *Closed, reopening not determined.*

▷ Return to the Campo Santa Maria Nova and turn right. After the Rio San Canciano, Calle Piovan and Calle Larga Giacinto Gallina, lined with several wine bars, will lead you to the Rio dei Mendicanti, beyond which you will come to the Campo Santi Giovanni e Paolo.

NEARBY
San Michele in Isola

Venetians and many famous visitors have chosen to be buried here.

This great white church – the first Renaissance church in Venice – was designed by Codussi. The façade includes a fine doorway, topped with a pediment and a statue of the *Madonna*. Two arched windows frame the central bay with its rose window. Note the shells in the lateral niches and how the radiating ribs disappear into the shell.

The interior extends down to a full set of choir stalls, presided over by *St Jerome* carved by the Flemish artist, Juste Le Court. The whole is enclosed beneath a sumptuous coffered ceiling. The sacristy ceiling, however, is later in date, painted by Romualdo Mauro. The **Emiliani Chapel**, on the left flank, is decorated by Guglielmo de' Grigi, known as "il Bergamasco" (the man from Bergamo).

Cimitero (Cemetery) – *Ask for a map at the entrance.* ⏱*Open year-round daily 7.30am–6pm (4pm Oct–Mar). 7.30am–noon 1 Jan, Easter, 25 Dec.*

Here lie Ezra Pound (1885–1972), Igor Stravinsky (1882–1971), Sergei Pavlovich Diaghilev (1872–1929) and Josif Brodskij (1940–96), a Russian poet and Nobel Prize winner (1987), who drew on Venice for his work entitled *Fundamentals for the Incurable*:

Condemned for his anti-American propaganda, **Ezra Pound**, the author of the *Cantos*, was first interned in a concentration camp and then in an asylum, before spending his last years in Italy. He is buried in the Evangelical section to the left on entering. **Igor Stravinsky**, the Russian composer, along with his associate **Sergei Diaghilev**, the émigré founder of the Russian Ballet, are buried in the Greek section, at the end. Also in San Michele Cemetery lie the musician Luigi Nono (1924–90) and the great Goldoni actor **Cesco Baseggio** (1897–1971).

Ca' D'oro★★★

The much photographed Ca' d'Oro is the jewel in the crown of the tranquil *sestiere* of **Cannaregio**. Its arches are as symbolic of the city's style and identity as its gondolas, and a visit here, gazing down across the river onto the Rialto fish market, is a quintessential part of the Venetian experience.

A BIT OF HISTORY

When Marino Contarini commissioned the construction of his *domus magna* at the beginning of the 15C, the French artist Jean Charlier, known as Zuane de Franza di Sant'Aponal, painted the façade in blue, black, white and around the architectural carving it was gilded, hence the name given to the *palazzo,* "House of Gold". The original gold may have long gone but the Ca' d'Oro remains the city's gold standard in Venetian Gothic domestic architecture. Several Lombard masters, followers of Matteo Raverti (active 1385–1436), were involved in the construction of the Ca' d'Oro and under the leadership of Giovanni (c.1360–1442) and Bartolomeo Bon (active 1441–64) the Venetian masters took over. The well-head at the centre of the courtyard is attributable to Bartolomeo Bon, the son of Giovanni. The figures represent the three theological virtues of Fortitude, Justice and Charity.

Nowadays it is the façade and its reflection in the Grand Canal which most captivates the visitor. After a long period of restoration, the subdued colours have regained their magical intensity and the delicate marble tracery and crenellation are complete. The façade is harmonious in its asymmetry, despite possible plans for a left wing.

The original structure commissioned by the Contarini was subject to various alterations requested by numerous owners who lived there over the course of the centuries. Restoration work started in the 19C, when Prince Troubetskoy bought the Ca' d'Oro as a present for the ballerina Maria Taglioni. The restoration was

not faithful to the original construction. At the end of the 19C, more accurate restoration work was undertaken by **Baron Giorgio Franchetti**, who was responsible for the implementation of the gallery that now houses a varied collection of paintings, Renaissance bronze sculpture and medals spanning seven centuries from the 11C to the 18C.

⚓ **Michelin Map:** (4, ET)
Vaporetto: Ca' d'Oro, San Alvise or Madonna dell'Orto.

▷ **Location:** The district of Ca' d'Oro stretches between the Grand Canal and the north lagoon: on the east, the Strada Nuova links it to the Campo dei Santissimi Apostoli and, from there, to the Rialto. On the other side, the Rio Terrà San Leonardo leads to the station (direction: Ferrovia) along the Ghetto. You can get to the Ca' d'Oro on line **1 (N):** reach the palace via the small Calle Ca' d'Oro. You can also get to the vaporetto stops on the lagoon: Madonna dell'Orto is accessible by joining, behind the Scuola dei Mercanti, Calle Larga, which continues on from the Campiello Piave; Sant' Alvise, via Calle larga Canossiana from the square. The two stops are served by lines **4.1, 4.2** (Murano) and **5.1, 5.2**.

☺ **Don't Miss:** The Ca' d'Oro with its gallery and the melancholy charm of the walk along the forgotten canals.

🕐 **Timing:** Allow half a day to explore this neighbourhood.

⚓ **Also See:** Neighbouring sights *Il GHETTO; SAN ZANIPOLO.*

Façade of Ca' d'Oro

© Mauro Bighin / Dreamstime.com

VISIT

 ⏰Open year-round 8.15am–7.15pm (2pm Mon); last admission 30min before closing. ⏰Closed 1 Jan, 1 May and 25 Dec. €8,50 (€10 with Palazzo Grimani). ✆041 52 00 345. www.cadoro.org.

Take a few moments to enjoy the handsome courtyard with its exquisite marble flooring and statuary. The staircase and well-head are original features. Both were ripped out of the palazzo, but reinstated by subsequent owners.

Galleria Franchetti★★

The first floor is devoted to Veneto-Byzantine art from the 11C to the 13C. Notable for its luminosity is the central panel of the polyptych dedicated to the Passion by **Antonio Vivarini** (c.1420–84), which depicts the Crucifixion. Another significant work is the English 15C Scenes from the Passion of St Catherine.

The highlight of the gallery is **Andrea Mantegna**'s uncompleted St Sebastian★★, set in a niche at the end of the corridor on the right. Note the memento mori attached to the candle stating Nihil

nisi divinum stabile est – Coetera fumus (Nothing if not divine is eternal – all the rest is smoke) and the fact that the candle has just been blown out by the wind which ruffles St Sebastian's hair. The surge in popularity of St Sebastian during the early Renaissance is thought to be associated with his martyrdom by multiple arrow wounds, a fate involving the similar searing pain endured by those afflicted with the plague.

The other was an opportunity for a painter to prove his worth by depicting the nude torso of the young man modelled upon Classical sculpture. The other saint invoked by the plague-stricken is the pilgrim **San Rocco**, who was believed to have protected Venice from the epidemic. The saint seems to indicate where the bubonic swellings have appeared by the position of his arms.

Among the bronzes, the work of **Pier Giacomo Bonaccolsi** (c.1460–1528) stands out. The official sculptor at the Gonzaga court at Mantua, he was better known for his emulation of sculptures in the Antique style – note the Apollo on display in one of the small showcases).

Note also the *Annunciation* which appears to be set in Venice itself and the *Death of the Virgin,* painted by **Vittore Carpaccio** (c.1465–1526) and his studio, for the Scuola degli Albanesi.

The *Flagellation* by **Luca Signorelli** (c.1445–1523) is to be found on the same floor, along with the vibrant sequence from the *Life of Lucretia* in two paintings by Biagio d'Antonio (active to 1508). The latter depicts the departure of Sextus Tarquin from the Roman camp at Ardea, the rape of Lucretia, her suicide and funeral. The *Virgin with Child and St John,* a tondo by Jacopo del Sellaio (1442–93), is also on display here.

Exhibits on the floor above include the *Portrait of the Procurator Nicolò Priuli* by **Tintoretto**; Flemish tapestries from the second half of the 16C; *Venus with a Mirror* by **Titian** (1490–1576), which is incomplete on the right-hand side; *Portrait of a Gentleman* by **Sir Anthony van Dyck** (1599–1641) and *Venus Asleep with her Lover,* by **Paris Bordone** (1500–71). Two specifically Venetian scenes are by **Francesco Guardi** (1712–93): *St Mark's Square,* and the *View of the Wharf towards the Basilica of Santa Maria della Salute.* Of great importance despite being very damaged are frescoes painted by **Giorgione** (c.1476–1510) and Titian for the façades of the **Fondaco dei Tedeschi.** All that remains of Giorgione's work is the *Nude.* Titian's work is still discernible in the frieze with the *Justice* and the great coat of arms. Other interesting works include: paintings by Flemish artists, notable for their domestic interiors and landscapes; *The Crucifixion* by a follower of Van Eyck, remarkable for topographical detail, particularly with regard to the fortified city that emerges from the background.

The Franchetti collection of ceramics is displayed in the adjoining Palazzo Duodo.

☙WALKING TOUR

▶ On leaving the Galleria Franchetti, turn left on Calle di Ca' d'Oro, then left onto Strada Nuova.

Strada Nuova

This bustling thoroughfare runs almost parallel to the Grand Canal. It is part of the throbbing artery that starts at the Santa Lucia Station, snakes through the Cannaregio *sestiere* and eventually leads to the Rialto. Opened in 1871, the street is vibrant with the uninterrupted flow of people as visitors shuttle to and from the station and the Rialto, and locals do their shopping. It is lined with all sorts of shops, particularly the stretch of Rio Terrà San Leonardo near the station and around the lively market. Fish stalls run the length of the Fondamenta della Pescaria, alongside the Cannaregio Canal. Stop for a treat in a bakery, or take a break at an outdoor cafe – this is a great location to watch Venetians and visitors go by.

The **Church of San Felice** houses *St Demetrius with his Follower* by Tintoretto (1518–94) (*www.sanfelicevenezia.it*).

▶ Turn right onto the Fondamenta San Felice, which runs alongside the Rio di San Felice.

This tranquil *rio,* facing the lovely **Sottoportego del Tagiapier,** which supports some palaces, has an attractive charm that is enhanced by the contrast between the green water, which reflects the colour of the shutters, and the sienna facades. At the point where the *fondamente* bends sharply to the left, you will see the **Ponte Chiodo,** the only surviving example of the Venetian bridges without a parapet that are often depicted in paintings, such as those that can be seen at the Museo Correr and at the Fondation Querini Stampalia Onlus (☙ *see PIAZZA SAN MARCO).*

The **Ramo della Misericordia** and the Fondamenta della Misericordia lead to the intersection of two canals: the Rio della Misericordia and the Rio di Noale; the colourful houses reflected in the water create a charming tableau.

After the bridge stands the **Scuola Nuova della Misericordia,** a building designed by Sansovino in 1534 as the "new" seat of the Order and built in brick, but never completed.

▶ Continue on the Fondamenta della Misericordia.

Campo dell'Abbazia

The centre of this square, paved in brick in a herringbone pattern, is marked by a fine well-head. Bordering on the Rio della Sensa and the Misericordia Canal, the *campo* is hemmed in by the **Church of Santa Maria della Misericordia**, otherwise known as Santa Maria Valverde after the island on which it was built in the 10C, and by the **Scuola Vecchia della Misericordia**. The Baroque façade of the church, the work of Clemente Moli (1651–59), contrasts sharply with the Gothic brick façade of the Scuola of 1451. Beyond the church, the canal opens out into the lagoon via the **Sacca della Misericordia**, a cove buffeted by the wind, from where the view stretches into the distance, punctuated only by the Island of San Michele, the tranquil cemetery on the water.

▶ Return to the Campo dell'Abbazia and walk alongside the Rio della Sensa on the Fondamenta dell'Abbazia.

Since the 19C, literature and the cinema have portrayed an image of Venice as a city of mists and silent swash, woefully eroded by water, wind and time. This image will accompany you as you walk under the arcades of the old abbey and continue on to the bridge that spans the **Rio dei Muti**. Courtyards glimpsed through an open gate, balconies, surprising or incongruous architectural details, small deserted workshops, walls bearing the scars of age: everything here contributes to the atmosphere of magic and decadence.

▶ Continue along Calle dei Muti, then turn left towards the Fondamenta dei Mori where you will come to the rio.

On the *fondamenta* is the house (no. 3399) where Jacopo Robusti, more commonly known as **Tintoretto**, lived and, in 1594, died. A statue of Maure, his head wrapped in a turban, marks the corner of the **Campo dei Mori**, where you will see three other statues from the 13C with sphinx-like expressions. They depict the three **Mastelli brothers**, incorrectly known as the Moors: in fact, these three merchants were from Moreo or the Peloponnese. On the corner, the character with an iron nose is *Sior Antonio Rioba*, the "Pasquino di Venezia" to whose nose Venetians used to attach satires addressed to politicians and prominent figures in the city.

▶ The Campo di Mori, on the right, provides access to the Rio della Madonna dell'Orto.

Madonna dell'Orto★

🕐*Open year-round Mon–Sat 10am–5pm (noon–5pm Sun and hols). ☏041 71 99 33. www.madonnadellorto.org.*

This is known as the Tintoretto Church, as it was the parish church of the Tintoretto family. The richly ornamented brick façade betrays the various stages of construction from its foundation in the 14C, through early Gothic and Renaissance periods. Patronage was entrusted to the miracle-working Madonna dell'Orto (Our Lady of the Garden) when a statue of the Madonna and Child was found in a sculptor's garden.

The spacious interior accommodates important works of art: *John the Baptist* by Cima da Conegliano (1459–1517); *St Vincent* by Jacopo Palma il Vecchio (c.1480-1528); *Martyrdom of St Lawrence* by Daniel van den Dyck (1614-63). Over the entrance to the Mauro Chapel is the *Presentation of the Virgin in the Temple* (1551) by **Tintoretto** (1518–94), whose burial place is marked by a slab in a chapel on the right. Other works by the master, as well as by his son Domenico and by Palma il Giovane, adorn the church.

Next to the church stands the **Scuola dei Mercanti**, seat of the Guild of Merchants since 1570, when it transferred itself there from the Frari. Palladio participated in its renovation (1571–72) and is responsible for the portal which overlooks the *fondamenta*.

The **Fondamenta Gasparo Contarini**, which will take you to the Sacca della Misericordia. On the way, you will notice on the other bank a palace whose harmonious proportions, gothic elements and corner pillar – the remains of a Roman altar – are all impressive; the most striking feature is the bas-relief depicting a man pulling a camel. The **Palazzo Mastelli del Cammello** belonged to a family from Morea who settled in Venice in 1112. Popular lore credits its name to the many vats (*mastelli*) filled with gold sequins that it possessed. The camel (*cammello*) alludes to the merchant caravans carrying riches of the Orient. Several fine palaces line the tranquil *rio*, including, right at the end, the **Palazzo Contarini dal Zaffo**, and a glimpse of its huge garden.

▶ Retrace your steps, pass the church and follow the Fondamenta della Madonna dell'Orto until the first bridge on your left. The narrow Calle Loredan leads to the Rio della Sensa. Turn right onto the Fondamenta della Sensa, then right again onto Calle del Capitello, and follow this until you reach the Campo di Sant'Alvise.

Sant'Alvise★

🕓*Open year-round Tue–Sat 10.30am–16.30pm (4pm Mon).* 🕓*Closed 1 Jan, Easter, 15 Aug and 25 Dec.* ✍€3 or Chorus Pass. 📞041 27 50 462. www.chorusvenezia.org.
The simple brick façade is pierced by a rose window and a portal. Originally Gothic in style, the façade was greatly modified during the 16C. The statue in the lunette is of St Louis of Anjou, who lived towards the end of the 13C and was named Alvise by the Venetians.
The 17C frescoes by Antonio Torri and Pietro Ricchi lend an evocative three-dimensional effect to the flat ceiling. The entrance area is overlooked by the *barco,* the choir stalls used by the nuns, supported by columns with 15C capitals and Gothic buttresses. Above the columns stand 15C statues of Christ

the *Redeemer* and *John the Baptist*. As you enter, note the 15C **tempera panel paintings** on the left, by a pupil of Lazzaro Bastiani (active 1449–1512). On the right wall are Tiepolo's *Flagellation* and *Crown of Thorns* (1740); his *Christ's Way to Calvary* (1749) is in the presbytery. The 16C wooden polychrome statue of Sant'Alvise shows the saint dressed in a Franciscan habit with a splendid crown.

After leaving the church, you can either head towards the lagoon to catch the vaporetto or retrace your steps towards the Fondamenta della Sensa. The Calle della Malvasia, facing the bridge, leads to the lively and popular Fondamenta degli Ormesini, whose little cafés provide a good opportunity to take a break.

▶ To get to the Campo di Ghetto Nuovo (🕓*see CANNAREGIO AND THE GHETTO*), turn right and cross the iron bridge on your left. To get back to the Strada Nuova, turn left onto the fondamenta and continue straight on until you reach the church of San Marziale, visible on your right after a bridge.

San Marziale

The austere exterior of the **Chiesa di San Marziale** (4, **ET**) contrasts sharply with its rich Baroque interior. The ceiling decoration is the work of Sebastiano Ricci (1659–1734).
Campo San Fosca is dominated by a church of the same name and a monument to the remarkable **Paolo Sarpi** (1552–1623), a Venetian monk and scientist. A fierce defender of the Republic, he stood against Rome when Pope Paul V claimed rights in the religious courts. His arguments were so well founded that the Pope finally conceded to Venice. An attempt to assassinate him took place soon afterwards. Fra Sarpi is also credited with discovering the dilation of the iris and making the first map of the moon.

Cannaregio and Il Ghetto★★

A wide pedestrian thoroughfare leads visitors from the station to the Rialto, the Cannaregio canal and its colourful facades and workaday atmosphere. The mysterious Ghetto is steeped in history and drama, whose tall houses give it the appearance of a fortress. This walking tour offers you, aside from its many contrasts, a wonderful change of scene.

A BIT OF HISTORY

Although signs in the Ghetto refer to *Vecchio* (old) and *Nuovo* (new) these should not be interpreted in any chronological sense to the area as a whole: they are merely references to the old and new foundries. In fact, the Jews were first confined to the Ghetto Nuovo – then a practically impenetrable fortified island. At the time, the houses were rather squat and low-lying; the area was subjected to a form of curfew at nightfall, after which time the drawbridge was raised and the area sealed off. It was only in 1866 that access to the Ghetto was freed up and Jews were granted the same rights as other Venetian citizens. As long as the Jews were obliged to stay there, however, they were at least protected.

Indeed, it was precisely because their community was confined to this small area that their houses climbed ever taller. It seems ironic, now, to think that Jews were prohibited from undertaking any kind of building work, be it on their

- **Michelin Map:** Vaporetto: Ferrovia, Ponte delle Guglie, San Marcuola
- **Location:** On the right bank of the Grand Canal, east of the city, the Cannaregio district, which stretches to the north lagoon, is crossed by a major waterway, the Cannaregio canal. The old Jewish quarter borders this canal. On the Grand Canal, the district is served by the Ferrovia and San Marcuola stops. The Cannaregio canal is traversed by vaporetti **4.1, 4.2** and **5.1, 5.2.** Stops at Guglie, Crea and Tre Archi.
- **Don't Miss:** The monumental Palazzo Labia and its attractive square.
- **Timing:** Allow 3 to 4hrs for a leisurely visit.
- **Kids:** The playground at Parco Savorgnan.
- **Also See:** Neighbouring sights: *CA' D'ORO.*

houses, their five synagogues, or their *scuole.* Instead, they became *strazzaroli* (rag dealers in secondhand clothes and goods), doctors, and bankers involved in moneylending activities: the colours of their stalls were red (*no. 2912*), green and black.

WALKING TOUR

Tour starting from Campo San Marcuola (at the vaporetto

Sign of the Times

An 18C notice in the Old Ghetto warns Jews converted to Christianity not to frequent the ghetto, nor the houses of other Jews, on pain of "hanging, prison, hard labour, flogging, pillory." The means by which the Serenissima authorities were to be informed was secret denunciation via the infamous holes in the wall known as **bocca di leone.** These tablets also advertise the dues to be expected by the accuser, paid in recompense from the property of the accused.

stop of the same name) marked in green on map p180.

San Marcuola.
The name is a rather puzzling contraction of two saints' names: Ermagora and Fortunato, though how this came to make up Marcuola is lost in the mists of time or perhaps Venetian dialect.
The original construction dates back to around the 10C, but the church was subsequently restructured during the course of the 18C. The façade of the square, which is a landmark overlooking the Grand Canal, was never completed. Inside, the altars are the work of Giovanni Morlaiter (1699–1781), who sculpted the high altar in the famous Church of La Salute. There is also a *Last Supper* by Tintoretto on the left wall of the chancel.

▶ The *rii* (plural, *rio*) Terrà de la Chiesa and del Cristo lead to the Rio Terrà San Leonardo. Follow the Rio Terrà Farsetti opposite.

After crossing the Rio della Misericordia, turn left onto the Fondamenta degli Ormesini. Grocery stores, fishmongers, bakeries (*panifici*), hairdressing salons straight out of the 1950s, and little cafés, which set out their tables on the quayside in fine weather, make up a picture of a Venice that is busy, workday and a far cry from the one you may have

discovered between the Rialto and St Mark's Square.

▶ Take the metal footbridge that leads to the Campo di Ghetto Nuovo.

Campo di Ghetto Nuovo★
This square recalls the most tragic moments in the more recent history of the Jews in Venice: reminders include a relief (1979) by the Lithuanian artist Blatas and a *Monument to the Deportees* (1993) referring to the 204 Jews who were deported from Venice by the Nazis; only 8 returned from the death camps.

Campo di Ghetto Nuovo

A. Serrano/ hemis.fr

At the same time, the square projects a picture of everyday tranquility where ancient Jewish traditions live on: workshops manufacture objects relating to the Jewish faith, and glass ornaments and cards bear images of rabbis for those who seek inspiration to devotion, or who just want to buy a memento of this special corner of Venice.

Museo Ebraico

🕐 *Open year-round Sun–Fri 10am–5.30pm (Jun–Sept 7pm).*
🕐 *Closed 1 Jan, 1 May, 25 Dec and Jewish festivals.* ⊚⊚€4 *museum only; Full Tour* €10. ⬥ *Guided tours of the synagogues, Sun–Fri hourly from 10.30am; last tour Jun–Sept 5.30pm, Oct–May 4.30pm. Guided tours to the ancient Jewish Cemetery, by reservation.* ℘*041 71 53 59. www.museoebraico.it.*

The **Jewish Museum** (which also includes the Ghetto synagogues) has assembled together many precious artifacts relating to Judaism including many decorative objects and ornaments connected with the sacred scrolls (⬥*see Box below*). Of all the Torah covers in the collection, the one featuring the Jews encamped, the manna and the hand of Moses issuing forth water from the rock is particularly precious.

Synagogues★★

Occupying the upper floors of various buildings, the five windows and the lanterns peeping out from under the roofs indicate the presence of a place of prayer. All five synagogues in Venice (the Italiana, Levantina, Spagnola, Canton and the oldest, Tedesca) share the same bifocal layout in which the pulpit (*bimà*) and the cupboard that contains the scrolls (*aròn*) are placed, one in front of the other, along the smaller side of the room, with the women's gallery above.

The Spagnola and Levantina Synagogues are situated in the Ghetto Vecchio, which was assigned to the Jews in 1541. The **Spagnola Synagogue** (**8, DT**), the largest, was rebuilt by Longhena in the 17C. Longhena and his followers were probably responsible also for the restoration of the Levantina Synagogue, which

is used during the summer months. The Tedesca (Ashkenazi), Canton and Italiana Synagogues are situated in Campo di Ghetto Nuovo.

The **Canton Synagogue** (**8, DT**), named either after the banker who commissioned its construction in the 16C or the Venetian term *canton* which refers to its corner position, is renowned for its series of rare illustrations along the upper section of the walls. Strict observation of the second commandment prohibits the representation of any creature in the sky, on land or in water, of God or of man; even a suggestion of landscape inside a synagogue could be considered a distraction from prayer. However, the most important moments of Jewish history are recounted here. These include: *the Sending of Manna from Heaven, the Parting of the Red Sea* (interestingly, a hand can be seen protruding from the water, a detail that might indicate that the artist was Egyptian), *Moses Bringing Forth Water from the Rock, the Ark of the Covenant, the Symbol of the Jewish People who Crossed the River Jordan.*

Canal de Cannaregio

To the north, the canal links the lagoon to the Grand Canal. Two bridges cross the Canal; the north bridge closer to the lagoon leads directly to Campo San Giobbe. Continuing toward the Grand Canal, you can reach Ponte Scalzi and the Santa Lucia train station.

▷ Facing the bridge, take Calle delle Canne as far as the Campo San Giobbe.

San Giobbe

⊶*Temporarily closed for renovation.* ℘*041 27 50 462.*
www.chorusvenezia.org
This church is dedicated to the Old Testament figure of Job. Antonio Gambello began construction in the late-15C and it was completed by Pietro Lombardo. The plain façade is broken by a Renaissance portal. St Francis and Job appear in the low relief enclosed in the lunette.
Interior features include the coat of arms of **Doge Cristoforo Moro** (1462–71), who is buried in the presbytery.

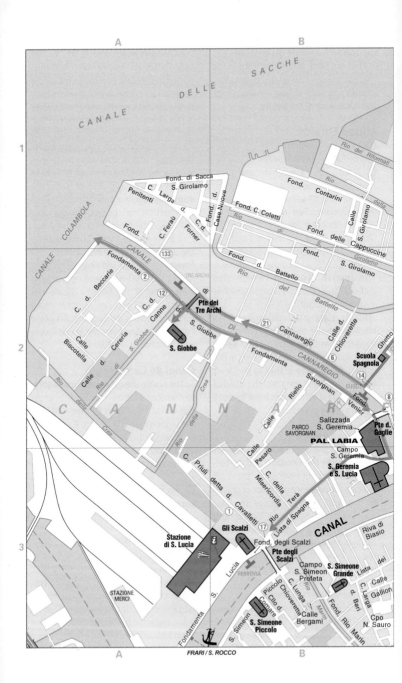

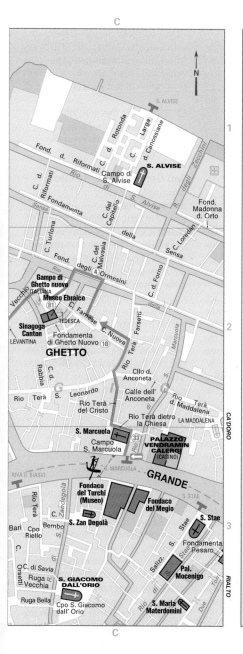

CANNAREGIO AND IL GHETTO

0 —————————— 150 m

WHERE TO STAY

WHERE TO EAT

▶ Return to the canal and turn right onto the Fondamenta di San Giobbe and Savorgnan.

Ponte delle Guglie (⓼, DT; B2)

Passing over the Ponte delle Guglie (1580) is practically obligatory, given that it is the bridge linking the railway station to the Strada Nuova. It takes its name, Bridge of the Gargoyles, from the architectural features that adorn the balustrade.

▶ When you arrive at the bridge, keep going straight ahead on the Fondamenta Labia.

Palazzo Labia★

Site is not open for visits.

The construction of this *palazzo*, built of Istrian stone, was commissioned in the late-17C by a wealthy family of Spanish merchants, to whom the building owes its name. The three façades, adorned with eagles – the family emblem – overlook Campo San Geremia, the Cannaregio Canal and a small square next to the Grand Canal. It was a prerogative of the Venetian nobility to have a residence overlooking the canal. The Labia family, who had paid to be listed in the **Libro d'Oro** (◔ *see History: 1789*) had to settle for a residence with a view of the Grand Canal, without actually overlooking it. In honour of Maria Labia's marriage in the 18C, **Giambattista Tiepolo** was commissioned to fresco the Salone delle Festa (Banqueting Hall); it would appear that the depiction of Cleopatra was inspired by her beauty. After the fall of the Republic, the family abandoned the *palazzo*, and when Napoleon handed it over to the Austrians, a long period of neglect began. In 1948 the palace was acquired by a wealthy Mexican oil magnate who organised a sumptuous ball in 18C costume to which the international jet set were invited. Abandoned again, restoration was postponed until the 1960s when it was bought by the Veneto arm of RAI, Italy's national television network, then put up for sale again in 2008, the city binding the sale to cultural use. Apartments arranged around the *salone*,

or main room, and the courtyard, include the Stanza degli Specchi (Hall of Mirrors), with *trompe l'oeil* walls; the Stanza del Mappamondo (Map of the World) and chapel adjacent; a corridor decorated with Cordoba leather; the Stanza dei Stucchi, hung with portraits of the Labia family; and a room with a lively 18C representation of the *Signs of the Zodiac*.

▶ Salizada San Geremia , which continues on from the Ponte delle Guglie, leads to the campo of the same name.

San Geremia e Santa Lucia

http://digilander.libero.it/santigeremiaelucia

Bathed in light, the interior of this 18C church is similar in plan to the Church of La Salute. It is here that the body of Santa Lucia lies. A Sicilian martyred under the persecution of Diocletian, she is the patron saint of the blind. Also of note is a painting by Palma il Giovane, *The Virgin Attending the Coronation in Venice*. The brick campanile, alongside, dates from the 13C.

Lined with shops (souvenirs) and restaurants, the **Rio Terrà Lista di Spagna** (lista indicated the zone near the embassies, which enjoyed diplomatic immunity), leads to Santa Lucia station.

Church of the Discalced (Barefoot) Carmelites

This church next to the train station was named for the Barefoot Carmelites, designed by Longhena, has a baroque facade of Carrera marble. Inside, the second chapel on the left aisle houses the tomb of the last doge of Venice, Lodovico Manin. Before it was destroyed during the First World War, the ceiling was decorated with frescoes by Tiepolo (the current highly ornate baroque-style decoration dates from 1934). However, some frescoes by the artist remain on the vaults of the first chapel on the left aisle, as well as an Apotheosis of St Teresa, created in 1722 (second chapel on the right aisle). The Chapel of the Holy Family is adorned with Murano blue-glass candelabra.

I Frari and San Rocco★★

A different Venice awaits you on this walk. You will discover a popular student city along the narrow streets interspersed with "campi", where locals gather to chat and enjoy the cool of the evening, and "fondamente" dotted with cafés and little restaurants. These lively areas also contain major works of art, such as the church of the Frari, renowned for its Titian altarpiece, and the Scuola di San Rocco, where one of the great Venetian painters, Jacopo Robusti, more commonly known as Tintoretto, realized his full potential.

🐾WALKING TOUR

♿Tour marked in green on map p186.

▷ Cross the Grand Canal on the Ponte degli Scalzi and turn right onto the Fondamenta San Simeone Piccolo.

Église San Simeone Piccolo
♿See p183.

▷ Return to the Ponte degli Scalzi and turn right onto Calle Lunga Chioverette which, after turning a right angle, crosses the Rio Marin. Continue on until you get to the church of San Simeone Grande.

San Simeon Grande
So-called to distinguish it from the Church of San Simeon Piccolo, the church is also known as San Simeon Profeta. Although its origins go back as far as 967, the building has undergone considerable remodelling, particularly in the 18C. The neo-Classical white façade dates from 1861.
The internal space is divided into nave and aisles by a series of columns crowned with Byzantine capitals and shrouded in heavy red damask drapes. Although the ornamentation is generally

▷ **Location:** From the Ponte degli Scalzi, opposite the station, to the San Pantalon church, this route enables you to explore the districts on the right bank of the Grand Canal. The beginning of the walk is served by the Ferrovia stops (right bank of the Grand Canal, lines **1, 2, 4.1, 4.2, 5.1, 5.2** and **N**) and Riva de Biasio (left bank, near the Campo San Simon Grando, lines **1, 5.1, 5.2** and **N**). You can also reach the Campo San Tomà from the stop of the same name via Calle del Traghetto Vecchio (lines 1, 2 and N).

▷ **Don't Miss:** Titian's masterpiece, *Assumption of the Virgin*, in the Maggiore Chapel within the Frari Church.

○ **Timing:** Allow a day.

👪 **Kids:** The Natural History Museum.

♿ **Also See:** Neighbouring sights: *I CARMINI, SAN ROCCO.*

heavy, there is an exquisite *Last Supper* by Tintoretto on the left of the entrance. On the left side of the church, the Campo San Simeon Grande (here, as nearly everywhere else, the place names painted on the walls are written in Ven-exiàn), which overlooks the Grand Canal and is equipped with a few benches, offers the opportunity to take a pleasant break. Alongside the Grand Canal, and a vaporetto stopping place, the Riva de Biasio immortalizes the name of a pork butcher, once renowned for his sguazzeto alla bechera, which drew customers from all over Venice, until it transpired that it was made from the flesh of young children! Needless to say, the reckless deli owner suffered an unenviable punishment commensurate with his crimes, but that didn't prevent the place, and even a vaporetto station, being named after him.

▷ Leave the campo via the sottoportego at the corner of the hotel Ai Due Fanali, turn right onto Salizada de la Chiesa, then left onto Lista Vecchia dei Bari, and finally bear left onto Calle Bembo after the Campiello Rielo.

San Zan Degolà

Dedicated to the beheaded John the Baptist, this church can trace its origins back to 1007, when the first parish church was built on the site. The terracotta façade is early 18C. A rose window is the main feature of the central section of the three-tier façade, framed by pilasters supporting a triangular tympanum. The relief on the right wall retells the story of John's decapitation.

As with the façade, a harmonious simplicity pervades the interior. The ceiling takes the form of an inverted ship's hull. The intense silence enhances the air of contemplation inspired by the frescoed chapels at the end of the side aisles.

▷ Leave the campo via the narrow Calle del Capiello then turn left onto Salizada del Fontego dei Turchi, which leads to the Grand Canal.

▲▲ Fondaco dei Turchi/Museo di Storia Naturale

&⏱*Open Tue–Sat 10am–6pm; Nov –May 10am–5pm (6pm Sat and Sun).* ⏱*Closed 1 Jan, 1 May and 25 Dec.* ✆€8. ✆041 27 50 206. *msn.visitmuve.it.*

A major renovation completed in 2012 brought new life to this 12–13C palace and former Turks' Warehouse that now houses the Natural History Museum. Abandoned from 1838 to 1865, the municipal authority later renovated it and transformed it into the Museo Correr. The building's present use was proposed in 1922. Vast, visually lively and varied, it is a perfect family outing. Displays are arranged by theme: palaeontology; natural collections, both as Curiosity Rooms as well as for study; and form and function in living things. The ground floor has an aquarium dedicated to regional coastal species (and out of

Museo di Storia Naturale

© Museo di Storia Naturale / Fondazione Musei Civici Venezia

view, the taxidermists' laboratories). The first floor has a display on the Venetian Lagoon. The second floor traces the path of life; fossils from Bolca near Verona illustrate the evolution of vertebrates, on to dinosaurs including the 12 ft/3.6m high Ouranosaurus skeleton and a giant crocodile skull. The theme then turns to collecting; a 16C-style Curiosity Room shows off specimens that were collected for their natural beauty and to amaze; other collections are grouped according to scientific classifications.

Retrace your steps, turn right onto Ramo Secondo del Megio and continue on until you reach the well-proportioned Ponte del Megio, which spans the Rio Fontego dei Turchi, bordered on the left by lovely palaces. Opposite, Calle del Pistor leads to the Palazzo Mocenigo and the San Stae church (⟲*see* Rialto) beyond the narrow Rio Ca' Tron, canopied by trees from a neighbouring garden.

▷ At the Ponte del Megio, turn right onto Calle Larga San Giacomo.

Campo San Giacomo dall'Orio

This is an endearing campo, one of those "intimate" places in Venice that you'll enjoy coming back to all the more for the many café and restaurant terraces that have taken up residence here. Shaded by plane trees and acacias, with a quirky shape and a layout reminiscent of the Campo Santa Maria Formosa (⚬ see PIAZZA SAN MARCO), in particular the position of its San Giacomo dall'Orio church, which presents its apses to the campo, this vast space is sometimes deserted but can become very busy in the morning and late afternoon. Elderly people and mothers occupy the benches, while children crisscross the square on roller skates or run around chasing a ball.

A few palaces stand alongside the campo, such as the Palazzo Pemma (immediately to your left), which shows hints of a lush garden when it is open, while on the left, facing the church, you can glimpse a floral, shaded terrace.

▶ Walk around the church to get to the Campiello del Piovan.

Bordered by a rio and the tables of a restaurant, this well-proportioned *campiello* skirts the facade of the church of San Giacomo.

San Giacomo dall'Orio★

🕓*Open year-round Tue–Sat 10.30am–4.30pm (4pm Mon).* 🕓*Closed Sun, 1 Jan, Easter, 15 Aug and 25 Dec.* ⬤*€3 or Chorus Pass.* ✆*041 27 50 462. www.chorusvenezia.org.*

The church was founded in 976 but most of its present fabric dates from 1225. The centre of the main façade features a Veneto-Byzantine patera with a statue in Istrian stone of the Apostle St James the Great standing above the portal. The bell-tower, erected in the 12C or 13C, is reminiscent of that on the island of Torcello. The three apses date back to different periods. The transept frontage dates from the 14C.

The Gothic lacunar **ceiling**, shaped like an inverted ship's hull, is striking. The nave is divided from its aisles by five baseless columns. Beside the entrance, David is depicted with excerpts from Psalm 150. The unusual stoop for the holy water is made of cipolin (onion) marble from Anatolia. Of the paintings in the choir stalls attributed to Schiavone

The Apostles in the Boat is the most likely to be by him. The organ was built by Gaetano Callido. It is likely that the Ionic column of ancient green marble, which was brought to Venice from Byzantium has been in the church since the 13C.

In the **New Sacristy** are Palma il Giovane's *Crucifixion with the Virgin and St John* and a version of *The Marriage at Cana* also thought to be by him. The **Santissimo Chapel**, is dedicated to faith in the Eucharist.

The **Old Sacristy** (*apply to the custodian*), besides its fine wood panelling, is decorated with a cycle of paintings by Palma il Giovane.

Set off along Calle Larga then turn left onto Calle dello Spezier to reach **Campo San Giovanni Decollato** (Campo San Zan Degolà, in Venetian dialect), where stands the church of the same name. This square, only a stone's throw from the incessant comings and goings of the Grand Canal, has an indescribable Venetian charm.

▶ Leave the Campiello del Piovan by crossing the rio via either the Ruga Vecchia or the Ruga Bella. From the Campo Nazario Sauro, take the Calle della Croce to get to the Rio Marin. Turn left at the latter.

This pleasant quay is made all the more so by a lovely patisserie-cum-tearoom that spreads its tables out on the right side of the Rio Marin (no. 784).

▶ Cross over at the end of the quay and turn left onto Calle dell'Ollio.

Scuola Grande di San Giovanni Evangelista

🕓*Open periodically when not hosting meetings; for opening days see the website.; 9.30am–5pm.* ⬤*€8. ✆041 71 82 34. www.scuolasangiovanni.it.*

The courtyard outside the Scuola of St John the Evangelist has been described as *"a little masterpiece of Venetian Renaissance architecture."*

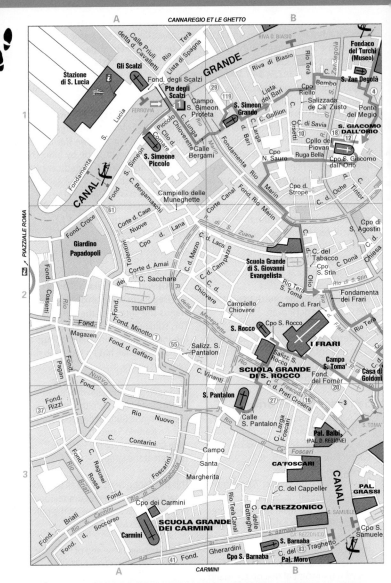

Salone, Scuola Grande di San Giovanni Evangelista

© J. Boulay / age fotostock

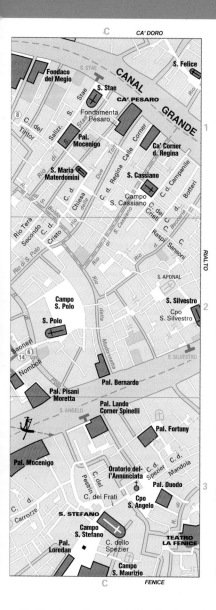

The Scuola was the second of the **Scuole Grandi** (👣 see I CARMINI: The Venetian Scuole) to be founded in 1201, and honoured by a confraternity of flagellants who attended religious processions stripped to the waist and whipping themselves with scourges. They are represented in the relief carvings dated 1349 at the front, which itself dates from 1454, when the large ogee windows were inserted.

The double stairway inside, lit with large arched windows, was built by Codussi. On the first floor, the oval windows were added by Giorgio Massari (1727), who raised the height of the **salone**. Various craftsmen are responsible for the decoration on the ceiling and the

Santa Maria Gloriosa dei Frari

© Stefano Scattolin/age fotostock

walls, including Domenico Tintoretto and Pietro Longhi.

The salone adjoins the Oratory of the Cross built to house Carpaccio's cycle of the *Miracles of the Relic of the True Cross,* now on display in the Accademia.

▶ Following on from Calle dell'Olio, Calle Magazèn then Rio Terà San Tomà on the left lead to the Fondamenta dei Frari, which will take you to the Campo dei Frari.

Campo dei Frari

🐾 **Good to know** – The name Frari is the abbreviation of Frati Minori, otherwise known as Friars Minor or Franciscans. This rather quirkily shaped campo is bordered by the Rio dei Frari, which is overlooked by the large Frari church. On the fondamenta, a few cafés and wine bars offer a pleasant place to stop before you visit the sanctuary.

Santa Maria Gloriosa dei Frari

🕐*Open year-round 9am (1pm Sun) –6pm.* 🕐*Closed 1 Jan, Easter, 15 Aug and 25 Dec.* 💶€3 or Chorus Pass. ✆*041 27 50 462. www.basilicadeifrari.it and www.chorusvenezia.org.*

This great church, Santa Maria Gloriosa dei Frari, is known simply as the Frari, which is derived from the abbreviation

of Fra(*ti Mino*)ri. It frequently draws comparison with the Church of Santi Giovanni e Paolo (🕐*see page 207*) because of its sheer scale and style. Monumental in stature, flanked by the second tallest campanile (70m/229ft 6in) after St Mark's, this building is strikingly magnificent, massive yet articulated with fine architectural detail, conforming to Franciscan archetypes, yet quite original. It impresses from every angle. The best view of the apses, the oldest part, is to be had from the Scuola di San Rocco (*opposite*); if contemplated from the bridge built by the monks in 1428, it appears just as breathtaking, its late-Gothic tripartite façade a masterpiece of design.

Exterior

The doorway is surmounted by a *Risen Christ* by Alessandro Vittoria (1581), flanked slightly below by the *Virgin with Child* and *St Francis* by Bartolomeo Bon (active 1441–64), supported on two finely crafted engaged columns. High above, inserted into the plain brickwork, are four circular window openings edged in white Istrian stone.

Over the side door into St Mark's or the Corner Chapel (*at the end on the left*) the Madonna is shown restraining the Christ child from struggling to break free.

Interior

The church is constructed in the form of a Latin cross. The nave is divided from the aisles by 12 huge cylindrical piers that soar up to the criss-cross of transverse and longitudinal timber beams underpinning the quadripartite vaults. The red and white floor tiles are from Verona.

The first noteworthy monument (*left aisle*) is neo-Classical and dedicated to **Canova** (1757–1822) (**1**). It was designed by the sculptor to commemorate Titian but was never completed. The allegorical figures before the pyramid represent Sorrow (portrait of Canova) with Venice (*left*), in the company of Sculpture (heavily veiled), Painting and Architecture. Beyond the Baroque monument to **Doge Giovanni Pesaro** is the famous

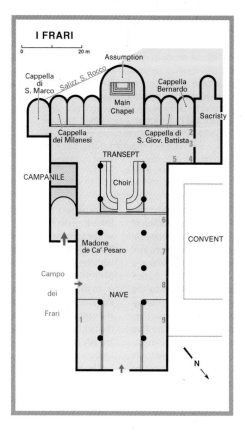

I FRARI

0   20 m

Assumption

Cappella di S. Marco

Salizz. S. Rocco

Cappella Bernardo

Main Chapel

Sacristy

Cappella dei Milanesi

Cappella di S. Giov. Battista

2

3

TRANSEPT

5   4

CAMPANILE

Choir

6

Madone de Ca' Pesaro

CONVENT

Campo

7

dei

8

Frari

NAVE

1   9

N

Madonna di Ca'Pesaro Chapel, dominated by Titian's altarpiece. Some commentators believe this represents the artist's wife.

Serving as a glorious harbinger to the Maggiore Chapel and Titian's *Assumption* are the 15C **choir stalls**, comprising 124 decorated stalls. The two organs on the right are signed Gaetano Callido (1794) and Giovanni Piaggia (1732) respectively. Beyond, early-17C paintings by Andrea Micheli, known as Vicentino, illustrate the Works of Corporeal Mercy (*left*) alongside his *Creation of the World*, the *Brazen Serpent*, a *Last Judgement* and the *Glory of Paradise* (*right*). In the left transept, the first chapel on the left is the St Mark's or Corner Chapel, which houses the *Triptych of St Mark* by Bartolomeo Vivarini (c.1432–91). High up on the wall opposite is *Christ's Descent into Limbo* by Jacopo Palma il Giovane.

The marble baptismal font with John the Baptist is by Sansovino.

Next comes the Milanese Chapel with its *Sant'Ambrogio* altarpiece by Alvise Vivarini and Marco Basaiti.

The **Maggiore Chapel** is the focal point of the magnificent perspective of the Frari Church. All points converge on Titian's **Assumption of the Virgin**, which was commissioned by the Franciscans in 1516. This major work, the first religious subject undertaken by the painter, caused the friars some consternation because of its unorthodox iconography. Instead of Mary's restful contemplation, the crowded painting shows the Apostles disturbed by the mystery of this supernatural event; *putti* and winged angels, singing and playing music, emphasise the upward movement of the composition, as the (nervous) Virgin looking ever upwards

The Council of Trent

Established in 1545 and dissolved in 1563, the Council of Trent aimed to encapsulate Catholic ideals in dogma and to structure its ministry by disciplinary reform. This ecclesiastical body confirmed the Church's sole right to interpret the Bible and underlined the role of the clergy as the only intercessors between man and God. The value of the seven sacraments was reaffirmed, and the practices of baptism and confirmation were ratified. The acknowledged existence of Purgatory, the invocation of saints, the veneration of relics, and the granting of indulgences were also endorsed and rationalised. Those opposed to the rationalisation of the Roman Church went on to precipitate the Counter-Reformation and found the Protestant faction.

towards God the Father is received in the Kingdom of Heaven in a triumph of light and colour. The brilliance of heaven is exaggerated by the careful portrayal of light from the realms of shadow and darkness on earth, via the more shaded zone occupied by angels, up to the explosion of bright light pushing the figure of the Virgin into bold perspective. Against the presbytery walls are two important monuments, one commemorating **Doge Nicolò Tron** by Antonio Rizzo – probably the most important Renaissance sculptural group in Venice (*left*) – and the other, from the 15C, to **Doge Francesco Foscari**, attributed to Nicolò di Giovanni Fiorentino.

In the right arm of the transept, the jewel of the Chapel of John the Baptist is the only Venetian work by **Donatello**, his *John the Baptist* depicted with the index finger of his right hand raised against Herod as a sign of admonition (unfortunately the finger is missing). Beyond the former Santissimo Chapel, now dedicated to Maximilian Kolbe, comes the Bernardo Chapel containing a *Polyptych* by Bartolomeo Vivarini (1482). *Before going into the sacristy note:*

♦ the equestrian monument to **Paolo Savelli** (d.1405) (2) who fought for Venice against the Carraresi;

♦ on the door to the sacristy, the 16C monument to **Benedetto Pesaro** (3) by Giovambattista Bregno. Between the columns that frame the doorway, note the Lion of St Mark's holding the closed Gospel: during periods of political conflict, Venice, unable to listen to the biblical teachings of

peace, would "close" the Gospel and leave it under the lion's paw;

♦ the terracotta monument to the **Blessed Peacemaker of the Frari** (4) with the 15C portrayal of the Baptism of Christ in the lunette;

♦ to the right of the transept, the monument to **Jacopo Marcello** (5), the captain of the Venetian fleet who died in 1488 during the conquest of the city of Gallipoli. The work is by Pietro Lombardo. The **sacristy** houses a splendid **Triptych** by **Giovanni Bellini**. Opposite is a lunette (1339) by Paolo Veneziano that was designed to be set above the Byzantine sarcophagus of **Doge Francesco Dandolo** (1329–39) in the adjacent Sala del Capitolo (⟞ *closed to the public*); the Capitolo was used for the periodic assembly of religious orders. The **Chapel of St Catherine of Alexandria** (6) is decorated with an altarpiece by Palma il Giovane, illustrating the saint's salvation from the torture of the wheel. In the next bay is the unusual statue of *St Jerome* (1504) (7) by Alessandro Vittoria, which recalls the style of Michelangelo.

The **altar of Purification** (8) is ornamented with a painting by Salviati. **Titian's Mausoleum** (9), hewn in marble from Carrara, was executed during the decade 1842–52. Titian, who died of the plague in 1576, was buried in the Frari in accord with his wishes, but by the end of the 16C all traces of his body had disappeared.

Directly opposite the marble pyramid with mourners is **Canova's Mausoleum,** built in 1827 by his pupils to a design Canova had made for Titian's tomb. Beside this is the **monument to Doge Giovanni Pésaro** (died 1669), complete with giant ragged-trousered Moors and decomposing bodies. The original work was by Longhena but the more graphic pieces are later additions by the German, Melchiorre Barthel. It has been called the most grotesque monument in the city – it is certainly one of the most bombastic.

▶ From the Campo dei Frari, walk alongside the rio of the same name, which leads to the Rio Terà. Take the first street on the right (Calle Secunda Saoneri), then turn right again (Calle Saoneri) and at the end of the street turn left onto Rio Terà dei Nomboli. Keep on until you reach Calle dei Nomboli.

Casa di Goldoni

♿🕐Open year-round Mon–Thur and Fri 10am–2pm (10am–5pm Sat and Sun). 🕐Closed Wed, 1 Jan and 25 Dec. ✆€5 or Museum Pass (♿ see p29). 📞848 08 20 00 or 041 427 30 892 (from abroad). www.carlogoldoni.visitmuve.it. It was in this *palazzo*, its small courtyard complete with a well and staircase, that the famous playwright **Carlo Goldoni** was born. The house is now home to the International Institute for Theatrical Research; one room serves as a small puppet theatre, housing works by Goldoni and Pietro Longhi.

▶ Return via Calle dei Nomboli and cross the Rio San Tomà to get to the campo of the same name.

Campo San Tomà

This lovely square with its simple, now deconsecrated church dates back to the 10C; it was remodelled in 1742. Straight ahead is the **Scuola dei Calegheri**, the guild of cobblers, which acquired the building in the 15C.

▶ Walk around the Scuola: behind it, Calle Prima leads to the Campo dei Frari.

San Rocco★★★

🕐Open year-round 9.30am–5.30pm. 🕐Closed 1 Jan and 25 Dec. ✆€10; no charge 16 Aug (St Rocco's feast day). 📞041 52 34 864. www.scuolagrandesanrocco.it.

Little is known of **San Rocco** (c.1295–1327), protector of the plague-stricken, other than he was born in Montpellier in southwest France. According to his Venetian biographer, Francesco Diedo, Roch travelled to Italy, where he miraculously cured plague victims (in Aquapendente, Cesena, Mantua, Modena, Parma…) with the sign of the cross until he, too, succumbed to the disease in Piacenza but recovered enough to return home. On his return to Montpellier, he was mistaken for a spy in Angers and incarcerated. He died there in prison.

San Rocco was particularly venerated in Venice, which as an important port was influential in spreading plague epidemics.

The Scuole di San Rocco was formed in 1478 and its prestige was enhanced (to Grande Scuole) in 1485 when the saint's relics were transferred to its care. The present headquarters was initiated in 1516 by Bartolomeo Bon, who was dismissed in 1524 after a major disagreement with the leaders of the Scuola. The project was then entrusted to Scarpagnino, who worked on the building until his death.

The magnificence of the Scuola resides in its interior decoration, which has an interesting history of its own. In 1564, a competition was launched for the decoration of the Salla dell'Albergo (*a small room on the first floor where the Chapter met*). Several illustrious artists, including Paolo Veronese, Andrea Schiavone, and Federico Zuccari, submitted their drawings, but **Tintoretto** quickly completed a painted panel for the ceiling and promptly donated his work as a gesture of devotion. In such circumstances, the work could not be refused, and so Tintoretto went on to furnish the entire Scuola with his paintings.

Spared from Napoleon's edicts, the Confraternity of St Roch is still active today. On 16 August each year, Venice

St Pantaleon

One of the patron saints of the city, Pantaleon (or Pantalon) was born to a pagan father and Christian mother. According to legend, he was reconciled to Christianity while employed as a physician at the court of Emperor Galerius at Nicomedia and denounced during the persecutions prescribed by Diocletian in 303. His cult was popularised in the Eastern Church, notably during the Middle Ages, when he was honoured as one of the patron saints of physicians. (*www.sanpantalon.it*).

celebrates the saint with traditional pomp and circumstance.

Exterior

Despite displaying a certain homogeneity, the façade draws together a variety of styles, most evident in the windows: those on the ground floor are early Venetian Renaissance and those above are Mannerist in design.

The rear façade, facing onto the canal, is simpler in format with a portico and finely carved details (note the heads on the pilasters on the first floor).

Interior★★★

Start upstairs by taking either of the two flights that feed into the single, grand staircase. Above, Scarpagnino's barrel-vaulted ceiling is painted with *St Roch Presenting the Sick to Charity, who Bears the Torch of Religion* by Giannantonio Pellegrini; the walls show *Venice with St Mark, St Roch and St Sebastian in Supplication for an End to the Plague* by Pietro Negri (1673) (*on the left*) – note the inclusion of the Church of La Salute, which was erected as a votive gesture at the end of the plague in 1630; and (*on the right*) *The Virgin Appearing to the Plague-stricken* (1666) by Antonio Zanchi.

Sala dell'Albergo

The most striking work of art in the Albergo Room is the huge and dramatic *Crucifixion* immediately opposite the door. In the left section of the entrance wall, the intensity of the scene in *Christ Appearing before Pilate* is concentrated by light focusing on the figure of Christ. In the middle section *Ecce Homo* is depicted, and to its left, *Christ Bearing the Cross*, a realistic rendering of the tragic journey, which Tintoretto populates with a weary cortège of figures moving in the opposite direction.

The *Three Apples* on the bench, reminiscent of Cézanne, is a fragment from the ceiling discovered above the door behind one of the capitals after four centuries.

Despite some controversy, the easel picture of *Christ Bearing the Cross* has been attributed to Giorgione and that of *Christ in Pietà* to his followers.

Sala Capitolare

In the large chapter house, subjects are based on the Old Testament (*ceiling*) and the New (*walls*).

The central ceiling panel depicts *The Brazen Serpent*, framed by two square panels depicting *Moses Striking the Rock* and *Manna Sent from Heaven*. The two large oval panels illustrate *Ezekial's Vision* and the *Fall of Man*. The other eight panels painted in green chiaroscuro conclude the Old Testament cycle.

On the side of the corridor is depicted *The Ascension*, followed by *The Pool of Bethesda*. *The Temptation of Christ* boasts a splendid Lucifer that echoes images of Eve tempting Adam.

On the wall opposite, the *Adoration of the Shepherds* is followed by the *Baptism*; in the central section opposite *The Ascension, The Resurrection of Christ* shows Christ seemingly bursting from the tomb as the two Marys walk in the morning light beyond; in *The Agony in the Garden*, the hour of the day imbues the scene with a faint reddish light. The focal point of perspective in *The Last Supper* is the bright halo hovering over the little figure of the Saviour.

The room also accommodates a large altarpiece, depicting the *Vision of St Roch* painted largely by Tintoretto, assisted by his son and studio; a *Self-Portrait* showing Tintoretto in a religious pose and one of his versions of *The Visitation*. *The Annunciation* however is by Titian, the two other easel canvases by Tiepolo.

Sala Terrena

On the ground floor hang Tintoretto's last canvases, dedicated to Mary. *The Annunciation* – a more "popular" version if compared to the aristocratic rendering by Titian – preceding *The Adoration of the Magi, The Flight into Egypt, The Massacre of the Innocent* (imbued some might say with a sharp sense of realism and desperate tragedy by a Tintoretto overwhelmed with grief at the death of his son), and a *Mary Magdalene*.

All Tintoretto's canvases conform to the aesthetic principles outlined by the Council of Trent, scorning all artifice and intellectual iconography in favour of a direct appeal to the common people.

San Rocco

The present façade of the church (🕐*Open year-round daily 9.30am–5.30pm (12.30am 1 Jan and 25 Dec)*). Built in the mid-1720s and remodelled in the late-18C. The statues of the *Saints* and the *Blessed* are by Marchiori and the Austrian-born Gianmaria Morlaiter. The portal, rose window and a few of the original Renaissance features survive on the side overlooking the *scuola*.

Above the entrance door, the **old organ door panels** painted by Tintoretto depict *The Annunciation* and *The Presentation of St Roch to the Pope*.

In the first side chapel of the left aisle, the altarpiece is by Sebastiano Ricci; the two tall panels by Pordenone show *St Martin* and *St Christopher,* and the panel below, *Christ Chasing the Moneychangers from the Temple,* is by Fumiani. Over the second altar is an *Annunciation and Angels* by Solimena. Four canvases by **Tintoretto** are to be found in the presbytery. On the other side of the church, towards the exit, the first altarpiece on the left is dedicated to *The Miracle of St Anthony* by Trevisani (1656–1746). In the middle, between the two altars, hang two more canvases by **Tintoretto**. The last altar is decorated with an altarpiece by Sebastiano Ricci.

▶ Take the alley (Calle Fianco la Scuola) that leaves from the left of the Scuola, and having crossed the Rio della Frescada, turn left onto Calle dei Preti Crosera, then immediately right onto Calle San Pantalòn, which leads to the campo of the same name, overlooking the Rio di Ca' Foscari and where stand the Palazzo Signolo-Loredàn and the church of San Pantalòn.

San Pantalon

Despite its unfinished façade (1668–86), this church recalls others in Venice such as San Marcuola and San Lorenzo.

Its main interest is its interior ornamented with an undisputed masterpiece by Fumiani comprising 60 canvas ceiling panels illustrating *The Martyrdom and Glory of St Pantaleon*a, executed between 1684 and 1704, and restored in 1970. The work is a tour de force of perspective, projecting the nave high into the sky. The presbytery decoration is by the same artist, often referred to as *fumoso* (meaning smoky) owing to his predilection for dark colours, so characteristic of a period tormented by ever-present death. To the left of the high altar, the small chapel, dedicated to a relic of the True Cross, houses *Paradise* (1444) by Antonio Vivarini. In the third chapel on the right is a work by **Veronese**.

▶ Beyond the rio, Calle della Chiesa leads to the Campo Santa Margherita, the starting point of the next walking tour (*🕐see I CARMINI*). To catch the vaporetto, return to Calle dei Preti Crosera, follow it to the end, then turn left onto Calle larga Foscari and, after the rio, right onto Calle Cristo, which will take you back to the Campo San Tomà. The vaporetto is at the end of Calle del Traghetto Vecchio, on the right of the church.

I Carmini★

This stretch of the **Dorsoduro** district includes a lively mix of university life with the daily markets in the **Campo Santa Margherita** and along the **Rio di San Barnaba**. Here waterborne greengrocers sell the freshest produce, including delicate artichokes from Sant'Erasmo. It is not difficult to find an eatery catering to students and tourists, or indeed a quintessentially Italian bar. There are plenty of shops catering for locals rather than just visitors and also the odd authentic *bottega*, particularly between San Barnaba and Campo di Santa Margherita, selling wood carvings and masks.

♙♙WALKING TOUR

Tour marked in green on map p196.

▶ Following on from the previous walking tour (*see I FRARI and SAN ROCCO*), from Campo San Pantalòn, cross the Rio di Ca' Foscari and get to the Campo Santa Margherita via Calle de la Chiesa.

Campo Santa Margherita

The distinctive features of this large square are the Scuola dei Varoteri (Confraternity of Tanners) and the stunted campanile of the former Church of Santa Margherita. Cafés, shops and market stalls add a buzz. Its relatively humble appearance derives largely from its position alongside the Rio della Scoazzera (meaning sewage channel), now running underground, which dissuaded the nobility from building patrician *palazzi* in its vicinity.

Scuola Grande dei Carmini★

Open daily 11am–5pm (4pm Nov–Mar). Closed 1 Jan and 25 Dec. €5. 041 52 89 420. www.scuolagrandecarmini.it.
The narrowest end of the Campo di Santa Margherita houses the Scuola dei Carmini (Guild of Dyers), devotees of the Virgin of

- **Michelin Map:** (**7**, CX) Vaporetto: Ca' Rezzonico, San Tomà or San Basilio
- **Location:** The Carmelite district is located on the right bank of the Grand Canal and bounded on the north by the rii dei Carmini, de Santa Margherita and de Ca' Foscari and on the south by the Rio Malpaga. The walk is described from the Campo Santa Margherita, following on directly from the previous walk. But you could also start this walk after arriving by vaporetto: get off at the Ca' Rezzonico (line **1**) stop or possibly at San Tomà (lines **1, 2** and **N**) or, on the Zattere, at the San Basilio stop (line **2**).
- **Don't Miss:** Ca'Rezzonico, an outstanding palazzo, exquisitely furnished. If you have time to see only one palazzo, this is the one.
- **Timing:** About half a day, plus 2hrs for Ca'Rezzonico.
- **Kids:** Children will enjoy watching the constant parade of all manner of watercraft on the Guidecca canal, including massive cruise ships.
- **Also See:** *ACCADEMIA, SAN ROCCO.*

Carmelo, borne out by the central picture on the ceiling of the Salone, *The Virgin in Glory Appearing to the Blessed Simon Stock, Consigning to him the Scapular* (a simple arrangement of two squares of white cloth tied together with strings over the shoulder, a standard part of the Order's costume). This panel and eight others were executed by **Giovanni Battista Tiepolo**. The **Sala dell'Archivio** is decorated with 18C wall hangings. On the wall next to the entrance to the **Sala dell'Albergo** is *Judith and Holofernes* by Piazzetta (1683–1754).

I Carmini

The simple Renaissance façade of this church and its 14C porch, decorated with Veneto-Byzantine pateras framing the portal on the left side, are in stark contrast to the rich decoration of the interior. At first sight, the red columns dividing the three aisles, the dark 17C and 18C paintings and the heavy black and gold of the statues lend a lugubrious atmosphere; yet the brightness of the internal space, the woodwork decoration so typical of such 14C churches, and its many paintings, soften the initial impression.

Dedicated to Santa Maria del Carmelo, the church contains some interesting works of art: among them are (*left aisle, near the entrance*) Padovanino's *San Liberale Saves Two Men Condemned to Death* and *St Nicholas between John the Baptist and Saint Lucy with Angels* by Lorenzo Lotto; (*right wall*) *Feeding of the Five Thousand* by Palma il Giovane; (*above the fourth altar, right aisle*) *Presentation of Christ in the Temple* by Tintoretto. Many of the paintings were restored by funds from the American Committee to Rescue Italian Art.

⊙ On leaving the church, cross the bridge and turn left onto the Fondamenta Briati then the Fondamenta Barbarigo, which skirt the Rio dei Carmini then the Rio di San Nicolò. Turn right onto Calle Rielo and follow the Rio de le Terese to the church of San Nicolò dei Mendicoli.

San Nicolò dei Mendicoli

The dedication of the church to the *Mendicoli* alludes to the beggars who used to live in the area, notably the *pinzochere* (impoverished religious women) who sheltered in the portico. Indications are that the church was founded in the 7C, although this building dates for the most part from the 12C, as does the massive bell-tower.

The central bay of the façade and its portico echo those of the Church of San Giacomo di Rialto. Inside, the wooden statuary dates to the 16C, when the iconostasis was given its present appearance. The paintings by followers of Veronese

(1528–88) depict *Episodes from the Life of Christ*.

⊙ Leaving the church, turn left to join the Fondamenta Lizza. Cross on the first bridge and take the Fondamenta di Pescheria (or de la Pescaria) to the church of Angelo Raffaele.

Beyond the **Church of Angelo Raffaele**, which contains the *Stories of Tobias and the Angel* purportedly by Gian'Antonio Guardi (1699–1760) on the parapet of the organ, Calle Nave branches off to the left towards the Church of St Sebastian.

San Sebastiano★★

🕐*Open year-round Tue–Sat 10.30am–4.30pm (4pm Mon).* 🕐*Closed 1 Jan, Easter, 15 Aug, 25 Dec.* ∞€3 *or Chorus Pass.* ℘041 27 50 462. *www.chorusvenezia.org.*

The true beauty of this church lies in its rich internal decoration: Vasari described Veronese's paintings as "joyous, beautiful and well-conceived". It is worth scanning the individual masterpieces before allowing time to absorb the overall effect.

Along the right side in the first side chapel hangs *St Nicholas* by **Titian** (c.1490–1576); in the third is a *Crucifixion* by Veronese (1528–88); the *Tomb of Livio Podacattaro*, Bishop of Candia (Cyprus), is by Sansovino (1486–1570); opposite, next to the organ, stands the **bust of Veronese** that marks the burial site of the master painter who so celebrated the beauty of the world with depictions of luxurious silk and velvet, buxom women in flesh and stone, surrounded by gold, glass and silver. It is the opulent quality of his art that renders the Church of St Sebastian unique; it was with this cycle of frescoes that the painter was preoccupied for the most significant part of his life.

St Sebastian recurs as the subject of many of the frescoes: above Podacattaro's tomb and behind the statue (*right*), the saint is shown pierced by arrows from archers on the wall opposite. His martyrdom is also depicted.

⊙ When you get to this point, you have two options: having crossed the

The Venetian Scuole

Instituted during the Middle Ages, the Venetian Scuole (literally meaning "school") were lay confraternities or guilds drawn from the merchant classes active in all aspects of everyday life, until the fall of the Republic. Patricians subscribed to the most prestigious Scuole, which excluded the poor, those engaged in morally dubious activities, and women, unless they were part of a member's family. Each Scuola had its own patron saint and **Mariegola**, a rule book and constitution of the guild. The Scuola di San Giorgio degli Schiavoni and the Scuola degli Albanesi were dedicated to assisting foreign workers financially and spiritually. Others were formed of artisans sharing a common trade. Those of a religious nature were known as the **Scuole di Battuti**, reflecting their penitential practices.

From the 15C, the Scuole were divided into *Scuole Grandi* and *Scuole Minori*, as resolved by the Council of Ten. At the time, some 400 Scuole were in existence: the buildings that housed the most important guilds were magnificent palaces, with their interiors decorated by famous artists.

bridge opposite the church, take the Fondamenta San Basilio, which leads to the Fondamenta Zattere al Ponte Lungo where you will find the S. Basilio vaporetto stop. From here, the 82 will take you to the island of Giudecca. To get to the Grand Canal, stopping to visit Ca' Rezzonico en route, take Calle de l'Avogaria opposite the bridge, which becomes Calle Lunga San Barnaba.

Campo San Barnaba

The buzz of this popular square is generated by a healthy mix of tourists and locals alike. It is confined by the simple white façade of the titular church, small shops, cafes and the food stalls along the Rio di San Barnaba near the Ponte dei Pugni. *Today the Chiesa di San Barnaba hosts an exhibition of machines designed by Leonardo da Vinci.* ○*Open year-round*

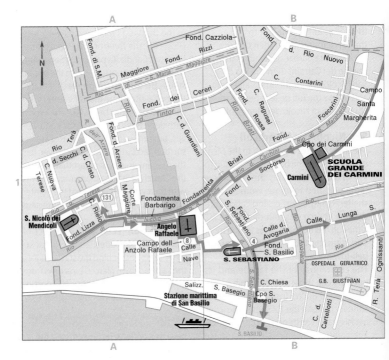

9.30am–7.30pm. €8. 339 79 85 464.
www.leonardoavenezia.com).

▶ To get to the Ca' Rezzonico palace, cross the Ponte dei Pugni, then turn right onto the Fondamenta Rezzonico, or, take Calle del Traghetto on the right of the church: from the vaporetto stop, a wooden pontoon provides direct access to the palace via the entrance overlooking the Grand Canal.

Ca' Rezzonico★★

The last *palazzo* to be designed by **Baldassare Longhena** was, in fact, completed by **Giorgio Massari** (c.1686–1766). It is markedly the product of two very distinctive masters who, despite their differences of opinion, worked towards the same end. **Henry James** (1843–1916) considered the Ca' Rezzonico to be such a majestic piece of architecture as to be almost mythological; Ruskin (1819–1900), who detested the Baroque style, likened the pilasters to "piles of cheeses." Originally commissioned for the Bon family, ownership was transferred incomplete to a family from Lake Como; one of

its progeny was to become Pope Clement XIII (1758).

Ca' Rezzonico was once owned by **Robert Browning** (1812–89) and his wife, the poet Elizabeth Barrett (1806–61), before passing to their son Robert (1849–1913). He was better known as "Pen", coined as an abbreviation of *penini*, which in Venetian dialect means small feet. Robert Browning junior was forced to sell the *palazzo* in 1906 when his divorce obliged him to return a large dowry.

Ca' Rezzonico now houses the **Museo del Settecento Veneziano** (Museum of 18C Venice).

Museo del Settecento Veneziano

Open 10am–6pm (5pm Nov–Mar); last admission one hour before closing. Closed Tue, 1 Jan, 1 May and 25 Dec. €10 *or Museum Pass (see p30).* 848 08 20 00 or (+39) 041 427 30 892 *(from abroad).*
www.carezzonico.visitmuve.it.
The visit begins with an enormous staircase, designed, as with the other state rooms on the *piano nobile,* to impress

I CARMINI

0   150 m

WHERE TO STAY

Tiziano.............................(131)

WHERE TO EAT

Casin dei Nobili..........................②
Da Toni....................................④
Osteria ai Pugni.........................⑥
Pane, Vino e San Daniele...............⑧
Ristoteca Oniga.........................⑩

guests and host elaborate Carnival fancy-dress parties. The **Salone da Ballo** (ballroom) is dominated by the great coat of arms of the Rezzonico family and frescoed by the master of *trompe l'oeil*, **Giambattista Crosato** (c.1685–1758). On the ceiling, *Apollo's Chariot* is flanked by the *Four Parts of the World*. Early-18C Venetian pieces include the ebony figurines and delicate chairs that once belonged to the Venier family. In spring, classical **musical concerts** are staged here.

The ceiling of the **Sala dell'Allegoria Nuziale** was frescoed by Tiepolo in 1757 for the society wedding of Ludovico, one of the members of the Rezzonico family,

Housed in the **Sala dei Pastelli** (Pastel Room) are portraits by **Rosalba Carriera** (1675–1757), including one of *Cecilia Guardi Tiepolo,* the wife of Giambattista Crosato and mother of the artist Lorenzo Tiepolo. The furniture is Rococo, delicate and ornamentally fanciful and over-decorative.

The **Sala degli Arazzi** (Tapestry Room) is hung with Flemish tapestries from the end of the late-17C that tell the story of Solomon and the Queen of Sheba. The furniture here is also Rococo. The frescoed ceiling from c.1756 is the work of Jacopo Guarana (1720–1808). Note the yellow lacquer door with chinoiserie decoration, very fashionable at the time.

The **Sala del Trono** (Throne Room) derives its name from the majestic golden throne adorned with nymphs, sea horses and *putti* that was used by Pope Pius VI on his visit to Venice in 1782. It is worth noticing Bernardino Castelli's particularly impressive portrait of *Pietro Barbarigo* (c.1780) set in its grandiose frame decorated with allegorical figures. The ceiling panel depicting *Merit* (crowned with laurel and attended by Nobility and Virtue) *Ascending to the Temple of Glory* was painted by **Tiepolo**.

Continue into the **portego**, where a golden sedan chair covered in red silk is kept. The doorway onto the stairs, is ornamented with two sculptures by Alessandro Vittoria (1525–1608).

In the **Sala del Tiepolo** (Tiepolo Room) the ceiling depicts *Virtue and Nobility Bringing Down Perfidy*. The four *Heads* on either side of the chimney are attributed to the sons of the great artist, Giandomenico (1727–1804) and Lorenzo Tiepolo (1736–76). Other notable works hung here include the *Portrait of the Architect Bartolomeo Ferracina* by Alessandro Longhi (1733–1813) The *bureau* in walnut is 18C; the games table with carved legs dates back to the late 17C/early 18C; the 17C cabinet was used as a strongbox. The next room is the **library**, furnished with gilded leather chairs and a clock made in London.

Despite its name, the **Sala del Lazzarini** houses only one work by this artist, *Orpheus Massacred by the Bacchants* (1698), displayed on the left as you enter the room.

In the **Sala del Brustolon**, the flowerstand table is decorated with an *Allegory of Strength*, personified by Hector. The 18C Murano chandelier is the best example of its kind to have survived intact from this period.

▷ Return to the portego for access to the second floor.

Upstairs in the *portego* are topographical works by **Canaletto**: *View over the Rio dei Mendicanti* and *View of the Grand Canal from Ca' Balbi to the Rialto Bridge*. Other works include those by Guardi, Piazzetta, Pellegrini and Strozzi.

Giandomenico's frescoes, which depict a crowd of peasants turned away from the viewer, once graced the Tiepolo Villa at Zianigo, near Mirano. They are now housed in a room at the end of the *portego*, on the right.

The **Sala del Clavicembalo** accommodates an early-18C harpsichord that gives the room its name. Works on display in the small corridor include *View of the Castel Cogolo* by Francesco Guardi (1712–39) in poor condition, *A Pastoral Scene* by Francesco Zuccarelli (1702–88) and *Teaching the Art of the Coroneri* (the *coroneri* being makers of crowns, rosaries and buttons) by Francesco Guardi.

The **Sala del Parlatorio** (Parlour Room) contains paintings by Pietro Longhi and two well-known pieces by Francesco Guardi: the *Parlour of the Nuns of San Zaccharia* and a miniature of *Palazzo Dandolo to San Moisé*.

▶ Access to the Sala del Longhi (Longhi Room) is back through the portego.

Among the 29 paintings by **Pietro Longhi**, note particularly his *Portrait of Francesco Guardi*. Longhi has been compared to England's William Hogarth as a social commentator of his times, although the depictions of quiet Venetian patrician domesticity are more benign than those of his English counterpart. The ceiling panel of *Zephyr and Flora* is by Tiepolo.

Chinoiserie predominates in the **Sala delle Lacche Verdi** (Green Lacquer Room). The *Triumph of Diana,* on the ceiling, is by Gian Antonio Guardi. Note the particularly evocative painting of the *Frozen Lagoon* (1788), by a follower of Francesco Battaglia.

The three frescoes in the **Sala del Guardi** (Guardi Room) are by **Giovanni Antonio**: *Venus and Love, Apollo* and *Minerva*. Little biographical detail exists about the Guardi brothers, Francesco (1712–93) and Giovanni Antonio (1699–1760), other than the fact that they relied on the tourist market for most of their trade. Francesco, the "Veduta" painter, uses paint freely to capture sparkling light in his topographical landscapes (a quality later admired and taken up by the Impressionists), whereas the elder brother animated his scenes with figures in a way that was to influence 18C British watercolour painting.

The **Alcova** (Alcove) is a reconstruction of a bedroom and boudoir; the pastel *Madonna* is by **Rosalba Carriera**. The 17C silver toilette service is the work of Augsburg silversmiths. Giandomenico Tiepolo is responsible for the ceiling of the wardrobe; the stucco decoration and the frescoes in the boudoir are by Jacopo Guarana.

Nello studio del pittore *by Pietro Longhi*

▶ Access to the third floor is via the portego.

The spacious **Pinacoteca Egidio Martini** houses a collection of paintings from the Venetian School dating from the 15C–20C. The visit of 18C Venice concludes with a reconstruction of the **"Ai Do San Marchi"** pharmacy.

▶ Leaving the palace, you can either catch the vaporetto or, alternatively, follow Fondamenta Rezzonico, turn right onto Calle delle Botteghe, then right again onto Calle della Malvasia. Finally, turn left onto Calle del Cappeller and continue straight ahead on Calle Foscari.

Ca' Foscari

A famous example of the Gothic style, Ca' Foscari was built in 1452 for the Doge Francesco Foscari. Today it accommodates the headquarters of the **University of Venice**. The approach from Calle Foscari is not ideal as the view of the *palazzo* is restricted by the crenellated wall that surrounds the courtyard. Bustling with student activity, the Ca' Foscari is best seen from the Grand Canal which, in turn, may be glimpsed from the salone on the ground floor, which hosts occasionl exhibitions (🦽*see Il CANAL GRANDE*).

▶ Cross the bridge over the Rio Foscari to get to Campo San Tomà (🦽*see I FRARI AND SAN ROCCO*).

© Ca' Rezzonico / Museo del Settecento Veneziano / Fondazione Musei Civici Venezia

La Giudecca

Once the island of Giudecca was dotted with the villas of wealthy Venetian nobles; today exclusive hotels are the only reminders of the luxurious living of the past. Not far from the Fortuny textile factory showrooms, the Molino Stucky flour mill was converted into a hotel, while another waterfront palazzo houses the local youth hostel. Here one of the churches took in girls without dowry to learn sewing and lacemaking skills. The origin of the area's name is either a reference to the Jews (giudei) who lived here, or perhaps an allusion to the 11C zudegà (judgement) that guaranteed land to noble families who had been exiled from elsewhere. Nowadays Giudecca island has a relaxed and peaceful atmosphere.

WALKING TOUR

Tour marked in green on map p200. Disembark from the vaporetto at the Palanca stop.

Location: The long and narrow island of Giudecca stretches along the south of Venice, separated from the Zattere and Dorsoduro by the wide Giudecca Canal, in constant movement with vaporetti, ferries from the island of Tronchetto, and even some large cruise ships. Line **2** (**N** after midnight) serves the Giudecca from Zattere (direction San Marco). It makes three stops on the island (Palanca, Redentore and Zitelle), before arriving at San Zaccaria by way of San Giorgio Maggiore.

You are going to explore the island's secret alleyways to discover a Venice that is more industrious and less prestigious than that of the opposite bank but just as endearing. The main "tourist" sites are located on the riverside, opposite the Zattere; you can therefore enjoy strolling along these fondamente, between the Mulino Stucky in the west and the Zitelle church in the east.

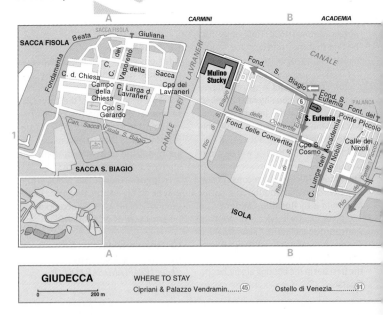

GIUDECCA	WHERE TO STAY	
0 ———— 200 m	Cipriani & Palazzo Vendramin.......(45)	Ostello di Venezia...........(91)

- **Don't Miss:** A long meander along the *fondamenta* following the canals that divide the island into its eight parts, from Mulino Stucky (now the Hilton hotel) east towards the Church of San Giorgio Maggiore.
- **Timing:** Allow 30–45min for the walk and visit of Redentore. Then stop in the Hotel Cipriani for lunch or afternoon tea; it's advisable to make advance reservations (*see Where to Stay in Your Stay in the City*).
- **Also See:** *SAN GIORGIO MAGGIORE.*

◗ Leave the vaporetto at Palanca and turn right along the Fondamenta di Ponte Piccolo, which becomes the Fondamenta Sant' Eufemia, then the Fondamenta San Biagio after the Rio di Sant' Eufemia.

Riva San Biagio

Planted with a row of shrubs, the Riva is also provided with benches: this is a perfect place to contemplate at leisure the other bank of the canal with its row of Zattere palaces, occupied by shipping companies on the right of ferry terminal. On the island side, a few dilapidated palaces soon give way to industrial facilities, such as the Fortuny warehouses (where they still make "artistic fabrics" using the original designs by Mariano Fortuny) and the Stucky mill.

Molino Stucky

This prepossessing but rather awkward construction, which would perhaps be more at home in Dickens' London, is the work of late-19C German architects. It takes its name from the Swiss entrepreneur who commissioned it and for decades was an empty landmark on the Venetian skyline.

The former flour mill now houses the luxurious **Hilton Molino Stucky Venice** hotel, boasting Venice's first rooftop hotel pool and a large spa.

◗ Retrace your steps to the church of Sant' Eufemia.

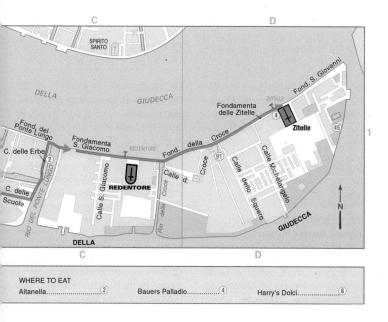

Sant'Eufemia

This is the oldest church on the island, its origins dating back to the 9C. Still graced with 11C Veneto-Byzantine capitals, the interior houses the colourful *San Rocco and the Angel* by **Bartolomeo Vivarini** (c.1432–91) (*first altar, right aisle*); the frescoed ceiling is by Giambattista Canal (1745–1825) and exalts the life of the saint to which the church is dedicated.

▷ Turn right onto the Fondamenta del Rio di Sant'Eufemia.

You will arrive at the **Campo San Cosmo**. On your left, beyond the *rio*, the **Fondamenta delle Convertite** houses a convent that has been converted into a women's prison. Further on are the old studios of the Scalera film production company, where scenes from **Luchino Visconti**'s *Senso* were shot in 1954. On the *campo* with its almost rustic appearance, the former Santi Cosmo e Damiano convent today houses a theatre centre and composer **Luigi Nono** archives.

▷ Follow the narrow street alongside the convent then turn right onto Calle Lunga dell'Accademia dei Nobili. Cross the Rio del Ponte Piccolo and continue straight ahead on Calle delle Scuole.

You will arrive in a modern district organized around the **Piazza Junghans**, which overlooks the lagoon and its wooded islands. Further on, the Rio del Ponte Lungo, which serves here as the "Grand Canal", is bordered by the Fondamenta Sant'Angelo (*turn left onto it*) and Calle delle Erbe, which leads to the Riva via a *sottoportego*.

▷ Turn right onto this street, cross the rio and follow the Fondamenta San Giacomo.

The view of Venice is magnificent: beyond Zattere, la Salute seems to emerge from the rooftops. In the distance you can see the Doge's Palace, and beyond it, the Riva degli Schiavoni. Closer by, the dome of San Giorgio Maggiore mirrors that of la Salute.

Il Redentore★

◷ *Open Tue–Sat, 10.30am–4.30pm (4pm Mon).* ◷ *Closed 1 Jan, Easter, 15 Aug, 25 Dec.* ⊜€3 *or Chorus Pass.* ☎*041 27 50 462. www.chorusvenezia.org.*
In 1576 Venice had been decimated by the plague, which had been raging for more than a year. **Doge Alvise Mocenigo** proposed that a new church be dedicated to the Redeemer, and every year thereafter honoured by a solemn procession.

Palladio was commissioned to design the church and sought to make it fulfil its votive function above all else. Its longitudinal axis was necessary for the long procession of clergy and dignitaries. The flat, rigorously Classical façade, set back from a flight of steps inspired by biblical descriptions of the Temple in Jerusalem, embodies an idealised view of the Catholic Church accommodating a modern, classically ordered building. Flooded with light, the unified interior is contained in a single nave lined with side chapels. As with the architecture, the paintings (by Bassano, Tintoretto and others) are arranged in such a way as to reveal their significance and unfurl the mystery of life as the procession progresses. In the **sacristy** hang a *Baptism of Christ* by Veronese and a *Madonna with Child and Angels* by Alvise Vivarini.

▷ Continue beyond the Rio della Croce on the Fondamenta della Croce.

Le Zitelle

The **Church of Santa Maria della Presentazione** was also designed by **Palladio**. The name *Zitelle* was coined from a reference to the girls without dowry, who were taught sewing and lacemaking in hopes they would not turn to lives of prostitution; they were accommodated in the adjoining hospice that forms part of the façade. Characteristic features of the main front include the dominant triangular tympanum, flanked by bell-turrets, over a semicircular window.

▷ The vaporetto Zitelle stop is opposite the church on the Fondamenta delle Zitelle.

San Giorgio Maggiore★

The island of San Giorgio Maggiore is not only thoroughly Venetian but provides first-rate views over the city. It does not detain visitors for long however as there are no bars nor restaurants here. For this reason alone, it is a "must" for anyone searching for a unique view of Venice and for those attracted to the serenity of monastic life, albeit only for an hour or so. It is also a must for Palladio fans.

A BIT OF HISTORY

The island's name relates to a church erected here in 790; the term *maggiore* is used to distinguish it from another island, San Giorgio in Alga. Since 982, the year a Benedictine monastery was founded here, the island's history has been associated with this monastic order. It became especially favoured by doges, who on 26 December would come and attend Mass in celebration of the Feast of St Stephen. However the island's moment of glory came with the arrival of **Andrea Palladio**, commissioned to redesign the church, which had already been rebuilt between 1400 and 1500.

The island's decline, coinciding with that of the Republic of Venice, was protracted into the 1850s. After both Napo-

- **Michelin Map:** (**9**, GHXY) Vaporetto: S. Giorgio
- **Location:** Positioned across from the tip of Giudecca, the island of San Giorgio Maggiore, recognizable by the dome of its church, faces the Piazza San Marco. To reach the island, take the vaporetto **2** and **N**.
- **Don't Miss:** The best possible view of Venice, from the church's bell-tower.
- **Good to know:** Take a bottle of water as there are no refreshment facilities. Accommodation is available in the monastery, call 041 52 27 827.
- **Timing:** The proposed tour takes about 2hrs.
- **Also See:** Neighbouring sights: *La GIUDECCA*.

leon and the Austrians had defiled the artistic beauty of the island, its finest buildings continued to be devastated by various armies passing through, including the Italian army using the dormitory as military stores during the Second World War.

The restoration of the island to its former beauty is largely due to the Cini Foundation and to the Benedictines, who, for more than 1 000 years, have faithfully preserved the original liturgical tradition

San Giorgio Maggiore

©P. Zelei/Getty Images

and Gregorian chants of San Giorgio, assisted by the Salesians, who are active in all fields of education and guidance. No one lives on the Island of San Giorgio besides these dedicated people. It is a place of retreat, of profound learning and deepest religious faith. Other than the monastery, there is nowhere to stay, nor anywhere to eat nor drink.

●●WALKING TOUR

San Giorgio Maggiore★★

🕐*Open Apr–Oct 9am–7pm; Sun 8.30– 11am and 2.30pm–6.30pm (Nov –May –sunset; Sun 11am Mass in Gregorian Chant).* ✆*church free, campanile €6.* 𝄞*041 52 27 827.*

The rebuilding of the church, to designs by Palladio, began in 1566. The front is dominated by a great triangular pediment supported by four columns: a feature borrowed from a Classical temple. The bright interior enhances the ample Latin cross space enclosed within its vaulted ceiling and apsed transepts. In the third chapel, *The Martyrdom of SS Cosmas and Damian* was painted by **Jacopo Tintoretto**, who also did the two large paintings in the presbytery. The main altar is ornamented with late-16C sculptures by Gerolamo and Giuseppe Campagna. The door to the right leads into the chapel (*open for Sunday services only*) decorated with Tintoretto's last work, his *Deposition from the Cross*.

The doorway in the left wall provides access to the **campanile**, given its present form by Scalfarotto in 1726. It offers the classic **view★★** over Venice.

Fondazione Giorgio Cini

Housed in a beautifully restored Benedictine monastery, this private institution is responsible for restoration work undertaken on many of Venice's monuments. It also stages important international conventions.

The foundation was founded by **Vittorio Cini** (1885–1977), a man who showed

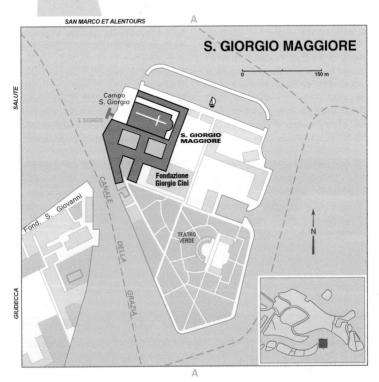

Riva degli Schiavoni from the church's bell tower

© Ruth Tomlinson / age fotostock

great courage and philanthropy during his life as a financier and government minister.

Library★

🕐 *Open during exhibitions only.* 🎫 *€10.* ♿ 🚻 *Only Guided tours (1hr) Sat–Sun 10am–5pm; guided tours available in English at 11am, 1pm, 3pm and 5pm (winter 11am, 1pm and 3pm).* 📞 *041 22 01 215. www.cini.it. Glass Tea House Mondrian. www.lestanzedelvetro.it.*

The library (1641–53) was designed by Longhena. It is decked with shelving and ornamented with carved wooden figures: the ceiling was decorated in the 17C Mannerist style.

Antique furnishing and objets d'art on the first piano nobile recreate the building's original character. Alongside thirty paintings of the Tuscan school are some fine pieces of applied arts: ceramics, porcelain (including a complete 275-piece 18C set by Cozzi), ivory caskets and badges, enamels, gold-work, candlesticks and chandeliers made in Murano, terracotta sculptures and furniture, including dressers, chests, bookcases, a rare Sienese marriage-chest of the mid-14th-century and an 18th-century Neapolitan sedan-chair.

Cloisters

This ancient monastery has two cloisters. The first, the **Chiostro dei Cipressi** (Cypress chloister) was designed by Palladio with paired columns and windows below curved and triangular pediments. This leads into the **Teatro Verde**, an open-air theatre with marble seats used during the summer. The second cloisters, which are older, were originally known as the **Chiostro degli Allori** (Laurel Chloister). Palladio worked with Veronese on the **Refectory** (*Refettorio*). For the end wall, Veronese painted a *Wedding at Cana,* a panel Napoleon had sent back to Paris, and which now hangs in the Louvre. Its replacement, representing *The Marriage of the Virgin,* is from the school of Tintoretto.

Glass Tea House Mondrian

Glass Tea House Mondrian, opened June 2014, offers a guided Japanese tea ceremony for two, which must be booked in advance. The structure is Hiroshi Sugimoto's first architectural work in Venice.

Dormitorio

The dormitory building is impressive for its sheer size (128m/420ft long) and lightness. Known as the *manica lunga*, meaning the long sleeve, it was conceived by Giovanni Buora at the end of the 15C. There are fine views from here towards the Riva degli Schiavoni.

On the outside is a 16C relief depicting *St George and the Dragon.*

Sant'Elena and San Pietro★

The Sant'Elena and San Pietro districts of the Castello *sestiere* are both peaceful and yet often vibrant too, as their green spaces – a novelty in Venice – attract crowds of locals. The view from the public gardens and the Park of Remembrance over the lagoon and St Mark's Basin is magnificent. Movement and activity pervade the area around the Rio di Santa Anna with its floating market, and extend to the bustling commercial activities of the only street (*via*) in Venice, to be named as such, Via Garibaldi.

🐾WALKING TOUR

🕭*Tour marked in green on map p208.*

▶ Disembark from the vaporetto at the Sant'Elena stop and turn right along the lagoon embankment.

A BIT OF HISTORY
Biennale

The 100-year plus history of this international exhibition of contemporary art (Esposizione Internazionale d'Arte della Citta di Venezia) is long and controversial. Even at its beginnings in 1895, it caused an outcry by exhibiting a painting by **Giacomo Grosso** described as "A casket with a cadaveric face coming out, while five naked young women surrounded him in despairing and lusty posing". Over a century later, it is often said that the Biennale thrives on conflict and controversy. No doubt it would be deemed a failure if it had not insulted or outraged a particular party for that year! The exhibition has always been held in the Giardini Publicci, where the pavilions host the various countries which elect to exhibit. It is held every odd-numbered year between June and November. www.labiennale.org.

- 🕭 **Michelin Map:** Vaporetto: S. Elena, Giardini Biennale
- ▶ **Location:** Further on from the Arsenal, the public gardens that host the famous Venice Biennale are well known to visitors and art and architecture lovers. The same cannot be said of the two districts that lie beyond it, Sant'Elena, which is somewhat unexpected here, and that of San Pietro in Castello, which is close to the heart of Venetians, who are still attached to their first cathedral. The Giardini and Sant'Elena vaporetto stops are served by **1, N, 4.1, 4.2, 5.1, 5.2** and **6**.
- 🕭 **Don't Miss:** Viale Garibaldi, a long pathway through a tree-shaded expanse lined with charming homes.
- 🕔 **Timing:** Allow 3hrs for a leisurely visit.
- 👫 **Kids:** The playground within the leafy grounds near the public garden.
- 🕭 **Also See:** Neighbouring sights: *ARSENALE*.

ISOLA DE SANT'ELENA

Up until the 11C, the island was known as *cavana* (refuge), as it provided sheltered anchorages to boatmen and fishermen. Its present name is derived from St Helen (c.257–336), mother of the Emperor Constantine, whose relics are housed in the church (first chapel on the right) and were brought to Venice in 1211, after the Fourth Crusade.

The small monastery, established in 1060, was built by Benedictine monks from Tuscany in 1407. Subsequent rebuilding was undertaken between 1439 and 1515.

During Napoleon's rule, the monastery was disbanded and its assets sold and dispersed; the church was used as a warehouse and troops were billeted in the convent buildings. During the late-19C and early 20C, the area around the church and monastery was extended and urbanised. Today, the church and convent accommodate Servite monks. This quarter is one of the cheapest parts of the city to dine out.

Church

On the far side of the Rio di S. Elena rises the Church of Sant'Elena, flanked by a stadium and military base. The Gothic façade is dominated by its portal (1467). The sculptural group above, by Antonio Rizzo, shows the Capitano da Mar (Sea Captain-General), **Vittore Cappello**, kneeling before St Helen. Through the gate to the left extend the cloisters. Erected in 1956, the campanile does not conform to the essentially Gothic structure of the church. Inside the luminous interior, a single nave terminates in an apse pierced with tall windows. The chapels radiate off the apse on the right.

👥 Parco delle Rimembranze

This Park of Remembrance is dedicated to soldiers who lost their lives in World War II. Children's play areas, green space and a skating rink make it a popular place for families on a sunny day.

Chiesa San Giuseppe

Beyond Viale Trento in a little square is the 16C church of San Giuseppe. In the first bay on the right is *St Michael and Lucifer Fighting over the Soul of Michele Bon* by Jacopo (1518–94) and Domenico (c.1560–1635) Tintoretto.

🔘 Cross the bridge just left of the square and follow Calle Correra to Fondamenta Sant'Anna. Turn right, cross the bridge on the left, and continue straight up Calle Larga San Pietro to the Church of San Pietro di Castello.

ISOLA DI SAN PIETRO DI CASTELLO★

This island was inhabited before the city of Venice was founded. Originally known as **Olivolo**, perhaps after its olive groves, the *sestiere* commemorates a castle (hence the name Castello) that was either built or found there by the earliest Venetians. Since time immemorial,

it has been the religious symbol of the city. Not only the seat of Bishop Castellano, and a dependent of the Patriarch of Grado, it still shelters the body of the first Patriarch of Venice, Lorenzo Giustiniani, who resided there in the 15C. The basilica stands in an open, grassy area, the venue for lively celebrations during the Feast of San Pietro di Castello.

San Pietro di Castello★

🕐 *Open year-round Tue–Sat 10.30am–4.30pm (4pm Mon).* 🚫 *Closed 1 Jan, Easter, 15 Aug and 25 Dec.* 🎫€3 *or Chorus Pass.* 📞 *041 27 50 462. www.chorusveneiza.org.*

The Church of St Peter at Castello was regarded as the official cathedral of Venice until 1807, when St Mark's was merely considered to be the doge's chapel. It was erected in the 8C on the foundations of a church that dates to 650. The façade conforms to Palladian design. On the right is the former late-16C Patriarchal Palace. The nearby campanile, which leans to one side, was rebuilt by Mauro Codussi (c.1440–1504). The 17C interior comprises a Latin cross with three aisles and a large dome. Above the main portal are represented *The Feast of the Jewish Passover* by Malombra and Vassillachi (16C–17C) (*right*) and *The Feast in the House of Simon* by Jacopo Beltrame (16C) (*left*).

In the left aisle note the painting on canvas by **Veronese** (1528–88) and in the left transept in the Gothic **Lando Chapel**, the mosaic altarpiece based on a cartoon attributed to Tintoretto. The antependium (altar front) comprises a 9C Veneto-Byzantine marble transenna (openwork screen) inlaid at the base with 2C or 5c mosaic on the floor. The **Vendramin Chapel** alongside is by Longhena: the *Madonna and Child with the Damned* is by Luca Giordano (1634–1705).

Returning down the right side, the marble seat known as **St Peter's Cathedra** is from Antioch: note the unusual back adapted from an Arab-Muslim funerary stele, decorated with inscriptions from the Koran in Cufic script.

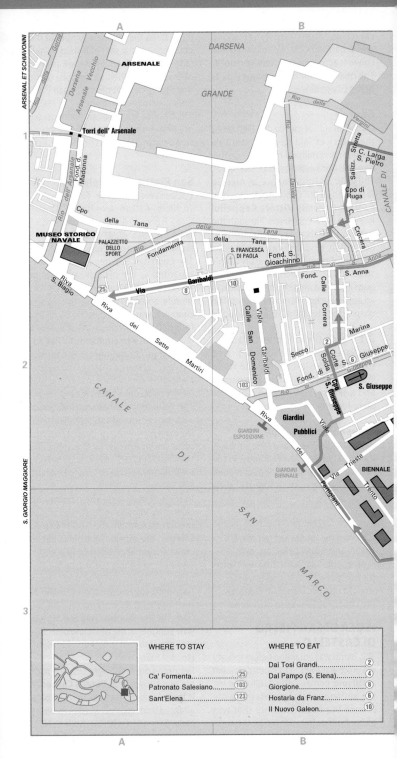

WHERE TO STAY

Ca' Formenta.....................㉕
Patronato Salesiano...........⑩③
Sant'Elena.........................①②③

WHERE TO EAT

Dai Tosi Grandi.......................②
Dal Pampo (S. Elena)..............④
Giorgione................................⑧
Hostaria da Franz....................⑥
Il Nuovo Galeon......................⑩

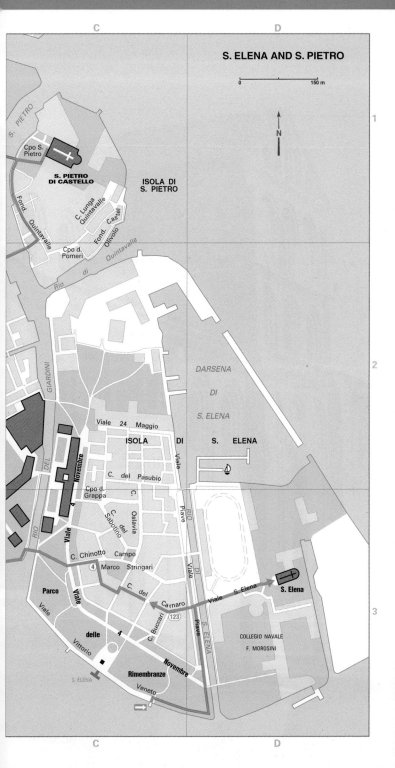

S. ELENA AND S. PIETRO

0 ————— 150 m

N

Cpo S.
Pietro

**S. PIETRO
DI CASTELLO**

ISOLA DI
S. PIETRO

C. Lunga
Quintavalle

Fond. Quintavalle

Fond. Castello
Olivolo

Cpo d.
Pomeri

Quintavalle

Rio   di   Quintavalle

GIARDINI

DARSENA
DI
S. ELENA

DEL

Viale   24   Maggio

ISOLA   DI   S. ELENA

Novembre

C.   del   Pasubio

Viale

RIO

Cpo d.
Grappa

C.

Oslavia

C. del Sabotino

Viale

RIO   DI   S. ELENA

Piave

C. Chinotto   Campo

4   Marco   Stringari

C.   del

Parco

Viale

Carnaro

123

C. Buccari

Viale   S. Elena

S. Elena

Viale

delle   4

Vittorio

COLLEGIO NAVALE
F. MOROSINI

Piave Viale DI S. ELENA

Rimembranze

Novembre

S. ELENA

Veneto

Basilica dei SS Maria e Donato, Murano

Islands and Lagoon

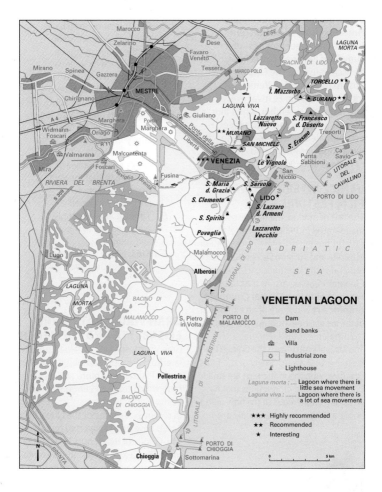

VENETIAN LAGOON

——	Dam
	Sand banks
🏛	Villa
✿	Industrial zone
⚓	Lighthouse

Laguna morta : .... Lagoon where there is little sea movement
Laguna viva : ...... Lagoon where there is a lot of sea movement

★★★ Highly recommended
★★ Recommended
★ Interesting

0   5 km

Il Lido ⚏ ☼ ☼

The Lido is Venice's seaside resort. Once sophisticated but now slightly decadent, for many visitors it is forever associated with the legacy of Luchino Visconti's *Death in Venice*, which was filmed at the Hotel des Bains, and haunted by the disconcerting yet majestic Hotel Excelsior, so reminiscent in style and sheer boldness of Ludwig of Bavaria's castle in Neuschwanstein. The Lido plays host to the glittering Venice International Film Festival every late August/September, when film directors, actors and critics meet, accompanied by their inevitable jet-setting entourage and crowds of curious onlookers.

VENICE INTERNATIONAL FILM FESTIVAL

The first of its kind, the film festival was inaugurated in 1932 at the Hotel Excelsior, on the initiative of Conte Volpi di Misurata and Luciano De Feo, Secretary General of the International Institute of Cinematographic Art. At that time, the **Festival of International Cinematographic Art** was more of an exhibition of the art of cinematography, organised to complement the Biennale.

The festival's top prize is the Golden Lion (Leone d'Oro) award. Many of the films that have won this in the past are small-budget arthouse productions that have remained anonymous to the film-going public at large. *www.labiennale.org*

A. Ajello/Michelin

ℹ Information: ☎ 041 24 24. www.veneziaunica.it.

▶ Location: Extending roughly north-south to the east of Venice, the Lido resembles a long, thin leg of land (7.5mi/9km long and around half a mile/0.8km wide), fronting the Adriatic Sea. The sandy stretch serves as a barrier island for the Venetian lagoon and a beach for Venetian residents. It is easy to get to the Lido: hop onto vaporetto line **1, 2, 5.1, 5.2, B** or **N** from Piazza San Marco and half an hour later you will arrive at Santa Maria Elisabetta.

Don't Miss: The beach in summer, though beware that the best stretches are privately owned.

🕐 Timing: Allow a couple of hours soaking in the sights and sounds.

👥 Kids: Biking around the island and the beach.

GRAN VIALE SANTA MARIA ELISABETTA AND THE BEACH

Gran Viale is the Lido's main thoroughfare; from the vaporetto stop, it stretches to the Piazzale Bucintoro (*accessible by bus*), which leads to Lungomare Guglielmo Marconi.

In recent years some of the Lido's best hotels have been converted for private use. Colourful beach huts line the seafront. The Casino, a golf club, bike rental, and an airport are also located here.

JEWISH CEMETERY

🕐 *Opening times call* ☎ *041 71 53 59.* *www.museoebraico.it.*

At the north end of the island, the old Jewish Cemetery, which dates from 1389, can be seen at San Nicolò.

Murano★★

From the water, Murano appears to be walled-in by its long line of furnaces. As you step off the vaporetto, you will be urged, even cajoled, to visit the glassworks. While the commercial aspect of the "invitation" can be irritating, it is well worth watching the various stages and processes. Murano is also an island of art in other senses too. Don't get so distracted by the tantalising glass shops that you forget to visit the island's two fine churches.

A BIT OF HISTORY

By the end of the 13C, glassmaking was so widespread in Venice that the threat of fire ravaging the city was ever constant. Countless small fires frequently broke out as a result of the widespread use of wood and candles; had these incidents not been contained, it would not have taken much for fire to spread quickly, with disastrous consequences. Finally, three nervous centuries later, the Grand Council decided to move the glassworks away from the city to Murano. This had the bonus that it would also help protect the secrets of the glassmaking process.

The most likely theory to explain the origins of glass is rooted in the ancient Orient where potters learned how glass was formed from silicon sand when glazing their ceramics by firing them in a kiln. The process was already in widespread use by the time the books of Job and Proverbs were written, as recorded in the Bible, and commonly practised in Egypt by the

▷ **Location:** Murano sits less than a mile to the northeast of Venice and is broken up by several wide canals. To get to Murano, board vaporetto line **3, 4.1, 4.2, 12, 13** and **N** at Fondamenta Nuove.

⊙ **Don't Miss:** The Museum of Glass and the Church of Santa Maria e San Donato, especially its mosaic floor.

⊙ **Timing:** Allow about 2hr 30min.

⊙ **Also See:** Neighbouring sights: *SAN ZANIPÒLO*.

4th millenium BC, as small objects found in datable tombs would imply. The colours blue and green were created by the addition of copper and cobalt oxide. The technique for blowing glass, however, as favoured by the Romans, came later. Before its arrival in Venice, glass was produced in Greece and Turkey. In 1203, following the occupation of Constantinople, Venice secured the "exclusive" collaboration of immigrant potters in exchange for preferential treatment from the Republic. However, the terms of agreement were ruthless; if the glassmakers refused to return to the city, they were hunted down and killed. Partly as a result of this the city's supremacy in glassmaking remained uncontested until the end of the 16C.

Venice and Murano have long lost their monopoly on the industry but even

Island of Murano in the lagoon

© Luke Daniek / iStockphoto.com

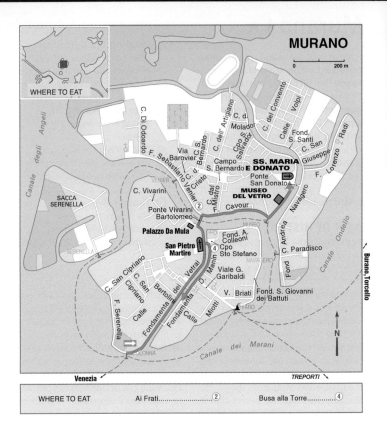

MURANO

0   200 m

WHERE TO EAT

WHERE TO EAT	Ai Frati.........................②	Busa alla Torre..............④

today, modern glass creations from Murano are considered works of art. Within everyone's budget are the *murrine,* which sparkle with colour, often set into costume jewellery, and the distinctive discs of kaleidoscopic patterns. The final effect of this unique glassworking technique is achieved by juxtaposing various coloured rods of glass that have been drawn in length and fused when molten. When the composite rods are then sliced crosswise, the famous discs of colour remain.

WALKING TOUR

From the vaporetto stop at Scalo Colonna, follow Fondamenta dei Vetrai. Tour marked in green on map above.

When you approach Murano on board the *vaporetto,* the island seems to be surrounded by a wall, which reveals itself to be made up of a long series of glassmakers' workshops. Get off at the first stop (Colonna) and, on the right bank of the Rio dei Vetrai, take the long **Fondamenta dei Vetrai**, whose name (**glassworkers' quay**) is a sign of the island's main activity. Shops follow one after another, giving you a glimpse of current production. Many of them have focussed on small souvenir pieces that are easy to carry away, with the result that, from an aesthetic point of view, quality is very variable.

On the other bank, a long *sottoportego* supports a gothic-style palace with ogee windows and a facade inlaid with coats of arms.

San Pietro Martire

Begun in 1363, this brick church was consecrated in 1417. Gravely damaged by fire, it was rebuilt in the Renaissance style before being subjected to further modifications over the ensuing few hundred years. A Renaissance main door is surmounted at the front by a large stained-glass window made of *rui*, small circular sections of Murano glass. Inside, the nave and aisles are apsed and endowed with **paintings★** by illustrious artists such as Salviati, Veronese, Tintoretto, Bellini and Palma il Giovane. *www.sandonatomurano.it.*

▶ At the confluence of the Grand Canal, follow the Fondamenta Da Mula.

Built in the 15C, the **palazzo Da Mula** has a very fine facade decorated, notably, with elements from an earlier Venetian-Byzantine style.

▶ Retrace your steps and cross the canal.

The **Canale degli Angeli**, bordered by a forest of paline and a few wooden pontoons, some of which are used for restaurant terraces, is enlivened by the comings and goings of the vaporetti, between which glide boats belonging to locals.

▶ After the bridge, turn right onto Fondamenta Cavour until you reach the Canale di San Donato, then turn left onto Fondamenta Giustinian.

Museo del Vetro★★

&⊙*Open 10am–6pm (5pm Nov–Mar).*⊙*Closed 1 Jan and 25 Dec.* ⊚€*10 (€12 inc Museo del Merletto) or Museum Pass (&see p30).* ✆*848 082 000 or (+39) 041 427 30 892 (from abroad). museovetro.visitmuve.it.* Palazzo Giustinian, which is undergoing a major renovation in 2014, shows the evolution of glassmaking over the centuries. It is a place to see quality before perusing shops and on some days even see glassblowing (Glass in Action at the Museo del Fornace). An archaeological section displays embalming tools, cups, utensils and necklaces. The physical processes practised by tradition and modern technology, includ-

ing coloured glass and *murrine,* are explained with illuminated panels and samples of raw materials. Developments in technique between the 15C and 18C are also defined. The height of artistry attained in the 15C is represented by a wedding cup, traditionally known as the **Barovier Cup**. The museum also houses a fine collection of modern glass and a museum shop. The renovation will be accompanied by the addition of an adjacent building to expand exhibit space.

Facing the museum, on the other bank of the canal, the Palladian-style **palazzo Trevisan** (1557), boasts a so-called *serliana* window (& *ST MARK'S SQUARE,* nearby).

▶ Continue along the quay until you reach Campo San Donato.

Basilica dei SS Maria e Donato★★

⊙*Open year-round Mon–Sat 9am–6pm, Sun 12.30am–7pm. www.sandonatomurano.it.* The **apse**, viewed first by most visitors, is a masterpiece of 12C Veneto-Byzantine art. Founded in the 7C, the original church was dedicated to the Virgin Mary. The incorporation of San Donato dates from the 12C, when his body, together with what remained of the dragon that he had slain, arrived from Cefalonia (the bones of the "dragon" are stored behind the altar). The church was considerably remodelled in the 12C: the mosaic floor was completed in 1141, and extensively restored during the mid-19C. Inside, five columns with Veneto-Byzantine capitals separate the nave from the aisles; the striking **mosaic floor★★** recalls that of the Basilica of St Mark. One particularly significant section between the second and third column on the right depicts two cockerels bearing a fox, and represents the defeat of Cunning by Vigilance. Above the apse, a 12C mosaic *Virgin in Prayer* stands alone, projected forward by the brilliant gold background.

Burano★★

Burano is the most colourful of the lagoon islands. At the doors and windows of the houses, painted in the brightest colours of the rainbow, a few women still work on their lace pillows while the men attend to their fishing nets and boats. Visitors may be hailed with friendly "invitations" from the locals selling *passementerie* (articles bordered in lace) displayed by the "lace-houses".

A BIT OF HISTORY

Venice has been known for lace-making since the 16C. The practice was first established in the palaces as a domestic activity, to be supervised by the noble ladies, before spreading to the hospitals and women's institutions where residents were obliged to take up the occupation.

Traditional production depended on the combined use of the needle and bobbin, and proliferated until the second half of the 17C, when demand was threatened by competition from France, which ironically had instituted an industry employing Venetian lacemakers. During the 18C the Venetian authorities were forced to take measures to halt the exodus of lacemakers; certain manufacturers such as **Raniere e Gabrieli** were granted preferential privileges and traditional methods were compromised, allowing for a simpler, bobbin-only technique to be used. Between the 18C and 19C, however, demand dwindled until eventually the production of lace for clothing was discontinued.

By the second decade of the 19C there were just two lace factories left, one in Venice and one on Burano, and needle-point continued as a private, domestic pastime. To safeguard designs and practices, a school was set up in 1872 and charged with the organisation and education of the lacemakers, and their production.

Today very little lace is made in the traditional way as it is so labour intensive – it is said that it takes three years for ten women to make a single medium-sized

- **Location:** Burano lies about 5mi/8km northeast of Venice just south of the island of Torcello. It takes about 45min to get from Fondamenta Nuove (line **12**, **14** and **N**) to Burano. The last stretch of the journey is along the Mazzorbo Canal, which separates Burano from the island of Mazzorbo. The two islands are linked by a wooden bridge.
- **Don't Miss:** Demonstrations by the lacemakers at the lacemakers museum.
- **Timing:** Allow a couple of hours.
- **Also See:** Neighbouring sights: *SAN FRANCESCO del DESERTO, TORCELLO.*

tablecloth. It is therefore very expensive and (buyer beware) any lace that is sold cheaply is almost certainly imported from China.

WALKING TOUR

Tour marked in green on map below.

Disembarking the *vaporetto,* you will be captivated by the cheerfulness of the place. The small, low – single- or two-story – fishermen's houses rendered in distinctive colours (which served to define the property of each family) are reflected in the canals, which are spanned by little wooden bridges and crowded with fishing boats. The alignment of these simple facades, with their windows outlined in white and their narrow doors, is broken only by a few aediculated skylights in the Roman-tiled roofs and by a forest of chimneys.

From the embankment, where the *vaporetti* pontoons are lined up facing the Torcello bell tower, the Via Marcello is the only way to reach the centre of this small agglomeration. When you reach the canal, turn left onto

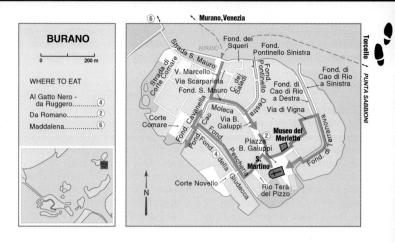

BURANO

0   200 m

WHERE TO EAT

Al Gatto Nero -
  da Ruggero............④
Da Romano...............②
Maddalena...............⑥

Fondamenta San Mauro, which leads to the main street, then via Baldassare Galuppi.

Via Baldassare Galuppi

Lined with cafés, restaurants and lace shops, this street is where most tourists congregate, to the point where it is sometimes difficult to move around between the groups.

Piazza Baldassarre Galuppi

The square is dominated by the austere façade of the 16C Church of San Martino and its 18C campanile, built by Andrea Tirali, which leans 1.85m/6ft 1in.

Inside is a *Crucifixion* by **Tiepolo** (*left aisle*) and, on the left of the presbytery, a great sarcophagus around which a miracle is said to have happened. It is explained in a painting, the *Miracle of the Children and the Urn,* attributed to **Alessandro Zanchi**.

The inhabitants of Burano also attribute the fact that they were spared from the plague in 1630 to the divine intervention of their patrons (the island of Torcello

was also saved). The skeletons of the three saints today lie in the altar below the sarcophagus.

Off the piazza on via Baldassare Galuppi opposite the Galuppi restaurant is Burano's most **colourful house**, known after the owner as Bepe's.

Museo del Merletto (Lace Museum)

◷ *Open 10am–6pm (5pm Nov–Mar).* ◷ *Closed Mon, 1 Jan and 25 Dec.* ⊜€5 *(€12 inc Museo del Merletto) or Museum Pass (* ♿ *see p30).* ☏ *848 082 000 or (+39) 041 427 30 892 (from abroad). museomerletto.visitmuve.it.* Important collection of collars, napkins, parasols, bedspreads, centrepieces, handkerchiefs and lace edgings are on display in this recently restored museum. Practical demonstrations by experts illustrate just how painstaking the traditional Burano methods are.

Fondamenta di Terranova

Just off the Piazza Galuppi, this quay with particularly colourful houses borders a rio that joins the lagoon opposite Torcello. There are beautiful views to be

Island of Artists

Not surprisingly Burano has long been a magnet for artists and a school of painting evolved here before the First World War. Like the houses, one of the characteristics of the Burano School is a strong use of colour. Pay a visit to the Restaurant Da Romano, a sponsor of the artists since 1947, to see examples of their work. The beautiful pastel coloured shades of the houses attract not only visiting tourists, French designer Philippe Starck owns several Burano houses.

had of these peaceful stretches of water from the jetty. You can return either via the same route or, having crossed the rio, via the peaceful Via di Vigna, which leads to the square.

Giudecca et Pescheria

If you want to explore the island further, this time in almost total solitude, take the Rio Terrà del Pizzo, on the right of the church, then Calle Providenza, via a *sottoportego*, which will lead you to the della Giudecca, flanked by the Fondamenta della Giudecca et della Pescheria. This is where you will discover the authentic Burano: lacemakers at work, fishermen repairing their nets, children chasing a ball on an otherwise deserted *campiello*. At the end of the *rio*, the Fondamenta Cao provides access to the banks of the lagoon where a walkway is under construction. In the distance, the silhouette of St Mark's bell tower seems to float in the mist.

▶ Retrace your steps along the Fondamenta Cao and continue straight ahead to reach the vaporetto jetty.

EXCURSION
San Francesco del Deserto★

The island is situated just south of Burano. The island where St Francis landed is still only accessible by private boat today. Take the vaporetto (9, 12, N) to Burano, then water taxi, or negotiate a ride with one of the fishermen. They depart from Burano where the canal meets the lagoon as it laps the water's edge in Piazza Galuppi – not far from the front of San Martino. The cost includes the 10 minute ferry ride and

waiting time; ask the boatman, who will make himself known, about the price. It is also possible to spend a few days in retreat with the monastic community by prior arrangement. ✆*Donation requested.* ☞*Visit by guided tour only (1hr) Tue–Sun 9am–11am and 3–5pm. www.sanfrancescodeldeserto.it.*

This little island is ideal for anyone seeking respite from commotion and crowds, particularly in high summer when the islands of the lagoon can get very busy. Before St Francis landed on the island on his way back from the Holy Land in 1220, San Francesco del Deserto was known as the *Isola delle due Vigne* (the Island of the Two Vines). Its name was changed when a house for Franciscan novitiates was established on the island in 1224. On four occasions the monastery played host to Bernardino of Siena, who may have paid for the well to be dug to collect water. Set into a wall in the cloisters is a 13C relief of two crossed arms, said to be the arm of Christ and the sleeved arm of St Francis.

Today around seven friars live here, their number augmented by novices who generally stay for a year or so.

Visit

A guided tour (1hr) with a Franciscan monk, takes in various paintings depicting the saint arriving on the island and the miracle of St Francis ordering the birds to be quiet and not to move during prayers.

The island's beautiful and vast cypress-scented **park** is possibly the most peaceful place in the whole Venetian archipelago. It overlooks the lagoon and affords a clear view of Burano.

Lagoon Life

The Venetian lagoon comprises a variety of active biological ecosystems, and is always an atmospheric sight, whichever time of year you visit. Sea birds rest on *bricole*, the orange-topped beacons that transform the maze of waterways into navigable channels; herons pick their way carefully through the rushes. Most disconcertingly, near Burano, you might see people sheltering from the sun under umbrellas or packing bags with handfuls of mussels, apparently floating in the water. As you get closer you will see that they are standing on barely visible spits of sand.

Torcello★★

The poet and critic, John Ruskin, wrote of the relationship between Torcello and Venice in melancholy terms: "Mother and Daughter, you behold them both in their widowhood". Hemmingway had a favourite retreat here, which is still in operation. A walk along the Fondamenta dei Borgognoni and on by the canal allows a full prospect of the unique lagoon landscape to unfold. Once more important than Venice, these days wild and overgrown, Torcello is an atmospheric near-ghost island, where only the stones can speak of its glorious past.

A BIT OF HISTORY

Near the **Ponte del Diavolo** (the Devil's Bridge) stands the religious complex of Torcello. Alongside are a handful of restaurants and possibly some itinerant lace sellers. It is incredible to think that in ancient times there were around 20 000 people (some estimates go as high as 50 000) living on the island while

- ▷ **Location:** Torcello lies about 5.5mi to the northeast of Venice. From Fondamenta Nuove, take the same line (**9, 12, N**) that goes to Burano, which is only minutes away from Torcello.
- ⏱ **Timing:** Allow a minimum of 2hrs to take in the atmosphere.

the glorious history of Venice was only just beginning.

During the period of barbarian invasions, the Lombards chased out the Byzantines (6C–8C) and established themselves in Aquilea, Padua, Altinum and Oderzo. The bishop and the inhabitants of Altinum moved to Torcello where, in 639, the church and probably the fortifications were built; it is the *torri* (towers) of such fortifications that gave rise to the name of the island. They were not the first inhabitants, however, as the Romans had already discovered the island and records show continu-

TORCELLO

0   200 m

N

WHERE TO EAT

Al Ponte del Diavolo.... ②
Locanda Cipriani......... ④

Canale di Torcello

Museo
S. Maria Assunta
Piazza Santa Fosca
Santa Fosca
④

Fondamenta dei Borgognoni
②
PONTE DEL DIAVOLO

TORCELLO

Barena Paltan

Canale Borgognoni

Canale Sant' Antonio

↘ Burano, Venezia

Locanda Cipriani

In 1934 Giuseppe Cipriani, the founder of Harry's Bar in Venice and the Hotel Cipriani in Giudecca, bought a modest wine and oil shop on Torcello. He transformed the shop into a small inn (*locanda*) with just a few guestrooms and a restaurant surrounded by a garden of flowers and vegetables and an unparalleled view of the churches of Torcello. In 1948 Ernest Hemingway stayed here and, when he wasn't out hunting ducks in the lagoon, was writing *Across the River and Through the Trees*. It may not have been his most famous novel but Hemingway devoted whole pages of it to Torcello and kept a special place in his heart for the island. As a result, the Locanda became a destination of choice for the exclusive world of stars and celebrities who often visited Venice in the post-War era. Six decades on it is still a charming unpretentious place, well worth a visit to eat, drink or stay overnight: *www.locandacipriani.com*.

ous fishing and glassmaking activities throughout the 5C and 6C.

Torcello's decline started around the 10C and mirrors the pace of the glorious ascent of Venice. When malaria infested the marshes, Torcello was abandoned by its inhabitants, who fled to Venice and Murano. Now there are only around 20 inhabitants who live here year round.

➤🐾WALKING TOUR

Refer to the map p221.

On disembarking from the *vaporetto*, walk along the **Fondamenta dei Borgognoni** next to the canal and enjoy the peaceful atmosphere of the lagoon, particularly if you're visiting out of season when tourists are more sparse. **George Sand**, who loved the rustic flavour of the island, was impressed by the "unimaginable silence that prevails over this landscape". Like **Hemingway**, who enjoyed staying at the *Locanda Cipriani* (*see p286*), where he would go duck shooting at the crack of dawn, you may be captivated by the unique atmosphere of this place, but you may also sense a certain melancholy, like **Ruskin,** who admired this phantom island from the top of the bell tower, only stones bearing witness to its former glory.

From the jetty, follow the quay, bordered by orchards, vineyards and the occasional house, alongside the Torcello canal. Like the Chiodo bridge in Venice

(*CA' D'ORO),* the **Ponte del Diavolo**, which spans the canal, has no parapet. A little further on stands the complex of historical buildings, which is distinguishable from afar by the high bell tower of the cathedral;although you can see it from Burano, is hidden from view once you draw alongside the island.

You will soon reach a green square, the centre of the old town, surrounded by the only remaining historical buildings.

COMPLEX OF HISTORICAL BUILDINGS

Open Basilica Santa Maria Assunta and Campanile 10.30am–6pm (10am–5pm Nov–Feb), Museo 10.30am–5.30pm (10am–5pm Nov–Feb). You can buy a ticket for all the island's historical buildings at the entrance to the basilica; €5 Basilica; €5 Campanile; €3 Museo; combined ticket Basilica and Museum €8; Basilica, Museum and Campanile €12. itorcello. it/visitare-la-basilica-di-torcello/ or www.veneziaubc.org.

Long ago, at the dawn of Venice's extraordinary story, thousands of men and women inhabited the island. Today, grass covers the relics of this past, accentuating the desolate ruins while adding to the magic of the place. You can see the remains of Roman buildings as well as the "seat of Attila", where the bishop of the person charged with administering justice presided. A silent witness of a bygone era, the cathedral stands near the remains of the baptistery of

Santa Fosca and two gothic palaces. The reunion of these buildings had a symbolic significance for the early church, which would place a baptistery in front of the cathedral and, next to it, the church of the martyr (Santa Fosca) or "martyrium",thus uniting the symbols of birth, life and death, the source of eternal life.

Basilica di Santa Maria Assunta

♿ *itorcello.it/visitare-la-basilica-di-torcello/*.

As recorded by the ancient **inscription** on the left of the altar, the cathedral dedicated to the Assumption was erected in 639, during the reign of Heraclius, Emperor of Byzantium. As such it is the lagoon's oldest building, and a splendid example of the Veneto-Byzantine style. In the 9C and 11C, it underwent modification. Little remains of the 7C baptistery other than fragments of the brick façade and its many pilasters. The 14C portico supported by the columns and pilasters also serves as a link to Santa Fosca.

The interior is divided into nave and aisles by columns. In contrast to the simplicity of structure, the decoration is opulent. The pavement is 11C. The choir, enclosed by Corinthian columns, is separated from the nave by a 15C iconostasis set with 11C Byzantine painted panels depicting the Madonna and Child flanked by the Twelve Apostles with, above, the Crucifixion from the same date. Between the columns nestle delicate Byzantine marble *plutei* carved with semi-symmetrical lions and peacocks. The Roman sarcophagus near the high altar contains the relics of St Heliodorus, the first Bishop of Altinum.

But most striking are the **ancient mosaics**★★ representing the Virgin and Christ. In accordance with Byzantine iconography, the Virgin is portrayed descending from Heaven.

The Last Judgement

The Last Judgement is the theme of the **mosaics**★★ (13C–14C) at the back of the basilica. The main elements of the scene, drawn from the Apocalypse, unfold from top to bottom and are divided into two sections: the Judgement below and the Death and Resurrection of Christ above. From the Crucifixion there follows the Descent into Limbo: Christ tramples over many keys and a devil reduced to miniature proportions while determinedly clutching Adam's hand. Behind is Eve, her hands covered for reasons of propriety; to the right stands John the Baptist, who may easily be recognised by his long hair and camel-hair shirt. Beyond rank the Prophets, and to the left, the two figures with halos are David and Solomon. At the far edges, the Archangels Michael (left) and Gabriel (right) stand guard.

Dominating the central section is the *Deisis*: Christ in glory enclosed within a mandorla, the aura of His divinity, surrounded by the symbols of the Passion. He is flanked by the Virgin and John the Baptist and by two angels.

Arranged symmetrically around the edge are the Apostles, including St Peter (left) and St Paul (right; here St Paul is included among the Twelve Apostles, on a par therefore with St Barnabas).

The lower section recounts the Triumph of the Cross. The angels' trumpets recall the dead from the sea monsters that devoured them. Below the souls are being weighed by St Michael, working to safeguard the salvation of those who deserve to be protected from the demons that burden the scale with bags of sins. To the left are the saved; to the right the damned. The seven devils portray the seven deadly sins – Pride, Avarice, Lust, Wrath, Gluttony, Envy, Sloth. The main figure is Lucifer, who holds the Antichrist and is sitting on Leviathan, the sea monster described in the Book of Job whose breath sets burning coals ablaze.

Torcello

Between the windows are aligned the *Apostles* (12C), and below the window St Heliodorusis. The mosaics of the intersecting vault harbour *Four Angels bearing the Mystic Lamb*, of a type found at Ravenna. The floral mosaic is populated with birds and animals which postdate those at San Vitale in Ravenna (7C), for these are also by artists from Ravenna, who came here while the church was being built.

Campanile – *itorcello.it/visitare-la-basilica-di-torcello/.* At the rear of the basilica stands the old bell-tower (12C). The climb is not difficult and the **view**★★ over the lagoon more than compensates for the effort.

Santa Fosca

This small church, in the form of a Greek cross, was built between the 11C and 12C. Its octagonal exterior is encircled by open arcading with columns capped by Veneto-Byzantine capitals. The interior, imbued with solemn silence, is enclosed below a round wooden roof.

Museo di Torcello

🕓 *10.30am–5.30pm (10am –5pm Nov–Feb).* 🚫 *Closed Mon, 21 Nov and hols.* ✆ *You can buy a ticket for all the island's historical buildings at the entrance to the basilica; €5 Basilica; €5 Campanile; €3 Museo; combined ticket Basilica and Museum €8; Basilica, Museum and Campanile €12.* ✆ *041 730761 itorcello.it/visitare-la-basilica-di-torcello/ or museotorcello. servizimetropolitani.ve.it/info/.*
Artifacts associated with the history of Torcello are displayed on two floors. Interesting pieces, some dating to the 9C, include capitals, pateras, tablets, a mid-15C wooden *Pietà* of the Venetian School, paintings from the Church of St Anthony of Torcello, a work from the studio of Veronese, books and documents which recount parts of the island's history, pages from the *Mariegola* and fragments of Venetian ceramics.

Chioggia

Although there is a Venetian quality about this lagoon fishing port – most notable in its canals and double-arched windows and other architectural detail – the atmosphere is very different. The traffic on pavements, roads and water is constant. Chioggia is one of Italy's busiest fishing ports and there's a frenetic urgency with which all local matters of marine and fishing business are dealt with in this working-class town.

A BIT OF HISTORY

One of the channels of the Brenta Delta was, in Antiquity, called *Fossa Clodia*, from which **Clodia**, Chioggia's former name, derives. In the 1C BC the Romans transformed it into a commercial harbour. The problems began in the 9C, following destruction from Charlemagne's son Pepin. Between the 11C and 12C, the saltpans constituted a major source of income for Chioggia. Between 1378 and 1381 it became the field of battle between the rival factions Genoa and Venice. The Serenissima was victorious, but Chioggia was annihilated.

Rebuilding began and continued over the ensuing century. Venice intended that Chioggia should be reinforced as a defence post for the lagoon.

The town of Chioggia grew up as close to the sea as possible, configured from these early times around Corso del Popolo and the Canale della Vena. Economic development was then halted: when the Brenta was diverted, the harbour gradually silted up, excluding large vessels. The canal that was dug separating the islet from the mainland served to consolidate defences. From the 16C fishing began to supersede the saltpans as the main industry. In the 19C Chioggia's isolation was in part breached by the building of the bridge carrying the Romea road. On the water, if you look carefully in some spots you can still see a trabucco, a traditional spindly wooden fishing pier, seen also in the 2011 film, *Io Sono Li* (*Shun Li and the Poet*).

Information: Via Cassiopea, 33, Sottomarina. ☎041 401 846. www.chioggiavenezia.it.

Location: Chioggia is not strictly a lagoon island, as it rests on two parallel islands, linked to terra firma by a long bridge. 12mi/19km south of Venice (as the crow flies), along the Adriatic Sea, and north of the Brenta Valley. From the Brenta villas, take the SS 309, which has beautiful views over the Venetian Lagoon. Bus service operates every 30min from Piazzale Roma to Chioggia-Sottomarina taking around 1hr. Or bicycle south from the Lido.

SIGHTS

The main street, the **Corso del Popolo**, runs parallel to the Canale della Vena – the Fossa Clodia of Ancient times – colourful and lively at its excellent 🐟**fish market** (open every morning except Monday) and ending at Piazzetta Vigo. The column bearing a winged lion marks the end of the Fossa Clodia. To cross the canal, walk over the stone bridge, the Ponte Vigo, built in 1685. The *corso* is dotted with the Duomo and several of the Chioggia churches, among them the Church of **San Andrea**, with its 11C Romanesque campanile rising from a square base. **San Giacomo** was rebuilt in the 18C; **San Francesco delle Muneghette** was founded in the 15C but rebuilt 18C.

At the far end of Chioggia, the **Isola di San Domenico** is reached by following Calle di San Croce, beyond Ponte Vigo. The two small museumsare the **Museo Diocesano d'Arte Sacra**, Sacred Art Museum (☎041 55 07 477. *en.turismovenezia.it/Chioggia*) and close by the **Museo della Laguna Sud** (041 55 00 911. *www.chioggia.org/museochioggia/*).

San Lazzaro degli Armeni ★

This island was especially loved by the Romantic poet Lord Byron, as he found the atmosphere lifted his ascetic spirit in times of melancholy. Today, it is no less evocative to visiting travellers. On arrival by vaporetto, tourists are greeted by charming Armenian monks who chaperone their charges and introduce them to this green, serene island.

MONASTERY
THE ARMENIANS AND THE MECHITAR COMMUNITY

The Armenians are an ancient people whose ancestry has been linked to Noah's Ark, which some believe "ran aground" on Mount Ararat, on the Armenian border. Armenia then extended from the Black Sea to Mesopotamia, where the mountains hide the sources of the River Tigris and River Euphrates. Today the Republic of Armenia is hemmed in between Turkey, Georgia, Azerbaijan and Iran.

The country was conquered on several occasions by the Arabs, Turks, Mongols, Tartars, Ottomans and Persians. During the First World War, its people were persecuted by the Turks, almost to the point of extinction. Subsequent diaspora saw the Armenians flee overseas, particularly to the United States.

▷ **Location:** The island is located west of the Lido, off the west side. It takes about 15min to get to the island of San Lazzaro degli Armeni on vaporetto **line 20** from Riva degli Schiavoni (San Zaccaria). Tours are scheduled to coincide with the vaporetto times – the talk begins on landing and continues through the monastery visit. Should you require more time on the island, catch the vaporetto that leaves at around 2pm and check for the departure time of the second return service.

◷ **Timing:** The tour takes about 1hr 15mins.

From the 14C, the island of San Lazzaro served as a leper colony until the last two leprosy sufferers were transferred to Venice (1600s).

Mechitar was given the island by the Venetian Republic and arrived here in 1717. The church was rebuilt. The pavement was lifted, the arches were made into lancet arches and the vaulted ceiling took the form of a starry sky. The original Romanesque church was built by the Benedictines, who subsequently remodelled it in the Gothic style.

Aerial view of San Lazzaro degli Armeni and the monastery

© Guido Alberto Rossi / Tips Images

Visit

👣Visit by guided tours only (1hr 30min), daily 3.25pm (vaporetto departs San Zaccaria 3.10pm). ⊛€6. ✆041 52 60 104.

Cross the simple cloister full of flowering plants, kept neat and tidy, to seek out the historical manuscripts that are a testament not only to the Armenian heritage, but also to the kindly Mechitar monks who dedicate themselves to preserving the Armenian culture. In total there are 10 monks plus 10 seminarians, and around 15 Armenian students who study Italian language and culture.

Visitors are then shown the refectory where the monks and the seminarists eat their meals in silence while the Scriptures are read out in classical Armenian. On ascending the stairs, note the fine Sienese terracotta relief from 1400 and part of a painting by Palma il Giovane depicting the *Martyrdom of St Catherine*: the central section of this painting is in St Petersburg.

As well as being an important centre of Armenian culture, the monastery also owns a collection of Flemish tapestries; paintings by Armenian artists; Greek, Phoenician and Assyro-Babylonian artefacts – there is even an Egyptian sarcophagus and mummy (the latter in a somewhat gruesome state of decay). Other treasures include tapestries, tables, statues, thrones and gold, silver, and jewels that the monks have either bought or received as gifts over the centuries. Indeed the collection is so grand that some visitors tend to raise an eyebrow at its ostentation. A highlight of the tour comes with a visit to the archive, a modern circular building containing over 150 000 volumes, including 4 000 Armenian Illuminated Manuscripts, some dating back 1 300 years.

The tour ends in a gift shop stocked with religious literature, postcards, and Armenian prints.

Mechitar

Mechitar (1676–1749) was born in Turkey. He was ordained into the Catholic Church before settling in Constantinople, where he founded a community of Uniate Armenian monks based on St Benedict's teachings and precepts of monasticism. The monks were forced to flee the city and take refuge in Morea, a Venetian territory. When Morea was lost to the Turks, the Venetian Republic granted the community the island of San Lazzaro. The Mechitarists devote themselves to education and missionary work. The Armenian liturgy differs from that of the Roman Church in that it does not acknowledge the Pope's primacy or infallibility.

Lord Byron (of Venice)

Lord George Gordon Byron (1788–1824) was a handsome youth with a colourful personality. After Cambridge, he took his seat in the House of Lords before travelling to Portugal, Spain, Malta, Greece and the Levant. The experience fired his imagination and he vowed to see Greece freed from Turkish rule. In 1812 *Childe Harold's Pilgrimage* was published, securing his reputation as one of the great Romantic poets. His liaisons with his half-sister and subsequent marriage however led to disrepute. Byron left England in 1816 for the last time. While in Venice he became attracted to the monastic life at San Lazzaro, finding the spiritual quietude he craved and from which he continually transgressed as his passions flared across the water. A plaque in the monastery quotes his thoughts on his time spent here, "the visitor will be convinced that there are other and better things even in this life". Fascinated with the Armenian community, he visited the island twice a week for around 6 months during which time he managed to learn their language in six months. He collaborated with the monks on an English-Armenian dictionary and would swim to San Lazzaro from the Palazzo Mocenigo in Venice.

Cortina d'Ampezzo with Monte Cristallo, Dolomiti
© Jose Fuste Raga / age fotostock

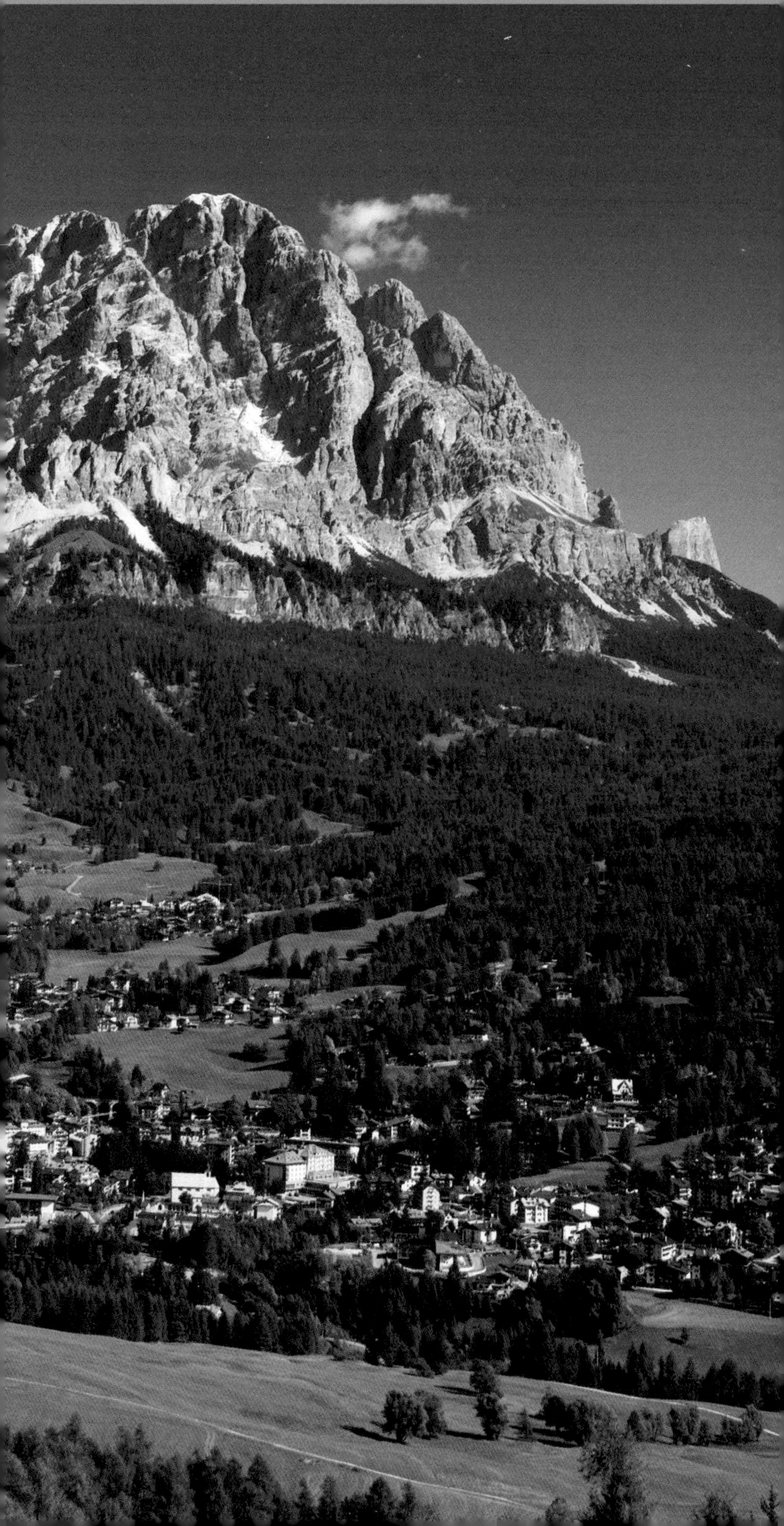

The Veneto

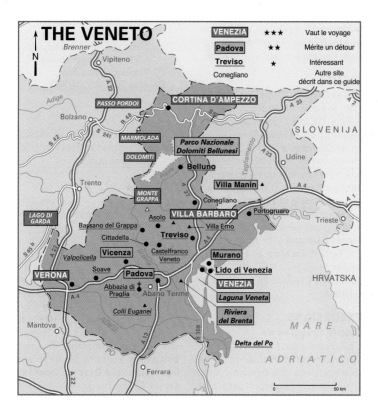

THE VENETO

N

VENEZIA	★★★	Vaut le voyage
Padova	★★	Mérite un détour
Treviso	★	Intéressant
Conegliano		Autre site décrit dans ce guide

Brenner

Vipiteno

Adige

Bolzano

S 42

PASSO PORDOI

MARMOLADA

DOLOMITI

Trento

LAGO DI GARDA

CORTINA D'AMPEZZO

SLOVENIJA

Parco Nazionale Dolomiti Bellunesi

● **Belluno**

Udine

Villa Manin ▲

Conegliano

MONTE GRAPPA

Asolo

VILLA BARBARO

▲ Villa Emo

Portogruaro

Trieste

Bassano del Grappa

Treviso

Cittadella

Castelfranco Veneto

Valpolicella

Vicenza

Murano

Lido di Venezia

VERONA

Soave

Padova

Abbazia di Praglia

Abano Terme

VENEZIA

Laguna Veneta

HRVATSKA

Colli Euganei

Riviera del Brenta

Delta del Po

Mantova

MARE

ADIGE

PO

Ferrara

A 13

S 309

ADRIATICO

0   50 km

Bassano del Grappa★★

Bassano del Grappa has grown up on the banks of the lovely River Brenta. It's an attractive place with painted houses and squares bordered by arcades. The main square is Piazza Garibaldi while the most famous sight is an attractive 13C covered bridge. The town is named after the majestic mountain, Monte Grappa, which looms nearby. Bassano is a well-known centre for the production of grappa.

- ▶ **Population:** 43 372
- ⌖ **Michelin Map:** 562 E 17 – Veneto.
- ℹ **Info:** Pza Garibaldi 36. ℘0424 51 99 17. www.bassanodelgrappa.gov.it.
- ▷ **Location:** The town lies on the S 47, 53mi/40km northwest of Venice.
- ☺ **Don't Miss:** The view of the famous covered bridge from just across the river (to the left) and a taste of grappa from the Nardini Distillery (est. 1779) or bars on the bridge.
- ⌚ **Timing:** Allow a day.
- ⌖ **Also See:** *PADOVA*, *TREVISO* and *VICENZA*.

SIGHTS

Museo Civico★ – ⌚*Open Tue–Sat 9am–7pm, Sun and hols 10.30am–1pm and 3–6pm.* ⌚*Closed 1 Jan, Easter and 25 Dec.* ⊚€5 (€7 inc Museo Remondini and Museo Ceramica). ℘0424 52 22 35.www.museibassano.it. The Municipal Museum has works by Jacopo da Ponte, aka **Jacopo Bassano** (1510–92), whose works, including **St Valentine Baptising St Lucilla**, show remarkable realism with dramatic contrasts of light.

Piazza Garibaldi – The square has the 13C **Torre di Ezzelino**, and the church of San Francesco (12C–14C) with a porch dated 1306 and a 14C Christ by Guariento.

EXCURSIONS

Monte Grappa★★★

32km/19.9mi N (alt. 1 775m/5 823ft).
The road heads up through forests and mountain pastures to the summit, from where there is a magnificent **panorama** out to Venice and Trieste.

Asolo★

14km/9mi E.
The attractive little town, dominated by its castle, is lined with frescoed palazzi. Robert Browning spent time here. Eleonora Duse, the Italian actress, is buried in the Sant'Anna cemetery.

Marostica★

7km/4.3mi W.
Piazza Castello★, the main square of this charming medieval town, serves as a giant chessboard for an unusual game of chess held in Sept every other year. *www.marosticascacchi.it.*

Cittadella

13km/8mi S.
A 12C Padovan stronghold with splendid city **walls★**.

Possagno

18km/11.2mi NW.
The birthplace of Neoclassical sculptor **Antonio Canova** (1757–1822). ☺⌚*Open Tue–Sun 9.30am–6pm.* ⌚*Closed 1 Jan, Easter and 25 Dec.* ⊚€10. ℘0423 54 43 23. www.museocanova.it. The impressive **Tempio Canoviano**, designed by Canova, contains his tomb and last sculpture, a **Descent from the Cross★**. ⌚*Open Tue–Sun 9am–noon and 3–6pm (winter 2–5pm). Ask the custodian for access to the dome.* ℘339 65 48 000.

Castelfranco Veneto★

26km/16.2mi SE.
Lovely birthplace of **Giorgione** (1478–1510) has his splendid **Madonna and Child with Saints★★** in the cathedral and a musem (⌚*Open year-round Tue–Thu 9.30–12.30am; Fri–Sun 9.30–12.30am and 2.30–6.30pm.* ⌚*Closed Easter and 25 Dec.* ⊚€5 (€6 inc Torre Civica or €8 inc Torre Civica and Theatre) ℘0423 73 56 26. www.museocasagiorgione.it).

Belluno★

This pleasant town with an attractive historic centre stands at the confluence of the River Piave and River Ardo and enjoys a spectacular Dolomite mountain backdrop.

VISIT

Walk along via Rialto through the 13C gateway, Porta Dojona (remodelled in the 16C), across **Piazza del Mercato★**, bordered with arcaded Renaissance houses and adorned with a 1409 fountain, along via Mezzaterra and Via Santa Croce to the gateway, Porta Rugo. Via del Piave offers an extensive **view★** of the Piave Valley.

Piazza del Duomo★ is surrounded by the late-15C Venetian-style **Rectors' Palace★** (Palazzo dei Rettori), the Episcopal Palace (Palazzo dei Vescovi) and the **cathedral** (Duomo), dating from the 16C with its Baroque campanile by Juvara. In the crypt there is a 15C **polyptych★** by the Rimini school. The Jurists' Palace (Palazzo dei Giuristi) houses the **Museo Civico** (Beginning 23 August 2016 the Museo Civico will remain closed for artwork renovations in preparation for moving the collections to Palazzo Fulcis.). *museo.comune. belluno.it*).

▶ **Population:** 35 870
ᚒ **Michelin Map:** 562 D 18 – veneto.
ᚒ **Info:** Piazza Duomo 2. ☎334 2813222. www.infodolomiti.it.
◉ **Location:** Belluno lies 70mi/112 km north of Venice on the A 27, en-route to the Dolomites.
ᚒ **Don't Miss:** Piazza Maggiore in Feltre.
◔ **Timing:** Allow half a day.
ᚒ **Also See:** *DOLOMITI.*

EXCURSION
Feltre
31km/19mi southwest.

Grouped around its castle, Feltre, has kept part of its ramparts and in **Via Mezzaterra★**, old houses, adorned with frescoes in the Venetian manner. **Piazza Maggiore★** is a beautiful square with noble buildings, arcades, stairways and balustrades. The **Museo Civico** displays some fine works by artists including Bellini, Cima da Conegliano, Ricci and Jan Massys (ᚒ◔*Open Sat and Sun 10.30am–1pm and 2.30–7pm; 10.30–12.30am and 4–7pm Oct–Jun).*◔*Closed 1 Jan, 25 and 26 Dec.* €4; ☎0439 88 52 41. *musei.comune.feltre.bl.it/MuseoCivico*).

Clock tower and a belfry, Piazza del Duomo, Belluno

Villas of the
Brenta★★

The Brenta Valley is a bucolic stretch of land where the doges elected to have their lavish country houses. Some Venetian families still follow this tradition today. Reflected in the quiet waters of the river, from Padua to the lagoon, these patrician villas possess that air of an exclusive, cultural country retreat were working farms that were crucial after the loss of trade to the New World.

A BIT OF HISTORY
A Troubled Past

By 1100 the Paduans and the Venetians were locked in conflict over who should have control over the Brenta River's course and therefore the hold on a strategic access point to the lagoon. After 1409, with the annexation of Padua, the Republic of Venice was assured definitive control of the River Brenta and thus started to invest in landed property along its banks. In an effort to limit the threat of damage from flooding, subsidiary canals were built. By the beginning of the 16C, opulent villas, set among extensive gardens, were being designed and built.

In 1840, after a disastrous flood, work was initiated on redirecting the river to flow into the lagoon at Chioggia, but infilling the delta proved so difficult that

Barchesse

Up until the end of the 17C, the *barchesse* (from *barca* meaning boat) were the outbuildings of the villas used for storing grain and "garaging" the boats, because it was prohibited to leave them moored along the canal. Frequently, throughout the 17C, the *barchesse* doubled up as sleeping quarters for use by the extra house guests invited to the great parties at the villas, which might go on for days.

Info: Villa Widmann. Via Nazionale 420, Mira Porte. ℘041 42 49 73. villawidmann.servizi metropolitani.ve.it/. The "Ville Card" provides reduced ticket prices for the individual villas along the Riviera del Brenta, as well as for transportation, shopping and some restaurants. ℘041 42 49 73. €2. www. rivieradelbrenta.com.

Location: The Brenta River skirts the city of Padua and arcs south. The villas lie along the Naviglio Brenta section, which empties into the Adriatic Sea at Porto di Brondolo near Fusina, to the south of Chioggia. The River Brenta links Padua to Venice by water, but access from either direction is easiest by road. If you are coming from the west along the A 4, exit at Padova Est. Follow the Noventana road and directions for Stra (SS 11). From Venice–Mestre, follow the signs for Riviera del Brenta and Malcontenta (SS 11).

Don't Miss: The Salone delle Feste at the Villa Pisani.

Timing: Allow 2 days for the driving itinerary and tour of the villas.

the water was directed farther down to run straight out to sea, as it does today at Brondolo.

Today the Brenta Valley, like Venice, survives as if by a pact made between nature and architecture. However, many find the area oppressive; heavy swirling mists and flooding exaggerate the cold in winter and the humid atmosphere in summer.

Allegorical Painting in the Brenta Villas

Frequent recourse to allegorical subject matter in the art of the 17C and 18C reflects the prevailing wish to assert the Venetian taste in "style": one that was inspired by a *joie de vivre*, a Humanist interest in Classical literature and a predilection for ostentation and luxury. The great battles at sea and on land were now over and Venice was to be celebrated as a proud combatant and conqueror. Now was the time to relish past glories and to enjoy the good life.

The Villas

The traditional villa was intended to provide the landowner with lodgings and a base for commerce while running his farm estate. Erected near the farm, it was built on a centralised plan, flanked by *barchesse* (*see Box, left*).

The villa's function as country home to which the landed gentry could retreat was secondary to supervising their tenanted farm, often their main source of income after loss of trade to New World routes that favoured other ports. By the 18C, country houses were all the rage among the Venetian nobility, who basked in luxury, while Venice sang its maritime trade swansong. The most popular holiday periods were the months of June, July, October and November, when the balmy evenings might be spent listening to a musical recital or watching a group of players.

Few of the many villas can be attributed to specific architects; however, given their artistic quality, it is generally acknowledged that they must have been designed to satisfy highly sophisticated and aesthetically discerning patrons.

Entertaining along the Brenta

Nobles or peasants, the Venetians shared the same taste for **farce**. Along the riverbanks, where people idled away the time with a good book, puppeteers found an ideal location in which to set up their theatres and animate their characters: Brighella, Harlequin, Columbine and Pantaloon. In the villa gardens, comic plays were staged. The numerous **sagre** (feast days) were always an excuse for throwing a party, when guests could sing and dance the night away in the magnificent villa ballrooms.

BOAT TOUR
Il Burchiello

The 18C traveller could choose to journey from Venice to Padua by boat or by carriage.

The boat was neither comfortable nor quick and fellow passengers would not always have been the most salubrious. The original *Burchiello*, built in Padua c.1700 and adapted from the **burchio** (canal barge) that was used in Venice to transport general goods, heralded an improvement in river transport. Passengers were accommodated on benches arranged around tables and protected by a canopy overhead. Further shelter against driving rain, biting winds or blinding sunshine was provided by decorative panels of inlaid wood and attractive drapes.

When travelling upstream, the barge was pulled by a yoke of horses. Travelling aboard the *Burchiello* became a pleasure to be experienced, but the legendary vessel did not survive long: the costly service was suspended when the Republic fell in 1797 and was not revived again until the 1960s when a modest vaporetto was put into service.

The present-day version of the *Burchiello* is modern, and very comfortable - in fact there are no less than 12 *burchielli* presently in service; eight are operated by the I Battelli del Brenta company (*049 87 60 233. www.battellidelbrenta.it*) and three routes by Il Burchiello (*049 87 60 233. www.ilburchiello.it*). Both operators offer various cruises and tours, usually Mar to Oct; contact them for details.

⇨ DRIVING TOUR

FROM PADUA TO FUSINA, VIA MIRANO

▷ Take the A4 to the Padova Est Exit. Follow the Noventana road towards Stra (SS 11).

Villa Foscarini Rossi

&.🕙*Museum open Mon–Thu 9am–1pm and 2–6pm (Fri 5pm); Sat –Sun and hols guided tours only 2.30–6pm.* 🕙*Closed Jan–Dec Sat –Sun and hols only.* ⊜ €7 *or Ville Card (🕙see p. 234).* ✆049 98 01 091. www.villafoscarini.it or www.museodellacalzatura.it.

This villa is named after its most eminent resident, **Marco Foscarini**, who was elected doge in 1762. The current Rossi family are famous for their shoes and several of the rooms open to the public are devoted to a very artistic and stylish display of shoes, past and present. The villa is neo-Classical in style, although modifications were made during the 19C.

Villa Pisani – La Nazionale

© Gino Cianci / Fototeca ENIT

The adjacent *barchessa* is older and in its hall frescoed allegorical scenes are set among *trompe l'oeil* detailing.

Villa Pisani – La Nazionale ★

🕙*Open year-round Tue–Sun 9am–7pm (winter 4pm); Labyrinth Tue–Sun 9am–7.15pm.* 🕙*Closed 1 Jan, 25 Dec.; Labyrinth Nov–March.* 🖵. ⊜€10; Park €7,50. ✆049 50 20 74. www.villapisani.beniculturali.it.

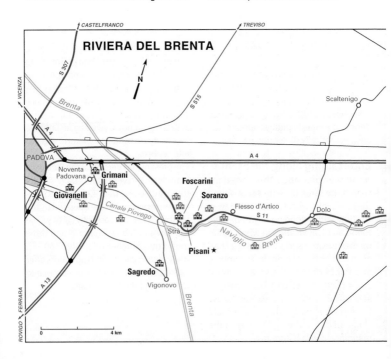

RIVIERA DEL BRENTA

CASTELFRANCO TREVISO

N

Scaltenigo

VICENZA

S. 307

Brenta

S 515

A 4

A 4

PADOVA

Noventa Padovana

Grimani

Foscarini

Soranzo

Fiesso d'Artico

Dolo

Giovanelli

Canale Piovego

Stra

Naviglio Brenta

S 11

Pisani ★

Sagredo

Vigonovo

Brenta

A 13

ROVIGO FERRARA

0   4 km

The residence of **Alvise Pisani**, elected doge in 1735, comprises a magnificent estate with stables and gardens designed by **Girolamo Frigimelica**, who also submitted plans for the villa. These proved to be too costly and were entrusted to **Francesco Maria Preti**.

During the 18C, the villa was endowed with sculpture and paintings, but when the Republic fell in 1797 the Pisani family was forced to sell it to Napoleon who, in turn, gave it to his adopted son Eugène Beauharnais, the Viceroy of Italy. Following the Austrian occupation in 1814, Villa Pisani accommodated several other famous figures, including Francesco Giuseppe, Maximilian of Austria, and Carlos IV of Spain. Soon after the unification of Italy, the villa returned to Italian ownership. It now belongs to the State.

Exterior

At first sight, the house appears to be modelled on a French château. The outside wall, enclosing extensive grounds at the rear, accentuates the horizontal design elements of the façade: the central, projecting Palladian-style bay is charged with decoration; the entrance itself is austerely monumental. Four Atlas figures support the loggia, and silhouetted against the sky, statues and pinnacles punctuate the corners of the pediments.

Beyond the entrance opens a gallery supported by columns, from which there is a magnificent view over the still water and the Palladian-style stables, fronted by their imposing entrance and figures of Zephyr and Flora, sculpted by **Giovanni Bonazza** and his son Tomaso.

Interior

Villa Pisani has 114 rooms in honour of Alvise Pisani, the 114th Doge of Venice. This most famous member of the Pisani family spent his summers here to keep an eye on the grain harvest and the wine production.

Climb the stairs to the left of the entrance, ornamented with wooden statues attributed to Andrea Brustolon, up to the **Sala del Trionfo delle Arti**s, named after the ceiling decoration executed by Giovan Battista Crosato.

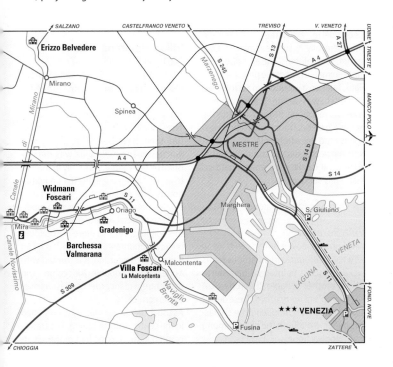

In the next room, dedicated to Bacchus and frescoed by Jacopo Guarana (1770), there is an implausible portrayal of an elephant, painted without first-hand knowledge (*on the wall through which you have come*); watch for the *casone*, a typical peasant dwelling in the Brenta region (*in a panel opposite the windows*). After the room where Hitler and Mussolini met in 1943, comes the Beauharnais suite, furnished with a small bed and the chapel housing an altar by Sansovino, which was brought here by Napoleon from the Church of San Gimignano in Piazza San Marco, which he ordered to be demolished.

The highlight is the vast **Salone delle Feste** in which sumptuous balls were held. The orchestra would play in the long minstrels' gallery. The striking fresco was the last to be painted by Tiepolo in Italy. Look for his signature motif, a parrot (*right corner*).

The Grounds

The great garden extends around a long pond which, although well integrated into the villa's landscape, is a modern addition. It was, in fact, dug in 1911 by the University of Padua to carry out studies on tidal forces. On the west side is the Belvedere folly, its steps seeming to wrap around two columns. The east side is the more animated part of the park: the Café-Haus, built on a mound and surrounded by a ditch, was designed as a summer-house for relaxation. Beyond, towards the exit, is a gazebo, from which a fine view opens onto the whole villa.

Note the nearby maze, a common feature in French and Italian Renaissance gardens that rarely survives.

▷ Proceed eastwards along the SS 11.

Villa Soranzo

Villa Soranzo, now a hotel (*℘041 44 50 27, www.villasoranzo.it*), is famous for its façade frescoes painted by Benedetto Caliari, brother of Paolo (Il Veronese). A fine example of *trompe l'oeil*, these depict a balustrade with monochrome characters peeping out from the niches among mythological figures.

▷ Continue through Dolo and at Mira, follow the directions to Mirano (7km/4mi from Mira) and the road along the canal.

Mirano

Also known as *Il Musone*, Mirano is a satellite of the Brenta Riviera. Although it is not blessed with all the features of the Riviera proper, it has the usual scenery of mills, aligned houses and villas. In **Mira Porte** the houses are terraced into long lines and the Brenta loops around them. Once there was a lock here that brought river trade. Today, the place survives as a small but thriving Veneto town, its piazza ringed with local bars. The Villa Widmann Foscari is 1mi/2km from here.

Villa Widmann Foscari Rezzonico

♿☉*Open year-round Tue–Sun 10am–1pm and 1.30–4.30pm.* ☉*1 Jan and 25 Dec.* ✆€5,50 *or Ville Card* (♿*see p234).* ℘*041 42 49 73. villawidmann. servizimetropolitani.ve.it/visita-la-villa/.* Goldoni, D'Annunzio and Stravinsky all stayed at this 18C villa. The highlight of its magnificent Rococo interior is the ballroom, complete with minstrels' gallery.

Villa Valmarana ai Nani

♿☉*Open year-round Tue–Fri 10–12.30am and 3–6pm (10am–6pm Sat –Sun).* ✆€10 *or Ville Card* (♿*see p234).* ▷*Guided tours (1hr) €3.* ℘*0444 32 18 03. www.villavalmarana.com.* The 18C Villa Valmarana would, at one time, have been flanked by two *barchesse*. The main villa was demolished by the Valmarana family in the 19C to avoid paying a wealth tax on luxury goods. The *barchessa* on the left was divided between six families who modified the original architectural layout of the building. Yet this mere outbuilding is truly monumental. Surrounded by an Italianate rose garden, it is fronted with a fine portico of double Doric columns. In the centre, a giant order of pilasters rises to the cornice.

As usual, the owner's family are glorified in the central **salone** ceiling. The fresco, painted in the second half of the 17C, is attributed to Michelangelo Schiavoni ('Il Chioggotto'), a follower of Tiepolo.

▶ Continue through Oriago and cross the swing bridge over the river.

Villa Gradenigo

🕐 *Open only by tour.* 🖉 *049 87 60 233. www.ilburchiello.it.*

One of the oldest villas on the Brenta, Villa Gradenigo has a square floor plan which was typical of the 16C. The frescoes decorating the garden front, despite their poor condition, are still discernible as the work of Benedetto Caliari, brother of Paolo, Il Veronese. Better preserved although not perfect are the frescoes inside. In the 19C the villa was divided into apartments, and several of the frescoes were irretrievably damaged. At one point in the early 20C, the *palazzo* even served as a laundry, the steam ironically being the coup de grâce for the paintings. Today the villa is a privately owned B&B.

In the reception room on the ground floor, which served as a *portego* – half house, half garden – are murals by Benedetto Caliari. The room is further decorated with friezes of festooned flowers and fruit and painted architectural elements which were first introduced into Venetian villa decoration by Veronese.

▶ Continue along the SS 11 then turn right, off the Venice road, in the direction of Malcontenta.

Villa Foscari La Malcontenta★

🕐 *Open Apr–Oct Tue and Sat 9am–noon.* 👝 €10. 🖉 *041 54 70 012. www.lamalcontenta.com.*

The elegant **Villa Foscari** known as **La Malcontenta** is designated a UNESCO World Heritage Site. The name comes from the controversial excavation of a canal called the *fossa dei malcontenti,* which has lent its name to the area of Malcontenta since 1458.

Since the 16C, the villa has been visited by various illustrious personalities including Henri III, the King of France. Having been used as a military hospital during the First World War, the villa is now back in the hands of the Foscari family, who use it as a summer home.

The House

When Foscari commissioned **Andrea Palladio** (1508–80), the idea was to build a residence in the style of Classical Antiquity: a central square fronted by a temple portico facing the Brenta. This projecting entrance, flanked by Ionic columns, gives the house a formal austerity relieved in part by rustication. The main rooms are accommodated on the *piano nobile*, the first floor, raised above ground level to avoid the risk of flood damage but also to provide enough space to contain the kitchens and storage areas.

The south-facing "back" overlooks the widest part of the garden: it is less formal than the main front, relieved with decorative touches such as the broken pediment and varied window heights. The arched "thermal" window was an idea borrowed from Roman baths.

It is the precise calculation of geometrical harmonies that is unique to the Villa Foscari, developed by Palladio with all measurements determined by the number four as a unit or as a multiple.

Interior

The main entrance to the villa leads into the Latin-cross shaped *salone*. Space is further enhanced by the fresco decoration by **Giambattista Zelotti**, complete with painted fluted Doric columns.

To the northwest of the *salone* is the **Stanza dell'Aurora** (Aurora Room) containing *Harvest*: a beautiful Venetian lady, the legendary Malcontenta, making her entrance; the dependent *studiolo* is dedicated to Bacchus and Venus. To the northeast, Prometheus is depicted on the ceiling with, on the walls, *Phaethon Struck Down by Jupiter* and *Caco Stealing Arms from Hercules*. The **Stanza dei Giganti** (Room of the Giants) presents a very different, apocalyptic scene of giants being crushed by huge boulders. These frescoes, initiated by **Battista Franco** and completed by Zelotti, recall the influence of the Mannerist painter-architect Giulio Romano (Palazzo del Tè in Mantua 1532–34).

Dolomiti★★★
The Dolomites

These high, pale-coloured mountains (Monti Pallidi) situated between the Veneto and Trentino-Alto Adige (South Tyrol), straddle the Italian-Austrian border and are legendary for the red tints they take on at sunset. The ski slopes here have long been famous as a winter playground for the Italian jetset, but there is plenty of interest here for less well-heeled visitors all year round.

A BIT OF GEOGRAPHY

The Dolomites are made of a white calcareous rock known as dolomite. Some 150 million years ago this land was submerged by the sea. On its sandy depths coral reefs and limestone began to shape these "Pale Mountains". Then about 70 million years ago the layers were violently compressed and forced to the surface.

The Dolomites were completed about 2 million years ago when glaciers softened and hollowed out the valleys.

The massifs – To the southeast rise the Pelmo (3 168m/10 393ft) and the Civetta (3 220m/10 564ft) massifs. To the south, near the peak of the Vezzana, the Pale di San Martino, streaked by fissures, divide into three chains separated by a plateau. The Latemar (2 842m/9 324ft) and the Catinaccio (2 981m/9 780ft) massifs, together with the Torri del Vaiolet (Towers of Vaiolet), frame the Costalunga Pass. To the north of the pass rise the Sasso Lungo and the vast Sella Massif (Gruppo di Sella). To the east, the chief summits in the

- ♿ **Michelin Map:**
  562 C 16–19 – Veneto – Trentino-Alto Adige
- ℹ **Info:** Veneto: Corso Italia 81, Cortina d'Ampezzo ℘0436 86 90 86. infodolomiti.it. Alto Adige/South Tyrol: Piazza Walther 8, Bolzano. ℘047 13 07 000. www.suedtirol.info.
- ▶ **Location:** In the Trentino-Alto Adige region, the Dolomites are reached by A 22 off the Brennero transalpine route. From the Veneto region take A 27.
- 🅿 **Parking:** Leave your car in the car park north of Chiusa if visiting the Convento di Sabiona.
- 👀 **Don't Miss:** Val Gardena and the panoramas from Tofana di Mezzo.
- 🕐 **Timing:** Allow for 3–4 days of skiing or walking.
- ♿ **Also See:** *BELLUNO*.

Cortina Dolomites are the Tofane, the Sorapis and the Cristallo. Finally, in the heart of the range, stands the **Marmolada Massif** (Gruppo della Marmolada, 3 342m/10 964ft).

Between Cortina and the Piave Valley the wooded region of **Cadore** boasts the Antelao (3 263m/10 705ft) and the triple peak, Tre Cime di Lavaredo (Drei Zinnen), which it shares with the Parco delle Dolomiti di Sesto in Alto Adige.

Flora and fauna – The Dolomite landscape is coloured by coniferous forests, crocuses, edelweiss, rhododendron, lil-

The Ladin Culture

Ladin is a curious ancient language which has its roots in the Latin language and is spoken by around 30 000 people in and around the Dolomites. It had emerged by the 5C as a direct result of the earlier Roman expansion into the mountainous regions. At Ciastel de Tor, in San Martino in Badia, the Museum ladin has an impressive exhibition on the Ladin culture. Artistic displays and creative use of the latest communications technology make for an interesting visit: 🕐*For opening days and hours see the website.* 🕐*Closed Nov, 25 Dec.* ⊛€8. ℘0474 52 40 20. www.museumladin.it.

Lago di Fedaia and Marmolada, Dolomiti

© Alberto Simonetti / iStockphoto.com

ies and alpine bluebells. Tourist activity drives away wild animals, but the Dolomites are still a refuge for many, including royal eagles and woodcock.

🚗 DRIVING TOURS

① STRADA DELLE DOLOMITI★★★
From Bolzano to Cortina – 210km/131mi – Allow at least two days.

This great Dolomite Road is not only a world-famous spectacular route but a perfect example of the science of road engineering.

Bolzano★
Capital of the Alto Adige, Bolzano lies on the A 22, the Brenner transalpine route, at the confluence of the Adige and the Isarco.It anchors one end of the wine road (*Strada di Vino*). The architecture of the town shows a marked Austrian influence, built largely between the 16C and 1918. At its heart centre is the Piazza Walther and the delightful **Via dei Portici★**. Don't miss the **Museo Archeologico dell'Alto★** (&🕐*Open Tue–Sun 10am–6pm; daily in Jul, Aug, Dec. 🕐Closed 1 Jan, 1 May and 25 Dec. ⊛€9. ☎ 0471 32 01 00. www.iceman.it.*), which illustrates the chronology of the South Tyrol from the last Ice Age (15000 BC) to the Carolingian age (AD 800) and houses the "Iceman," known as "Ötzi," whose preserved remains were found by German mountain climbers in the Ötzi Alps, in 1991. The nearby **Renon Plateau★** (Ritten) is dazzlingly green and fertile, dominating the Isarco Val-

ley (Eisacktal) between Bolzano and Ponte Gardena. It can be reached by car from Bolzano north or the funicular at Soprabolzano in Bolzano.

Gola della Val d'Ega★
This narrow gorge, the Ega Valley, with pink sandstone walls, is guarded by the **Castel Cornedo**.

Passo di Costalunga★
From this pass on the Dolomite Road there is a **view★** over the Catinaccio on one side and the Latemar on the other.

Vigo di Fassa※※
🛈 *Strada Rezia 10. ☎0462 60 96 00. www.fassa.com.*
This resort, in a picturesque site★ in the Val di Farsa, is a mountaineering centre in the Catinaccio Massif. The multi-lingual Ski School (*Piazza J.B.Massar 1. ☎0462 76 31 25. www.scuolascivigo.com.*) is recommended.

Canazei※※※
🛈 *Piazza G. Marconi 5. ☎0462 60 96 00. www.fassa.com.*
Canazei lies in the heart of the massif, between the Catinaccio, the Towers of Vaiolet (Torri del Vaiolet), the Sella Massif and the Marmolada. This is the usual base for excursions in the Marmolada mountain range.

▷ At Canazei turn right onto the P 641.

This road affords very fine **views★★** of the Marmolada range and its glacier. As one comes out of a long tunnel a lake, **Lago di Fedaia★**, suddenly appears.

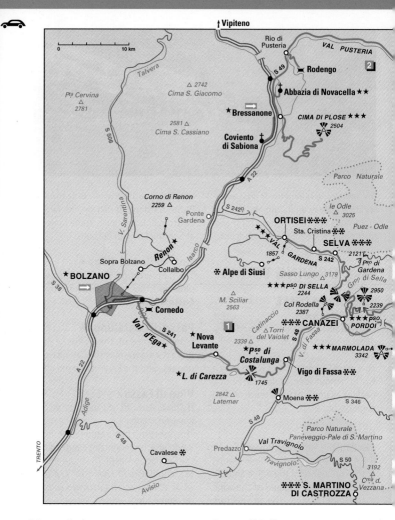

Marmolada★★★

☐ ☎0437 52 29 84.
www. funiviemarmolada.com.
This is the highest massif in the Dolomites, famous for its glacier and fast ski-runs. The **cable car** from Malga Ciapela goes up to 3 265m/10 712ft offering wonderful **panoramas★★★** of the Cortina peaks (Tofana and Cristallo), the Sasso Lungo, the enormous tabular mass of the Sella Massif and in the background the summits of the Austrian Alps including the Grossglockner.

◓ Return to Canazei then after 5.5km/3mi turn left.

Passo di Sella★★★

Linking the Val di Fassa and Val Gardena this pass offers one of the most extensive **panoramas★★★** in the Dolomites, including the Sella, Sasso Lungo and Marmolada massifs.

Val Gardena★★★

☐ www.val-gardena.com.
This is one of the most famous, most beautiful and most visited valleys in the Dolomite. The inhabitants still speak a language which was born during the Roman occupation: the Ladin dialect. Skilful local woodwork can be seen in shops in Selva (Wolkenstein), Santa Cristina and Ortisei (St Ulrich).

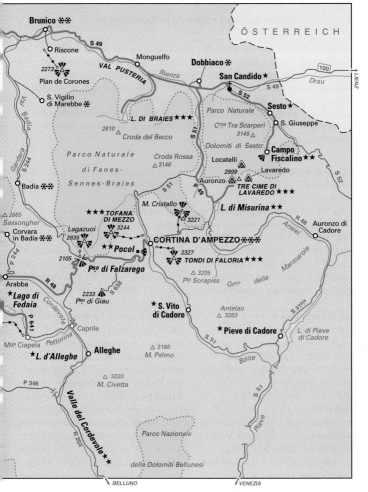

Selva Val Gardena✳✳✳
🛈 *Str. Mëisules 213.* 📞*0471 77 79 00.*
www.val-gardena.com.
This resort lies at the Sella Massif base and is a renowned craft centre as well as one of the leading ski resort in the Alps.

Ortisei (St Ulrich)✳✳✳
🛈 *Str. Rezia.* 📞*0471 77 76 00.*
www.ortisei.com or
www.val-gardena.com.
From Ortisei (St Ulrich) a cable car climbs up to **Alpe di Siusi**✳ (Seiser Alm), a 60km2/23sq mi plateau in a delightful **setting**✳✳ overlooking the Sasso Lungo and the Sciliar. This is an excellent base for excursions to suit all abilities.

▷ Return to the Dolomite Road.

Passo Pordoi★★★
The highest pass (2 239m/7 346ft) on the Dolomite Road lies between huge blocks of rock with sheer sides and shorn-off tops.

Passo del Falzarego
Nearing Cortina the pass cuts through the Tofane and skirts the barren land-scape of the Cinque Torri (literally, Five Towers), which are said to have inspired Tolkein when he wrote *The Lord of the Rings.*

The Legend of the Pale Mountains

Legend has it that a prince who lived at the foot of the Alps married the daughter of the King of the Moon. The young girl loved flowers and meadows but she so desperately missed the pale mountains of her home that she felt compelled to return to the Moon. The Prince was unable to go with her because the brightness of the moon would blind him. Some dwarfs came to his aid and made some skeins of thread from the moon's rays, weaving them into nets which they placed on the mountains, turning them into the required pallid shades of the Mountains of the Moon. The princess was thus able to return to her prince.

Cortina d'Ampezzo✿✿✿

🛈 *Corso Italia 81. ✆0436 86 90 86. www.infodolomiti.it.*

Cortina, the capital of the Dolomites, is a winter sports and summer resort with a worldwide reputation.

Set in the heart of the Dolomites at an altitude of 1 210m/4 000ft it is an excellent excursion centre for discovering the magnificent **mountain scenery★★★**.

Tondi di Faloria★★★

Cable car service to Faloria from Via Ria di Zeto. From Cortina d'Ampezzo to Tondi di Faloria: in winter, "Tondi," "Girilada," "Vitelli," "Rio Gere" and "Bigontina" chairlifts .
✆0436 25 17. www.dolomiti.org or cortinacube.it.

From the summit a grand panorama may be enjoyed. Excellent ski slopes.

Tofana di Mezzo★★★ – *"Freccia del Cielo" cable car. ✆0436 5052. www.freccianelcielo.com.* A cable car climbs to 3 244m/10 743ft, for a superb panorama of the mountain.

Belvedere Pocol★★ – *www.servizi-ampezzo.it. ✆0436 86 79 21. Hourly bus service from Piazza Roma, Cortina.* Lying to the southwest, this viewpoint affords a wonderful sunset view of Cortina.

② VAL PUSTERIA AND SURROUNDING AREA

This itinerary begins in Bressanone and continues into the Pusteria Valley.

Val Pusteria, or Pustertal, is bordered to the south by the Dolomites and by the central Alps to the north. From the end of the 13C until the 16C it belonged to the County of Gorizia and formed part of the Strada d'Alemagna, a road which linked Venice and Germany.

Bressanone (Brixen)★★

🛈 *Viale Ratisbona 9. ✆0472 83 64 01. www.brixen.org.*

Set at the confluence of the Rienza and Isarco rivers, Bressanone is an elegant Tyrolean town that enjoys an exceptionally high number of sunshine hours. Conquered by the Romans in 15 BC, it then belonged to Bavaria and Austria, until 1919 when it became Italian.

Duomo – This Baroque cathedral has a neo-Classical west front and luminous interior decorated with golf leaf frescoes and Romanesque **cloisters.★**

Palazzo vescovile – Commissioned by Prince-Bishop Bruno de Kirchberg after 1250, the palace underwent numerous alterations but retained its superb **courtyard★**. It now houses the vast **Museo diocesano★** (🕐*Open Mar–Oct Tue–Sun 10am–5pm (winter daily).* 🕐*Closed 24 and 25 Dec.* ✆€5 (€8 incl Hofburg). *✆0472 83 05 05. www.hofburg.it.*) containing a wonderful set of polychrome **wood carvings★★** (Romanesque and Gothic Tyrolean), **altar pieces★** carved in the round dating from the Renaissance, the cathedral **treasure★** and **Nativity scenes★** dating from the 18C to 20C.

▶ Head south towards Chiusa (Klausen).

Monastero di Sabiona

🕐*Open year-round 8am-5pm; Church of Our Lady Jul–Sept Tue–Sat 2–5pm.*
✆0472 84 74 24. www.klausen.it.
🅿 *If you can, leave the car in the car*

park north of Chiusa (Klausen), from here it is 30min on foot.

This spectacularly located convent of Benedictine nuns (known as the Acropolis of the Tyrol)dates back to the 17C. It was built on the rock where the bishop's palace had stood, the palace having burnt down after being struck by lightning in 1535.

▶ Turn around and head in the direction of Bressanone, turning right onto the road for Plose.

Plose★★
Alt 2 446 m/8 031ft.
A cable car from Valcroce and then another from Plose enable visitors to enjoy a wonderful **panorama★★★** of the Dolomites and the Austrian mountains.

▶ Retrace your steps and continue along the S 49. The Abbazia di Novacella is 3km/2mi north of Bressanone.

Abbazia di Novacella★★
Open year-round by guided tour only (italian and German only) Mon–Sat 10am, 11am, 2pm, 3pm, 4pm. Reserve in advance. €7. 0472 83 61 89. www.abbazianovacella.it .
The abbey, known in German as Kloster Neustift, was founded in 1142 and run by Augustinian monks. The courtyard contains the **Well of Wonders** decorated with "eight" wonders of the world, one of which is the abbey itself. The Bavarian Baroque **church** has an ornate interior and **Rococo** library of 76 000 rare books, and manuscripts. A new organ was installed May 2014.

▶ Return to the SS 49 and continue north to Rio di Pusteria. Close by stands the Castello di Rodengo.

Castello di Rodengo
Open by guided tour only (1hr) 1 May–15 Oct Sun–Fri 11.30am–2.30pm (also 3.30pm 15 Jul–31 Aug). €5. 328 16 51 332.
The Castle of Rodengo is decorated with the oldest known cycle of Romanesque

(13C) frescoes with a profane theme: the epic poem *Iwein* by Hartmann von Aue.

Bruneck (Dietenheim)✼✼
This is the main town in the Pusteria Valley. The beautiful open-air **Südtiroler Landesmuseum für Volkskunde** (South Tyrol Museum of Folk Traditions)★ (*Open Easter–Oct Tue–Sat 10am–5pm, 6pm Jul–Aug; Sun and hols 2–6pm. Closed Mon. €7. 0474 55 20 87. www.volkskundemuseum.it.*) comprises the stately late 17C residence of Mair am Hof and its grounds of 3ha/7 acres, which includes many and various types of rural buildings brought here from other parts of the region. These include a hayloft, a farm, grain store, and a mill, the oldest building dating as far back as 1497.

▶ From Bruneck head in the direction of Dobbiaco. After Monguelfo turn right to Lago di Braies (signposted).

Lago di Braies (Prager Wildsee) ★★★
Alt 1 495m/4 905ft. This shimmering lake can be circumnavigated in around an hour. It is the starting point of some rather arduous mountain footpaths.

▶ Proceed through the Pusteria Valley. Turn right before Dubbiaco in the direction of Cortina. Follow directions for Misurina and then for Tre Cime di Lavaredo. The last stretch is a toll-road.

Tre Cime di Lavaredo★★★
From the *rifugio* (refuge) at Auronza the Lavaredo shelter is reached in half an hour. From there the Locatelli shelter is reached in an hour. This last stretch offers spectacular views of the Tre Cime (Three Chimneys) range. The Tre Cime can also be reached from Sesto, along path 102, which leads to Locatelli in two and a half hours.

▶ On the way back from Tre Cime a stop at Lago di Misurina is recommended.

Lago di Misurina★★

Alt 1 759m/5 770ft.

This lake is set among a plantation of fir trees and is an excellent starting point for excursions to the surrounding mountains, from the Tre Cime di Lavaredo to the Cristallo.

Dobbiaco (Toblach)✳

Dobbiaco was an important town in the Middle Ages, standing at the crossroads with the main Strada dell'Alemagna.

San Candido★

This pretty village has the most important Romanesque church in the Alto Adige. The **collegiata★** dates from the 13C. Most striking is the *Crucifixion*, a 13C wood sculptural group with Christ's feet resting on Adam's head.

▶ At San Candido turn right for Sesto leaving the Pusteria, which eventually leads to Austria.

Sesto★

Sesto overlooks the Dolomites and offers a huge variety of footpaths and alpine excursions. The **Monte Elmo funicular** makes distances shorter. For a peaceful walk, path 4D crosses the forest and high pastures and affords views of the Meridiana del Sesto.

▶ At San Giuseppe (Moos) the Val Fiscalino leads to **Campo Fiscalino★** offering stunning views of the Meridiana di Sesto and Cima dei Tre Scarperi.

VISIT
Valle del Cordevole★★

The road from Caprile to Belluno is lined with hilltop villages. **Alleghe** on the **lake★** is a good excursion centre.

San Martino di Castrozza✳✳✳

A good starting point for excursions.

Pieve di Cadore★

🔲 *www.infodolomiti.it.*

The birthplace of the great artist, **Titian**, the town church holds one of his works and his family house **Casa**

del Tiziano is now a museum 🕐*Open Tue–Sun 10–12.30am and 3.30–6.30pm (7pm Jul and Aug); 6 Jan–1 May by reservation only.* 🕐*Closed 1 Jan and 25 Dec.* ⊜€3; ☎0435 32 262. *www.magnifica comunitadicadore.it.* Also of interest is the **Cadore Museum** situated in the Palazzo della Magnifica Comunita. Worth a second glance is the unusual but interesting **Museo dell'Occhiale** (Spectacles Museum) (☎*www.museo dellocchiale.it*) displaying over 2 600 examples of reading glasses, dating from the Middle Ages to the modern day.

ADDRESSES

SPORT AND LEISURE

DOLOMITI – MOUNTAIN FOOTPATHS

The Dolomites have a dense network of footpaths. Whether you are an expert climber or simply want to take a peaceful walk, there is a vast choice of routes for those wishing to get a better look at the Monti Pallidi. Maps and guides listing paths, mountain huts and bivouacs are on sale just about everywhere.

Some mountain pathways include:
No 2 (Bressanone–Feltre): This path crosses the Plose, the Puez Group, the Gardenaccia, the Sella and the Marmolada massif.

No 3 (Villabassa–Longarone): This path winds its way through Val Pusteria, the Croda Rossa, Misurina, the Cristallo, the Sorapis and the Antelao.

No 4 (San Candido–Pieve di Cadore): This track goes through the Sesto Dolomites, the Cadini di Misurina and the Marmarole.

To be fully prepared for a mountain excursion it is advisable to contact the tourist offices listed left.

TREKKING AND CLIMBING

Gruppo Guide Alpine Scuola di Alpinismo – *Corso Italia 69/a Cortina d'Ampezzo.* ☎*0436 86 85 05. www.guidecortina.com.* This company use only experienced mountain guides and offer a wide variety of organised year-round excursions for children and adults alike including hiking, orienteering, climbing courses for all levels, off-piste skiing, ice climbing and trekking.

Padova★★

Padua

Padua is home to some of the finest historical and artistic sights in the Veneto. The city's cultural and artistic heritage dates back to the 13C and 14C when its university was one of the very best in Europe, the Scrovegni Chapel had become a landmark in Renaissance Art and the Basilica di Sant'Antonio (Basilica del Santo) was founded as a major site of pilgrimage.

A BIT OF HISTORY

There are few traces of ancient *Patavium,* which was one of the most prosperous Roman cities in the Veneto during the 1C BC owing to its river trade, its agriculture and the sale of horses. In the 7C Padua was destroyed by the Lombards, and from the 11C to 13C it became an independent city-state. The city underwent its greatest period of economic and cultural prosperity under the enlightened rule of the lords of Carrara (1337–1405). In 1405 Padua came under the sway of the Venetian Republic and remained a loyal subject until 1797 when the Venetian Constitution was abolished by Napoleon.

The City of St Anthony the Hermit – This Franciscan monk was born in Lisbon in 1195 and died at the age of 36 in the environs of Padua. He was a forceful preacher and is generally represented holding a book and a lily. St Anthony is buried in the Basilica which has long been one of Italy's major pilgrimage sites.

A Famous University – The University of Padua, founded in 1222, is the second oldest in Italy after Bologna. Galileo was a professor and its students included Renaissance scholar Pico della Mirandola, the astronomer Copernicus and the poet Tasso.

Art in Padua – In 1304, **Giotto** came to Padua to decorate the Scrovegni Chapel, with a superlative cycle of frescoes.

In the 15C the Renaissance in Padua was marked by **Donatello**, another Florentine, who stayed in the city from 1444 to 1453. Also in the 15C, Paduan art flourished under the influence of the Paduan artist, **Andrea Mantegna** (1431–1506), a powerful painter and an innovator in the field of perspective.

- ▶ **Population:** 211 560
- **Michelin Map:** 562 F 17 – Veneto
- **Info:** Galleria Pedrocchi. ℰ049 20 10 080. Stazione Ferrovie dello Stato. ℰ049 20 10 080. www.turismopadova.it.
- **Location:** Padua is 24mi/40km west of Venice.
- **Don't Miss:** Giotto's frescoes in the Scrovegni Chapel, the Basilica del Santo, the University.
- **Timing:** Allow at least two day to explore Padua.
- **Also See:** *Riviera del BRENTA, TREVISO, VENEZIA, VICENZA.*

SIGHTS

Scrovegni Chapel (Capella degli Scrovegni) ★★★

Open year-round 9am–7pm. The chapel may only be visited by supervised tour (20min allowed in chapel). Reservations compulsory and must be made at least 24hrs in advance. (see box below for more details on visiting). Closed 1 Jan,1 May, 25 and 26 Dec. €13 or PadovaCard (see p252). ℰ049 20 10 020. www.cappelladegliscrovegni.it.

The chapel was built in 1303 by Enrico degli Scrovegni. His father had been an infamous usurer, condemned to eternal damnation by Dante (in the Inferno) and this monumental offering was his son's attempt to save his soul. In 1303 he commissioned Giotto (1267–1327), then at the height of his career, to fresco the building from top to bottom in religious imagery; the result is widely recognised as one of the milestones in the history of art. Before the Scrovegni Chapel such images were stylised icon-like representations; Giotto brought life and humanity to his subjects. To get the most out of your visit it is highly recommended

Visiting the Scrovegni Chapel – Practicalities

The Scrovegni Chapel is one of the most precious places in all Italy and strict visiting rules are in place to preserve it for future generations. For centuries visitors to the chapel were inadvertently accelerating the decaying process of the frescoes simply by breathing and perspiring in here. In May 2000 an access building was installed, with a special air-conditioned waiting-room which reduces the body temperature of visitors (and filters out other pollutants), while they watch a short introductory film. This means that they can enter the chapel without further jeopardizing its fragile condition and the condition of the frescoes is now stable though restoration is an ongoing process.

The number of visitors each day is strictly limited to timed tickets and only 25 people per visit. Pre-booking is required (at quiet times you might be able to purchase a same-day ticket). You can pay by credit card up until the previous day. You must collect pre-paid booked tickets at the Eremitani Museum ticket office (100 metres away) one hour before the assigned time of entry, then arrive at the entrance of the air-conditioned waiting-room outside the Scrovegni Chapel five minutes before the allotted visiting time. Late visitors will not be admitted into the chapel, and will have to pay again and re-book.

To buy tickets on the day and collect prepaid tickets, go to the office at Piazza Eremitani. The ticket fee includes Eremitani Museum and the Zuckermann Palace.

that you see the excellent Sala Multimediale (multimedia room) in the Eremitani Museum complex (◔ see below) before the chapel. A short film and interactive computer screens give the background to the project and shows how frescoes are created. There are no guides or interpretation in the chapel itself so you need to answer all your questions here.

The remarkable cycle of 39 frescoes, with colours still as bright as the day they were painted, illustrates episodes in the lives of Joachim and Anna (the parents of the Virgin), episodes in the Virgin Mary's life, and Christ's life and death. Highlights are *Flight into Egypt, Judas' Kiss,* the *Entombment* and the saturated cobalt-blue ceiling sprinkled with golden stars. On the lower register powerful monochrome figures depict the Vices and Virtues. A powerful and graphic *Last Judgement* on the west wall completes the cycle. On the altar stands an often overlooked masterpiece of a **Virgin★** by the Tuscan sculptor Giovanni Pisano.

Chiesa degli Eremitani ★★

www.cappelladegliscrovegni.it.
In the Cappella Ovetari of the 13C church of the Hermits (*the second on the right of the Cappella Maggiore*) are fragments of frescoes by **Mantegna**; *Martyrdom of St James on the north wall, Assumption in the apse and Martyrdom of St Christoper on the south wall.* The Lady Chapel (Cappella Maggiore) has splendid frescoes by **Guariento**, Giotto's pupil.

Museo Civici agli Eremitani★

♿◔*Open year-round Tue–Sun 9am–7pm.* ◔*Closed 1 Jan, 1 May, 25 and 26 Dec.* ◉ €10 *inc Palazzo Zuckermann and multimedia room;* €13 *inc multimedia room, Cappella degli Scrovegni, Palazzo Zuckermann, or PadovaCard* (◔ *see p252).* ℰ*049 82 04 551. www.cappelladegliscrovegni.it.*

The Civic Museums complex is a collection of three separate museums and the **Sala Multimediale** (◔ *see above*).

The main building, which includes the Scrovegni Chapel ticket office, is in the cloisters of the former Eremetani monastery. This houses the extensive **Museo Archeologico** (Archealogoical Museum) with its superb Roman section, and above the three thousand paintings or so that make up the **Museo d'Arte-Medioevale e Moderna** (Medieval and Modern Art Museum). These span the period from the 14C to 19C and include works by Giotto, Bellini, Giorgione, Tit-

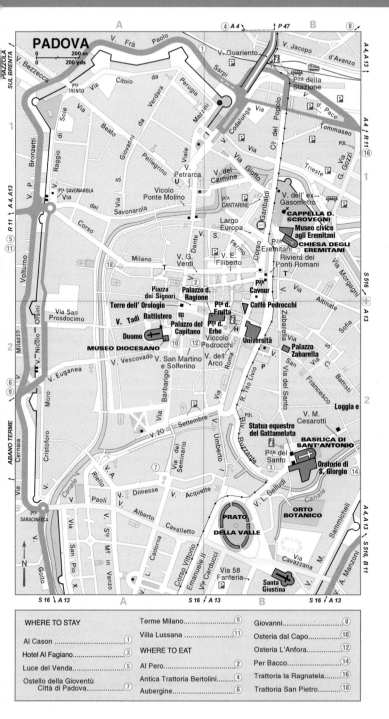

PADOVA

0 — 200 m
0 — 200 yds

ian, Bassano, Veronese, Tintoretto and Tiepolo alongside a large Flemish and Dutch collection.

Across the road, housed in the Palazzo Zuckermann, is the **Museo Arti Applicate e Decorative & Museo Bottacin**, which is split between and the famous numismatic Bottacin collection.

The former contains more than 2 000 Applied and Decorative Arts pieces: glass, intaglio and inlay work, ceramics, silver, ivory, jewellery, Oriental antiquities, textiles and fabrics, and furniture. Many of these are on display for the very first time since recently being transferred from the storeroom of the Museum of Medieval and Modern Art. They illustrate the various types of artefacts made and used in Padova between the Middle Ages and second half of the 19C,

The Bottacin Collection comprises some 50,000 coins, medals and seals making it one of the most important collections of its kind in the world.

Basilica del Santo (Sant'Antonion)★★

&⊙*Open Basilica daily 6.20am –6.45pm (7.45pm Mar–Oct); Anthonian Museum: Tue–Fri 9am–1pm, Sat–Sun 9am–1pm and 2–6pm; Scuola di Sant Antonio: 9am–1pm and 2–6pm.*⊙*Closed 1 Jan, Easter and 25 Dec.* ⊛€2,50 (Anthonian Museum) or PadovaCard (⌚see p252); €3; €5 (inc Sala Priorale and Oratorio di San*

PadovaCards

The PadovaCard (48hrs or 72hrs) gives admission (add €1 booking fee) to the Scrovegni Chapel, to important sights and museums, free public transport and many other discounts for €16 or €21, little more than the cost of the standard ticket for the Scrovegni Chapel. Alternatively there is the Museums All Year Long Card which is cheaper, but does not include transport. Valid for one adult plus one under age 14 years.

Giorgio). ☎049 82 25 652. www.santantonio.org.

In front of the basilica Donatello erected an **equestrian statue★★** of the Venetian leader **Gattamelata** (the nickname of Erasmo di Narni). This bronze was the first of its size to be cast in Italy.

This lavish building, often described as a poor man's St Mark's, began construction immediately after the death of "Il Santo" in 1231. The exterior is an imposing sight in Romanesque Gothic style with eight domes and spires of eastern inspiration that make it look almost like a mosque. The **interior★★** is equally impressive, sumptuously decorated with a multitude of monuments. The magnificent nave is divided by huge pillars and the main attraction is the **Cappella del Santo★★**, location of the tomb/altar of St Anthony (Arca di Sant'Antonio) by Tiziano Aspetti (1594). The magnificent nave is divided by huge pillars and the main attraction, the Capella del Santo, lies to the left. This 16th-century marble confection is mostly the work of Tullio Lombardo and Jacopo Sansovino, adorned with 21st century photographs of healed limbs and various other votive offerings which attest to the ongoing miraculous powers of St Antonio. Next to this is the Chapel of the Black Madonna, the Saint's original resting place.

The main altar is decorated with acclaimed bronze statues and reliefs by Donatello. Behind here is the **Treasury Chapel** with some of the church's most valuable relics. These include a thorn from Christ's crown and the tongue, jawbone and larynx (labelled, *apparato vocal*) of St Anthony. Apparently when his body was removed to the basilica 32 years after his death, the tongue had remained completely intact – a miracle attributed to his great oratorical skills.

On the walls are 16C **high reliefs★★**. In the chancel the **high altar★★** has bronze panels (1450) by Donatello. The third chapel has **frescoes★** by Altichiero (14C), a Veronese artist.

There is a fine **view★** of the building from the cloisters, to the south, which are chock-a-block with tombs, monuments and plaques. The **Magnolia (Chapter)**

Courtyard with its 200-year old magnolia tree is particularly beautiful.
The **Oratorio di San Giorgio** (St George's Oratory) is decorated with 21 **frescoes★** (1377) by Altichiero.
In the adjacent **Scuola di Sant'Antonio**, are 18 16C **frescoes★** relating the life of St Anthony. Four of these are by Titian. (To visit the Oratory you may have ask one of the guardians, who can be found in the adjacent building which connects the Oratory to the little church on the right, the 'Scoletta'.

Palazzo della Ragione★

Enter by the Scala delle Erbe off the Piazza delle Erbe. ♿ *Entrance on via VIII Febbraio.* 🕐 *Open Open daily 9am–7pm (6pm Nov–Jan).* 🕐 *Closed 1 Jan, 1 May, 25 and 26 Dec.* 👝€6 or PadovaCard (👝 see p252). ✆049 82 05 006. padovacultura.padovanet.it.

The former Law Courts are set between two of the city's liveliest squares, the **Piazza della Frutta★** and the **Piazza delle Erbe★**, named after the colourful daily markets that take place.

Built in 1218–19 the Palazzo boasts the largest undivided hall in Europe. Known as the **Salone★★** the hall measures 79m long, 27m wide and 26m high, with a magnificent upturned wooden ships-keel style roof. The four walls are covered by a beautiful intriguing cycle of 333 astrological and religious frescoes designed by Nicola Miretto in 1425–40. In total they stretch some 217 linear metres. Pick up a leaflet at the front desk. There is also a Foucault pendulum (Italian author Umberto Eco wrote a book entitled *Foucault's Pendulum*, although not about this one).

Unmissable is the hall's largest permanent exhibit, **Il Cavallo Ligneo★** (The Wooden Horse). This magnificent equine giant stands over 4m tall (5.75m including its plinth) and dates from 1466. It is thought to have been made for a fair or joust, perhaps on the Prato della Valle next to the Basilica del Santo and is probably modelled after Donatello's Gattemelata monument, though the architect is unknown.

Piazza dei Signori

This is one of the city's most beautiful squares, headed by the Palazzo del Capitanio, built 1599–1605, with a **Torre dell'Orologioa** (astronomical clock tower) made in 1344. On the corner of the square with Via Monte de Pieta is the Loggia della Gran Guardia, completed in 1523.

Università★★

🕐🚶 *Visit by guided tours only (45min) Mon–Sat; for opening hours see the website* 🕐 *Closed Sun and hols.* 👝€7. ✆340 34 73 772. www.unipd.it/universita/patrimonio-artistico-culturale/visite-guidate/visite-guidate-palazzo-bo.

Established in 1222, the University of Padua was among the first in Europe. Its main block, right in the centre of town, is known as the Palazzo del Bo (or to its students, simply Il Bo) – bo meaning ox, after an inn that once stood here. As you ascend the stairs the statue of Elena Cornaro Piscopia (1646–84) is a reminder how enlightened the university was for its time, in allowing her to become the very first woman in the world to receive a doctorate degree. Upstairs is an ancient relic of the University's most famous lecturer, the raised desk-cum lectern from which Galileo taught physics from 1592 to 1610. Even this is eclipsed however by the first permanent **Teatro Anatomico★★** (Anatomy Theatre) in the world, built for the university in 1594, by Fabricius. His student William Harvey studied at Padua in 1602 and formulated the (then) very controversial theory of the circulation of the blood from the heart, after watching dissections in the University theatre. Another famous Padua graduate was Fallopius (of Fallopian tubes fame) who attended here in 1561. The structure – a round wooden amphitheatre that once held up to 250 students – is still perfectly intact though no longer strong enough to stand on. Visitors are offered a curious worm's-eye view, looking up through a hole from beneath the theatre.

Caffè Pedrocchi★

This beautiful landmark neo-Classical café, established 1831, is famous as being the place where the student rebellion against the Austrians was played out in 1848. The lower floor is a grand cafe while upstairs (*piano nobile*) is the **Museo del Risorgimeno** (Museum of Independence) (🕐*Open year-round. Upstairs museum Tue–Sun 9.30am–12.30pm and 3.30–6pm.* 🕐*Closed 1 Jan, 1 May, 25 and 26 Dec.* ✆€4). ✆*049 82 04 541. padovacultura.padovanet.it*).

Chiesa Santa Giustina

This 16C church, dedicated to St Justina boasts an **altarpiece★** by Veronese.

Orto Botanico

🕐*Open daily Apr–Sept 9am–7pm; Oct 9am–6pm; Nov–Mar 9am–5pm.* 🕐*Closed 1 Jan and 25 Dec.* ✆€10. ✆*049 82 73 939. www.ortobotanico.unipd.it.*
These botanical gardens, laid out in 1545, contain many exotic species including a palm tree, planted in 1585, made famous by Goethe who was apparently inspired by it to write essays and scientific works on plants.

EXCURSIONS

Colli Euganei★

The Euganean hills, south of Padua, are of volcanic origin and were appreciated in Roman times for their hot springs and wines.

Abano Terme♨♨♨

11km/7mi southwest.
www.abanomontegrotto.it.
Shaded by pines, this is one of Italy's most famous thermal spa towns. The adjacent resort of **Montegrotto Terme** is also a first-class spa resort.

Monselice★

27km/17mi southwest.
This town (Latin name *Mons Silicis*; granite mountain) was an ancient Roman mining community. The upper terrace of the Villa Balbi with its Italian garden affords a lovely **view★** of the region.

Arquà Petrarca★

27km/17mi southwest.
It was here that the poet **Petrarch** (1304–74) died. **Petrarch's house★** is open to the public. Exhibits include memorabilia and autographs of visitors such as Carducci and Byron. 🕐*Open daily Mar–Oct 9am–12.30pm and 3–7pm; Nov–Feb 9am–noon and 2.30–5.30pm.* 🕐*Closed 1 Jan, 1 May, 25 and 26 Dec.* ✆€4. ✆*0429 71 82 94. www.arquapetrarca.com.*

Montagnana★

47km/29mi southwest.
Impressive 14C **ramparts★★** reinforce this town. The **Duomo**, by Sansovino, contains a *Transfiguration* by Veronese.

Delta del Po★

Once a malaria-infested marshy district, this is now a fertile agricultural area and a designated nature reserve. The Chioggia–Ravenna road traverses flat expanses stretching away to the horizon. Clumps of poplars and umbrella pines, canals spanned by curious bridges, and fishing boats add touches of colour and a special charm. The area to the south of the Valli di Comacchio lagoons has a melancholy beauty.

Abbazia di Pomposa★★

96km/60mi southeast. 🕐*Open Tue–Sun 8.30am–7.30pm.* 🕐*Closed 1 Jan, 1 May, 25 Dec.* ✆€5. ✆*0533 71 91 19.*
This Benedictine abbey was founded in the 6C and enjoyed fame in the Middle Ages due to its musical heritage. The fine pre-Romanesque **church** in the style typical of Ravenna is preceded by a narthex whose decoration exemplifies the Byzantine style. The nave has some magnificent **mosaic flooring** and two holy water stoups, one in the Romanesque style and the other in the Byzantine style. The walls bear an exceptional cycle of 14C **frescoes**. From right to left the upper band is devoted to the Old Testament while the lower band has scenes from the Life of Christ; the corner pieces of the arches depict the *Apocalypse*. On the west wall are a *Last Judgement* and in the apsidal chapel *Christ in Majesty*.

Treviso★

Treviso sits at the heart of an important agricultural and industrial area. The old centre, surrounded by waterways and what remains of the city walls, is a delight and includes an area of Venetian-style canals.

▸ **Population:** 83 777
- **Michelin Map:** 562 E–F 18
- **Info:** Via Fiumicelli 30. ℘0422 54 76 32. www.visittreviso.it.
▹ **Location:** Treviso is 23 mi/37km north of Venice, linked by the SS 13.
- **Don't Miss:** Chiesa di San Nicolo and the Villa Maser.
- **Timing:** Allow at least a day to visit the city.
- **Also See:** *PADOVA, VENEZIA.*

A BIT OF HISTORY

Treviso flourished under Carolingian rule in the early Middle Ages. However, in 1237 the city fell under the tyranny of Ezzelino da Romano and subsequently endured over a century of torment and civil war as authority passed from hand to hand. Treviso made a pact with Venice in 1389, which heralded a long period of prosperity and saw another period of construction, this time in the Venetian Gothic style. In 1509 the city began to play a key role in Venice's defence of the south. The current walls and gates date back to this period.

In 1797 Treviso – and Venice itself – fell to Napoleon, and was subsequently subsumed into the Austrian domain until 15 July 1866.

Allied bombings in 1944 killed thousands and many historic landmarks were destroyed.

VISIT
Piazza dei Signori★

Alongside the piazza, the centre of town is landmarked by the monumental medieval **Palazzo dei Trecento★** (1207) complex which also includes the **Palazzo del Podestà**, with its huge Torre Civica, and the Palazzo Pretorio.

The effect of the devastating air raid on the city in 1944 is illustrated by photographs in the arcades below the buildings and a dark line marked on the side of the Palazzo dei Trecentro shows the level at which it had to be painstakingly reconstructed. Restaurants and cafes now cluster around here. Behind these buildings, almost hidden from view are the former **Monte di Pietà** (old pawn shop, closed to the public) and the two atmospheric **medieval churches** of Santa Lucia and San

Vito (*Open 9am–noon. ℘0422 54 76 32. www.santaluciatreviso.it*). The former contains frescoes by Tomaso da Modena. Just the other side of the Piazza Indipendenza is another seamlessly reconstructed medieval structure, the **Loggia dei Cavaliere**, with some of its original 13th-century frescoes still intact.

Chiesa di San Nicolò★

This large Romanesque-Gothic church contains interesting frescoes, especially those on the columns by Tommaso da Modena. In the Onigo Chapel there are portraits of people from Treviso by Lorenzo Lotto (16C). The *Virgin in Majesty* at the far end of the chancel is by Savoldo (16C). The adjoining **monastery** has portraits of famous Dominicans by Tomaso da Modena.

Museo di Santa Caterina★

Open Tue–Sun 9am–12.30pm and 2.30pm–6pm. €6. ℘0422 65 84 42. www.museicivicitreviso.it.

Housed in the former convent of Santa Caterina is a fine exhibition of art and archaeology from the 5C BC up to the 1900s, with outstanding paintings by Bellini, Titian, Lorenzo Lotto, Jacopo Bassano and other masters. The star attraction however is in the deconsecrated church next door which houses the **Santa Orsola (Ursula) cycle of frescoes** and the **Capella degli Innocenti frescoes**, both masterpieces by Tomaso da Modena.

Duomo

The 15–16C cathedral has seven domes and a Romanesque crypt. In the Chapel of the Annunciation (Cappella dell'Annunziata) there are frescoes by Pordenone and on the altarpiece an *Annunciation* by Titian.

Chiesa di San Francesco

Viale Sant'Antonio da Padova.
This church in the transitional Romanesque-Gothic style has a fine wooden ceiling, the tombstone of Petrarch's daughter and includes the tomb of one of Dante's sons, as well as frescoes by Tommaso da Modena.

EXCURSIONS

Villa di Maser (Villa Barbaro)★★★

29km/18mi northwest on the SS 348.
Open Apr–Oct Tue–Sat 10am–6pm (11am–6pm Sun and hols); Nov–Mar Sat–Sun and hols 11am–5pm. Closed Easter Sun, 9 Dec–5 Feb. €9. 042 39 23 004. www.villadimaser.it.
This famous villa was built in 1560 by Palladio for the Barbaro brothers: Daniele, Patriarch of Aquileia, and Marcantonio, ambassador of the Venetian Republic. The interior was decorated 1566–8 with a splendid cycle of **frescoes★★★** by Veronese and has been declared a World Heritage Site and has a winery.

Conegliano

28km/17mi north.
via XX Settembre 61. 0438 21 230. www.conegliano2000.it.
Conegliano is surrounded by hills clad with vineyards famous for producing excellent Prosecco white wine. This was the birthplace of **Cima da Conegliano** (1459–1518), a gifted colourist. The **Duomo** has a fine **Sacra Conversazione★** by the artist. (0438 22 606). The **castello** houses the Museo Civico (Open Nov–Mar 10am–12.30pm and 2.30–6pm (6.30pm Apr–May and Sept–Oct; 7pm Jun–Aug). €2,50; 0438 22 871) and affords a lovely **panorama★** of the town. By the cathedral the **Sala dei Battuti** (Open year-round Tue–Sat 2.30–6.30pm, Sun and hols 10–noon. donation) has 15C and 16C

Venetian and Lombardstyle **frescoes★**. Vino in Villa, the annual wine festival dedicated to DOCG Prosecco wines of Conegliano Valdobbiadene– sparkling, semi-sparkling and still – is held the third weekend in May in the 13C Santo Salvatore di Susegana Castle. During that event, many wineries open their doors to visitors. *vinoinvilla.it* (*see p21) or www.prosecco.it.*

Vittorio Veneto

41km/26mi north.
Viale della Vittoria 110. 0438 57 243. www.turismovittorioveneto.gov.it.
The name of this town recalls the great victory of the Italians over the Austrians in 1918. The two separate, but adjacent towns of Ceneda (now the southern half) and Serravalle (the northern half) were unified into a single town. In Ceneda the **Museo della Battaglia**, restored May 2014, is installed in a 16C loggia with a frescoed portico by Sansovino (Open Tue–Fri 9.30–12.30am and 3–6pm. 0438 57 695. www.marcadoc.it or www.museobattaglia.it). Serravalle is the older town withperiod charm. The church of **San Giovanni** has 15C **frescoes★**.

Portogruaro★

56km/35mi east.
Via Cimetta 1. 0421 73 558. www.portogruaroturismo.it.
Two fine main streets lined with attractive porticoes flank the river banks and there are numerous palaces. On the **Corso Martiri della Libertà★★** (the busiest of the shopping streets) not far from the 19C cathedral and its leaning Romanesque campanile is the strange **Palazzo Municipale★**, built in a late-Gothic style (14C). Behind the palace is the river with two 15C watermills and a small 17C fishermen's chapel with its own landing-stage.
In the Via del Seminario stands the **Museo Nazionale Concordiese** (Open daily 8.30am–7pm. Closed 1 Jan, 1 May and 25 Dec. €3. 0421 72 674) with fine Roman exhibits and palaeo-Christian artefacts from Concordia Sagittaria (*3km/2mi south*), a Roman colony founded in 40 BC.

Verona★★★

Verona stands on the banks of the Adige against a hilly backdrop. It is the second most important art centre in the Veneto region after Venice. The fashionable Piazza Bra is linked by Via Mazzini to the heart of the old town.

A BIT OF HISTORY

Verona reached the peak of its glory under the Scaligers who governed for the Holy Roman Emperor from 1260 to 1387. It then passed to the Visconti of Milan before submitting to Venetian rule from 1405. Verona was occupied by Austria in 1814 and became part of the Veneto with Italy in 1866.

Pisanello – Artists of the Veronese school were influenced by Northern art from the Rhine Valley and they developed a Gothic art which combined flowing lines with a meticulous attention to detail. Antonio Pisanello (c.1395–c.1450), a great traveller, active painter, prodigious medal-maker and enthusiastic draughtsman, was the greatest exponent of this school. His painting, with soft colours, meticulous details and flowing lines, was reminiscent of the rapidly disappearing medieval world.

●●WALKING TOUR

Arena di Verona★★

&⃠ *Open Tue–Sun 8.30am–7.30pm (Mon 1.30-7.30). Schedule may vary performance days.* ⃠*Closed 1 Jan and 25 Dec.* ⃝€10 or VeronaCard. ✆045 80 05 151. www.turismoverona.eu or www.arena.it.

This magnificent amphitheatre, among the largest in the Roman world, was built to accommodate 25 000 spectators in 44 tiers. It is built of blocks of pink marble, flint and brick and thus probably dates from the late 1C. Mid-June to September it is the venue for a world-famous opera season. The topmost row offers a **panorama★★** of the town in its hilly setting, which on a clear day reaches as far as the Alps.

▶ **Population:** 258 765
&⃗ **Michelin Map:** 561, 562 F 14–15.
ℹ **Info:** Via degli Alpini 9. ✆045 80 68 680. www.tourism.verona.it. The VeronaCard (one or two day; €18 or €22) offers a savings on multiple sights.
⃝ **Location:** Verona lies between Venice (120km/75mi east) and Lake Garda (30km/19mi) west.
⃝ **Don't Miss:** The Arena (catch a summer opera performance if possible); Castelvecchio and Ponte Scaligero; San Zeno Maggiore.
&⃗ **Also See:** *PADOVA*.

Castelvecchio and Ponte Scaligero★★

⃠*Open daily Tue–Sun 8.30am–7.30pm (Mon 1.30–7.30pm).* ⃝€6. ✆045 80 62 611. www.turismoverona.eu.

This splendid fortified complex was built in 1354 by Cangrande II Scaliger. It is now home to the superb **Museo d'Arte** collection★★, with Veronese art from the 12C to the 16C, showing links with Venice and the International Gothic movement. There are frescoes by local artists and canvases by Stefano da Verona, Pisanello, Giambono, Carlo Crivelli (a splendid Madonna of the Passion), Mantegna and Carpaccio as well as the Bellinis.

The rooms on the upper floor contain works from the Renaissance period by Veronese artists: Morone, Liberale da Verona (Virgin with a Goldfinch), Girolamo dai Libri and Veronese. There are also Venetian works by Tintoretto, Guardi, Tiepolo and Longhi. Also on display are jewellery and sculpture.

⃝ Follow Corso Cavour, home to the **church of San Lorenzo**, then continue to the Porta dei Borsari (1C AD). Continue along Corso Porta Borsari.

Piazza delle Erbe★★

The "Square of Herbs" was the former Roman forum. Markets still take place mornings, though in recent years they have become very touristy. In the middle of the square stand the market column; the *capitello* (a rostrum from which decrees and sentences were proclaimed) by the 16C governors (*podestà*). Also look for the fountain known as the Verona Madonna, with a Roman statue symbolising the town, and a Venetian column surmounted by the winged Lion of St Mark (1523).

Palaces and old houses, some with pink marble columns and frescoes, frame the square: on the north side is the Baroque **Palazzo Maffei**.

In Via Cappello (No 23) is the **Casa di Giulietta** (Juliet's House); in fact it is a Gothic palace which is said to have belonged to the Capulet family; the famous balcony is in the inner courtyard (free access). ()*Open daily Tue–Sun 8.30am–7.30pm (Mon 1.30–7.30pm).* ()*Closed 1 Jan and 25 Dec.* €6 (with *Tomba di Giulietta* €7). 045 80 34 303. *casadigiulietta.comune.verona.it.*

Piazza dei Signori★★

Take Via della Costa to reach this elegant square. On the right is the 12C **Palazzo del Comune** (Town Hall), also known as the Palazzo della Ragione, dominated by the **Torre dei Lamberti** (()*Open daily 9.30am–7.30pm (Sat–Sun 11am–7pm)* ()*Closed 1 Jan and 25 Dec.* €5 (€8 inc modern art museum) or VeronaCard. 045 92 73 027. *www.turismoverona.eu*),

Romeo and Juliet

The setting for this apocryphal drama was Verona in 1302, when political conflict raged. The tragic young couple immortalised by Shakespeare belonged to rival families: Romeo to the Montecchi (Montagues), who were Guelphs and supported the Pope, and Juliet to the Capuleti (Capulets), who were Ghibellines and supported the Emperor.

a tower built of brick and stone and with an octagonal upper storey. This building is connected by an arch with the **Palazzo dei Tribunali** (Law Courts), formerly the Palazzo del Capitano (Governor's Residence) which is also flanked by a massive brick tower, the Torrione Scaligero. The **Loggia del Consiglio** on the opposite side is an elegant edifice in the Venetian-Renaissance style. At the far end of the square, the late-13C **Palazzo del Governo** with its machicolations and fine Classical doorway (1533) by Sammicheli was initially a Scaliger residence.

Arche Scaligere★★

()*Open Tue–Sun 10am–1pm and 3–6pm.* €1. *www.turismoverona.eu.* The Scaliger built their tombs between their palace and their church. The sarcophagi bear the arms of the family, with the symbolic ladder (*scala*). Theses elegant Gothic mausolea are surrounded by marble balustrades and wrought-iron rails, and are decorated with carvings of religious scenes and statues of saints in niches. Over the door of the Romanesque church of **Santa Maria Antica** is the tomb of one of the more infamous of the family "Cangrande" I (d.1329) with his equestrian statue above.

Sant'Anastasia★

()*Open daily Mar–Oct 9am–6pm (1–6pm Sun and hols); Nov–Feb 10am–1pm and 1.30–5pm (12.30–5pm Sun and hols).*€2,50. *www.chieseverona.it.*

This church was begun at the end of the 13C and completed in the 15C. The campanile is remarkable and the façade is pierced with a 14C double doorway adorned with frescoes and sculpture. The lofty interior contains several masterpieces: four figures of the Apostles by Michele da Verona; Pisanello's famous **fresco★** (above the Pellegrini Chapel, to the right of the high altar) of St George delivering the Princess of Trebizondaea (1436), which has an almost surreal combination of realistic precision and Gothic fantasy; 17 **terracottas★** by Michele da Firenze in the Cappella Pellegrini; and the **fresco★** showing Knights of the Cavalli

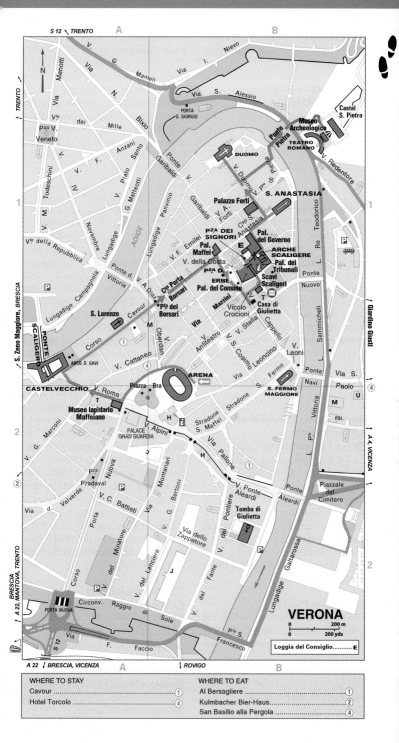

VERONA

0 ____ 200 m
0 ____ 200 yds

Loggia del Consiglio.......... E

WHERE TO STAY		WHERE TO EAT	
Cavour .... ①		Al Bersagliere .... ①
Hotel Torcolo .... ④		Kulmbacher Bier-Haus.................................... ②
		San Basilio alla Pergola .... ④

family being presented to the Virgin (1380) by the Veronese artist, Altichero (first chapel in the south transept).

Palazzo della Ragione – Galleria d'Arte Moderna

🕐 *Open Tue–Sun 11am–7pm; Oct–Jun Tue–Fri 10am–6pm (11am–7pm Sat–Sun and hols).* ✆€8. ☎ 045 80 01 903. *www. palazzodellaragioneverona.it.* New museum of modern art opened April 2014.

Duomo Santa Maria Assunta★

🕐 *Open Mar–Oct 10am–5.30pm; Nov–Feb 10am–1pm and 1.30–5pm. 1.30–5pm Sun and hols.* ✆€2,50. *www.chieseverona.it.*

The cathedral has a 12C Romanesque chancel, a Gothic nave and a Classical-style tower. The remarkable main doorway in the Lombard-Romanesque style is adorned with sculptures and low reliefs by Maestro Nicolò. The interior has pink marble pillars. The altarpiece (*first altar on the left*) is decorated with an *Assumption* by Titian. The marble chancel screen is by Sammicheli (16C).

Teatro Romano and Museo Archeologico★

🕐 *Open Tue–Sun 8.30am–7.30pm (1.30–7.30 pm Mon).* ✆€4,50. ☎045 80 00 360. *museoarcheologico.comune. verona.it.*

The Roman theatre dates from the time of Augustus but has been heavily restored. Regular summer theatrical performances are staged here. Above the theatre a former monastery houses the small archaeological museum with a lovely view over the city.

Castel San Pietro

Take the stairway which leads off Regaste Redentore. St Peter's Castle dates back to the Visconti and the period of Venetian rule. The terraces afford splendid **views**★★of Verona.

San Fermo Maggiore★

🕐 *Open daily Mar–Oct 10am–6pm (1–6pm Sun and hols); Nov–Feb 10am–1pm and 1.30–5pm (1–5pm Sun*

and hols). ✆€2,50. ☎ 045 59 28 13. *www.chieseverona.it.*

The church, dedicated to St Firmanus Major, was built in the 11C–12C and remodelled at a later date. The façade is in the Romanesque and Gothic styles. The aisleless church is covered by a stepped, keel-shaped roof. By the west door the Brenzoni mausoleum (1430) is framed by a **fresco**★ of the Annunciation by Pisanello.

San Zeno Maggiore★★

Access via Largo D. Bosco.

🕐 *Open daily Mar–Oct 8.30am–6pm (12.30am–6pm Sun and hols); Nov–Feb 10am–1pm and 1.30–5pm (12.30–5pm Sun and hols).* ✆€2,50. *www.chieseverona.it.*

St Zeno is one of the finest Romanesque churches in northern Italy. It was built on the basilical plan in the Lombard style in the 12C. The façade is decorated with Lombard bands and arcading; the side walls and campanile have alternate brick and stone courses. In the entrance porch resting on two lions, there are admirable bronze **doors**★★★ (11C–12C) with scenes from the Old and New Testaments. On either side are low reliefs by the master sculptors Nicolò and Guglielmo (12C). On the tympanum of the doorway is a statue of St Zeno, patron saint of Verona.

The imposing interior has a lofty, bare nave with a cradle roof flanked by aisles with shallow roofing. On the high altar is a splendid **triptych**★★ (1459) by Mantegna. There are 14C statues on the chancel screen and a curious polychrome statue of St Zeno laughing in the north apse.

Tomba di Giulietta

🕐 *Open Tue–Sun 8.30am (Mon 1.30pm)– 7.30pm.* ✆€4,50. ☎045 80 00 361.

Juliet's supposed tomb is in the atmospheric cloisters of the church of San Francesco al Corso. On display in the adjoining **Museo degli Affreschi G.B. Cavalcaselle** are cycles of frescoes coming from buildings dating from the Middle Ages to the 16C century.

Vicenza★★

Strategically located at the crossroads of the routes that link the Veneto with the Trentino, Vicenza is now a busy commercial and industrial centre, renowned for its textile industry and as a gold-working and trading centre. But above all it is the home of the great Renaissance architect, Palladio.

A BIT OF HISTORY

The ancient Roman town of Vicetia became an independent city state in the 12C. After several conflicts with the neighbouring cities of Padua and Verona, Vicenza sought Venetian protection at the beginning of the 15C. This was a period of great prosperity, when Vicenza counted many rich and generous art patrons among its citizens and it was embellished with an amazing number of palaces.

Andrea Palladio

Andrea di Pietro della Gondola (1508–80) was born in Padua and apprenticed at the age of 13 as a stonemason. He came to Vicenze three years later and worked for two of the most eminent stone cutters in the city, mingling with the city's leading architects. One of these, Giangiorgio Trissini took him under his wing and named him Palladio, after the goddess Pallas Athene (representing Strength and Wisdom). Given the enormous wealth of the Venetian Empire these were fertile times for architects with a plentiful supply of rich citizens who wanted to affirm their status through the outward appearance of their city houses and country villas (&see VILLAS OF THE BRENTA). It was in the latter area where Palladio was to achieve his greatest fame though remarkably he didn't receive his first public commission (the Basilica at Vicenza) until the relatively advanced age of 38. His *Quattro Libri dell' Architettura*, Four Books on Architecture was later to become the profession's bible. In Britain, Inigo Jones and Sir Christopher Wren were close followers.

- ▶ **Population:** 112 953
- **Michelin Map:** 562 F 16
- **Info:** Piazza Matteotti 12. ☎ 0444 32 08 54. Piazza dei Signori 8. Museum Card Vicenza €15. www.vicenzae.org.
- **Location:** Vicenza lies 75km/47mi west of Venice along the A 4.
- **Don't Miss:** Piazza dei Signori, the Teatro Olimpico and the frescoes by Giovanni Battista at the Villa Valmarana ai Nani.
- **Timing:** Allow a day for a visit.
- **Also See:** *LAGUNA VENETA, PADOVA, VERONA.*

In addition to palazzi and villas he was also to find fame in Venice designing the churches of San Giorgio Maggiore and the Redentore.

In total there are 66 bodies of work that Palladio designed and completed during his lifetime, with many more collaborations, and projects finished after his death. His pupil, Vicenzo Scamozzi (1552–1616), completed several of these works and carried on his style.

VISIT
Piazza dei Signori★★

Like St Mark's Square in Venice, this is an open-air meeting-place recalling the forum of Antiquity. As in the Piazzetta in Venice, there are two columns, here bearing effigies of the Lion of St Mark and the Redeemer.

With the lofty **Torre Bissara★**, a 12C belfry, the **Basilica Palladiana ★★** (🕑 *For opening hours see www.museicivicivicenza.it*), built 1549–1617, occupies one whole side of the square. The elevation is one of Palladio's masterpieces, with two superimposed galleries in the Doric and Ionic orders, admirable for their power, proportion and purity of line. The great keel-shaped roof, destroyed by bombing, has been rebuilt. Despite its name the building was *not*

Piazza dei Signori

© bluejayphoto/istockphoto.com

a church but a meeting-place for the Vicenzan notables. The 15C **Monte di Pietà** (municipal pawn shop) opposite, its buildings framing the Baroque façade of the church of San Vincenzo, is adorned with frescoes. The **Loggia del Capitano★**, formerly the residence of the Venetian Governor, which stands to the left, at the corner of the Contrà del Monte, was begun to the plans of Palladio in 1571 but left unfinished.

Teatro Olimpico★★

&.◎*Open year round Tue–Sun 9am–5pm. ◉€11 or Museum Card Vicenza (&see p259). ✆0444 96 43 80. www.teatrolimpicovicenza.it.*
This splendid building in wood and stucco was designed by Palladio in 1580 on the model of the theatres of Antiquity. The tiers of seats are laid out in a hemicycle and surmounted by a lovely **colonnade** with a balustrade crowned with statues. The **stage★★★**is one of the finest in existence with its superimposed niches, columns and statues and its amazing perspectives painted in *trompe l'oeil* by Scamozzi who completed the work.

Corso Andrea Palladio★

This, the main street of Vicenza, and several neighbouring streets, are embellished by many palaces designed by Palladio and his pupils.

At the beginning is the **Palazzo Chiericati**, an imposing work by Palladio; at No 147 the 15C **Palazzo Da Schio** in the Venetian-Gothic style was formerly known as the Ca d'Oro (Golden House) because it was covered with frescoes with gilded backgrounds. The west front of **Palazzo Thiene** overlooking Contrà S. Gaetano Thiene was by Palladio, while the entrance front at No 12 Contrà Porti is Renaissance, dating from the late 15C. The **Palazzo Porto-Barbaran** opposite is also by Palladio.
At No 98 the **Palazzo Trissino** (1592) is one of Scamozzi's most successful works. Next is the Corso Fogazzaro, where the **Palazzo Valamarana** (1566) at No 16 is another work by Palladio.

Pinacoteca★

&.◎ *Limited access to the Palladian wing. Open year round Tue–Sun 9am–5pm. ◉Closed 1 Jan and 25 Dec. ◉€5 or Museum Card Vicenza (&see p259). ✆0444 22 28 11. www.museicivicivicenza.it.*
The collection of paintings includes Venetian Primitives (*The Dormition of the Virgin* by Paolo Veneziano); a **Crucifixion★★** by Hans Memling; canvases by Bartolomeo Montagna (pupil of Giovanni Bellini), Mantegna and Carpaccio, one of the most active artists in Vicenza. There are Venetian works by Lorenzo Lotto, Veronese, Bassano,

Piazzetta, Tiepolo and Tintoretto as well as Flemish works by Brueghel the Elder and Van Dyck.

Santa Corona

The church was built in the 13C. Works of art include: a **Baptism of Christ★★** by Giovanni Bellini (*fifth altar on the left*) and an **Adoration of the Magi★★** (1573) by Veronese (*third chapel on the right*). The fourth chapel on the right has a coffered **ceiling★**, adorned with gilded stucco, and a *Mary Magdalene and Saints* by Bartolomeo Montagna. The cloisters house the small **Museo Naturalistico-Archeologico** (Museum of Natural History and Archaeology) ○*Open year round Tue–Sun 9am–5pm (summer 10am–1.30pm).* ○*Closed 1 Jan and 25 Dec.* ◉€3,50 or Museum Card Vicenza (⌖see p259). ℘044 43 20 440. www.museicivicivicenza.it.

Duomo (Santa Maria Annunziata)

○*Open year round daily Mon–Sat 10.30–noon and 3.30–5.30pm (Sun 10.30–12am).* ℘0444 32 09 96.
Built between the 14C and 16C, the cathedral has an attractive colourful Gothic façade and a Renaissance east end. Inside is a fine **polyptch★** (1356) by Lorenzo Veneziano.
Also in Piazza Duomo (no. 6) is a Roman cryptoporticus (1C BC–1CAD), open the second Sun of the month (inquire at tourist office).

EXCURSIONS

Villa Valmarana ai Nani★★

2km/1mi south by the Este road and then the first road to the right.
○*Open year-round Tue–Fri 10–12.30am and 3–6pm(10am–6pm Sat–Sun and hols).* ◉€10. ℘0444 32 18 03. www.villavalmarana.com.
The villa dates from the 17C. Both the mainhouse and the Forestiera buildings are adorned with splendid **frescoes★★★** by Giovanni Battista (Giambattista) Tiepolo and his son Giovanni Domenico. A caffè is on the premises.

La Rotonda★

2km/1mi southeast, off the Este road.
○*Open interior only 12 March–first week Nov Wed and Sat ; garden year round 10–noon and 3–6pm (winter 10–12.30am and 2.30–5pm).* ○*Closed 1 Jan and 25 Dec.* ◉€10 interior; €5 garden. www.villalarotonda.it.
The Rotonda is one of Palladio's most famous creations and has inspired many other masterpieces worldwide. The gracefully proportioned square building is roofed with a dome and fronted on each side by a pedimented portico, making it look like an ancient temple.

Basilica di Monte Berico and Monti Berici★

2km/1mi south by Viale Venezia.
○*Open year-round daily 6am–12.30pm and 2.30–7pm (winter 6pm).* ℘0444 55 94 11. www.monteberico.it.
As the Viale X Giugno climbs uphill, it is lined with an 18C portico and chapels. On the summit is the Baroque basilica roofed with a dome. Inside, there is a Pietà (1500) by Bartolomeo Montagna. From the esplanade there is a wonderful **panorama★★** of Vicenza, the Venetian plain and the Alps.

Montecchio Maggiore

13km/8mi southwest on the S 11.
www.comune.montecchio-maggiore.vi.it.
Novelist Luigi del Porta of Vicenza set the original story of Romeo and Juliet in Montecchio Maggiore in 1552 and the town's two adjacent ruined 10C castles are known as the castles of Romeo and Juliet respectively. From here there are **views★** of the Po Plain and Vicenza.
On the outskirts, on the Tavernelle road, the **Villa Cordellina-Lombardi** has one room entirely covered with **frescoes★** by Tiepolo. ⌖○*Open Apr–Oct Tue and Fri 9am–1pm (also 3–6pm Wed–Sun); Nov–Mar only reservation.* ◉€3. ℘0444 90 81 60. www.provincia.vicenza.it.

Palazzo Cavalli Franchetti from Ponte dell'Accademia

Where to Stay

Although Venice has a wide range of accommodation, visitors should be aware that prices can be high and value for money difficult to find. Venice is now a travel destination throughout the year. The city officially defined high season as 1 Feb–30 Nov. Although summer weather can be hot and damp, which makes sightseeing extremely tiring, don't expect discounts. **It is advisable to book as far in advance as possible**, especially for dates during Carnival. Like Rome and Florence, Venice and some other Veneto cities have instituted a hotel tax, which applies to each occupant per night at fees that range from €0.60 to €5 based on type of accommodation, location, and season. Information on accommodation in Venice is available from the official tourist board website, www. turismovenezia.it. The red **Michelin Guide Italy,** updated on a yearly basis, also provides a detailed list of recommended hotels and restaurants in Venice.

OUR SELECTION

Our price categories are for a double room in high season. Given the significant seasonal variations, this classification is based on average prices and to help compare pricing among different hotels. Most prices quoted include breakfast. You are strongly advised to enquire beforehand and to check the rates that apply to your stay. In the summer, visitors are advised to verify that lodgings have air conditioning (especially for the basic or inexpensive premises).

☺ **A bit of advice** – The **Michelin Guide Italia** is updated every year and includes a very wide selection of hotels and restaurants.

VENICE HOTEL TAX

In Summer 2011, Venice initiated a tourist tax for hotel rooms, like that launched earlier in the year for the cities of Rome and Florence. The fee is per person, not per room. The tax will vary according to the category of hotel, its neighborhood, and whether the tourist season is high or low. The tourist tax regulations identify three territorial areas and two periods (high season and "other"). The territorial areas are: Venice historic centre, Giudecca and the islands dedicated mainly to accommodation (e.g. San Clemente); islands of the Venetian Lagoon (e.g. Lido, Murano, Burano, etc.); and mainland. In 2016, the total days considered high season are 300 days. Keep in mind that in summer during even years, when the Biennale is not on, there may be some good discounts toward late July and August, even if the tax rates are for high season. Overall, these distinctions can be helpful if you want to avoid crowds or to find lower hotel rates. Here are the periods of high season:
1) 1 Jan–Sun after 6 Jan; 2) the period of Carnival; 3) the first Wed before Easter–following Tuesday; 4) 1 Apr–31 Oct; 5) the week that includes the 8 December; 6) 23–31 Dec.

CHOOSING YOUR AREA

Wherever you end up in Venice, you should enjoy quiet nights. The neighbourhood atmosphere varies by districts within the *sestieri*. If you like to laze in the sunshine on a café on the square, then opt for an area around a *campo* like **Santo Stefano** or, on the other side of the Grand Canal, **Santa Margherita** or **San Giacomo dall'Orio**. If you fancy an old-fashioned, slightly melancholy charm, then opt for the *sestiere* of **Dorsoduro**, between San Barnaba and La Salute. And if you thrive on hustle and bustle from the moment you get up, then try the **Riva degli Schiavoni**, the area around **St Mark's Square** or the **Rialto**, or around the **Strada Nuova**.

Pensione La Calcina, Zattere

© Gwen Cannon / MICHELIN

HOTELS

Traditional hotels, known as *alberghi*, are located throughout the city. Prices vary according to location, comfort levels and views.

🐾 **A bit of advice** – Don't rely exclusively on the number of stars to determine a hotel's quality.

PENSIONI, LOCANDE AND AFFITACAMERE

Generally, these are more informal than traditional hotels and often occupy a single floor of a building. With a small number of rooms, these places have the feel of a family hotel or guesthouse and can often be quite classy. Generally you will pay less in these types of establishments than in the hotels.

BED AND BREAKFASTS

There are numerous bed and breakfast establishments in Venice, in all categories and all prices. As with hotels, you will have to eat lunch and dinner out.
www.interhome.fr
www.bedandbreakfast.com
www.bbitalia.it

APARTMENTS

The rental market is well developed in Venice. For those staying several days, an apartment allows you to play at being a Venetian and to save money on meals.

Venice Apartments – Italy - collecting keys point +39 335 56 84 147 or 329 22 88 914; United Kingdom - offices: 0740 44 96 964 (WhatsApp free international calls, from abroad United Kingdom +447404496964). www.veniceapartments.org.

RELIGIOUS INSTITUTIONS

Institutions run by religious orders providing tourist accommodation often at attractive prices. Some of them run genuine *case per ferie* offering accommodation of a standard comparable to a small hotel. Usually the atmosphere is spartan (often with no air conditioning) though invariably spotlessly clean. Note that few of these places accept credit cards, some impose a curfew and some are only open during the main visitor season, July–September. Also, some may require the occupant to vacate the premises for a certain number of hours during the day.

YOUTH HOSTEL

Venice's youth hostel boasts a superb canalside location on the island of Giudecca. It belongs to Hostelling International and is only open to holders of annual youth hostel membership. Accommodation in single-sex dormitories.
For more youth hostelling information, contact www.hiusa.org/hostels/international-hostels or www.aighostels.it (only italian).

CAMPSITES

Venice has no campsites in the city, but many sites along the coastline are accessible by *vaporetto*, offering accommodation in tents or furnished bungalows. A few campsites are in the Marghera-Mestre-Tessera area, as well as a site on the **Lido**, near San Nicolò (℘041 526 74 15. www.campingsannicolo.com).

ACCOMMODATION BY AREA

GRAND CANAL

🔊 **A bit of advice** – The best rooms in certain hotels have views of the Grand Canal. Our listings here follow the route of the canal from north to south.

LEFT BANK

Ovidius and Sturion – See Rialto, p267.

RIGHT BANK

Ca' Nigra – See I Frari and San Rocco, p271.

San Cassiano and Rialto – See Rialto, p267.

Palazzo Sant'Angelo sul Canal Grande – See Around La Fenice, p268.

Pensione Accademia "Villa Maravege" – See Accademia, p268.

PIAZZA SAN MARCO

🔊 *Map p115.*

INEXPENSIVE

Foresteria Valdese B1 – *Palazzo Cavagnis, at the end of Calle Lunga S. Maria Formosa, Castello 5170. ℘041 528 6797. www.foresteriavenezia.it. Various price bands.* This institution, run by the Union of Waldesian and Methodist Churches, occupies an attractive palazzo beside the Rio S. Severo, next to SS. Giovanni e Paolo.

Istituto San Giuseppe A1 – *Ponte della Guerra (behind S. Zulian), Castello 5402. ℘041 522 5352.* The institution is housed in an attractive p just beyond the Rio coming from San Zulian. A very nice place to stay, five minutes from St Mark's Square, with huge air-conditioned rooms.

EXPENSIVE

San Marco A2 – *Calle dei Fabbri, S.Marco 877. ℘041 520 4277. www.sanmarcohotels.com. 55 rooms. ☎.* Comfortable and couldn't be closer to St Mark's Square, if lacking a little in charm.

Paganelli B2 – *Riva degli Schiavoni, Castello 4182. ℘041 522 4324. www.hotelpaganelli.com. 22 rooms. ☎.* A family place facing St Mark's basin. A few rooms at the front benefit from the view.

Villa Igea B2 – *Campo S. Zaccaria, Castello 4684. ℘041 241 0956. www.hotelvillaigea.it. 17 rooms. ☎.* This remarkably well-located annex of the Hotel Savoia e Jolanda offers well-kept rooms, some facing the church of S. Zaccaria.

Ca' dei Conti B1 – *Fondamenta di Remedio (a stone's throw from S. Maria Formosa), Castello 4429. ℘041 277 0500. www.cadeiconti.com. 15 rooms. ☎.* A harmonious façade on the corner of a romantic canal spanned by little bridges. Very comfortable rooms furnished in the 18C style, and a *cortile* (courtyard) for breakfast.

LUXURY

Concordia A1 – *Calle Larga S.Marco, S. Marco 367. ℘041 520 6866. www.hotelconcordia.com. 55 rooms. ☎.* Very close to St Mark's Square: even though the entrance to the hotel is at the rear, some of the rooms face onto the Piazzetta dei Leoncini and offer wonderful views of the basilica and the campanile.

Savoia e Jolanda B2 – *Riva degli Schiavoni, Castello 4187. ℘041 520 6644. www.hotelsavoiajolanda.com. 51 rooms. ☎.* This pleasant hotel overlooking St Mark's Basin has a restaurant with terrace dining on the Riva in good weather.

Palazzo Priuli B1 – *Fondamenta dell'Osmarin, Castello 4979/b. ℘041 277 0834. www.hotelpriuli.com. 10 rooms. ☎.* Commissioned in the 14C by Antonio Priuli, of a dynasty of doges, this palazzo stands at the junction of two *rii*, and boasts a fine stone staircase and a large hall with a beamed ceiling. Each room has unique decor.

Danieli B2 – *Riva degli Schiavoni, Castello 4196.* ✆*041 522 6480. www.star woodhotels.com/danieli. 225 rooms.* ⌨. Palazzo Dandolo, home to the Hotel Danieli since 1822, suggests a dream world. Columns, banisters, galleries and intricate stonework form the incredible décor that seduced Dickens, Wagner, Balzac, Proust and Sand.

Metropole B2 – *Riva degli Schiavoni 4149.* ✆*041 52 05044. www. hotel metropole.com. 67 rooms.* ⌨. Sumptuous touches of the Orient and textiles by Fortuny and Bevilacqua merge with sleek Art Deco objects, accented with antique clocks and fans. Its lovely Met restaurant has a Michelin star, while the Oriental Bar is the spot for a glass of Champagne or a cocktail.

RIALTO
♿*Map pp136–137.*

EXPENSIVE, LEFT BANK
Rialto B2 – *Riva del Ferro, S. Marco 5149.* ✆*041 520 9166. www.rialtohotel.com. 79 rooms.* ⌨. Just by the *vaporetto* landing stage. As you can imagine, the view over the Grand Canal and the bridge is sublime. Lots of groups.

EXPENSIVE, RIGHT BANK
Antica Locanda Sturion B2 – *Calle del Sturion, S.Polo 679.* ✆*041 523 6243. www. locandasturion.com. 11 rooms.* ⌨. Just 100 metres from Rialto Bridge, and a 10 minute walk from Saint Mark's Square, Antica Locanda Sturion offers a tranquil environment with immediate access to Venice and its monuments. Book an elegant 18th century-style room equipped with modern comforts.

Locanda Ovidius B2 – *Calle del Sturion, S. Polo 677A.* ✆*041 523 7970. www. hotellocandaovidius.com. 15 rooms.* ⌨. These two hotels occupy two floors of the same building facing onto the Grand Canal, south of the Rialto Bridge. Besides the exceptional view, the very pleasant service makes either hotel a delight.

San Cassiano (Ca' Favretto) A1 – *Calle della Rosa, S. Croce 2232.* ✆*041 524 1768. www.sancassiano.it. 36 rooms.* ⌨. A period residence set in an ancient palazzo faces onto the Grand Canal,

opposite the Ca' d'Oro: each room is different, and the room overlooking the Grand Canal on the *piano nobile* is exceptionally charming.

LA FENICE
♿*Map pp142–143.*

MODERATE
Locanda San Samuele A1 – *Salizada S. Samuele (the street leading from the* vaporetto *stop of the same name), S. Marco 3358, upstairs at the end of the courtyard.* ✆*041 520 5165. www.hotelsansamuele.com. 10 rooms (some without bathrooms).* This pretty guesthouse suggests traditional Venetian living.

Locanda Fiorita B1 – *Campiello Novo (or delle Morti), S. Marco 3457A.* ✆*041 523 4754. www.locandafiorita.com. 10 rooms.* ⌨. A welcoming guesthouse offering comfortable, charming rooms on a theatrical little *campiello.*

Domus Ciliota A1 – *Calle delle Muneghe (from the* campo *via Calle delle Botteghe), S. Marco 2976.* ✆*041 520 4888. www.ciliota.it. 51 rooms.* The former Augustinian monastery (1448), renovated in 1999, is near Campo S. Stefano and Palazzo Grassi. All the institute's rooms have a shower, television, minibar, air conditioning. Credit cards accepted.

Locanda Art Decò AB1– *Calle delle Botteghe (opposite the church of S. Stefano), S. Marco 2966.* ✆*041 277 0558. www.locandaartdeco.com. 6 rooms.* Tiny but magnificently located and furnished *locanda*; the attic room is lovely, but beware the ceiling beam!

EXPENSIVE
Serenissima C1 – *Calle Goldoni (near Campo S. Luca), S. Marco 4486.* ✆*041 520 0011. www.hotelserenissima.it. 37 rooms.* ⌨. This simple, pleasant hotel is close to St Mark's Square and offers rooms decorated with modern paintings.

Palazzo del Giglio B1 – *Campo S. Maria del Giglio, S. Marco 2462.* ✆*041 271 9111. www.hotelgiglio.com.* ⌨. The sienna-coloured terrace and green shutters face the *campo.* Very comfortable in an excellent location by the *vaporetto.*

LUXURY

Kette B1 – *Piscina San Moisè, S.Marco 2053.* ✆ *041 520 7766. www.hotelkette.com. 63 rooms.* ☕. Set in an evocative 16C residence, right by La Fenice, on the corner of a quiet street that leads only to the Rio dei Barcaroli.

Gritti Palace B1 – *Campo S. Maria del Giglio, S. Marco 2467.* ✆ *041 794 611. www.thegrittipalace.com. 85 rooms.* To "live like a doge", try this former home to Doge Andrea Gritti, a palazzo that conjures images of film stars, alighted for the Film Festival, posing on the hotel's terrace. Gritti seems to float on the Grand Canal. As for the interior, a €35 miilion restoration completed in 2013 kept Gritti's charm in every detail adding lavish new perks.

Flora B1 – *Calle dei Bergamaschi (to the left of the Calle Larga 22 Marzo), S. Marco 2283A.* ✆ *041 520 5844. www.hotelflora.it. 44 rooms.* ☕. A remarkably well-located hotel right by St Mark's Square and La Fenice, in a small palazzo at the end of a quiet street, offers a flower-filled garden to enjoy breakfast.

Santo Stefano A1 – *Campo S. Stefano, S. Marco 2957.* ✆ *041 520 0166. www.hotel santostefanovenezia.com. 11 rooms.* ☕. A discreet hotel set in a tall building, with rooms all facing onto the *campo* and catching the morning sun. You can breakfast outside the hotel, with plants to shield you from the gazes of passers-by.

Palazzo Sant'Angelo sul Canal Grande A1 – *Ramo del Teatro de S. Angelo, S. Marco 3878B.* ✆ *041 241 1452. www.sinahotels.com. 26 rooms.* ☕. This superb palazzo with its private landing stage on the Grand Canal offers huge rooms and bathrooms equipped with whirlpool baths, some of them facing out onto the prestigious Grand Canal.

ACCADEMIA
☕ *Map p153.*

MODERATE

Ca' San Trovaso A1 – *Fondamenta delle Eremite (access via the no-through-road), Dorsoduro 1350.* ✆ *041 241 2215. www.casantrovaso.com. 6 rooms.* ☕. Beside the Rio delle Eremite, behind the church of S. Trovàso, this inexpensive hotel (by Venetian standards, at least) is in a district noted for its melancholy charm.

EXPENSIVE

Pensione Accademia "Villa Maravege" B1 – *Fondamenta Bollani, Dorsoduro 1058.* ✆ *041 521 0188. www. pensioneaccademia.it. 27 rooms.* This fine Neoclassical residence is fronted by an attractive statue-filled garden, where the Rio della Toletta meets the Rio S. Trovàso, and makes for a charming place to stay.

Agli Alboretti B1 – *Rio Terrà Antonio Foscarini, Dorsoduro 884.* ✆ *041 523 0058. www.aglialboretti.com. 23 rooms.* ☕. One of the nicest hotels you will find, with a garden shaded by an arbour, and welcoming staff. Very comfortable.

Belle Arti B1 – *Rio Terrà Antonio Foscarini, Dorsoduro 912A.* ✆ *041 522 6230. www.hotelbellearti.com. 67 rooms.* ☕. A very pretty garden with a fountain surrounded by a covered gallery adds to the appeal of this comfortable hotel.

LUXURY

Ca' Pisani B1 – *Rio Terrà Antonio Foscarini, Dorsoduro 979A.* ✆ *041 240 1411. www.capisanihotel.it. 29 rooms.* ☕. Class and refinement with the Ponte dell'Accademia on your doorstep. Rooms have various themes, from the plush red brocade Doge's room to Marco Polo's Oriental room.

LA SALUTE
☕ *Map p155.*

INEXPENSIVE

B&B Cà Fujiyama A1 – *Calle Lunga San Barnaba, Dorsoduro, 2727A.* ✆ *041 72 41 042. fujiyama.life. 4 rooms.* ☕. Venice as gateway to the East… This little guesthouse is run by a Japanese couple. Spotlessly clean, cozy atmosphere, attentive hospitality and refined décor including a few Japanese prints and pieces of furniture. In the back, the small raised garden does nothing to diminish the zen! Tearoom in the afternoon.

MODERATE

Messner A1 – *Rio Terrà dei Catecumeni, near the Fond. Ca' Balà, Dorsoduro 216.* ℰ*041 522 7443. www.hotelmessner.it. 38 rooms.* ☕. An elegant, comfortable structure located just a few metres from the Basilica di S. Maria della Salute.

ZATTERE

MODERATE

Hotel La Calcina A1 – *Zattere ai Gesuati, Dorsoduro 780.* ℰ*041 520 6466. www.lacalcina.com. 26 rooms.* ☕. Only a photograph in the entrance hall remains of the *locanda* where Ruskin stayed in 1876. A restoration has re-created its former appearance, rooms furnished with simple early 20C furniture and hardwood floors. The hotel boasts a wonderful location on the Giudecca Canal. Its restaurant, La Calcina, has good food, reasonable prices, and terrace tables on the Giudecca Canal.

LUXURY

American Dinesen A1 – *Fondamenta Bragadin (Campo San Vio), Dorsoduro 628.* ℰ*041 520 4733. www.hotelamerican.com. 34 rooms.* ☕. This was the area where Venice's American expats used to gather, including Ezra Pound, who lived on the nearby Fondamenta Ca'Bala. With its flower-bedecked windows, this comfortable hotel will satisfy the most demanding of guests.

SCHIAVONI AND ARSENALE
☕*Map p161.*

LUXURY

Liassidi Palace A2 – *Calle della Madonna/Ponte dei Greci, Castello 3405.* ℰ*041 520 5658. www.liassidipalace hotel.com. 30 rooms.* ☕. A large courtyard stands in front of this refined 18C palazzo. A very comfortable choice, with an excursion to Murano included in the price.

SANTI GIOVANNI E PAOLO
☕*Map p168.*

EXPENSIVE

Locanda SS. Giovanni e Paolo C3 – *Calle dell'Ospedaleto (on the right-hand side of Barbaria delle Tolle, just after the church), Castello 6401.* ℰ*041 522 2767. www.locandassgiovannipaolo.it. 8 rooms.* ☕ €8. A modest *locanda* well located near the statue of Condottiere Colleoni.

Locanda Ca' La Corte B3 – *Calle Bressana, on the corner of Fond. dei Felzi, Castello 6317.* ℰ*041 241 1300. www.locandalacorte.it. 14 rooms.* ☕. A charming hotel with floral window displays, occupying an attractive 16C residence facing onto the Rio S. Giovanni Laterano. A *cortile* and tasteful interiors complete the picture.

Ca' d'Oro A2 – *Corte Barbaro (via the Salizada del Tentor from Campo SS. Apostoli), Cannaregio 4604.* ℰ*041 241 1212. www.venicehotelcadoro.com. Closed 24–25 Dec. 27 rooms.* ☕. The rooms of this pleasant little hotel are arranged around a *corte* with access to the Rio di Ca' d'Oro via a *sottoportego.*

Giorgione A2 – *Salizada del Pistor/ Calle Larga delle Proverbi (at the corner of Campo di SS. Apostoli), Cannaregio 4587.* ℰ*041 522 5810. www.hotelgiorgione. com. 76 rooms.* ☕. This hotel occupying a whole block encloses a nice flower-filled garden with a fountain, away from the bustle of the *campo.*

CA' D'ORO

INEXPENSIVE

Casa Cardinal Piazza – *Fondamenta Gasparo Contarini, Dorsoduro 3539A.* ℰ*041 721 388. www.casacardinalpiazza.org. 24 rooms.* ☕. An institution offering sober hospitality on the canalside walkway leading from the Madonna dell'Orto to the Sacra della Misericordia.

MODERATE

Locanda Ca' le Vele – *Calle delle Vele, 3969, Cannaregio.* ℰ *041 24 13 960. www. locandalevele.com - 6 rooms. Closed Jan.* ☕. Located in a 17th-century palazzo overlooking a romantic canal, this locanda is a charming place to stay, with traditional Venetian rooms that have exposed beams, marble and Murano lights. Breakfast is served in the rooms.

LUXURY

Ai Mori d'Oriente – *Fondamenta della Sensa, Cannaregio 3319.* 📞 *041 711 001. www.morihotel.com. 48 rooms.* 🛏. With a bar facing onto the quiet *rio*, this newcomer features Moorish décor in this 15C palazzo, sure to satisfy discerning guests.

Boscolo Venezia (formerly Grand Hotel dei Dogi) – *Fondamenta Madonna dell'Orto, (Calle Larga Piave) Cannaregio 3500.* 📞 *041 220 8111. venezia.boscolohotels.com. 66 rooms.* 🛏. This out-of-the-way district makes an unusual setting for this kind of luxury hotel. The 17C palazzo has period frescoes that contrast with contemporary art on exhibit, while its extraordinary huge park leads down to the lagoon and private landing stage. A place for well-heeled guests in search of the quiet life.

Ca' Sagredo – *Campo S.Sofia, Ca' d'Oro, Cannaregio 4198/99.* 📞 *041 241 3111. www.casagredohotel.com. 42 rooms.* 🛏 **€28.** This marvellous 13C palazzo is named after the last Venetian aristocratic family to own the building, who took it over in the 18C. You'll be amazed by Andrea Tirali's monumental staircase, Pietro Longhi's immense fresco of the *Fall of the Giants*, the *portego* decorated with paintings by Andrea Urbani, the music room adorned with gilding and mythological frescoes by Gaspare Diziani, and the Tiepolo room, a tribute to the city painted by the artist.

CANNAREGIO AND IL GHETTO

MODERATE

Ca' San Marcuola C3 – *Ca' Marcuola (from the Strada Nuova via the Rio Terrà del Cristo), Cannaregio 1763.* 📞 *041 716 048. www.casanmarcuola.com. 16 rooms. Closed Dec–Jan.* 🛏. This renovated hotel equipped with a lift is located close to the *vaporetto* stop of the same name, making it a very acceptable choice.

Abbazia B3 – *Calle Priuli dei Cavaletti, Cannaregio 68.* 📞 *041 717 333. www.abbaziahotel.com. 48 rooms.* 🛏. Part of the Barefoot Carmelites' monastery, the tranquil atmosphere and rigorous elegance make this hotel a lovely stay close to the station. The refectory, with its benches and pulpit, is used as a bar, and the cloister garden is a perfect place to read, paint, or sip a drink.

Ca' Dogaressa B2 – *Fondamenta di Cannaregio (access via the Calle del Sottoportego Oscuro) 1018.* 📞 *041 275 9441. www.cadogaressa.com. 6 rooms. Closed 3 weeks Dec.* 🛏. The soberly decorated rooms in this little hotel are well equipped, adorned with painted furniture in the Venetian style, as well as very pleasant bathrooms. The hotel also has a terrace, and breakfast is served beside the canal when the weather is good.

Tre Archi A2 – *Fondamenta di Cannaregio 923.* 📞 *041 524 4356. www.hoteltrearchi.com. 24 rooms.* 🛏. This hotel with rooms decorated in the local style occupies a lovely palazzo overlooking the canal. As a further bonus, the flower-filled garden is an example of the sort of secret garden you can find in the city.

GHETTO

Locanda del Ghetto C2 – *Campo di Ghetto Nuovo, Cannaregio 2892.* 📞 *041 275 9292. www.locandadelghetto.net. 6 rooms. Closed Jan 15–30.* 🛏. This former synagogue constitutes the Ghetto's only accommodation option: a comfortable little *locanda* offering kosher breakfasts.

LUXURY

B4 Bellini B3 – *Lista di Spagna, Cannaregio 116A.* 📞 *041 524 2488. www.b4bellinivenezia.com. 97 rooms.* 🛏. The rooms of this hotel are all very different, ranging from the very sober to the almost sumptuous. Some have views onto the Grand Canal. A high-end hotel on the road to the station boasting refined décor and impeccable service.

I FRARI AND SAN ROCCO
♿ *Map pp186–187.*

INEXPENSIVE

Casa Caburlotto A3 – *Fondamenta Rizzi, S. Croce 316/318.* 📞 *041 710 877. www.sangiuseppecaburlotto.com. 52 rooms. Closed 25–26 Dec.* 🛏. A university hall of residence open all year round, offering simple, comfortable rooms in a peaceful area of S. Croce, beyond the Rio Nuovo. Curfew at 11pm.

MODERATE

Casa Mimma B1 – *Calle degli Orsetti, S. Croce.* 📞 *041 52 43 461. www.casa mimma.it. 6 rooms.* 🚇. A simple but pleasant hotel boasting a nice garden for breakfast on sunny days. Well equipped rooms with garden views.

Ca' Foscari B3 – *Calle de la Frescada (continuation of Calle Lunga Foscari), Dorsoduro 3887B.* 📞 *041 710 401. www. locandacafoscari.com. 12 rooms (some without bathrooms).* Extremely simple but well located right by the *campo*, this *locanda* is one of the city's few bargain accommodation options.

Casa Rezzonico A3 – *Fondamenta Gherardini, Dorsoduro 2813.* 📞 *041 277 0653. www.casarezzonico.it. 6 rooms.* 🚇. Renovated rooms, some facing onto the *rio*, a garden hosts breakfast in the sunshine and a *campo* on your doorstep.

Gardena A1 – *Fondamenta dei Tolentini, S. Croce 239.* 📞 *041 099 3670. www. gardenahotels.it. 19 rooms.* 🚇. This extremely comfortable hotel beside an attractive canal has been renovated and decorated with murals.

Falier A2 – *Salizada S. Pantalon, S. Croce 130.* 📞 *041 710 882. www.hotelfalier.com. 19 rooms.* 🚇. A good choice for those in search of a peaceful stay, close to Campo S. Margherita and the church of S. Pantalòn.

EXPENSIVE

Ai Due Fanali B1 – *Campo S. Simeone Grande, S. Croce 946.* 📞 *041 718 490. www.aiduefanali.com. 16 rooms.* 🚇. Occupying the former Scuola S. Simeone, this little hotel on a quiet *campo* facing onto the Grand Canal is notable for its peaceful atmosphere as well as its refinement. They also rent apartments overlooking St Mark's Basin.

Locanda San Barnaba B3 – *Calle del Traghetto, Dorsoduro 2785-2786.* 📞 *041 241 1233. www.locanda-sanbarnaba.com. 12 rooms.* 🚇. A stone's throw from the Ca' Rezzonico *vaporetto*, this discreet but pleasant choice occupies a 16C palazzo with a nice cortile.

Al Sole A2 – *Fondamenta Minotto, S.Croce 134/136.* 📞 *041 244 0328. www. alsolehotels.com. 51 rooms.* 🚇. A hotel set in a fine old palazzo with a façade featuring an attractive loggia. Some of the rooms have views over the garden, whilst others face the *rio*. In the attractive bar, the exposed beams of the ceiling are supported by columns adorned with capitals, and the hotel is also equipped with a lift, a rarity.

LUXURY

Ca' Nigra Lagoon Resort B1 – *Campo S. Simeone Grande, S. Croce 927.* 📞 *041 275 0047. www.hotelcanigra.com. 22 rooms.* 🚇. You access this hotel through a lovely garden with an immaculate lawn. It was opened in 2006 in a historic palazzo facing onto the Grand Canal, Rio Marin and the *campo*. The luxurious interior mixes period details with contemporary design. Breakfast is served on a flower-filled terrace overlooking the Grand Canal.

I CARMINI
♿ *Map pp196–197.*

EXPENSIVE

Tiziano A1 – *Calle Riello (near S.Niccolò dei Mendicoli), Dorsoduro 1873.* 📞 *041 275 0071. www.hoteltizianovenezia.it. 14 rooms. Closed Jan 7–28.* 🚇. A very well-kept and welcoming hotel in an extremely quiet district.

GIUDECCA
♿ *Map pp200–201.*

INEXPENSIVE

Ostello di Venezia D1 – *Fondamenta delle Zitelle, Giudecca 86.* 📞 *041 877 8288 www.hostelvenice.org. 18 rooms.* 🚇. Venice's youth hostel boasts a superb location opposite the Zattere.

LUXURY

Belmond Hotel Cipriani D1 – *Giudecca 10.* 📞 *041 240 801 (reservetion 0185 2678 451). www.belmond.com/hotel-cipriani-venice. Closed Nov 13–mid Mar. 95 rooms.* 🚇. A symbol of true, made-to-measure elegance and taste, in a location away from the hordes, and with a small spa.

SANT'ELENA AND SAN PIETRO
🕲 *Map pp208–209.*

MODERATE
Ca' Formenta A2 – *Via Garibaldi, Castello 1650.* 📞 *041 528 5494. www.hotelcaformenta.it. 14 rooms.* 🖥. A charming little hotel occupying a renovated house with a façade painted ochre-pink, almost on the corner of the Riva. A good choice near the centre on the edge of a working-class district.
Patronato Salesiano Leone XIII B2 – *Calle S.Domenico (almost at the mouth of the Rio S. Giuseppe), Castello 1281.* 📞 *041 041 523 0796. www.salesianivenezia. it/alloggi.html. Closed Dec and Jan. 33 rooms.* 🖥. Well located in a very 1950s-style residence, opposite the Island of Sant'Elena.

EXPENSIVE
Sant'Elena C3 – *Calle Buccari (at the corner of Calle del Carnaro), Castello 10.* 📞 *041 271 7811. www.hotelsantelena.com. 77 rooms. Closed Jan 7–31.* This Best Western chain hotel stands in a quiet, very un-Venetian-looking district. The plus points are the peace and quiet and the comfortable surroundings, but on the minus side, Sant'Elena is away from everything, but has a vaporetto stop.

IL LIDO
MODERATE
Atlanta Augustus – *Via Lepanto 15.* 📞 *041 526 0569. www.hotelatlant augustus.com. Closed mid Nov–Mar. 37 rooms.* 🖥. A large Art Nouveau building beside a canal. The rooms on the *piano nobile* have generous balconies, and the two suites on the roof-terrace have wonderful views.
Byron – *Via M. Bragadin 30 (behind the Hotel des Bains, a stone's throw from Lungomare Marconi).* 📞 *041 526 0052. www.byron-hotel.com. Closed Nov– mid Mar. 37 rooms.* 🖥. Comfort and tranquillity in this tastefully appointed little hotel in a green residential district.

EXPENSIVE
Villa Laguna – *Via Sandro Gallo 6 (100m to the right of the vaporetto landing stage).* 📞 *041 526 1316. hotelvillalaguna. com. Closed Dec 11–26. 20 rooms.* 🖥. A pink villa with a pleasant garden and a location on the lagoon looking towards Venice.

LUXURY
Grande Albergo Ausonia & Hungaria – *Gran Viale S. Maria Elisabetta 28.* 📞 *041 242 0060. www.hungaria.it. 77 rooms. Closed Jan 8–Feb 7.* 🖥. An extraordinary Art Nouveau palace dating from 1905, with a façade covered in painted tiles. The hotel has been fully renovated to suggest some of the unique atmosphere of its heyday. Thai spa.
Excelsior – *Lungomare G. Marconi 41.* 📞 *041 526 0201. www.hotelexcelsior venezia.com. Closed Nov–Mar. 197 rooms.* 🖥. With its incredible architecture, this vast hotel on the beach is a sight in itself! Since 1908, it has symbolised a certain art of appearing in public… During the Film Festival, fans camp out in front of the entrance, whilst the stars discreetly leave via the underground passage leading to the private dock and the canal heading to the lagoon.

CHIOGGIA
MODERATE
Grande Italia – *Rione S. Andrea 597 (on Piazzetta Vigo).* 📞 *041 400 515. www. hotelgrandeitalia.com. Closed Nov–Dec 28. 56 rooms.* 🖥. This large, restored Belle Époque-style manor house faces onto the lagoon. A very comfortable hotel with a refined atmosphere.

CERTOSA
MODERATE
Venice Certosa Hotel – *Isola della Certosa.* 📞 *041 277 8632. www.venice certosahotel.com. 18 rooms.* 🖥. Open year-round, situated next to Vento di Venezia boatyard where you can see historic boats being restored, this friendly informal hotel is a dream for anyone wishing to escape the crowds of San Marco, as well as for sailors and boating enthusiasts, who often dock their craft and plan excursions. Lovely outside patio with small garden to relax and plenty of land for children to run about in. Their complimentary evening taxi service makes it easy to go into the centre for dinner or a concert. The

restaurant, which also has a terrace, serves cuisine based on Venetian tradition.

MAZZORBO

INEXPENSIVE TO EXPENSIVE

Venissa Ostello – *Fondamenta Santa Caterina 3. ✆041 527 2281. www.venissa.it. 5 rooms. Closed Nov–Mar.* ☕. This small estate house on the edge of the lagoon and Venissa vineyard has two options: inexpensive rooms with shared bath, or more expensive with private bath. Try La Dorona, the estate's limited-production wine. The restaurant, in a separate building, has talented chef Antonia Klugmann who earned a Michelin star in 2014, a mastery blends local produce, tradition and interesting creative touches and well-selected wines. Enquire about Venissa's complimentary taxi service.

PADOVA

Map p249.

INEXPENSIVE

Ostello della Gioventù Città di Padova – *Via Aleardo Aleardi 30. ✆049 87 52 219. www.ostellopadova.it.* A centrally located youth hostel with simple accommodation suitable for all kinds of visitors, including families.

MODERATE

Al Cason – *Via Frà Paolo Sarpi 40. ✆049 66 26 36. www.hotelalcason. com. 48 rooms.* ☕. A little out of the centre but close to the railway station. Family run with fairly basic facilities and simple but high-quality cooking.

Hotel Al Fagiano – *Via Locatelli 45. ✆049 87 50 073. www.alfagiano.com. 37 rooms.* ☕ *€5.*Only 100m/110yds from the Basilica di Sant'Antonio, a pleasant hotel with attractively furnished rooms.

Villa Goetzen –*Via G. Matteotti, 6, Dolo. 18km W/11.19mi of Padova. ✆041 510 2300. www.villagoetzen.it. 12 rooms.* ☕. On the edge of the Brenta, this 18th-century villa has charming rooms. Local cuisine served in the restaurant.

Terme Milano – *Viale delle Terme 169, Abano Terme, 13km/8mi SW of Padova. ✆049 86 69 444. www.termemilano.it. Closed Jan–Feb. 89 rooms.* ☕ In the pedestrian-ised area of Abano, this hotel offers indoor and outdoor pools to help you make the most of the thermal waters. Gym and tennis court.

Villa Lussana – *Via Chiesa 1, Teolo, 21km/13mi SW of Padova. ✆049 99 25 530. www.villalussana.com. Closed Jan 6–Feb 15. 7 rooms.* ☕. An attractive hotel in an Art Nouveau villa with fine views over the Colli Euganei.

VICENZA

MODERATE

Hotel Victoria – *Strada Padana (in the direction of Padova) 52, 7km/4.3mi E of Vicenza on the SS 11. ✆0444 91 22 99. www.hotelvictoriavicenza.com. 123 rooms.* ☕. Reasonable prices and comfortable surroundings. Offers good-sized rooms and apartments. In summer guests can use the open-air pool. Not far from the motorway and yet a few minutes from the centre.

EXPENSIVE

G Boutique Hotel – *Via A. Giuriolo 10. ✆0444 32 64 58. www.gboutiquehotel. com. 16 rooms.* ☕. Behind a classic exterior lie super-stylish rooms that don't cut on comfort. Location close to the Teatro Olimpico.

VERONA

Map p257.

It is worth noting that during trade fairs and exhibitions the hotels tend to put their prices up so check before booking a trip. Otherwise good accommodation can be found at reasonable prices outside the city.

MODERATE

Cavour – *Vicolo Chiodo 4. ✆045 59 01 66. www.hotelcavourverona.it. Closed 7 Jan–20 Feb. 19 rooms.* ☕ *€12,50.* The main benefit of this hotel is its quiet, central location between Castelvecchio and Piazza Bra. Simply furnished rooms.

Hotel Torcolo – *Vicolo Listone 3. ✆045 80 07 512. www.hoteltorcolo.it. Closed Dec 17–25 and Jan 8–17. 19 rooms.* ☕. Simple but pleasant rooms, each decorated in a slightly different style. Wifi available.

Where to Eat

The city's finest restaurants are listed in the **Michelin Guide Italy**, which is updated annually. Venice also has a wide choice of less formal establishments serving light meals, drinks and snacks (🍷 *for assistance with local dishes, see Introduction: Food and Wine*). Visitors should be aware that it is nearly always cheaper to drink at the bar than at a table; be sure to check prices before ordering. Provided below is a selection of *osterie*, trattorias and *pasticcerie* grouped under their respective neighbourhoods. The coin symbols here denote the price of a dinner meal consisting of an appetizer, an entree and a dessert (without drinks). Note that most restaurants in Venice include a *coperto*, a small charge (€2–€3 perhaps) for incidentals such as bread. Tips are sometimes, but not always included in the bill – always check to avoid tipping twice!

DINING OPTIONS

A **bàcaro** *(pl.bàcari)* or **osterìa** *(pl. osterìe)* is a very simple type of establishment that serves wine and a simple food menu. A *cichetteria* serves *cichèti* and wine, sometimes a few rice or pasta dishes. An **enoteca's** *(pl. enotèche)* purpose is to sell wine, but because generally Italians do not drink wine unless they also eat something, you can count on at least some snacks, simple platters, or a hot dish to accompany the wines. A **pizzeria** (and sometimes *forno*) is an establishment with a pizza oven (look for woodburning), and some specialise only in pizzas. The distinction among various terms for establishments is blurring in Italy. Traditionally a **locanda** is an "inn" or a "guesthouse", and may have a few rooms; a **trattorìa** meant modest but plentiful food, but now may be very upscale; or a **taverna** had dining, and finally, a **ristorante** was a bit more formal. Now it's best to consult the menu.

OUR SELECTION

We are keen to include all areas of Venice, so that you can combine exploration of the city with gastronomic discoveries. This is why we have included some bars, *enoteche* and *bàcari* in the restaurant section if they have a place where you can sit down and order some cooked food.
Our prices reflect the cost of a two-course meal with a carafe of wine.

BUSINESS HOURS

Most restaurants keep fairly restricted hours and are earlier than in Rome and the South: lunch *(pranzo)* is eaten between midday and 2pm, and dinner *(cena)* from 7.30–8pm onwards. A few places in tourist areas either offer continuous service or some options in between. When hunger strikes outside of traditional mealtimes, *bàcari* typically have been a resource, often open all day, but may close quite early (around 9pm).

SIT-DOWN MEALS...

Some places advertise tourist menus at bargain prices, sometimes quite aggressively. Check exactly what is included in the price before you sit down, and do not expect too much in the way of originality or quality. It would be a shame to look no further, because Venetian cuisine offers a wealth of flavours. You can eat very well in Venice without making a huge hole in your budget. Some down-to-earth restaurants frequented by working people and students offer dishes that are traditionally as tasty as the portions are large. Some high-end restaurants offer a reduced menu or tasting menus at lunchtime at reasonable prices.
🍷 **A bit of advice** – Prices for fish are sometimes given per 100g *(etto)*. An extra amount for bread and the cover charge *(pane e coperto)* is usually added to your bill, and service is not always included.

'La Dolce Vita'

Venice is full of little spots for sitting back and quite literally enjoying *"La Dolce Vita"*:

SAN MARCO
Venchi Chocolate – *Calle dei Fabbri 989.* ℘*041 241 2314.* Imaginative anddelicious ice creams, a Venice favourite.
Le Cafè – *Campo Santo Stefano 2797.* ℘*041 523 7201. www.lecafevenezia. com.* This excellent *pasticceria* has outside tables and light lunch fare.

DORSODURO
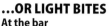 **Bar La Calcina** – *Zattere, Dorsoduro 780,* ℘*041 520 6466.* The homemade ice cream is better than in most of the gelaterie. Watch water vessels on the Giudecca Canal. Pleasant for lunch, dinner, or snacks.

LA GIUDECCA
Harry's Dolci – *Fondamenta S. Biagio 773.* ℘*041 522 4844. www.cipriani.com. Closed Tue and Nov–Mar.* This restaurant-cum-*pasticceria* is a little less expensive than Harry's Bar.

...OR LIGHT BITES
At the bar
Standing at the bar of one of the city's *bàcari*, you can eat *cichèti* or *crostini* – little snacks like Spanish tapas. This Venetian tradition is ideal for a quick bite at lunchtime and even more so at aperitif time. Every evening, young people meet up to enjoy the ritual of a *giro di ombra* (wine bar crawl): *òmbra* is dialect for an inexpensive glass of wine served at the bar to wash down your *cichèti*.

Take away
Panini and **tramezzini** are takes on the sandwich and do a good job of banishing the midday hunger pangs. Italian creativity can be seen in fillings such as *prosciutto crudo* with artichoke hearts, mortadella, anchovies and cheeses. Also, don't forget that a **pizza al taglio** (pizza slice) makes an excellent snack.

A bit of advice – You usually go first to the cash desk to pay for what you want to eat or drink. (Some items like pizza al taglio or cured meats or cheeses must first be weighed.) You can then go to the counter to collect your purchase in exchange for the receipt.

WHEN IN VENICE
The Piazza San Marco is famous for its *gran caffès* and almost equally infamous for the prices they charge. Just bear in mind that when you pull up a chair in one of these establishments, that you are not *just* buying a drink or a meal; rather you are taking up an exalted position in what Napoleon (supposedly) once called Europe's finest drawing room. There are several cafes around the square but two are world famous: the **Caffè Florian** (*www. caffeflorian.com*)

Caffè Florian in Piazza San Marco

© Gwen Cannon / MICHELIN

275

Piazza San Marco

© ventdusud/iStockphoto.com

and the **Caffè Quadri** (*www.alajmo. it*). Opened in 1720, Caffè Florian is not only Venice's most venerable cafe but perhaps the oldest in the country. The Quadri, in its present incarnation, opened in 1830, though a coffee shop once traded on the same site – perhaps the first ever in Venice – and is thought to have dated back to 1683. If you really want to push the boat out, take a seat outside either of these aristocratic *grand dames* (not forgetting to have a good look inside to admire their magnificent interiors) , and enjoy the music of a live orchestra. Dancing in the piazza is encouraged, and many would argue it is the best way to get your money's worth. The best cuisine on the piazza is at Quadri. A few steps away from the piazza on Calle Vallaresso, is Venice's most famous watering hole, **Harry's Bar** (*Calle Vallaresso 1323. ℘041 528 5777. www.cipriani.com*). The haunt of Hemingway, this stylish bar and restaurant continues to be the stomping ground of the glitterati, who come here for the trademark Bellini cocktail (sparkling Prosecco and white peach juice) as well as its good traditional cuisine. Like the caffès in the square, it is ferociously expensive, but sometimes money isn't everything.

RESTAURANTS BY AREA

PIAZZA SAN MARCO
🕭*Map p115.*

😊 **A bit of advice** – For other eating options in and around the square, see the entries under La Fenice (*p279*) and Schiavoni and Arsenale (*p281*).

MODERATE

All'Aciugheta B1 – *Campo SS. Filippo e Giacomo, Castello 4357. ℘041 522 4292.* The sidewalk tables of this trattoria are often packed with tourists, while the rustic dining room tends to be favoured by locals. Food quality has slipped in recent years, but their "pranzo dei operai", lunch specials for workers, are quite reasonable.

Alla Rivetta B1 – *Salizada S. Provolo, Between St Mark's Square and Campo S. Zaccaria, Castello 4625. ℘041 528 7302. Closed Mon.* A wide choice of *cichèti* right by S. Zaccaria.

Enoiteca Mascareta B1 – *Calle Longa di S. Maria Formosa, Castello 5183. ℘041 52 30 744. www.ostemaurolorenzon.com.* A wine bar serving up plates of *cichèti* (marinated fish, ham and cheese, platter of Italian cheeses) or hot dishes (allow €35 for a full meal) in an inviting atmosphere.

Al Mascaròn B1 – *Calle Lunga S.Maria Formosa, Castello 5225. ℘041 522 5995. www.osteriamascaron.it.* A renowned *osteria* serving authentic cuisine. Best to book ahead!

EXPENSIVE

Bistrot de Venise A1 – *Calle dei Fabbri, S. Marco 4685. ✆041 523 6651. www. bistrotdevenise.com*. A chic bistro-style lounge with an elegant zinc bar, dining room, and sidewalk seating. Sergio's passion for Venetian culinary history has put a few historic dishes on the menu, such as *bisato de vale*, roast eel flavoured with oranges in wine, cinnamon and bay. Most of the menu explores traditional and contemporary cuisine. Some 500 wines are available here by the glass, more by the bottle.

Alle Testiere B1 – *Calle del Mondo Nuovo (between Salizada S. Lio and Campo S. Maria Formosa), Castello 5801. ✆041 522 7220. www.osteriailletestiere.it. Closed Sun and Mon and Dec 22–Jan 10*. This little restaurant is renowned for its seafood and its bold flavour combinations: from John Dory with citrus fruit to *capesante* (scallops) with liqueur or *canestrelli* with lemon and mint. For less adventurous tastes, there is also a selection of grilled fish.

LUXURY

Quadri A2 – *Piazza S. Marco 121. ✆041 522 2105. www.alajmo.it. Closed Mon*. In the refined red-walled rooms overlooking St Mark's Square and bedecked with Murano glass chandeliers, this restaurant brought in a new chef in 2011 and Michelin star in 2012, emphasising new twists plus some traditional favourites.

Do Leoni B2 – *Riva degli Schiavoni, Castello 4171. www.londrapalace.com. ✆041 520 0533. Closed Jan*. The restaurant of the Hotel Londra Palace is another Venetian institution. Panoramic terrace in summer with unobstructed view of the lagoon. Booking essential.

Harry's Bar A2 – Don't overlook Harry's bar for a meal. Prices are extravagant, but quality is high. Arrigo Cipriani personally inspects his own suppliers, going up to Norway to procure salmon and so on. The menu leans toward Venetian tradition. Sunday's *osso buco* makes good, hearty comfort food. Upstairs has a view of St Mark's Basin. Best to dress the part or you won't find a seat in these musical, magical chairs.

RIALTO

♿*Map pp136–137.*

GRAND CANAL

☺ **A bit of advice** – On either side of the canal, downstream from the Rialto, on the **Fondamenta del Vin** or the **Riva di Ferro**, there are numerous restaurants with terraces, more renowned for their views than for their cuisine.

BÀCARI CRAWL

Around the edges of the market, you will find numerous littlebars, some of which appear in our selection (Vini da Pinto, Bancogiro, All'Arco) as they are also restaurants. You can adopt the Venetian habit of sampling various *cichèti*, often delicious, sampling a variety of wines in each place, gradually building up to a meal on the move.

INEXPENSIVE, LEFT BANK

Rosticceria Gislon B2 – *Calle della Bissa, S. Marco 5424. ✆041 522 3569*. Self-service style, but high quality, with a wonderful choice of Venetian dishes! You can eat at the bar, take a seat at one of the tables on the ground floor or sit down in more comfortable surroundings upstairs.

Ai Rusteghi B2 – *Corte del Tintor (access from S. Bartolomeo via Calle de la Bissa and the* sottoportego *on the left), S. Marco 5513. ✆338 760 6034. www. airusteghi.com*. Giovanni's wines are the focus of this small, rustic and often crowded spot, offering good panini. Wines change frequently, attracting local sommeliers and enthusiasts to sample also from smaller wineries, but prices are not posted, so do ask. Some courtyard seating.

INEXPENSIVE, RIGHT BANK

The Erberia is a particularly lively part of Venice both at lunchtimes and in the evenings. With its lively atmosphere, it's also the perfect place to enjoy an *òmbra* with some *cichèti*.

Al Mercà B1 – *Campo Bella Vienna (Erberia), S. Polo 213. ✆346 83 40 660. Closed Sun*. A place to make you feel like a real Venetian. Order a drink at the tiny bar facing onto the *campo*, choose from one of the many delicious *panini* and hang out with the locals taking a break before going back to the office. An enjoyable experience!

Pronto Pesce A1 – *Pescheria Rialto, S. Polo 319 (near Campo delle Beccarie). www. prontopesce.it.* ✆*041 822 0298 Closed Sun and Mon and mid Aug–mid Jan.* A little place with a nice menu of *cichèti*, or you could also try the delicious fish dishes. On Saturdays at 1pm, Venetians flock here for the *risotto di pesce*, with tourists hard on their heels!

All'Arco B1 – *Calle dell'Occhialer (a stone's throw from the Ruga S. Giovanni via the Sottoportego dei Do Mori), S. Polo 436.* ✆*041 520 5666. Closed Sun.* This tiny place is known for its *crostini*, has an excellent choice of wines and is always packed when the market is in full flow.

Cantina Do Mori B1– *S. Polo 429.* ✆*041 522 54 01.* Authentic *bàcaro* dating from 1462 and serving up very good *cichèti*.

Antico Dolo B2– *Rugo Rialto. S.Polo 778.* ✆*041 522 6546. www.anticodolo.it.* The little red-walled dining room of this *osteria* offers tripe, *crostini*, *polenta* and *bacalà mantecà* at mealtimes, along with a tasting menu. *Òmbre* and *cichèti* throughout the day.

Vini Da Pinto B1 – *Campo delle Becarie, S.Polo 367.* ✆*041 522 4599. www. ristorantevinidapinto.it.* The time to come for a glass of white wine with a few *cichèti* is during your morning shopping trip. Otherwise, the place has succumbed to the lure of the tourist trade and the dishes served at the tables in the square are nothing special.

Bancogiro B2 – *Campo San Giacometto, S. Polo 122.* ✆*041 523 2061. www. osteriabancogiro.it . Closed Mon and Jan 7–28.* "Bank exchange" might seem a peculiar name for an *enoteca*! But centuries ago this palazzo was the site of one of Venice's first banks. Wine from the bar, plus the little dining room upstairs serves unpretentious but flavoursome food. Try the "pregnant" (stuffed) sardines!

MODERATE, LEFT BANK

Al Vagon B1 – *Sottoportego del Magazen (close to Campo SS.Apostoli), Cannaregio 5597.* ✆*041 523 7558. www.alvagon.com. Closed Tue and Dec–Jan.* Honest Venetian food in a nicely turned-out dining room beside a canal, a little way from the crowds heading from the Rialto to the station, beneath a *sottoportego*.

MODERATE, RIGHT BANK

Al Nono Risorto A1 – *Sottoportego de la Siora Bettina (Campo S. Cassiano, beyond the rio of the same name), S. Croce 2338.* ✆*041 524 1169. Closed Wed.* A modest place, with a shaded terrace facing onto the *campo*. The pasta and pizza are popular with the locals.

Pane, Vino e San Daniele A1 – *Calle Boteri, S. Polo 1544.* ✆*380 410 8446 (mobile). www.panevinorialto.it. Closed Sun, Aug 2 weeks and 2 weeks before Carnival.* Like its sister establishment on Campo de l'Anzolo San Rafaele *(see I Carmini)*, this place is devoted to the famous *prosciutto crudo* from Friuli. An attractive, rustic dining room offers a choice of *cichèti* and dishes of the day on the chalk board and pleasant service.

Poste Vecie B1 – *Rio delle Beccarie/ Pescheria Rialto, S. Polo 1608.* ✆*041 721 822. www.postevecie.com. Closed Tue.* A little wooden bridge leads to this *trattoria* known as the "old post office", which it once was. It's also the city's oldest *trattoria*, dating back to the 16C. The fine old dining room spills over into the garden with its pergola when the weather is good. The house speciality is *seppie* with polenta.

EXPENSIVE, LEFT BANK

Al Graspo de Ua Lounge B2 – *Calle dei Bombaseri (between Campo S.Bortolomio and the Grand Canal), S.Marco 5094A.* ✆*041 520 5644. Closed Mon.* This restaurant nestling in a particularly narrow street has regained its former glory, which is good news for food lovers. Comes recommended, so it would be wise to book ahead.

Fiaschetteria Toscana B1 – *Salizada S. Giovanni Grisostomo (at the corner of Calle del Scaleter), Cannaregio 5719.* ✆*041 528 5281. www.fiaschetteriatoscana. it. Closed Tue, Wed lunch, Jul last week and Aug 3 weeks.* One of Venice's fine restaurants: don't miss moeche, lagoon crabs, when they are in season. Fish roasted in a salt crust is a speciality, but is also served grilled and fried. In these elegant surroundings, you can also choose from dishes like sea bass risotto with *Prosecco* or *carpaccio di cèrvo* (venison) with balsamic vinegar, or even a juicy Chianina steak. And why not start with a few oysters or a plate of *scampi* with lemongrass and honey? Sidewalk dining on the *campo* when the weather is good.

EXPENSIVE, RIGHT BANK

Vecio Fritolin A1 – *Calle della Regina (behind Campo S. Cassiano), S. Croce 2262.* ℘*041 522 2881. www.veciofritolin.it. Closed Mon and Tue lunch.* A traditional little place with a big reputation offering dishes based on produce from the nearby markets (try the swordfish tartare with olives and lemon), as well as delicious pasta made by the owner with quality fare.

Alla Madonna B2 – *Calle de la Madonna, S. Polo 594. ℘041 522 3824. www.ristoranteallamadonna.com. Closed Wed.* Traditional cuisine and a bustling atmosphere in its several rooms.

LUXURY, NEAR CAMPO S. POLO

Da Fiore A2 – *Calle del Scaleter (from Campo S. Polo via the Calle and Ponte Bernardo), S. Polo 2202. ℘041 721 308. www.dafiore.net. Closed Sun and Mon and Ago 7–22.* Always cited by other restaurateurs as a top place to dine, this is one of Venice's two Michelin-starred restaurants. In a narrow little street a stone's throw from S. Polo.

LA FENICE

⌖*Map pp142–143.*

MODERATE

Enoteca Al Volto B1 – *Calle Cavalli, connecting Campiello de la Chiesa (S. Luca) to the Grand Canal, S. Marco 4081. ℘041 522 8945. Closed Dec 24–25.* An *enoteca* set in a peaceful *calle* where you can take a seat and enjoy the *ombre* and *cichèti*.

Al Bacareto A1 – *Calle delle Boteghe (facing Campo S. Stefano, S. Marco 3447. 041 528 9336. www.osteriaalbacareto.it (in Italian). Closed Sun and Aug 3 weeks.* A long-standing restaurant serving up Venetian specialities, from the excellent, widely renowned *sarde in saòr* to *fegato* and *baccalà mantecato*. Or you could simply enjoy some *cichèti* at the bar with a glass of house wine.

Ai Assassini B1 – *Rio Terrà degli Assassini, S. Marco 3695. ℘041 528 7986.*

www.osteriaaiassassini.it. Closed Sun, Jan 7–14 and Aug 1 week. In a little street leading to the Rio San Luca, this small restaurant occupies the ground floor of an attractive building adorned with pairs of windows and serves a daily special to its regulars.

EXPENSIVE

Antica Carbonera C1 – *Calle Bembo (1st on the left after the Teatro Goldoni), S. Marco 4648. ℘041 522 5479. www.anticacarbonera.it. Closed Tue.* In a dining room decorated with objects and furniture from the yacht that belonged to Archduke Rudolph (of Mayerling fame!), you can enjoy classic Venetian cuisine, with both seafood and meat specialities.

Acqua Pazza B1 – *Campo S. Angelo, S. Marco 3808-3810. ℘041 277 0688. www.veniceacquapazza.com. Closed Mon, Jan and Aug 15 about 5 days.* This restaurant serves Neapolitan cuisine (essentially fish and shellfish) and boasts an additional attraction: its tables on the *campo*, with a view of the leaning bell tower of S. Stefano.

Ai Mercanti C1 – *Corte Coppo, Calle dei Fuseri, S. Marco 4346A. ℘041 523 8269. Closed Sun and Mon lunch.* A restaurant on a quiet little square close to the Scala del Bovolo offers a light lunch at a reasonable price. Evening tasting menus of Venetian cuisine, sometimes with a twist.

LUXURY

Antico Martini B1 – *Calle delle Veste/Campo S. Fantin, S. Marco 1983. ℘041 522 4121. www.anticomartini.it. Closed 3 weeks.* On the same square as La Fenice, you will find one of Venice's traditions, serving local and international cuisine, although the service could be a little better organised.

La Caravella B1 – *Calle Larga 22 Marzo, S. Marco 2399. ℘041 520 8901. www.restaurantlacaravella.com.* An elegant restaurant and a stalwart of Venetian fine dining: in the dining room or the inner courtyard you will enjoy carefully prepared food. Reasonably priced lunch menus.

ACCADEMIA
⚐ *Map p153.*

⊛ **A bit of advice** – On the **Zattere**, several restaurants set out their tables on decks over the canal facing the island of Giudecca. The best traditional cuisine is at La Calcina (*p280*), while Lineadombra serves stylish modern cuisine, and all have superb views! (*p280*)

INEXPENSIVE
Al Bottegon (Cantine del Vino gia Schiavi) B1 – *Fondamenta Nani, S. Trovaso (opposite the church), Dorsoduro 992.* ☎ *041 523 0034. www.cantinaschiavi.com. Closed Sun and August the first 3 weeks* This *bàcaro* (wine bar) offers a wide choice of traditional *cichèti*. An unmissable experience and an ideal place for a quick meal standing at the bar.

MODERATE
Taverna San Trovaso B1 – *S. Trovaso, Dorsoduro 1016.* ☎ *041 520 3703. www.tavernasantrovaso.it.* This pleasant canal-side *taverna*, a stone's throw from the Accademia, offers a wide choice of traditional dishes, such as *sepia* in its own ink served with polenta. Very popular with Venetians.

Ristorante San Trovaso B1– *Calle Larga Nani, on the corner of Rio Terrà Carità, Dorsoduro 967.* ☎ *041 523 0835. www.ristorantesantrovaso.it.* This offshoot of the *taverna* of the same name is located close by in a former warehouse and a courtyard.

Antica Locanda Montin A1 – *Fondamenta Borgo, Dorsoduro 1147.* ☎ *041 522 7151. www.locandamontin.com.* This traditional *trattoria* on a quiet canalside boasts a pleasant courtyard shaded by an arbour. It also has a few rooms available to rent.

Ai Quattro Feri A1 – *Calle Lunga S. Barnaba, Dorsoduro 2754.* ☎ *041 520 6978. Closed Sun and Jun.* In a bright little dining room with rustic décor, you can enjoy a peaceful meal thanks to the calm, attentive service. The "slow food" menu changes daily, according to what can be found in the markets. They only serve fish dishes. You choose your *antipasti* at the bar, then move on to generous main courses.

EXPENSIVE
La Rivista Wine&Cheese Bar B1 – *Rio Terrà Antonio Foscarini, Dorsoduro 979A.* ☎ *041 240 1425. www.restaurant larivista.com. Closed Mon.* This restaurant attached to the Hotel Ca' Pisani owes its name to a canvas painted in 1925 by Fortunato Depero for the *Rivista Illustrata del Popolo d'Italia*. The short menu focuses on local produce, cooked in a fairly innovative style. Service is both polished and friendly. Good list of local wines.

LA SALUTE
⚐ *Map p155.*

EXPENSIVE
Cantinone Storico A1 – *Fondamenta Bragadin, Dorsoduro 660.* ☎ *041 523 9577. www.cantinonestorico.it/ristorante-venezia.htm.* A little dining room and some tables along the Rio di San Vio in good weather provide the setting for this pleasant restaurant, very popular with English-speaking customers and renowned for its fish and shellfish.

LUXURY
Ai Gondolieri A1 – *Fondamenta de l'Ospedaleto (opposite the Ponte del Fornage, across the canal from the Guggenheim Museum), Dorsoduro 366.* ☎ *041 528 6396 or 348 808 9829. www.aigondolieri.com.* The owner Giovanni knows his wines. Meat specialities include the famous Venetian-style *fegato* (liver) served with polenta, the beef filet with Refosco wine gravy and potato timbale, and home-made desserts including sorbets. A magnet for tourists, but still serves good food.

ZATTERE
EXPENSIVE
Ristorante La Calcina, *Dorsoduro 782.* ☎ *041 520 6466. www.lacalcina.com. Closed Nov 21–Dec 15.* The wood terrace hangs right at the Zattere's edge, perfect for ship- and boat-watching. The ample menu selection offers fish, meat, and good vegetarian dishes, plus pasta, salads, and the Zattere's best gelato, handmade the traditional way.

LUXURY
Lineadombra B1 – *Zattere ai Saloni, just before the Dogana, Dorsoduro 19.*

☎041 241 1881. www.ristorante
lineadombra.com. Closed Tue (only winter)
and Nov–Feb. A restaurant serving
refined cuisine, either on the deck
in fine weather or in the minimalist
dining room: mille-feuille of *scampi
in saòr with apples*, sea bass fillet with
vanilla potatoes, or grilled *capesante*
with yoghurt and saffron, as well as
marinated raw fish and home-made
pasta. Good wine list and attentive
service. Alessio is a knowledgeable,
friendly sommelier, so don't hesitate to
ask for suggestions.

SCHIAVONI AND ARSENALE
Map p161.

INEXPENSIVE
Alle Alpi da Dante A2 – *Corte Nova,
Castello 2877.* ☎041 528 5163. This *osteria*
far from the tourist haunts at the end
of a *sottoportego* may not be much to
look at, but it is popular with the locals.
Enjoy a glass of house wine with a few
crostini and practise your *venexiàn* on
the regulars.

MODERATE
Da Remigio A2 – *Salizada dei Greci,
Castello 3416.* ☎ 041 52 30 089.
Closed Mon evening and Tue. Among
timeless streets, this bistro honours
traditional Venetian specialties: *pesce
spada affumicato* (smoked swordfish
carpaccio), *fritelle, zabaglione*…

EXPENSIVE
Al Covo B3 – *Campiello della Pescaria, to
the right of the Riva degli Schiavoni, just
before Ca' di Dio, Castello 3968.* ☎041
522 3812. www.ristorantealcovo.com.
Closed Wed and Thu. A highly regarded
restaurant, even though, from the
outside, nothing appears to set it apart
from the rest. A little terrace on the
square and an attractive dining room
with exposed beams. Three tasting
menus and renowned desserts.
Corte Sconta B2 – *Calle del Pestrin,
Castello 3886.* ☎041 522 7024. www.
cortescontavenezia.com. *Closed Sun,
Mon, Jan 8–30 and Jul 26–Aug 17.* In a
little street right by the entrance to
the Arsenale is one of the city's best
restaurants, with a particular reputation
for its sometimes unusual *antipasti*. The
little dining room leads to a pleasant

courtyard, always packed. Enjoy
specialities such as the home-made
pasta and excellent fish, either grilled
or in sauce, and Lucia's well-selected
wines. Booking is essential.

LUXURY
MET A3 – *Riva degli Schiavoni,
Castello 4149.* ☎041 520 5044 www.
hotelmetropole.com. *Closed Mon and Jan
9–31.* In this superb restaurant with
innovative cuisine – and a Michelin
star – the atmosphere is tranquil and
service attentive, as befits prestigious
Hotel Metropole, facing St. Mark's Basin.

SANTI GIOVANNI E PAOLO
Map pp168-169.

MODERATE
Al Ponte B2 – *Calle Larga G. Gallina,
Cannaregio 6378.* ☎041 5286157 348 764
3274. You will find this *osteria* just at the
end of the bridge on your way from SS.
Giovanni e Paolo. Specialities include
salt cod with courgette flowers *(baccalà
e fiori di zucca fritti)* or with olives and
peppers. The million-dollar question is
how to bag a table without turning up
at opening time.
Un Mondo DiVino B2 – *Salizada S.
Canciano, Cannaregio 5984A.* ☎041 521
1093. A wonderful *bàcaro* in a former
beef butcher's premises, which proudly
proclaims its previous incarnation. The
place gets very busy, and not only will
you not be able to sit down, you also
risk having to tuck into your *òmbra*
and *cichèti* in the street, along with
most of your fellow customers. This is
a small price to pay for the delicious
food, however, especially since the
atmosphere is extremely convivial.
Osteria-Enoteca Giorgione A2 – *Calle
dei Proverbi, Cannaregio 4582A.* ☎041 522
1725. www.osteriagiorgione.com. Under
new management, this locale employs
avant-garde cooking techniques,
celebrating local foods and making
room for Oriental influences in its
menu. A good wine selection makes
room for local vintners and emerging
winemakers.
La Perla A2 – *Rio Terrà dei Franceschi
detta la Botesela, Cannaregio 4615.* ☎041
528 5175. *Closed Wed, Aug and Dec 24–26.*
Pizza aficionados will find a very wide

choice at this decent pizzeria, including some unusual options.

Bandierette C3 – *Barbaria delle Tole, Castello 6671.* 📞*041 522 0619. Closed Mon evening, Tue, Aug 2 weeks and Dec.* Near the *campo* and the Ospedaletto church, this purveyor of wines and spirits has a pleasant dining room where you can enjoy dishes such as the excellent *capesante* (scallops), with the added bonus of service with a smile.

Da Alberto B2 – *Calle Piovan (extension of Calle Larga Giacinto Gallina leading from Campo SS. Giovanni e Paolo to the Chiesa dei Miracoli), Castello 5401.* 📞*041 523 8153. Closed Jan 8–16 and Jul last week.* A minuscule dining room where you'll be offered the dish of the day written up on the slate. Either book or be prepared to wait.

Da Alvise B2 – *Fond. Nuove, Cannaregio 5045A.* 📞*041 520 1515. www.ristorante daalvise.it. Closed Mon (in winter), Nov 5– Mar 4.* A pleasant resta urant opposite the lagoon, not far from the *vaporetto* stop. Fish specialities.

EXPENSIVE

Vecia Cavana A2 – *Rio Terrà dei SS. Apostoli, Cannaregio 4624.* 📞*041 528 7106. www.marsillifamiglia.it. Closed Aug last 2 weeks and Jan last 2 weeks.* Away from the busy thoroughfares, this restaurant is worth the detour for its traditional yet inventive cuisine: dishes like smoked swordfish or tuna, octopus mosaic or succulent aubergine *tortino* are followed by grilled fish (swordfish, sole, sea bass) or the more traditional *seppie in nero* served with the lightest polenta.

Osteria Boccadoro B2 – *Campiello Widman (from Campo S. Maria Nova via the narrow Calle Widman), Cannaregio 5405A.* 📞*041 521 1021. www.boccadorovenezia.it. Closed Mon and Jan.* This huge place with a terrace on a nice little square offers a delicious selection of shellfish.

CA' D'ORO

INEXPENSIVE

Ai Promessi Sposi B3 – *Calle dell'Oca (between Campo de SS. Apostoli and the Strada Nuova), Cannaregio 4367.* 📞*041 241 2747. Closed Mon and Wed lunch.* Cichèti and local cuisine served either in the little courtyard or the dining room with walls covered in classic 7-inch singles.

Cà d'Oro Alla Vedova B3 – *Calle Pistor (following on from the landing stage for the Ca' d'Oro vaporetto, beyond the Strada Nuova), Cannaregio 3912.* 📞*041 528 5324. Closed Thu and Sun lunch.* Another *bàcaro* that often gets packed: booking advised.

MODERATE

Al Marinèr A2 – *Fond. Ormesini (near the Ponte dell'Aseo), Cannaregio 2679.* 📞*041 720 036. Closed Sun, Dec and Aug 2 weeks.* In this very simple locals' *trattoria* in a down-to-earth district offers dishes like shrimp brochettes or stuffed mussels.

Da Rioba B2 – *Fond. della Misericordia, Cannaregio 2553.* 📞*041 524 4379. www. darioba.com (in Italian). Closed Mon and Aug 2 weeks.* On one of Cannaregio's fantastic canalside walkways blessed with the midday sun, this *osteria* has a few tables beside the water and a convivial atmosphere in the dining room when it fills up with regulars. Classy cuisine based on fresh fish, with home-made desserts to complete the picture. Good Italian wine list. Booking advised in the evenings.

EXPENSIVE

Il Paradiso Perduto B2 – *Fondamenta della Misericordia – Cannaregio, 2540.* 📞*041 720 581. Closed Tue, Wed, Dec 10–27 and Jan 7–early carnival.* Very well known in Venice for its authentic local cuisine, as well as a favourite meeting place for jazz enthusiasts.

Vini da Gigio B3 – *Fond. S. Felice, Cannaregio 3628A.* 📞*041 528 5140. www.vinidagigio.com. Closed Mon–Tue, Dec 25–26–31 and Jan 1.* A restaurant overlooking a nice *rio* and occupying several little rooms with beamed ceilings. The tasty shrimp and pumpkin risotto is good to start. Fish is served marinated, grilled or in sauce, and there are meat dishes on offer as well. Laura makes good desserts. The place is popular with tourists, but the food is still good and has a good wine list. Booking recommended.

Al Fontego dei Pescatori B3 – *Sottoportego dei Tagiapera or Calle Priuli or de la Racchetta, Cannaregio 3726.* 📞*041 520 0538. www.alfontegodeipescatori.it.* Whether you arrive via the *sottoportego* on the Rio San Felice or through the garden by the street, you will not regret your choice. Run by a former fishmonger in the market in this former warehouse where jazz plays in the background. Loris knows where to find the best local fish and shellfish, and how to serve it.

Anice Stellato A2 – *Fond. della Sensa, Cannaregio 3272.* 🕿 *041 720 744. www. osteriaanicestellato.com. Closed Mon and Tue (Open Tue evening April –Sept), Nov–Dec 2 weeks and Aug 16–30.* This little restaurant entices people from all over Venice into a district far from the main thoroughfares. Fish lovers are lured by the innovative cooking and the subtle use of sometimes unexpected spices like the Star Anise of its name. The restaurant stays open between mealtimes, offering a choice of *cichèti*.

CANNAREGIO AND IL GHETTO
🕭*Map pp180–181.*

MODERATE
Alla Fontana B2 – *Fond. di Cannaregio 1102 (on the corner of Calle delle Chioverette).* 🕿 *041 715 077. Closed Mon.* This wine bar frequented by a very local crowd also operates a little restaurant serving tasty food. Tables on the canalside when weather is good.

Ai Canottièri A2 – *Fondamenta S. Giobbe, Cannaregio 690.* 🕿 *041 476 1035.* Under new management a little café serving up daily specials to hordes of students from the nearby university.

Da A'Marisa A2 – *Fond. di S. Giobbe, Calle della Canna, Cannaregio 652B.* 🕿 *041 720 211. Closed Sun–Tue evening.* Carnivores take note! This is one of the few special-ist meat restaurants in Venice, with good reason, as it is run by a family of butchers. Excellent food in generous portions.

GHETTO

INEXPENSIVE
Al Cicheto B3 – *Calle della Misericordia, 376, Cannaregio 367A.* 🕿 *041 71 60 37. Closed Sat lunch and Sun.* A tiny wine bar located near the station. Good wine selection, excellent *cicheti* and typical Venetian dishes.

MODERATE
Gam Gam B2 – *Fond. di Cannaregio and Sottoportego del Ghetto Vecchio, Cannaregio 1122.* 🕿 *366 25 4505.*

gamgamkosher.com. Closed Fri evening, Sat and Jewish holidays. A few tables beside the canal and some more in the little street leading to the heart of the Ghetto, where you can sample a range of high-quality kosher cuisine, such as hummus, moussaka, couscous, fish with haraimi sauce, and pastries.

Bentigodi di Chef Domenico C2 – *Calle Nuove (between the Rio Terrà S. Leonardo and the Ghetto), Cannaregio 1423.* 🕿 *041 822 3714. www.bentigodi. com. Closed Sun evening and Mon.* This pleasant restaurant offers a wide choice of *cichèti* and innovative pasta dishes. Good wine list.

All'Antica Mola C2 – *Fondamenta Ormesini (opposite the Campo di Ghetto Nuovo), Cannaregio 2800.* 🕿 *041 717 492. Closed Wed, Jan 7–22 and Ago 1–15.* A little interior courtyard and a dining room decorated with maritime trophies provide the setting for this very simple, popular restaurant.

EXPENSIVE
Alla Palazzina B2 – *Rio Terrà S.Leonardo, at the corner of the Ponte delle Guglie, Cannaregio 1509.* 🕿 *041 717 725. www. ristoranteallapalazzina.it.* This restaurant with its wood-panelled walls and hidden garden offers several fish-based tasting menus, and occupies a stunning little palazzo. Gondoliers like to lunch here, a sign that their trade is lucrative and the food is good.

I FRARI AND SAN ROCCO
🕭*Map pp186–187.*

MODERATE
Il Réfolo B1 – *Campiello del Piovan (set back from Campo S. Giacomo dall'Orio) –S. Croce 1459.* 🕿 *041 524 0016. www. dafiore.net.* A place to enjoy a pizza or a more elaborate dish on a little square bordered by a canal, but be warned that it gets very busy and it may be wise to book for an evening meal.

Al Ponte B1 – *Ponte del Megio (at the corner of Calle Larga leading to Campo S. Giacomo dall'Orio), S. Croce 1666.* 🕿 *041 719 777. Closed Sun and Jan.* At the end of the "millet bridge", so-called because the area used to be occupied by millet and wheat warehouses, you will find this *trattoria* serving excellent fish specialities.

Capitan Uncino B1 – *Campo S.Giacomo dall'Orio, S. Croce 1501.* 📞 *041 721 901. www.tavernacapitanuncino.it. Closed Wed.* Tables on the *campo* shaded by an acacia tree. Fish and seafood specialities: try the *scampi alla buzzara* with polenta, or the grilled sea bass *(branzino)*.

La Zucca C1 – *Calle del Tintor, near the Ponte del Meggio, S. Croce 1762.* 📞 *041 524 1570. www.lazucca.it. Closed Sun.* A restaurant offering varied, creative cuisine at reasonable prices, which is quite a rarity for Venice. Amidst the *zucca* (pumpkin)-themed décor, you can enjoy numerous dishes renowned for their vegetable accompaniments: the artichokes, aubergines, marrows, zucchini and leeks do the lagoon's market gardeners justice, whilst the delicious desserts are a gourmet delight. The restaurant is highly regarded, so booking is advised.

Trattoria S. Tomà B3 – *Campo S.Tomà, S. Polo 2864A.* 📞 *041 523 8819. www. trattoriasantoma.com. Closed Tue and Jan.* Tables spill out into the *campo* and an interior courtyard. Service with a smile.

Dona Onesta B3 – *Calle Larga Foscari, where it meets the Rio de la Frescada (not far from Ca' Foscari), Dorsoduro 3922.* 📞 *041 710 586. www.donaonesta.it.* An excellent *trattoria*: the *sarde in saòr* with raisins and pine nuts are exemplary and the grilled fish (sea bass, sole…) is remarkable. Diligent, friendly service.

La Patatina C2 – *Calle del Saoneri, S. Polo 2741.* 📞 *041 523 7238. www.lapatatina.it (in Italian).* A nice, lively, traditional restaurant offering a vast choice of very hearty dishes (often based on potatoes, as the name suggests), to eat at the bar or sitting peacefully in the company of the ever-hungry crowd of students from the nearby Ca' Foscari, or local employees.

EXPENSIVE

Antica Besseta B1 – *Salizada de Ca' Zusto, S. Croce 1395.* 📞 *041 721 687. www. anticabesseta.it (in Italian). Closed Tue(only in winter) and Jan 9–20.* Traditional Venetian cuisine. A few tables in the street under a pleasant climbing vine.

Da Ignazio C2 – *Calle dei Saoneri, S. Polo 2749.* 📞 *041 523 4852. www.trattoriada ignazio.com (in Italian). Closed Sat and Aug 2 weeks and Jan 2 weeks.* This elegant little restaurant with nicely dressed tables offers excellent fish specialities. Good wine list.

I CARMINI
♿ *Map pp196–197.*

INEXPENSIVE

Osteria ai Pugni C1 – *Fondamenta Gherardini (Ponte dei Pugni), Dorsoduro 2836.* 📞 *346 960 7785. osteriaaipugni.com. Closed Sun (only summer) and Aug 1 week.* A nice, simple little place to drink an *ómbra* and nibble on a *cichèto*.

Da Toni B1 – *Fondamenta S.Basilio, Dorsoduro 1642.* 📞 *041 523 8272.* Beside the *rio*, a stone's throw from the church of S. Sebastiano and the port, you can join local workers tucking into the tasty home-made pasta.

MODERATE

Casin dei Nobili C1 – *Calle Casin dei Nobili (facing Campo S. Barnaba), Dorsoduro 2765.* 📞 *041 241 1841. Closed Thu.* The kind of place where Venetian noblemen would have consorted with women of easy virtue, although the atmosphere these days is much less racy. The restaurant, with its little dining room and a courtyard separated from the street by a wall, offers grilled meats, pasta and dishes of the day.

Pane, Vino e San Daniele A1 – *Campo dell'Anzolo Rafael, Dorsoduro 1722.* 📞 *041 523 7456. www.panevinoesandaniele.net. Closed Wed, Aug 3 weeks and Jan 2 weeks.* A place devoted to the famous *prosciutto crudo*, which you can enjoy as it comes with a glass of wine or prepared with bread *gnocchi* or pasta. Friendly service and an adjoining shop.

EXPENSIVE

Ristoteca Oniga C1 – *Campo S. Barnaba, Dorsoduro 2852.* 📞 *041 522 4410. www. oniga.it.* This restaurant-cum-wine bar is popular amongst local artists and offers carefully prepared traditional Venetian cuisine (delicious polenta with *seppie in nero* or salt cod), as well as more innovative creations such sea bass *in crosta* served with a grape risotto.

GIUDECCA
📍 *Map pp200–201.*

MODERATE

Altanella C1 – *Calle delle Erbe, Giudecca 268. ☎041 522 7780. Closed Mon, Tue and Dec–Jan and Aug 2 weeks.* On fine days, the dining room of this discreet trattoria opens out onto the Rio del Ponte Lungo by way of a vine-shaded terrace. Very popular with locals, as well as anyone with a taste for true Venetian cuisine.

LUXURY

Harry's Dolci B1 – *Riva San Biagio, Giudecca 773. ☎041 522 4844. www. cipriani.com. Closed Tue and Nov–Mar.* On the way to the Molino Stucky, you will find this off-shoot of the legendary Harry's Bar in Calle Vallaresso. The restaurant boasts an attractive dining room with white-tiled walls and a ceiling with exposed beams. You can sample the inventive cuisine thanks to two daily set meals, whilst the terrace on the *riva* offers a magnificent view.

Bauers Palladio Ristorante L'Ulivo D1 – *Fond. delle Zitelle, by the church of the same name, Giudecca 33. ☎041 520 7022. www. bauerhotels.com.* Even if you decide not to stay in this annex of the famous hotel, which is housed in the chiesa delle Zitelle's former convent school for girls, you can still enjoy snacks at lunchtime in the garden behind the building, or barbecue dishes in the evening.

SANT'ELENA AND SAN PIETRO
📍 *Map pp208–209.*

MODERATE

Giorgione A2 – *Via Garibaldi, Castello 1533. ☎041 522 8727. www.ristorante giorgione.it. Closed Wed and Dec 1 week.* A place serving honest local cuisine, with musical entertainment sometimes provided by a singer with a guitar. Amiable, speedy service.

Dal Pampo (S. Elena) C3 – *Calle Generale A. Chinotto, Castello 24. ☎041 520 8419. www.osteriadapampo.it. Closed Tue.* A few tables in the street in the residential district of Sant'Elena. The sight of the owners sorting through porcini mushrooms gathered from the nearby forests on one of the tables in the little dining room sums up the family atmosphere of this welcoming place, which is an unexpected treat.

Dai Tosi Grandi B2 – *Calle Secco Marina, Castello 985. ☎041 241 2299. www. trattoriadaitosigrandi.it . Closed Tue.* The success of this *trattoria-pizzeria* right by the Biennale has brought expansion and the addition of a nice little garden.

EXPENSIVE

Il Nuovo Galeon B2 – *Via Garibaldi, Castello 1308. ☎041 520 4656. www. ilnuovogaleon.com. Closed Tue and Jan.* On the corner of the *viale* leading to the Giardini Pubblici, this elegant place is one of the city's high-quality restaurants.

LUXURY

Hostaria da Franz B2 – *Salizada S.Antonin, Castello 3499 . ☎041 522 0861. www.hostariadafranz.com. Closed Tue and 3 weeks in Jan and 1 Jul.* An attractive dining room, classy surroundings and a terrace on the canal looking out on to the *campo*. With the Biennale not far away, da Franz sets out to create a sufficiently sophisticated atmosphere to attract the art world and its entourage.

IL LIDO

MODERATE

Andri – *Via Lepanto 21. ☎041 526 5482. Closed lunch (excluding hols) and Nov– Mar (Open only by reservation).* A restaurant set in an amazing villa with a lovely carved stone loggia. The terrace is set under a genuine miniature virgin forest. Very reasonable menu based on fish and seafood.

La Sfera – *Via Lepanto, on the corner of Via Enrico Dandolo. ☎041 526 0252. Closed Dec 1– Jan 31.* A place serving up the classics of Venetian cuisine in a canalside location.

MURANO
📍 *Map p216.*

EXPENSIVE

Ai Frati – *Fond. Venier 4. ☎041 736 694. www.aifrati.com. Open luncht only.Closed Thu.* For those in search of a simple *trattoria* serving seafood dishes.

Busa alla Torre – *Campo S. Stefano 3. ☎041 739 662. Closed evenings.* A *trattoria* occupying a red building with a loggia. Tables are laid out in the quiet *campo*, away from the bustle of the dock.

BURANO
Map p219.

A bit of advice – There is a string of restaurants and *trattorie* on either side of Via Baldassare Galuppi. Some can be invaded by groups, especially in summer: so if you arrive in the morning, it would be a good idea to book a table when you get there or cross the footbrige to Mazzorbo. The vaporetto (41/42) runs in the evening, so to avoid the crush linger for the sunset and have an early dinner.

EXPENSIVE

Da Romano – *Via San Martino Destra, Burano 221.* ℘*041 730 030. www. daromano.it. Closed Sun evening, Tue and Jan–Feb 10.* In the birthplace of a proud local sailor, Giovanni Tomadelli (1861–1926), this traditional restaurant was a haven for artists, who sometimes paid their tabs with works of art. They still maintain good quality, in spite of the influx of tourists.

Al Gatto Nero - da Ruggero – *Fond. de la Giudecca, Burano 88.* ℘*041 730 120. www.gattonero.com. Closed Sun evening, Mon, Jul 1 week and November 7 – Dec 4.* In a peaceful canalside location, away from the crowds. This was very "in" for seafood specialities, but recently locals complain that the prices have gone up while quality teeters a bit up and down.

MAZZORBO

MODERATE

Maddalena – *Mazzorbo 7C, by the canal, at the LN vaporetto stop, or on foot from the Burano landing stage, following the shoreline and crossing a wooden bridge. Fondamenta Santa Caterina, 7B.* ℘*041 730 151. www.trattoriamaddalena.com. Closed Thu.* Charming Raffaella and Beppino have run this trattoria for more than 50 years. This large orange villa has a slightly wild-looking garden beside the canal that produces one of the best salads you'll ever taste.

Venissa – *Fondamenta Santa Caterina 3 Mazzorbo, by the canal, at the LN vaporetto stop, or on foot from the Burano landing stage, following the shoreline and crossing a wooden bridge or call for their water taxi.* ℘*041 52 72 281. www.venissa.it. Lunch and dinner.* *Closed Tue and Nov–Apr 13.* Antonia Klugmann, who has earned a Michelin star for Venissa, seeks the freshest quality ingredients from as nearby as possible, which she then combines into innovative cuisine inspired by Venetian tradition for a meal to be savoured in this garden atmosphere near the Dorona vineyards, which is all managed by the Bisol winery. Lovely wine selection.

TORCELLO
Map p221.

EXPENSIVE

Al Ponte del Diavolo – *Fondamenta dei Borgognoni 10/11.* ℘*041 730 401. www. osteriaalpontedeldiavolo.com. Closed Mon and mid Nov–mid Feb.* A restaurant boasting a very pretty veranda with rattan chairs and a "gazebo" in the heart of the magnificent garden. It is only open at lunchtime, and the menu leans heavily on seafood (tuna tartare with capers, tagliolini with cuttlefish ink and marinated *scampi*, baked *branzino* (sea bass), or thinly sliced tuna with sauce and rosemary). A favourite, also, of other restaurateurs.

LUXURY

Locanda Cipriani – *Piazza Santa Fosca 29.* ℘*041 730 150. www.locanda cipriani.com. Closed Tue and Jan–Feb.* Hemingway's former bolt-hole right by the abbey is seductively calm and authentic, and the refined cuisine is a delight.

CHIOGGIA

MODERATE

El Fontego – *Piazzetta XX Settembre 497.* ℘*041 550 0953. www.fontego.it. Closed Mon, Nov 10 days and Jan 2 weeks.* A pizzeria and fish restaurant.

PELLESTRINA

MODERATE

Da Celeste – *Via Vianelli 625B.* ℘*041 967 355. www.daceleste.it. Closed Wed and Nov–Feb.* Fish lovers will be in their element in this restaurant decorated with modern paintings and boasting a large terrace looking out onto the lagoon.

CERTOSA

MODERATE

Ristorante Il Certosino – *Venice Certosa Hotel Polo Nautico Vento di Venezia.* ✆*041 520 0035. www.ristoranteilcertosino.com. Closed Wed (only Feb–Apr and Oct–Nov) and Dec–Jan.* (Vaporetto 4.1/4.2 toward Murano, stop is by request, so ask the attendant when you board.) A lovely evening out begins when you step off the *vaporetto*, walk down the wooden pier, enter the boatyard where craftsmen are restoring antique boats, and settle in for a delicious meal on the patio in the garden or in this simply decorated restaurant. Venetian tradition is the focus here. Limited but good wine selection. Don't worry about the return trip in the evening, just book the complimentary water taxi.

PADOVA
ⓑ *Map p249.*

MODERATE

Antica Trattoria Bertolini – *Via Altichiero 162, Altichiero, 5km/3mi N of Padova.* ✆*049 600 357. www.bertolini1849. it. Closed Sat, Sun evening, Aug 2 weeks and Dec 26–Jan 5. 14 rooms.* Just outside Padova, this long-standing restaurant serves good traditional dishes. Close to the motorway, it's also a good place to stay for travellers.

Aubergine – *Via V. Ghislandi 5, Abano Terme, 13km/8mi SW of Padova.* ✆*049 86 69 910. www.aubergine.it. Closed Tue, 2 weeks between Jul–Aug and 10 days between Feb–Mar.* A good choice if you are staying in Albano for the spa. Pizzas are also served.

Da Giovanni – *Via P. Maroncelli 22.* ✆*049 77 26 20. www.ristorantedagiovannipd.it. Closed Sat lunch, Sun, and Aug.* A historic restaurant that's worth seeking out for good homemade pasta and tasty stews.

Osteria dal Capo – *Via degli Obizzi 2.* ✆*049 66 31 05. www.osteriadalcapo.it. Closed Mon lunch and Sun and Ago 7–28.* A traditional trattoria just a stone's throw from the cathedral. Specialities from Padova and the Veneto.

Osteria L'Anfora – *Via del Soncino 13.* ✆*049 65 66 29. Closed Sun.* Good for just a drink or a meal in an attractive, informal setting at the heart of the ghetto.

Trattoria San Pietro – *Via San Pietro 95* ✆*049 87 60 330. Closed Sun and public hols.* A renowned trattoria in the historic centre, with elegant, carefully presented decor. Tables are limited, so reservations are essential.

EXPENSIVE

Belle Parti – *Via Belle Parti 11 , Altichiero, 5km/3mi N of Padova.* ✆*049 875 1822. www.ristorantebelleparti.it. Closed Sat.* In an elegant environment including paintings on the walls, mirrors and woodwork, the menu changes with the seasons, providing a range of succulent meat and fish dishes.

VICENZA

MODERATE

Al Pestello – *Contrà Santo Stefano 3.* ✆*0444 32 37 21. Closed Thu and Jan.* Specialising in local cuisine, there is also a lovely outdoor area.

Antica Osteria da Penacio – *Via Soghe 22, Arcugnano, 10km/6.2mi S of Vicenza on the S 247.* ✆*0444 27 30 81. www.penacio.it. Closed Wed , Thu lunch and 10 days Feb and 10 Nov.* Creative cuisine using local ingredients and lovely presentation. The family has presided for several generations. Warm, welcoming, elegant-rustic décor.

VERONA
ⓑ *Map p257.*

INEXPENSIVE

Al Bersagliere – *Via Dietro Pallone 1.* ✆*045 80 04 824. www. trattoriaalbersagliere.it. Closed Sun, Mon and Aug 10–31.* A typical little trattoria, where you can eat in the cellar dining room or at tables outside.

Kulmbacher Bier-Haus – *Via Marconi 72.* ✆*045 59 75 17. www.kbh.it. Closed Sat lunch.* This Bavarian tavern offers generous servings of tasty food in a convivial atmosphere.

MODERATE

San Basilio alla Pergola – *Via A. Pisano 9.* ✆*045 52 04 75. www.trattoriasanbasilio. it. Closed Sun and Jan the first week.* With its rustic-style dining rooms and splendid wooden floors, there is a pleasant, country feel to this restaurant. Complementing the ambience is the chef's traditional but imaginative cooking.

Entertainment

Venice at night is magically romantic and atmospheric. The play of lights on the lamplit canals and floodlit *palazzi* is a special sight to remember, especially from the vantage point of a slow gliding gondola. Evening entertainment is low key, though widespread in venues from theatres to churches. Few bars and cafes stay open past 11pm. Since the time of Goldoni and Pietro Longhi, Venice has been the perfect backdrop for theatre. Festivals and drama are still very much a part of life in this scenic city.

INFORMATION

The tourist office has a free calendar of Shows and Events on a monthly basis (see *Planning Your Trip*): evening performances are listed day by day. The office also offers a free, event-packed booklet entitled **un Ospite di Venezia**: see the Venice by Night section.

Information is also available online at www.unospitedivenezia.it and www. turismovenezia.it (click on Events); both sites are also in English. At the weekend the magazine of the daily newspaper, **Il Gazettino,** provides comprehensive coverage of the shows, exhibitions and festivals held in Venice, as well as concerts and recitals in churches and public buildings. Information on theatre, cinema and concerts in Venice is also available at www.culturaspettacolovenezia.it. Simplest of all, large posters announcing events are plastered throughout the streets so keep your eyes peeled.

VENICE

NIGHTLIFE

LATE BARS, LOUNGES AND PUBS

Bacaro Jazz – *S. Marco 5546.* *041 528 249. www.bacarojazz.com. 11–2am.* Jazz is the theme at this lively cocktail bar. Near the Rialto Bridge, it serves panininand simple Venetian specialities like *fegato*.

Birreria Forst – *Calle delle Rasse, S. Marco 4540.* *041 523 0557. 9.30am-11pm.* A typical brasserie where gondoliers meet, with a range of beers and German-style black-bread sandwiches.

Bistrot de Venice – *Calle dei Fabbri, S. Marco 4685.* *041 523 6651. www. bistrotdevenise.com. Open to 1am* (also see Restaurants). The kitchen serves to midnight and a savvy sommelier offers a few hundred wines by the glass

Centrale – *Piscina Frezzaria, S. Marco 1659B.* *041 887 6642. www.caffe centralevenezia.com.* A glamorous nightspot near La Fenice (before- or after-theatre dining) in the atmospheric 16C Palazzo Cocco Melin, with soft lighting, designer armchairs, sofas, Mediterranean cuisine and cocktails.

Devil's Forest – *Calle degli Stagneri 5185.* *041 520 0623. www.devilsforest.com. Closed Mon.* A pleasant brasserie for a glass of beer and *panini.*

Dogado Lounge – *Via Cannaregio, S. Marco 3660A.* *041 520 8544.* Good value food by day in a smart cafe downstairs, while by night it is a smart wine bar, with a full a la carte restaurant and roof terrace with garden-style swing loungers.

Aida performed at the Arena di Verona

© Ennevi Foto / Courtesy of Fondazione Arena di Verona

Antico Martini – *Calle del Cafetier, S. Marco 2007.* ✆ *041 522 4121. www. anticomartini.it.* Drinks and restaurant with inside garden. Runs nearby **Vino Vino** wine bar.

Al Paradiso Perduto – *Fondamenta de la Misericordia, Cannaregio 2540.* ✆ *041 720 581. Closed Tue-Wed.* Enjoy homemade *primi* (first courses), *fritti* (fried) and grilled fish in this long-term favourite *osteria.*

HOTEL BARS

A way to enjoy the ambience of the city's great hotels without the high cost of a room is to have a drink at the Hotel Bauer, Danieli, Metropole, or the Gritti Palace. Enjoy your cocktail in the bar or on the outdoor terrace, offering stunning nighttime views with royal service.

PERFORMING ARTS

The main theatres are:

Gran Teatro La Fenice *Campo San Fantin, S. Marco 1965.* ✆ *041 786 511. www.teatrolafenice.it.* The city's beloved opera house also hosts ballet and jazz concerts.

Teatro Goldoni *Calle del Teatro, S. Marco 4650B.* ✆ *041 24 02 011. www. teatrostabileveneto.it/Goldoni.* Plays and occasional concerts

Teatro Fondamenta Nuove *Fondamenta Nuove, Cannaregio 5013.* ✆ *041 522 44 98. www.teatrofondamenta nuove.it.* Programme includes jazz, contemporary music and dance.

Teatro Malibran *behind the church of San Giovanni Grisostomo, Calle Stretta Morosini, Cannaregio 5864.* ✆ *041 786 511. www.teatrolafenice.it.* Plays, operas and classical concerts.

OTHER CLASSICAL CONCERT VENUES

Churches and Scuoli

A Vivaldi concert in one of the city's historic **churches** is a highlight of any visit. Get the tourist office's Shows and Events calendar and watch the street posters. Churches holding performances usually display a printed announcement at the entrance steps a few days in advance of the event.

Many of the **scuoli,** such as Grande di San Teodoro, San Giovanni Evangelista, and San Rocco, offer evening performances of classical music, often in masks and period costumes. Be prepared to pay in cash, as credit cards are generally not accepted. Plan to arrive early to get good seats and to admire the wall and ceiling art.

STREET MUSIC

One of the delights of Venice is the variety of live classical music heard on so many streets and church entrance steps, both day and night.

CINEMA

The Venice International Film Festival is the world's oldest film festival (www. labiennale.org). The Lido and the city's squares host open-air cinemas showing films competing in the festival. Year-round the small **Casa del Cinema-Videoteca Pasinetti** (*Palazzo Mocenigo, San Stae 1990.* ✆ *041 524 1320. www.comune.venezia.it*) shows some films in their original language.

VERONA

OPERA

The opera seasons draw large crowds to the famous Arena to watch famous perennials such as Aida, Carmen and Madame Butterfly, from June to September. Ticket prices range from over €150 for the front row of the stalls, to just over €100 for numbered seats on the steps. Numbered seats low down are more comfortable than the stone steps but on hot nights it can be airless and stuffy and your view of the stage may be restricted. Sit high up for a breath of air and of course a grandstand view. As may be expected in an open-air venue acoustics are imperfect – the best sound is reckoned to be halfway down the tiers. An unreserved seat on the stone steps (gradinata) starts at under €25. ✆ 045 800 5151. www.arena.it.

Other venues to check for performances are churches throughout the Veneto region, historic *palazzi,* and the Palladian and other historic villas.

Shopping

Shopping in Venice is a treat. So many small shops greet visitors, showcasing glass, textiles, masks and other products that are unique to the area. In some, it is possible to watch specialists at work. Most shops are open Mon–Sat, 8am–1pm and 3.30–7.30pm. Credit cards are accepted in most stores. Venice has never been a place to seek out bargains, but remains a wonderful place for fine craftsmanship for the observant visitor to discover amidst the many tourist-oriented shops (many do not permit photos.)

VENICE STREETS

Calle Larga 22 Marzo – *West of Piazza San Marco.* Designer boutiques, glitzy shops, including shoe and handbag.
Mercerie – *Between Pizza San Marco and the Rialto Bridge.* Upscale boutiques selling leather goods, luggage, clothing, housewares and other merchandise.
Rio Terà Lista di Spagna – *Just east of the train station.* Here you'll find a wide variety of glass, clothing and souvenir shops.
Strada Nuova – *Near Ca' d'Oro in the Cannaregio district.* Bakeries and restaurants intermingle with souvenir stalls, gift, food and clothing stores. Pricey gift and clothing shops dot the **Procuratie Nuovo** bordering Piazza San Marco and heavyweight designer boutiques along **Calle Vallaresso,** just west of the Piazza, leading to Harry's Bar.

VENICE

COSTUMES AND MASKS

To hire a typical Venetian Carnival costume contact **Il Prato**, Calle delle Ostreghe 2456/9, San Marco, 041 523 1148, www.ilpratovenezia.com or **Atelier Nicolao**, Cannaregio 5590, 041 520 70 51, www.nicolao.com. Masks are sold everywhere; if you are looking for a good quality Venetian mask, opt for one made of *carta pesta* (papier-mâché). Reputable shops include **Ca' Macana**,

the original is at Dorsoduro 3172, another at 1169, and by appointment a workshop to make their own masks at 3172, 041 27 76 142, www.camacana. com; **La pietra filosofale**, San Marco 1735 (Frezzeria, near Fenice Theatre); and **Tragicomica**, San Polo 2800 (Calle dei Nomboli, near Campo San Tomà, between San Polo and i Frari), 041 72 11 02, www.tragicomica.it. **Carta Alta** (041 2771132, www.cartaalta.com) mask worshop (not open to visitors) is on the Giudecca; their masks are sold in various shops including **Fabris Leda** (S. Marco 702).

TRADITIONAL STATIONERY

Quality paper can be bought in many shops in the city, including **Alberto Valese's** (Campo Santo Stefano 3471, San Marco, 041 5238830, www. albertovalese-ebru.it). Everything a graphomaniac could want can be found in the shops in Calle della Mandola, between Campo Manin and Campo Sant'Angelo, and Calle del Piovan, between Campo San Maurizio and Campo Santo Stefano. The **Legatoria Piazzesi** (Campiello della Feltrina, between Santa Maria del Giglio and San Maurizio, 041 520 1978, www.legatoriapiazzesi.it) stocks beautiful cards printed using old-fashioned Venetian methods.
Gianni Basso's (Calle del Fumo 5306, Cannaregio), near the Fondamenta Nuove, where the vaporettos leave for the islands, produces a range of quality stationery, personal bookplates and business cards, embossed and printed using traditional methods.

TEXTILES, GLASS, LEATHER

Shops specialising in textiles, glassworks, dolls and puppets abound in Venice. In business since 1700, **Mario Bevilacqua** (Campo S. Maria del Giglio, S. Marco 2520, bevilacquatessuti.com) has gorgeous textiles and decorative trimmings, tie-backs, embroidery and velvet in the great tradition of Venetian fabrics; some are still woven on period looms. A collector, too, they even have some vintage Fortuny textiles here; another shop is in Castello, this is most atmospheric.
Venice has fine textile shops that specialise in velvets, silks, and brocades,

for clothing or interior design. **Giuliana Longo** (Calle del Lovo, S. Marco 4813, www.giulianalongo.com) in the family trade since 1901, is wedged into her tiny hat shop with a lovely variety, from wool felt or velvet with feathers, to hand-made Montecristi panama hats, or a reasonably priced doge's hat for Carnival. **Bottega Veneta** (Campo S. Moisè, San Marco 1461, www.bottegaveneta.com) crafts some of Italy's finest leather purses and bags near Vicenza, their trademark being their artisans' complex *intrecciato* (braided) weave. On a more economical scale, **Benetton** shops abound and clothes are manufactured worldwide, but the company still operates out of Treviso.

Glass stores are common in Venice, although quality varies greatly and much of it comes from Asia. These 11 companies make their glass exclusively on Murano: Anfora, DinoRosin Arte Studio, Effe, Formia, Galliano Ferro, Gino Cenedese, Linea Vetro, NasonMoretti, Nuova Biemmeci, S.a.l.i.r, Seguso Viro. The Museo del Vetro can help locate some of the local glass artists; the small museum shop often displays their work.

MODEL BOATS

The shop window of **Gilberto Penzo's** near i Frari (Calle Seconda dei Saoneri 2681, San Polo, 𝄢041 524 6139, www.veniceboats.com) specialises in historic Venetian model boats, gondolas and *bricole* made from wood. The shop sells model kits, construction plans, reliefs, rowlocks and nautical ex-votos.

COFFEE

Venice has excellent *torrefazioni* (coffee roasters). **Marchi** (Cannaregio 1337, www.torrefazionemarchi.it) roasts beans, sells them whole or ground, also has a small bar. Other brands are **Girani** (Castello 3727, www.caffegirani.it), **Doge** (bar at Calle dei Cinque, San Polo 609) and **India** (bar at Campo Santa Margherita, www.indiacaffe.it).

CONFECTIONERY

Volpe (in the Ghetto, Cannaregio 1143) sells Jewish bread and pastries. **VizioVirtù Cioccolateria** (Castello 5988, www.viziovirtu.com) makes chocolates.

VERONA

Via Mazzini and **Corso Porta Borsari** display top quality clothing and shoes. On the former look for **Libreria Ghelfi & Barbato** (at no 21) with its beautiful shopfront, a fine selection of books and fine food and wine. An old shop **La Salumeria** (Corso Sant'Anastasia) is crammed with Italian foodstuffs. **Rossi** bakes excellent breads and has enough treats to concoct a gourmet picnic. **Stradone Porta Palio** is known for its antique shops. The **Mercato di Piazza Erbe** (fruit, vegetables, and tourist fripperies) is a shadow of its former self.

PADOVA

Designer fashions are found around the **Piazza Cavour** and particularly on **Via San Fermo** with prices going stratospheric around the **Galleria Borghese**. **Rinascente**, on Piazza Garibaldi, is a mid-range department store. On via Calvi Pietro Fortunato, just off Piazza Cavour, is **Racca** (www.pasticceriaracca.com), a wonderful ice cream seller established 1933.
The town's other main shopping street is **Via Roma** with a selection of general shops for most budgets. Between the Piazza delle Erbe and the Duomo, **Via Daniele Manin** is a pretty arcaded street, lined with shops selling cut-price clothes, shoes and accessories, popular with the university students.
Padova is famous for its goldsmiths. On **Via Davila** are jewellers and silversmiths including **Roberto Callegari** at no 8, and at no 6 **L'Antiquario Gemmologo**. Other fine goldsmiths are **Alberta Vita**, **Mario Pinton**, and **Paolo Marcolongo**. Padua is excellent for **markets**. Its daily fruit and vegetable markets are renowned for their quality. The weekly general market is each Saturday on the Prato della Valle; on the third Sunday of every month, some 200 antiques and collectibles vendors set out their stalls.

MOLO (PROVINCE OF VICENZA)

Guerrino Lovato moved his mask collection from Venice (🔊*see photo*) to set up a museum **Museo Mondonovo Maschere** (*www.museialtovicentino.it*). He made masks for Stanley Kubrik's *Eyes Wide Shut*, as well as for Branaugh, Zeffirelli and La Fenice. Mask workshop at www.maskedart.com.

INDEX

INDEX

INDEX

INDEX

MAPS AND PLANS

THEMATIC MAPS

MAPS AND PLANS

The Districts of Venice

Islands and Lagoon

The Veneto

COMPANION PUBLICATIONS

MICHELIN MAPS

For planning in-depth trips in the Venice region, this guide may be used in conjunction with:

Michelin map 562 Italy
Covers the northeast of Italy and includes an index of towns.
Scale 1:400 000.

For visitors travelling throughout Italy, we recommend:

Michelin Road Atlas Italy
A useful spiral-bound atlas with an alphabetical index of 70 towns and cities. Scale 1:300 000.

Michelin map 735 Italy
a practical map which provides the visitor with a complete picture of Italy's road network. Scale 1:1 000 000.

INTERNET

Michelin is pleased to offer a route-planning service on the Internet:
www.travelguide.michelin.com
www.viamichelin.com

Choose the shortest route, a route without tolls, or the Michelin recommended route to your destination; you can also access information about hotels and restaurants from *The Michelin Guide*, and tourist sites from *The Green Guide*.

MAP LEGEND

	Sight	Seaside Resort	Winter Sports Resort	Spa
Highly recommended	★★★	⛱⛱⛱	❋❋❋	♯♯♯
Recommended	★★	⛱⛱	❋❋	♯♯
Interesting	★	⛱	❋	♯

Tourism

◉▭▭	Sightseeing route with departure point indicated	AZ B	Map co-ordinates locating sights
🏛🕈🏛🕈	Ecclesiastical building	ⓘ	Tourist information
▨ 🕌	Synagogue – Mosque	⚞ ⋰	Historic house, castle – Ruins
▭▭	Building (with main entrance)	⌣ ✿	Dam – Factory or power station
■	Statue, small building	✩ ⋒	Fort – Cave
ⱦ	Wayside cross	⚓	Prehistoric site
◎	Fountain	▼ ♈	Viewing table – View
●━●━▶	Fortified walls – Tower – Gate	▲	Miscellaneous sight

Recreation

🏇	Racecourse	🏃	Waymarked footpath
⛸	Skating rink	◈	Outdoor leisure park/centre
≋ ▨	Outdoor, indoor swimming pool	🎿	Theme/Amusement park
⟁	Marina, moorings	♈	Wildlife/Safari park, zoo
⌂	Mountain refuge hut	⊛	Gardens, park, arboretum
□▬■▬□	Overhead cable-car	⊜	Aviary, bird sanctuary
🚂	Tourist or steam railway		

Additional symbols

═══ ═══	Motorway (unclassified)	⊙ ⊚	Post office – Telephone centre
❶ ❶	Junction: complete, limited	▨	Covered market
⊏⊐ ═══	Pedestrian street	⋅×⋅	Barracks
⌁═══⌁	Unsuitable for traffic, street subject to restrictions	△	Swing bridge
⊞⊞ ⋯⋯	Steps – Footpath	⌣ ✕	Quarry – Mine
🚆 🚐	Railway – Coach station	Ⓑ Ⓕ	Ferry (river and lake crossings)
□⊦⊦⊦⊦⊦□	Funicular – Rack-railway	⟼⟼	Ferry services: Passengers and cars
⟼ ◉	Tram – Metro, underground	⟿	Foot passengers only
Bert (R.)…	Main shopping street	③	Access route number common to MICHELIN maps and town plans

Abbreviations and special symbols

H	Town hall (Municipio)	**T**	Theatre (Teatro)
J	Law courts (Palazzo di Giustizia)	**U**	University (Università)
M	Museum (Museo)	🏛	Palace, villa
P	Local authority offices (Prefettura)	**8** EX	Map number and grid reference locating sights on maps **2** - **11**
POL.	Police station (Polizia) (in large towns: Questura)		

MICHELIN IS CONTINUALLY INNOVATING FOR SAFER, CLEANER, MORE ECONOMICAL, MORE CONNECTED... BETTER ALL-ROUND MOBILITY.

Tyres wear more quickly on short urban journeys.

?

TRUE!

You tend to accelerate and brake more often when driving around town so your tyres work harder!
If you are stuck in traffic, keep calm and drive slowly.

Tyre pressure only affects your car's safety.

?

FALSE!

Driving with underinflated tyres (0.5 bar below recommended pressure) doesn't just impact handling and fuel consumption, it will shave 8,000 km off tyre lifespan.
Make sure you check tyre pressure about once a month and before you go on holiday or a long journey.

If you only encounter **winter weather from time to time** - sudden showers, snowfall or black ice - **one type of tyre** will do the job.

?

TRUE!

The revolutionary **MICHELIN CrossClimate** - the very first summer tyre with winter certification - is a practical solution to keep you on the road whatever the weather.

Fitting **2 winter tyres** on my car guarantees maximum safety.

FALSE!

In the winter, especially when temperatures drop below 7°C, to ensure better road holding, all four tyres should be identical and fitted at the same time.

2 WINTER TYRES ONLY = risk of compromised road holding.

4 WINTER TYRES = **safer handling** when cornering, driving downhill and braking.

If you regularly encounter rain, snow or black ice, choose a **MICHELIN Alpin tyre**. This range offers you sharp handling plus a comfortable ride to safely face the challenge of winter driving.

MICHELIN

MICHELIN IS COMMITTED

▶ MICHELIN IS **GLOBAL LEADER IN FUEL-EFFICIENT TYRES** FOR LIGHT VEHICLES.

▶ **EDUCATING OF YOUNGSTERS IN ROAD SAFETY,**
NOT FORGETTING TWO-WHEELERS LOCAL ROAD SAFETY CAMPAIGNS WERE RUN IN **16 COUNTRIES** IN 2015.

QUIZ

1 TYRES ARE BLACK SO WHY IS THE MICHELIN MAN WHITE?

Back in 1898 when the Michelin Man was first created from a stack of tyres, they were made of natural rubber, cotton and sulphur and were therefore light-coloured. The composition of tyres did not change until after the First World War when carbon black was introduced. But the Michelin Man kept his colour!

2 FOR HOW LONG HAS MICHELIN BEEN GUIDING TRAVELLERS?

Since 1900. When the MICHELIN guide was published at the turn of the century, it was claimed that it would last for a hundred years. It's still around today and remains a reference with new editions and online restaurant listings in a number of countries.

3 WHEN WAS THE "BIB GOURMAND" INTRODUCED IN THE MICHELIN GUIDE?

The symbol was created in 1997 but as early as 1954 the MICHELIN guide was recommending "exceptional good food at moderate prices". Today, it features on the MICHELIN Restaurants website and app.

If you want to enjoy a fun day out and find out more about Michelin, why not visit the l'Aventure Michelin museum and shop in Clermont-Ferrand, France:
www.laventuremichelin.com